Alvin Fayette Lewis

History of Higher Education in Kentucky

Alvin Fayette Lewis

History of Higher Education in Kentucky

ISBN/EAN: 9783744764674

Printed in Europe, USA, Canada, Australia, Japan

Cover: Foto ©ninafisch / pixelio.de

More available books at **www.hansebooks.com**

[*Whole Number 256*

UNITED STATES BUREAU OF EDUCATION.

CIRCULAR OF INFORMATION NO. 3, 1899.

CONTRIBUTIONS TO AMERICAN EDUCATIONAL HISTORY.

EDITED BY HERBERT B. ADAMS.

No. 25.

HISTORY OF HIGHER EDUCATION

IN

KENTUCKY.

BY

ALVIN FAYETTE LEWIS, A. M., PH. D.,

Professor of History in the University of Arkansas.

WASHINGTON:

GOVERNMENT PRINTING OFFICE.

1899.

LETTER OF TRANSMITTAL.

DEPARTMENT OF THE INTERIOR,
BUREAU OF EDUCATION,
Washington, D. C., June 26, 1899.

SIR: I have the honor to transmit for publication as a circular of information the twenty-fifth in the series of contributions to American educational history edited by Prof. Herbert B. Adams. The present number treats of the State of Kentucky, and is by Dr. A. F. Lewis, some time president of the Seminary West of the Suwanee River, in Tallahassee, Fla. In this monograph Dr. Lewis has undertaken to cover, with considerable detail, all phases of education in Kentucky, and has brought together a great mass of facts of much educational importance and but little known.

It will be recalled that Kentucky entered early on the work of education, for by the close of the war of the Revolution a charter had been given to Transylvania Seminary, from which grew the Transylvania University, long and favorably known throughout the West and Southwest.

The public-school system, which was also organized at a comparatively early date, is treated, and the literature of education, extensive although fragmentary in character, is reviewed in a series of bibliographies appended to the various historical sketches.

Very respectfully, your obedient servant,

W. T. HARRIS, *Commissioner.*

Hon. E. A. HITCHCOCK,
Secretary of the Interior.

CONTENTS.

LIST OF ILLUSTRATIONS.

PREFATORY NOTE.

In the preparation of this monograph the writer has been kindly assisted by many college officers and others, who have furnished information and cooperated in other ways, but whom it would be impossible here to thank by name. He desires, however, to express especially his obligations to J. W. Black, Ph. D., acting professor of history in Georgetown College, Kentucky, in 1891–92, and now professor of history in Colby University, Maine, for the preparation of the sketch of the former institution; to Hon. E. P. Thompson, ex-superintendent of public instruction, for courtesies extended in connection with the use of the Collins collection and other important historical material in the State capitol; to H. H. White, LL. D., the learned ex-president and professor emeritus of Kentucky University, for the loan of a transcript of the minutes of the trustees of Transylvania University and for valuable data in regard to that institution and Kentucky University, and also to R. T. Durrett, LL. D., the distinguished president of the Filson Club of Louisville, Ky., for the free use of his unsurpassed library of Kentucky history, for personal suggestions, and other assistance.

The facts used in the introduction have been gathered from the remainder of the monograph. Much information has been obtained from Reports of the Commissioner of Education, from catalogues, correspondence and personal interviews with the present executive officers of the different institutions—information usually not mentioned explicitly. Where no other authority is given, a sketch has been prepared exclusively from one or more of these sources.

Chapter I.

INTRODUCTION—GENERAL SKETCH.

Partly for covenience of treatment, and partly because the periods are in a general way epoch-making, the history of education in Kentucky may be divided into five parts, as follows: (1) From the settlement of the State to 1820; (2) from 1820 to 1830; (3) from 1830 to 1850; (4) from 1850 to 1870; (5) from 1870 to the present time. It is to be constantly borne in mind, however, that the dates selected are only approximate and not exact points of division, and that the movement, or movements, specially characterizing one period, as a rule, have their beginning in the previous one, and sometimes extend, at least in a modified form, through one or more subsequent ones. An attempt will be made here only to give the main characteristics of each of these periods, their most interesting individual features being reserved for more detailed treatment in connection with the history of the systems and institutions most closely associated with each.

THE PERIOD UP TO 1820.

The first thing that strikes our attention in the educational history of Kentucky is the early establishment of schools at its various stations, or settlements, notwithstanding the extremely unsettled condition of its affairs, and the great difficulties and dangers, especially from the Indians, which constantly beset its early inhabitants. The pioneers in the settlement of the State were largely from the Valley of Virginia, having entered Kentucky through Cumberland Gap, and were chiefly of Scotch-Irish descent. The leaders among them especially were men of more than the average intelligence and culture,[1] and we see them early taking steps to promote the diffusion of useful knowledge among themselves and their descendants.

[1] Marshall says of the early settlers (History of Kentucky, Vol. I, p. 442): "And what may be assumed with great confidence as a truth is that there were to be found in this population as much talent and intelligence as fell to the lot of any equal number of people, promiscuously taken, in either Europe or America." The "Kentucky Society for Promoting Useful Knowledge" existed as early as 1787, as is shown by a notice of one of its meetings in the Kentucky Gazette of December 1, 1787. The issue of August 2, 1788, also contains a notice of a "Society for Improvement in Knowledge." A marked evidence of at least political acumen is to be found in the discussions of "The Political Club," which existed at Danville from 1786 to 1790, and, independent entirely of all similar discussions, anticipated in its debates a number of the amendments to the Constitution of the United States that were subsequently adopted. See "The Political Club," by Thomas Speed, Louisville, 1894.

So the beginnings of education in the State are almost coincident with its foundation. Within about a year after the first permanent settlement had been established at Harrodsburg in 1774, when it was yet uncertain to whom the territory now composing Kentucky, belonged, as is shown by the organization of the Transylvania Company,[1] we hear of a school being taught at Harrodsburg, probably in the spring of 1776, by Mrs. Coomes,[2] the wife of one of the settlers, and that, too, when Indians were skulking around the station, ready at any moment to fall upon the unwary inhabitants. Some of Daniel Boone's companions had just been killed by them, and their outrages had just driven many prospective settlers back to Virginia. These are rather unusual circumstances for a school to be taught under, especially by a woman; but such were the surroundings of the first school taught in Kentucky.

Other similar schools were soon established, as that of John May at McAfee's Station in 1777, of Joseph Doniphan at Boonesboro in 1779, and of John McKinney at Lexington in 1780, within one year after the establishment of the town. The perils faced by these and other brave pioneers of education in Kentucky are illustrated by the fact that several of them were either killed by the Indians or suffered bodily harm from wild animals.[3]

We do not know just who attended these early schools or what was taught in them, but they were probably mainly intended for the younger children of the stations where they were located, and were of quite an elementary character. They were the first types of the early private and neighborhood schools, commonly called "Old-field," or "Hedge-row," schools, of which a more extended notice will be given later.

Schools of a higher grade, however, soon appeared. John Filson,[4] the surveyor, adventurer, and first historian of Kentucky, as well as teacher, established a seminary in Lexington in or before 1784. The pioneer Baptist preacher, Rev. Elijah Craig, established one at Georgetown early in 1788,[5] and during the same year the celebrated Dr.

[1] In regard to the character and organization of the Transylvania Company, see Chapter III, p. 44.

[2] See Spalding's Sketches of the Early Catholic Missions of Kentucky, p. 34; also Collins's History of Kentucky, Vol. I, p. 486.

[3] John May was killed by the Indians in the early part of 1790 while going down the Ohio River in a boat (Collins's History of Kentucky, Vol. II, p. 570). John McKinney was mangled by a wild-cat while teaching at Lexington in May, 1783 (Collins, Vol. II, p. 226). John Filson, one of the teachers mentioned below, was killed by the Indians in the latter part of 1788 near Cincinnati, Ohio, of which he was one of the founders, under the name of Losantiville (Collins, Vol. II, pp. 432-433).

[4] See reference to Filson's death above, as also Collins, Vol. I, p. 640, and Vol. II, p. 183; also The Life and Writings of John Filson, by R. T. Durrett, LL. D., Louisville, 1884.

[5] There is an advertisement of the early establishment of this school in the issue of the Kentucky Gazette (see Chapter III for description of this old newspaper) for January 5, 1788.

James Priestly took charge of Salem Academy[1] at Bardstown (then called Bairdstown), which had been preceded there, as early as 1786, by a school taught by a Mr. Shackleford. This school, under Dr. Priestly's management, was for some time one of the most noted in the State, and in it many of the great public men of the early history of Kentucky received the principal part of their education.

The founding of private high schools continued steadily, in conjunction with another movement to be presently noticed, until Winterbotham,[2] in 1795, could truthfully say, in writing of Kentucky's educational facilities: "Schools are established in the several towns, and in general regularly and handsomely supported;" and Marshall[3] states, referring in general to the period we are considering:

> There are many educated and more means to be applied in that way than most other countries could afford, while a general propensity for giving and receiving literary instruction was obviously a prevailing sentiment throughout the country.

The other movement just referred to is the most striking feature of the State's early educational history, and is so interesting as to demand of us, in another connection, a more extended treatment. It consisted in the inauguration of a system of local and State patronage of secondary and higher education. Lexington, soon after its establishment, reserved land for Latin and English schools, and by this inducement, as early as 1787, caused Mr. Isaac Wilson, late of Philadelphia College, as he describes himself in an advertisement in the Kentucky Gazette,[4] to open Lexington Grammar School; but State patronage of higher education came even earlier, as Transylvania Seminary, one of the first[5] "publick schools," or seminaries, of learning in the Mississippi Valley, of which we shall hear more later, was endowed by an act of the Virginia legislature in 1780, and further endowed and chartered in 1783, and other foundations and endowments by the mother State and by Kentucky herself followed rapidly, until soon a State educational system was developed quite unusual in its circumstances and quite in advance of the ideas of the day elsewhere, in this country at least.

The main thing of interest in Kentucky's educational history, up to about 1820, is the development of this splendid system of higher edu-

[1] For the incorporation of this academy see Chapter II, p. 22. The first advertisement of this school in the Kentucky Gazette occurs on November 29, 1788; others occur later. For something of Dr. Priestly and the school of Mr. Shackleford, see Collins, Vol. II, pp. 35 and 200.

[2] United States of America and the West Indies, p. 156.

[3] History of Kentucky, Vol. I, p. 443.

[4] In the issue of January 26, 1788, which says the school is again opened. The tuition in this school, as in most others of its class, was £4 per annum (the pound being equivalent to $3.33), and advertisements state that good boarding could be obtained at from £8 to £9 per annum. The tuition was usually paid one-half in cash, the other in property, such as produce of various kinds, while board was paid altogether in property.

[5] For the antiquity of this school see Chapter III.

cation, composed, as projected, of a State university and at least one subsidiary academy in each county, and probably intended to be supplemented later by a system of more elementary schools. The subsidiary academies were quite fully developed, and reached their culmination during this period, while Transylvania University was fairly inaugurated, and the foundations laid for the short but brilliant career upon which it was about to enter. The more elementary schools were, however, never connected with this system, and have only been established in any perfection in quite recent years, and then on an independent basis.

The main current of early public education in Kentucky began at the top and extended downward. We have first the university or college and then the public school. This is not to be wondered at, as it was, as a rule, true in all the older States. A number of the prominent men among the early Kentucky settlers were themselves college men and among the founders of colleges in Virginia. Naturally their first attempt to promote education in the new State, according to the prevailing ideas of the time, especially in Virginia, from which most of them came, took shape in the form of an institution of higher learning. It was remarkable, however, that in their hands this institution should have been planned to become the head of a great State system of public education, embracing even elementary schools—a conception in advance of public opinion at the time, in this country at least.

PERIOD FROM 1820 TO 1830.

This period is marked by the downfall of the magnificently conceived university system of which we have just been speaking. Even before 1820 the system of correlated academies had reached its culmination, and had, for various reasons, been acknowledged, in the way it was being conducted, as a failure by discerning public men. Soon after that date the plan had been really abandoned as a State enterprise. The State academies did not, however, disappear at once, but many of them continued as local high schools, and some of them after a time even developed into colleges. Augusta, Georgetown,[1] and, in fact, many of the earlier colleges of the State were built upon old academies, whose funds they inherited.

Public patronage, between 1820 and 1830, was confined almost exclusively to Transylvania University, which under Dr. Holley's administration, beginning in 1818, entered upon a peculiarly brilliant and successful era of its history, soon, however, to have its prospects blighted and its decline brought about by the unfortunate plan of its

[1] Augusta was founded on Bracken Academy and Georgetown on Rittenhouse Academy. In these cases the older academies were perhaps more prominent than in that of other colleges, but Transylvania University grew out of Transylvania Seminary and Centre College was at least partially based on Danville Academy, as was Southern College on Warren Seminary, while Louisville College was a development of Jefferson Seminary, and other colleges were more or less directly connected with older academies.

organization and the state of public opinion, especially in regard to religious questions.

It is interesting to note that this institution was not, as in the case of many of the early colleges of the older States, founded by some church organization, mainly to prepare young men for the ministry, but that it was founded by the State and was from the first considered a State institution, although never fully under direct State control, and its avowed purpose, as expressed in its first charter, was to prepare young men for the service of the State. The way in which it was managed, however, presents a curious blending of state and church control, for it was also founded under church auspices, and, for the greater part of its history, was under quasi denominational management. This double management by church and state, to a considerable extent, at one time or another, extended throughout the whole of the early Kentucky university system, and, especially by the denominational jealousies it aroused, had a very disastrous effect. The system's plan of management, as will be noted later, was in other respects also not such as to secure the greatest responsibility and the highest efficiency.

These things were largely instrumental in preventing the upbuilding of a grand system of public higher education and in causing the State to withdraw from her early policy of liberality toward education. Kentucky was certainly quite liberal toward Transylvania Seminary and the early academies, especially in the matter of the donation of public lands and the exemption of these from taxation, as well as in her direct appropriations, although the latter were never large. The land grants were, however, not sufficient to make the system self-sustaining or to pledge the State to its further sustentation, while the control assumed and the responsibility required were not requisite to secure proper efficiency. When the original plan had thus been wrecked, we see the State so far reversing her original policy that for a long time she refused to make adequate provision for her public schools, and, even as late as 1865, declined to give the fund needed to make the Congressional land grant of 1862 for agricultural colleges available for the highest educational uses, but left it to a denominational institution to make for her the most out of the limited endowment furnished by the General Government.

Even during the period we are now considering Transylvania University began to lose her hold upon the public good will, and denominational colleges began to spring up, as so many centers of opposition, and to compete with the university for public patronage. Centre and St. Joseph's in 1819, St. Mary's in 1821, Augusta in 1822, Cumberland in 1826, and Georgetown in 1829, arose in rapid succession. Their competition was not greatly felt for a time, but was destined to grow to strong proportions in the succeeding period.

The failure of the academy system did, however, cause public attention, even during this period, to be turned to the need of elementary schools, and public opinion was sufficiently aroused on the question t cause the legislature of 1821 to appoint a commission to investigate th subject and to report upon it to that body. This commission, compose of Hon. William T. Barry and other prominent public men, made, i 1822, an able report in favor of a system of public schools, embodyin excellent ideas in regard to how it could be inaugurated. The legisl ture was also induced to create a small literary fund to support such system, but nothing further was then accomplished.

PERIOD 1830 TO 1850.

Prior to the beginning of this period, Transylvania University ha been abandoned by the State in so far as the bestowal of public patro age was concerned, although nominal legislative control was sti retained. The neglect of the State was, however, somewhat supplie by private and local munificence, and the University long remaine eminently useful, especially through its professional departments, bu it may be said to have now entered into a condition of gradual declin Several attempts were made during this time to resurrect its prowes under partial denominational control. Baptists, Episcopalians, Pre byterians, and lastly Methodists were successively called to the aid its waning fortunes, but, as a rule, with indifferent success, althoug the powerful church influence which Dr. Bascom was able to bring t its assistance for a time seemed to revive the university's departe glories. When this, too, had to be withdrawn, in 1849, it sank eve lower than before.

The peculiar feature of the period between 1830 and 1850 was th development and further multiplication of denominational colleges, movement already begun in the previous period partly in oppositio to Transylvania University and partly to supply needs which it coul not then meet.

It now became the settled policy of each important denomination i the State to have its own representative institution. Several these had already been founded, but had not been strong competito of the university, owing to their lack of funds and equipment. Thes were now strengthened and others established, so that most of the pron inent denominational colleges of the State may be said to date the existence or their importance as educational factors from this perio Centre, St. Joseph's, and Augusta, especially, soon began to be we known, and others, as Bacon and Shelby in 1836, were founded. Th movement continued until, Collins tells us in his Sketches,[1] in 184 Kentucky had more colleges than any other State in the Union.

Special professional schools, especially of medicine, also began to l established. The first of these to amount to anything was the Loui ville Medical Institute, now the medical department of the Universit of Louisville, founded in 1837, as a direct competitor of the medic department of Transylvania University.

---

[1] Sketches of Kentucky, p. 272.

The founding of denominational institutions and of special professional schools has continued through all the subsequent educational history of the State and has led to an unfortunate multiplicity of new and separate institutions, whereas an enlargement of those already existing would have been far more preferable. One result has been that although the name has been frequently used, there has never been a real university in the State, even in the extensive use of the term, with all the usual departments and a complete faculty and equipment in each. Another result has been that the colleges of the State have been quite insufficiently endowed. The State has never fully committed herself to the policy of sustaining a well-endowed university, while other institutions have become too numerous to receive large amounts from local and denominational beneficence which has been the source of almost all of the endowment of the various institutions. No single individual, either within or without the State, has given a large amount to any single institution, and almost all that has been contributed has been given wholly by the people of the State, principally through the various religious denominations. Various communities have contributed with great liberality to institutions located in their midst without regard to denominational connections, and Presbyterians, Baptists, Methodists, Christians, and other denominations have done nobly for their respective institutions, but local demand or denominational jealousy has called into existence a multitude of colleges, each of whose share in the general bounty has been necessarily small among a people generally well-to-do but not wealthy. The funds received have usually only been sufficient to give them fairly good buildings and equipment, but have left them no endowment. So they have had to struggle on, mainly supported by tuition fees, many of the older institutions of the State having been, during the greater part of their history, rich only in the spirit of devotion to sound learning.

The fact that Kentucky colleges have been so largely unendowed mainly accounts for the many ups and downs in their history. As long as local and denominational influence and their own good work have kept their halls filled with students they have had fair success, but when, for any reason, the number of their students has declined, they have declined in like manner, and the history of the State is strewn with the wrecks of educational enterprises. Cumberland, Shelby, Eminence, and others are so many examples of a checkered career, ending finally in dissolution.

Lack of endowment and strong competition have also compelled most of the colleges to do a great deal of what is really preparatory and not college work, which has hampered their usefulness and necessarily vitiated their standard to a considerable extent. This we shall see applies especially to the female colleges of the State, which arose mainly in the period succeeding the one we are now considering, and for whose multiplicity we shall see there have been special reasons.

The period of which we are now speaking also witnesses the first inception of a State public-school system. The law of 1838 established this in a rather imperfect form it is true, but gave to it what was a great gain—a regular organization. Its operations were greatly hindered for some time by the smallness of the "literary fund" upon which it was based and by the fact that this fund was not properly husbanded; but the system made really substantial progress during this time in the crystallization of public opinion in its favor, and especially in the fact that the "literary fund," by the third constitution of the State, which went into effect in 1850, was inviolably devoted to public-school education.

PERIOD FROM 1850 TO 1870.

This era is noticeable for an unsuccessful attempt, made in 1856, to revive Transylvania University as a State institution in the form of a State normal school—a much-needed addition to the public-school system. After a short trial of two years, owing to the lack of proper public support, this effort had to be abandoned, and the history of the university as in any sense a State institution was ended. After this it sank into a school of merely secondary rank.

Again, an attempt was made in 1865 to build on its ruins a great university in the name of the State, but really under what was denominational, but not intended to be sectarian, control. This plan was splendidly devised and seemed for a time likely to succeed, but it, too, was doomed to be wrecked. So Kentucky University, instead of becoming what it promised to be, an institution overshadowing all others, was forced to take the position simply of one of the principal colleges of the State.

Special professional schools have, during this and the subsequent period, continued to increase in numbers, especially at Louisville, until that city, with its six medical colleges and other professional institutions, has become one of the largest centers of professional education in the country.

The further multiplication of denominational institutions also continued apace. Female colleges especially, whose numbers up to this time had been comparatively unimportant, were founded in rapid succession, and soon became so numerous that almost every prominent denomination in the State had two or more representative institutions. In addition to these many communities founded local institutions to supply their own needs, which, as a rule, unfortunately aspired to become colleges. This of course led to sharp competition and in many cases to unsound educational methods and practices.

The number of female colleges particularly which have been established in Kentucky since about 1850 has become almost legion, their multiplicity being due partly to the fact, as noted later, that girls were for a long time excluded from almost all the institutions of higher learning in the State, and partly from the fact that in so far as it was deemed necessary for them to be educated at all it was thought that their education should be more of an ornamental character and otherwise of a different type from that pursued by boys. These circumstances, in conjunction with the inefficiency of the public-school system for a long time and the consequent demand of localities for institutions suited to their own peculiar needs, have caused a large number of female schools to spring up, which unfortunately have in most cases been ambitious to be colleges, at least in name, and to confer diplomas if not degrees. Almost every school for girls in the State either bears the name of college or claims to do college work; in reality the work done by most of them is largely secondary and even to some extent primary. No attempt has been made in this monograph to give the history of all these schools. Only those have been treated a considerable part of whose work appears to be of collegiate rank. As it has been found very difficult to apply any absolute line of demarkation, it is probable that a number of institutions have been omitted quite as worthy of notice perhaps as some of those treated, but in general the same line of division has been followed as that used of late in the reports[1] of the United States Commissioner of Education.

In one respect particularly a great educational advance was made in Kentucky between 1850 and 1870. The public-school system may in that period be said to have first become firmly established in the hearts of the people of the State, largely through the efforts of State Superintendent Breckinridge in its behalf, and an educated public sentiment, aroused by him and others, called forth the act of 1869, which made public education really effective by granting it, by State taxation, a more ample revenue. The opening of the educational year 1870 marks the practical establishment of an effective public-school system in Kentucky.

PERIOD SUBSEQUENT TO 1870.

This is especially noted for the continual growth of a sound public opinion upon almost all educational questions.

An enlightened public sentiment has of late caused the State to return to her early liberal attitude toward public education, and no just complaint can now be made in regard to the way she supports the one institution she still controls—the Agricultural and Mechanical College—or her public-school system. All school property has lately been exempted from taxation,[2] and the State college now receives a liberal contribution in the form of a regular State tax, while the effectiveness of the public schools has been greatly increased by considerable addi-

[1] These reports class female colleges under division A, embracing a few institutions of the highest rank, such as Wellesley and Vassar, and division B, which includes all others. All the female colleges of Kentucky come under division B.

[2] According to the provisions of the constitution of 1891, as interpreted by a recent decision of the court of appeals.

tions to the "literary fund" and also by increasing the State tax levied for the support of the system. This attitude of the State is a characteristic feature of the present period, but is not the only one of interest.

A system of graded schools has also been established, by the aid of additional local taxation, in all the towns and cities of any size in the State. This largely supplies a pressing need for secondary instruction, and also relieves the colleges of the necessity of maintaining at least such large preparatory departments as formerly.

Most of the colleges, moreover, have largely added to their endowments within the past few years through private and denominational gifts. Several of them now have fairly good endowments for the work they undertake.

Many of the male colleges have of late opened their doors to women as well. This has continued so far that coeducation may now be said to be almost a generally accepted policy in the State. It has had at least one good effect in obviating the necessity of the further multiplication of female colleges.

Quite a contrary and hopeful movement has even taken place lately in the conversion of several of these colleges into avowedly secondary schools, and the founding of such schools in various communities where formerly the establishment of a college would have been attempted. The opening of the Vanderbilt Training School at Elkton, and of the various preparatory schools of Central University and Kentucky Wesleyan College, are so many illustrations of this praiseworthy spirit. A commendable disposition has also been shown to stop the further founding of separate professional schools, as those lately established have been opened in conjunction with the older colleges, and the older professional schools have shown a tendency to affiliate with established institutions for which they furnish professional departments, as was illustrated in November, 1897, when the Kentucky School of Medicine became the medical department of Kentucky University.

Several of the colleges of Kentucky have always been noted for their attachment to sound scholarship. Fortunately these, as a rule, have been able to increase their endowments along with others. So while higher education in Kentucky is still considerably hampered by a too great multiplicity of colleges and their consequent lack of ample endowments, yet its condition is one of greater hopefulness for the future. The needs of the public school system of the State will be more fully noticed in another connection, but it, too, may be truthfully said to be making favorable progress.

Chapter II.

SOME INTERESTING FEATURES OF EARLY EDUCATION.

A STATE UNIVERSITY SYSTEM.

This system, which has already been referred to as one of the striking features of the early educational history of Kentucky, may be said to have had its beginning in the act of the Virginia assembly, of May 1780, endowing Transylvania Seminary. For while the plan had not then been originated, and this school was soon to develop into Transylvania University, and become, in a sense, the head of the system after this transformation, yet it was at first intended to be of the same character as that afterwards taken by the other seminaries or academies (these words are always synonymous in early Kentucky educational history), the first part of the general plan to be fully developed, and was the model for the others in its original conception and especially in the method of its endowment by the State.

The original endowment act of Transylvania Seminary seems to have been copied largely in all of the first, at least, of the later academy acts. This act,[1] for its spirit if for nothing else, is worthy of being quoted at length. It reads as follows:

Whereas it is represented to the general assembly that there are certain lands within the county of Kentucky, formerly belonging to British subjects, not yet sold under the law of escheats and forfeitures, which might at a future day be a valuable fund for the maintenance and education of youth, and it being the interest of this Commonwealth always to promote and encourage every design which may tend to the improvement of the mind and the diffusion of useful knowledge, even among its remote citizens, whose situation a barbarous neighborhood and a savage intercourse might otherwise render unfriendly to science: Be it therefore enacted, That 8,000 acres of land within the said county of Kentucky, late the property of Robert McKenzie, Henry Collins, and Alexander McKee, be, and the same are hereby, vested in William Fleming, William Christian, John Todd, Stephen Trigg, Benjamin Logan, John Floyd, John May, Levi Todd, John Cowan, George Meriwether, John Cobbs, George Thompson, and Edmund Taylor, trustees, as a free donation from this Commonwealth for the purpose of a public school, or seminary of learning, to be erected within the said county as soon as the circumstances of the county and the state of its funds will admit, and for no other use or purpose whatsoever.

Thus was planned the first school in Kentucky established under State patronage and one which, at the time of its establishment soon afterwards, was truly in a "barbarous neighborbood" in so far as the proximity of Indian warriors was concerned.

[1] See references to this act in Chapter III.

The need of such an institution and the plan of securing its endowment seem to have been first seen by the Rev. John Todd, a prominent Presbyterian minister of Louisa County, Va., and his nephew, Col. John Todd,[1] then a representative from the county of Kentucky in the Virginia assembly. The advice and influence of the former, coupled with the ability and efforts of the latter, seem, mainly at least, to have induced the legislature to pass the act of endowment, an act in advance of Virginia's usual educational policy at that day and the more unusual as occurring in the midst of one of the most gloomy periods of the Revolution and one specially trying to her. The Todds are therefore to be given the very highest praise for the inception of the plan, and their names should for all time to come be placed high on Kentucky's roll of honor.

Transylvania Seminary was further endowed and incorporated in May, 1783,[2] owing, as we shall see, largely to the influence and efforts of Judge Caleb Wallace, when its endowment was exempted from taxation by the State, the latter being another feature of its organization appearing in the general academy plan. These are the principal ways in which this seminary may have influenced the founding of the academies, and so its history will not be traced further in this connection.

The first of the academies, subsequently appearing as a part of the regular system, of which we hear is Salem Academy, located at Bardstown and incorporated by Virginia in 1788.[3] It does not seem, at that time, to have received any land endowment, though it did later from Kentucky herself, and seems for a time to have been a private or local classical high school. In this capacity, we have seen,[4] it obtained quite a reputation under the noted Dr. James Priestly as master. It was later incorporated into the general academy system. Indeed, it seems that when this system had come into full operation schools of higher education, supported merely by private or local means, were generally forced by its competition either to become part of the system or to suspend operations.

The first acts of the Kentucky legislature on the subject of academies are the act of December 12, 1794,[5] incorporating Kentucky Academy at Pisgah, near Lexington; one soon after, of uncertain date,[6] incorporating Bethel Academy, in Jessamine County, and a third, on December 15, 1795,[7] establishing Franklin Academy at Washington,

[1] For the connection of the Todds, and also of Judge Wallace, with the founding of this seminary, see Foote's Sketches of Virginia, second series, pp. 47–48. Further references to Colonel Todd are found in Chapter III.

[2] References to this act are given in Chapter III.

[3] Littell's Laws of Kentucky, Vol. III, p. 579.

[4] In Chapter I, p. 13, where references are given in regard to Dr. Priestly's connection with it.

[5] For this act see Chapter III.

[6] A note in regard to this act is to be found in Chapter VII.

[7] Littell's Laws of Kentucky, Vol. I, pp. 296–298.

in Mason County. These acts were similar in scope to the Transylvania Seminary act of 1783, but gave no endowment of public land as that had done.

The first really important acts connected with the academy system proper are the two acts of February 18, 1798, the first[1] of which reincorporated Bethel Academy, giving it the plan of management subsequently used for the later academies, the second[2] of which endowed Kentucky, Franklin, Salem, and Bethel academies, and Lexington and Jefferson seminaries (the last two established by the act at Lexington and Louisville, respectively), with 6,000 acres of land each, to be vested in cooptative boards of trustees, as provided for in the case of Bethel, and to be held free from taxes.

The Bethel act gave to the trustees "all powers and privileges that are enjoyed by trustees, governors, or visitors of any college or university within this State not herein limited or otherwise directed." The president of the academy was also required to be "a man of the most approved abilities in literature." As shown by various advertisements and notices in the Kentucky Gazette and elsewhere, "Latin, Greek, and the different branches of science"[3] were required to be taught in at least most of these academies, thus furnishing to their students the elements of a fairly good classical education, not much emphasis, as a rule, being put upon the sciences. The powers conferred upon the academies by their acts of incorporation were sufficient for their conversion into colleges without any further change of charter, as actually occurred in some instances.

The second act of February 10, 1798, itself, and especially the sentiment of its latter part, should add imperishable renown both to its promoter and to the legislature that passed it. The last part of sections 5 and 6 of the act read as follows:

And whereas it is generally true that people will be happiest whose laws are best and best administered, and that laws will be wisely and honestly administered in proportion as those who form and administer them are wise and honest; whence it becomes expedient for promoting the public happiness that those persons whom

---

[1] Toulmin's Acts of Kentucky, pp. 469-470, and Littell's Laws of Kentucky, Vol. II, p. 174.

[2] Toulmin's Acts of Kentucky, pp. 470-472; Littell's Laws of Kentucky, Vol. II, pp. 107-109, and Bradford's Laws of Kentucky, Vol I, pp. 100-102.

[3] From the advertisement of Lexington Grammar School on January 26, 1788. This and such advertisements as that of Rev. Mr. Craig, on Jaunary 5, 1788, which speaks of "the teaching of the Latin and Greek languages, together with such branches of the sciences as are usually taught in public seminaries," indicate in a general way what was actually taught. The general act of incorporation of December 22, 1798, says (Toulmin's Acts of Kentucky, p. 474): "It shall be left wholly in the discretion of the said several trustees what subjects shall be taught in the said several academies, whether the English languages, writing, arithmetic, mathematics, and geometry only; or the dead and foreign languages and the other sciences which are generally taught in other academies or colleges in this Commonwealth."

nature hath endowed with genius and virtue should be rendered, by liberal education, worthy to receive and able to guard the sacred deposit of the rights and liberties of their fellow-citizens, and that to aid and accelerate this most desirable purpose must be one of the first duties of every wise government. (Sec. 6.) Be it therefore enacted, That all the lands within the bounds of this Commonwealth, on the south side of Cumberland River below Obey's River, which are now vacant and unappropriated, or on which there shall not be, at the passage of this act, any actual settler under the laws of this State for the relief of settlers south of Green River, shall be, and the same are hereby, reserved by the general assembly to be appropriated, as they may hereafter from time to time think fit, to the use of seminaries of learning throughout the different parts of this Commonwealth.

We certainly have here an epoch-making act, one which is in general on the model of the great ordinance of 1787 (in regard to the Northwest Territory), by which it may have been influenced, but its spirit seems rather to have been drawn from that of the old Virginia land grants to Transylvania Seminary. It is certainly a noteworthy thing, for the time, to see a State thus setting apart a considerable area of its lands for the purpose of establishing a system of public secondary and higher education. This is certainly an important enunciation of principle, but it was not simply to be a barren announcement of a theoretical attitude toward education in the future, but was soon to bear substantial fruit.

Winchester Academy, in the town of the same name, was established and endowed on the same plan and in the same way by an act of December 19, 1798,[1] and on December 22, 1798, were passed two acts, the first[2] in reference to Bourbon Academy and the second[3] in reference to nineteen others, which, especially if taken in connection with an act of the same date incorporating Transylvania University, are the culmination and completion of all the previous academy acts, contemplating as they do a grand State university system. They are really a continuation of the acts of the previous February, which serve as preambles to them, but are of wider import, and so more remarkable and epoch making. The act establishing Transylvania University, occurring as it does on the same day, it certainly seems should be taken in close conjunction with them, all being parts of one general plan.

These acts endow as before, out of the reservation previously set aside, the twenty academies named with 6,000 acres of land each, and also confer on each board of trustees the right to raise by lottery—a very common practice in those days and one considered by the best people as legitimate[4]—$1,000 to pay for locating the lands and other preliminary expenses. Section 3 of the second act establishes the gen-

[1] Littell's Laws of Kentucky, Vol. II, p. 217

[2] *Ibid*, Vol. II, p. 237.

[3] Toulmin's Acts of Kentucky, pp. 473-475, and Littell's Laws of Kentucky, Vol. II, pp. 240-246.

[4] For instance, some of the most prominent citizens of the State were, on February 4, 1812, authorized to raise $1,000 by lottery to complete a church on the public square at Frankfort. (Collins's History of Kentucky, Vol. I, pp. 26-27.) Another example of the moral ideas of the time is given in a notice in the Kentucky Gazette of August 20, 1788, which offers to give whisky for the erection of a church.

eral principle of granting a similar landed endowment by the State to academies in each county, by conferring upon the several county courts, in the counties having no academies, the right to a donation of 6,000 acres of land each, and does not even confine them to the Cumberland River reservation, but says they may locate their donation for academies that may be established on "any waste and unappropriated land."

The part of the charter of Transylvania University to be taken in connection with this general academy act is section 3, which, after stating that the seat of the university may be moved from Lexington by a vote of two-thirds of the trustees, adds, "and, on the concurrence of the same number, they may, from time to time, establish at the seat of the university, or elsewhere, one or more schools as nurseries of the said university." Circumstances seem to indicate that this had reference to the academy plan established at the same time and that it was aimed to make Transylvania University the head of a splendid scheme of public higher education, consisting of a central State university with correlated preparatory academies in every county of the State—truly a noble conception, for the main credit of which Judge Caleb Wallace's biographer[1] thinks he is undoubtedly entitled. If the act of February 10, 1798, "contains in its closing sections certain sentiments and provisions that reflect enduring luster on the State of Kentucky,"[2] it is certainly no great exaggeration to say that the combined acts of December 22, 1798, "established the most enlightened, practical, and complete system of education that could at that time be witnessed in America or perhaps anywhere else in the civilized world,"[3] and that there are no brighter pages in the statute books of Kentucky than those that record these acts.

As already indicated, no doubt the main influence in the passage of these acts was that of Judge Caleb Wallace, one of the early justices of the supreme court of Kentucky. While a resident of Virginia he had been among the founders of what are now Hampden-Sidney College and Washington and Lee University,[4] and, on coming to Kentucky, had become a member of the board of trustees of Transylvania Seminary in 1783, when, as a member of the Virginia legislature from Kentucky, he secured its reendowment and first incorporation. He later became a trustee of Kentucky Academy, and, in 1798, was laboring to build up the latter institution by securing for it an ample landed endowment. He was also one of the principal promoters of its union with Transylvania Seminary into Transylvania University, and seems to be

[1] Rev. W. H. Whitsitt, D. D., LL. D., ex-president of the Southern Baptist Theological Seminary, Louisville, Ky., in his Life and Times of Judge Caleb Wallace, Louisville, 1888.

[2] Whitsitt's Life and Times of Judge Wallace, p. 130.

[3] *Ibid*, p. 135.

[4] For Judge Wallace's connection with these institutions see Foote's Sketches of Virginia, first series, pp. 393-397, 442-444, and 458.

the one who conceived the magnificent university system of which we have just been speaking. We also have reason to believe that he contemplated the later addition to the system of public elementary schools which would, according to his ideas and those generally prevalent at the time, form the capstone of this beautiful educational structure. The part he played in the early educational history of Kentucky entitles his name to be placed even higher than that of the Todds among the State's benefactors, as he had even wider conceptions than they of the State's educational needs and of the means of supplying them. It can in no wise be ascribed to any fault of his that his splendid ideas were never fully realized; yet such was unfortunately the case. This grand system, so auspiciously planned, was never to be put into operation as a whole, and, as such, developed in all its capabilities, and was soon to be recognized as a failure.

Other academies were rapidly established and that part of the system was in quite full operation for a time, the movement continuing until 1820 or later, by which time as many as forty-seven county academies had been established and endowed with from 6,000 to 12,000 acres of land each, usually with the former amount. Evidences of the lack of public interest in the system and its ill success, however, soon began to appear in the frequent bills passed by the legislature allowing more time for the location of the academy lands and appointing new trustees where the old ones had resigned or acted improperly. A tendency to get more and more out from under State control soon displayed itself on the part of the trustees by their getting greater and greater rights in regard to the disposal of the land endowments, until finally, by an act of January 26, 1815,[1] they were given the absolute right of disposing of all their lands, provided only the funds were invested in stock of the Bank of Kentucky, the aim of the legislature in this case, it appears, being rather to bolster up the stock of the bank than to improve the condition of the seminaries.

Public utterances, showing the lack of success of the system, soon began to appear. Governor Slaughter, in his message of December 3, 1816, says that the academy fund "had proved inadequate to meet the enlightened and liberal view of the legislature," and by December 2, 1817, he recognizes the academies as failures. We find the committee on education of the State senate, in October, 1820, calling for additional help for the languishing seminaries, and Governor Adair, in his message of October 16, 1821, says the seminary funds "have been generally rendered inefficacious by negligence or indiscretion on the part of those to whose care the donations had been confided." The system had then for some time been practically abandoned as a State enterprise, the only further public patronage extended to it being an act of January 31, 1816,[2] making general the exemption from taxation of all seminaries

[1] Littell's Laws of Kentucky, Vol. V, pp. 163-164. [2] *Ibid.*, Vol. V, p. 331.

of learning, and an act of February 14, 1820,[1] giving all fines and forfeitures in the various counties to the respective seminaries located within them. This aid was, however, not very considerable and was insufficient to arrest the decline which had in most cases already set in, few of the academies, as the commissioners of 1822[2] inform us, being, in 1815, able to raise a fund sufficient to support good schools.

The reasons for the failure of the plan are not difficult to find, and have already been indicated to some extent. They may be enumerated as follows:

(1) The idea was in advance of the public opinion of the time. The people were preoccupied with other matters, partly necessary, such as driving back the Indians and providing for their own physical wants, but their leaders were largely engrossed in acquiring wealth in a prosperous and growing State, and they themselves too often considered the clearing, the tobacco patch, and the cornfield the best schools for their children, as McMurtrie[3] says in reference to Jefferson Seminary: "The clamors of Plutus drowning the modest accents of the muses." The legislature at this time seems to have considered the establishment of a State bank and the floating of its notes of vastly greater importance than the fostering of the academies. This lack of public sympathy for the movement would no doubt have been overcome if the more elementary schools had been added to it and the people had become attached to it by its being brought into more direct and intimate contact with them, but unfortunately the system was never sufficiently developed for this to be the case.

(2) The endowments were in many cases insufficient to accomplish their purpose, not because most of the lands set apart were poor and wild lands of little value, although some of them were no doubt of this character, but because these lands were really not sufficient in amount to support such a system well, and, moreover, much of them, in order to the speedy establishment of the schools, had been pushed into the market too hastily and disposed of at a great sacrifice, as was to be the case later, probably in a less degree, with the Congressional land grant of 1862 for agricultural colleges.

(3) The principal reason for the failure of the academies is to be found in the faults of the plan whereby their management was provided for and carried out. The trustees were self-perpetuating bodies and, as such, little responsible to public authority. Besides there was no adequate provision for calling them to account for their actions. Butler[4] calls them so many "promiscuous and irresponsible trustees." This opened the way for the primary cause of failure—speculation with and squandering of the funds, sometimes innocently, but often deliberately

[1] Littell and Swigert's Statutes of Kentucky, Vol. I, p. 596.

[2] Report of the commissioners appointed to collect information and prepare and report a system of common schools, p. 17.

[3] Sketches of Louisville, p. 124.

[4] History of Kentucky, p. 188.

and criminally. The endowments were at first well guarded by law, not more than one-eighth of the land being allowed to be sold for incidental expenses and providing buildings and apparatus, but subsequent acts gave the trustees too much discretion in disposing of the lands and opened the way "for the subsequent destruction of the endowment by incompetent or scheming men." It was too often the case that speculators bought the land and the money was all put in one costly building, unoccupied and useless, "a monument of the folly of its projectors."[1] Sometimes not even such a poor result was obtained from the endowment.

There was no general plan and no uniform means were adopted to secure the success of the whole system. Some few schools, through the wise management of their trustees, escaped the general wreck and retained their usefulness, some of them, as Bracken and Rittenhouse academies and Jefferson Seminary,[2] even becoming colleges afterwards. But the following, taken from Marshall,[3] written in 1824 in reference to Kentucky Seminary at Frankfort, is, alas too often, the record of the others:

> But being afflicted with the country disease—multiplicity and bad government—it has languished and revived alternately, in the building erected for it, until it has neither acting trustee, teacher, nor student, as it is believed.

While the academy plan as a whole was thus unfortunately a failure, yet it was not entirely so. Many of the schools long remained as important local educational factors, and one good result almost invariably came from the plan of endowment. Most of forty-seven counties of the State were able to buy a lot and build on it a fairly good school building, where a teacher could be supported by tuition and where many living near by were able to secure the elements of an education of which they would otherwise have been deprived. They were often able to pay at least a large part of their board and tuition in country produce, a thing they would not have been able to do elsewhere. Professor Chenault[4] sums up the educational result of the experiment by saying that "many of our early lawyers, doctors, ministers, and other professional men obtained all their education in these seminaries."

It is a great pity, both for the cause of education in Kentucky and elsewhere, that the great capabilities of this early educational system were never fully realized. Collins[5] has considered it a safe assumption to estimate that the seminary lands under proper management would have realized for each county an average permanent and productive school fund of at least $60,000, in many cases very much more than this amount—truly a magnificent financial foundation for a State educational system. Its comparative failure does not detract from the high meed of praise due the originator of this great educational project, whose abuses he could not well have foreseen and which certainly had in it the very greatest and grandest possibilities.

---

[1] Professor Chenault, in Smith's History of Kentucky, p. 703.

[2] See note to Chapter I, p. 14.

[3] History of Kentucky, Vol. II, p. 336.

[4] Smith's History of Kentucky, p. 697.

[5] History of Kentucky, Vol. I, p. 502.

BIBLIOGRAPHY.

A greater or less amount of information has been obtained from the following works in the preparation of this section:

Sketches of Virginia, by Rev. W. H. Foote, D. D., Philadelphia; first series, 1850; second series, 1855.

A Historical, Geographical, and Philosophical View of the American United States and the West Indies, by W. Winterbotham; 4 volumes, London, 1795.

A Description of Kentucky, by Harry Toulmin, 1792.

File of the Kentucky Gazette, 1787-1860 (old newspaper preserved in the Lexington city library).

A History of Kentucky, by Humphrey Marshall; first edition, 1 volume, Frankfort, 1812; second edition, 2 volumes, Frankfort, 1824.

A History of Kentucky, by Mann Butler, A. M., M. D.; first edition, Louisville, 1834; second edition, Louisville and Cincinnati, 1836.

Sketches of Kentucky, by Lewis Collins, Cincinnati and Maysville, 1847.

A History of Kentucky, by T. S. Authur and W. H. Carpenter, Philadelphia, 1852.

A History of Kentucky, by R. H. Collins, LL. D.; 2 volumes, Covington, 1874; the largest and best of the histories of Kentucky.

A History of Kentucky, by N. S. Shaler (American Commonwealth series), Boston, 1885.

A History of Kentucky, by Hon. Z. F. Smith, Louisville, 1886 (especially valuable for the article on education in Kentucky by William Chenault, LL. D.).

A History of Kentucky, by W. H. Perrin, J. H. Battle, and G. C. Kniffen, Louisville and Chicago, 1888; mainly compiled from other histories, but containing considerable new educational matter.

The Laws of Kentucky, by John Bradford, Lexington: Vol. I, 1799; Vol. II, 1807.

The Public and Permanent Acts of Kentucky now in force, together with Acts of Virginia in regard to Rents, Land Titles, and the Encouragement of Learning, by Harry Toulmin, Frankfort, 1802.

The Statutes of Kentucky, Comprehending also Laws of Virginia and Acts of Parliament now in force, by William Littell, Frankfort, 1809-1819.

A Digest of all the Laws of Kentucky, together with Virginia and English Laws still in force, by William Littell and Jacob Swigert, Frankfort, 1822.

Collections of Acts of the Legislature, published by order of the two Houses from time to time.

Messages of the governors of the State, published in the journals of the two houses of the legislature, from time to time.

Reports of committees on education of the two houses, published in like manner.

A History of Federal and State Aid to Higher Education, by Frank W. Blackmar, Ph. D., Washington, 1890.

The History of the Presbyterian Church in Kentucky, by Rev. Robert Davidson, D. D., New York, 1847.

Early Catholic Missions in Kentucky, 1787-1827, by Right Rev. M. J. Spalding, Louisville, 1844.

The Life and Writings of John Filson, by R. T. Durrett, LL. D., Louisville, 1884.

The Life and Times of Judge Caleb Wallace, by Rev. W. H. Whitsitt, D. D., LL. D., Louisville, 1888.

The Biographical Encyclopedia of Kentucky, published by J. M. Armstrong & Co., Cincinnati, 1878.

A History of Fayette County, Ky., by Robert Peter, M. D., edited by W. H. Perrin, Chicago, 1882.

Sketches of Louisville and Its Environs, by H. McMurtrie, M. D., Louisville, 1819.

Report of the Commissioners Appointed by the General Assembly to Collect Information and Prepare and Report a System of Common Schools, Frankfort, 1822.

Articles on Education in Kentucky, by T. M. Goodknight, A. M., in the Southern School, Lexington, from June 1, 1893, to July 31, 1894 (extend up to February, 1844).

The American Journal of Education (especially volumes 4 and 5), edited by W. Russell, 5 volumes, Boston, 1826-1830.

The American Annals of Education (especially volume 1), edited by W. C. Woodbridge, 6 volumes, Boston, 1831-1836.

Barnard's American Journal of Education, 16 volumes, Hartford, 1855-1866.

THE OLD-FIELD SCHOOLS.

Existing at the same time with the academies were a species of schools which are probably frequently met with elsewhere in the early history of the States, especially south of New England, but which had, in Kentucky, a somewhat characteristic development and a local color. They were also for a long time a considerable factor in her educational system, lasting, as they did, up to comparatively recent times, and only being displaced by the present public-school system in its later and more complete form. These facts entitle these schools, although not strictly lying within the scope of this monograph, to something more than a passing notice.

They were ordinarily denominated "Old-field"[1] schools, and were the kind of schools mainly existing until the last generation in the more remote agricultural districts of the State, where access to the academies, which were located in the towns, was difficult. They were long the only means of education available to a large part of the rural population, they and the academies constituting the two principal streams of education in the early history of the State. As we have seen, the very earliest schools of the State, as those of Mrs. Coomes, at Harrodsburg, in 1776; of May, at McAfee's, in 1777; of Doniphan, at Boonesboro, in 1779, and of McKinney, at Lexington, 1780, the four schools antedating Transylvania Seminary, were all probably of this type.

As soon as a community was fairly settled one of the first things undertaken was the building of a schoolhouse, also usually a church, partly by joint subscription, but mainly by joint labor, to meet their educational as well as spiritual needs. These schoolhouses, especially in early days, were of the most primitive pattern. They were built of logs, usually unhewn, the cracks being at most only half chinked, with "stack"[2] chimneys, and clapboard doors and windows, the latter as a rule being without frames or panes, although greased paper was sometimes used in lieu of glass. There was often no floor at all except the earth, and if there was, it was made of rude puncheons—split logs, with the hewn side turned up. The only desks to be had were the same rude puncheons, fixed in various ways, with legs inserted in auger holes or otherwise, at the proper height for sitting and writing, and without, as a rule, any backs of any kind to them. The only

[1] The name probably arose from the fact that the schoolhouses were usually built in some old clearing, often a spot formerly occupied by the Indians for agricultural purposes. The term "Hedge row" is applied to them by Professor Shaler (History of Kentucky, page 139), but the writer has never seen the term used elsewhere in reference to them, nor has he ever heard it used in western Kentucky, where the name "Old-field" is frequently used by elderly people.

[2] A name applied to a rough chimney built of logs and daubed with mud.

really comfortable thing about the whole structure in winter was the glow of the great fireplace, where huge logs were generously heaped, and in summer the breezes which circulated almost unhindered through the poorly chinked cracks.

In this rude educational house a teacher was installed and supported, as far as it could be called a support, by the pro rata subscriptions of the farmers of the neighborhood, a common rate of tuition being £1 7s. a year per pupil. The tuition fees were mostly paid in such articles as tobacco—then a legal tender in Kentucky, bear bacon, buffalo steak, jerked venison, furs, pot metal, bar iron, linsey, hackled flax, young cattle, pork, corn, or whisky, usually not over one-fourth of it being paid in money, a rare commodity on the then frontier.

Some of the teachers of these early schools, as Doniphan, were men of high standing, often following, for a great part of their time, the calling of a surveyor, then an honorable and lucrative one; but most of them were not, the character of the teacher and the methods he used being often almost as primitive as the house he occupied. He was usually some elderly man, of that or an adjoining neighborhood, who was supposed to have some education, but whose main qualification for the position was often that he did not know how, or did not care, or have the energy to do anything else, having probably failed in everything else he had undertaken; or he was some stranger, a traveling Irishman, or Englishman, or a wandering Yankee, whose qualifications for the place were presumed from the fact that he had seen a good deal of the world.

These men could not have made teaching a profession, as their wages were very low. When teaching, however, they were required to take up early and turn out late, giving short recesses and noon intermissions, the idea being that they must earn their money. They were otherwise practically under no supervision, except such as the pupils chose to put upon them, and taught according to their own peculiar theories, temperaments, and habits. They were often as rough and passionate as they well could be, and liberal in their use of the rod, even knocking down impertinent pupils; while, on the other hand, some of them allowed the scholars to do as they pleased. All, as a general thing, had written rules, which were frequently read and usually vigorously enforced, the pupils often dreading the frown and birch of the master more than the screams of the wild animals they sometimes heard on their way to and from the lonely schoolhouse.

The instruction given in the first of these schools consisted of reading, writing, and ciphering to the rule of three. The teacher had to be an expert penmaker, but his instruction in writing rarely extended beyond "capitals" and "large joining-hand."[1] Geography and arithmetic were taught orally—the former especially—often in doggerel verse, which was frequently sung in recitation and in studying, the pupils who were not reciting adding to the monotonous uproar of

[1] Perrin, Battle and Kniffen's History of Kentucky, p. 220.

the class by studying aloud, as they were usually allowed to do. The only text-books used at first were Dilworth's Speller and the Bible; later Webster's Spelling Book and Murray's English Reader and Grammar were introduced. Afterwards more mathematics and some classical instruction were added to the course in many schools, thus materially enlarging the education offered.

As already remarked, practically the only supervision to which the teacher was subjected was exercised by the pupils. This was regulated by custom, with which the patrons of the school never in any way interfered as long as it was at all within reason. It only concerned such things as treats upon certain recognized occasions, the granting of holidays, and similar matters, and was enforced by the larger boys of the school, who rode the teacher upon a rail, ducked him in some convenient spring or pond, or otherwise made things so unpleasant for him that he was forced to yield. A very common practice was "to turn him out" until he granted the desired concession. This is well illustrated by the following characteristic incident taken from an article by Col. R. T. Durrett, in the Louisville Courier-Journal, of April 2, 1881:

> On the 28th of April, 1809, the first show, as the boys called it, occurred in Louisville. It was the exhibition of an elephant, and there was a general uprising in all the schools for a holiday. The Jefferson Seminary and the schools at the head of which were teachers conversant with the habits of the place gave the boys a holiday without trouble, but there was a New England teacher, recently come to the charge of one of the log schoolhouses, who could not understand why the boys were to be permitted to lay aside their books a whole day to see an elephant. He would not grant the holiday asked and the boys went to work in the usual way to make him yield. On the morning of the 28th the Yankee teacher, as they called him, came to his schoolhouse and found the door well barred with benches, fence rails, and logs of wood, and the boys all inside laughing at his futile attempts to get in. They promptly told him the terms upon which the fort would be surrendered, which were simply to give them that day as a holiday, so they could go to see the elephant. The teacher was indignant, and not being able to get through the door, climbed upon the roof and attempted to descend the chimney. For this contingency the boys had prepared a pile of dry leaves, and when the teacher's legs appeared at the top of the chimney the leaves were lighted in the fireplace. Down came the teacher, for having once started he could not go back and the flames scorched him and the smoke smothered him, so that he was the powerless autocrat of the school and knight of the ferule. He gave the holiday and went home to lay up for repairs, as the boys expressed it, and the boys went to the show as if nobody had been either burnt or smoked.

Such were the methods of discipline and of teaching in the "old-field" schools, which, as has been said, were to be found in many parts of Kentucky until the last period of her educational history. In fact, some of somewhat similar type, in so far as schoolhouses at least are concerned, are still to be found in the out-of-the-way parts of the State; but their methods are far in advance of the primitive ones we have just described. These, for several generations, furnished to a large part of the agricultural population of the State the rudiments of an education which they would otherwise have been unable to secure.

They were of great service in their day and time, being for a long period practically the only schools accessible to many, especially to girls, whose education must otherwise have been almost entirely neglected.

BIBLIOGRAPHY.

Smith's History of Kentucky; Perrin, Battle and Kniffen's History of Kentucky.

Proceedings of the Crittenden County Teachers' Institute, Marion, Kentucky, 1877.

A History of Russellville and Logan County, by A. C. Finley, Russellville, 1878 and 1879.

Articles on Kentucky education, in the Louisville Courier-Journal for January 2, 9, 16, 23, and 30, 1881, by R. T. Durrett, LL. D.

Sketches of Montgomery County, by Richard Reid, Mount Sterling, 1882.

EARLY FEMALE EDUCATION.

It is an interesting fact that, although the first teacher in Kentucky was a woman, there were for a long time few schools at all for girls in the State, and these usually of the poorest and most primitive kind. Girls were excluded entirely from the early academies, and the only schools to which they had access, with few exceptions, were of the "old-field" type just described. The educational advantages offered in these were very limited as a rule, and the surroundings, at least, not calculated to be very refining. Professor Chenault, quoting from Felix Grundy, tells us that the teachers of these early schools, which girls generally had to attend if they received any education at all, "were often destitute both of a knowledge of polite literature and good manners."[1]

For a considerable period the only schools in the State claiming to give girls an ordinary grammar-school education were those of Rev. John Lyle, at Paris, and of Mrs. Keats, at Washington, Mason County. Our information in regard to these schools is very meager and can be given in a few words:

REV. MR. LYLE'S SCHOOL.

The Rev. John Lyle was one of the Presbyterian ministers prominent in the early history of Kentucky. We find him attempting to supply the great lack of educational facilities for girls, by opening, in 1806, at Paris, the first[2] female seminary in the West, if not in the United States. Mr. Lyle appeared to advantage as a teacher, and soon had a flourishing school of some 200 or more[3] pupils. He continued his school until 1809 or 1810,[4] when he is said[5] to have closed it because

[1] Smith's History of Kentucky, p. 699.

[2] Collins's History of Kentucky, Vol. I, p. 26.

[3] Collins's History of Kentucky, Vol. I, p. 26, says there were from 150 to 300 pupils, while page 483 of the same work gives the number as from 150 to 200. Foote's Sketches of Virginia, first series, page 551, says the school sometimes had more than 200 pupils.

[4] Collins (Vol. I, p. 483) says he declined to teach in 1809, while Sprague (Annals of the American Pulpit. Vol. IV, p. 179) says he withdrew from the seminary about 1810.

[5] By Foote and Sprague, as above.

others connected with the enterprise refused to allow the Bible to be read publicly in the school. Mr. Lyle then went into the active work of the ministry, in which he labored with success for many years afterwards.[1] His severing his connection with the school seems to have broken it up, as we do not hear of it again.

MRS. KEATS'S SCHOOL.

The other female school in the State at this period, which is also said[2] to be one of the most celebrated in the West at the time, was that taught by Mrs. Louisa Fitzherbert Keats, and was located at Washington, for some time the most important town in Mason County. Here, we are told, the daughters and wives of many of the distinguished men of the State were educated. The school was opened in 1807 and closed in 1812. We do not know for what reason.

OTHER EARLY FEMALE SCHOOLS.

Just at the time of the closing of Mrs. Keat's school, Loretto Academy was opened in what is now Marion County, and was followed, in 1814, by Nazareth Academy, in Nelson County. Not long afterwards, in 1825, Mrs. Tevis and her husband established Science Hill at Shelbyville. Four years earlier Lafayette Seminary had been founded at Lexington. This last school, while having a considerable attendance and reputation for a time,[3] does not seem to have had an extended history. Loretto, Nazareth, and Science Hill were, however, long the principal seats of female education, not only in Kentucky, but in the Southwest generally, and are still flourishing in their educational usefulness. They will, on this account, although a considerable part of their work is now to be classed as secondary and so lying outside the scope of this monograph, demand a more extended consideration at our hands in connection with the history of the female colleges of the State.

BIBLIOGRAPHY.

Foote's Sketches of Virginia, first series.

Collins's Sketches of Kentucky.

Collins's History of Kentucky.

Sketches of Paris and Bourbon County, by G. R. Keller and J. M. McCann, Paris, 1876.

The Annals of the American Pulpit, by Rev. W. B. Sprague, D. D., LL. D., 9 volumes, New York, 1859-1869.

---

[1] From Collins and Sprague, as above, we learn he was born in Virginia, in 1769; was educated at Liberty Hall (now Washington and Lee University), and was licensed to preach the Gospel in 1795. He came to Kentucky as a Presbyterian missionary in 1797 or 1798. His death occurred in 1825.

[2] Collins's History of Kentucky, Vol. II, p. 557.

[3] An annual announcement of the seminary for 1825 says it was visited by Lafayette on May 16, 1825. It then had nine instructors and one hundred and thirty-five pupils, and in the previous four years had had altogether three hundred and sixty-six pupils. It is said to furnish every facility "for making thorough and accomplished scholars."

SECOND MEDICAL BUILDING OF TRANSYLVANIA UNIVERSITY. ERECTED 1840, BURNED 1863.

CHAPTER III.

TRANSYLVANIA UNIVERSITY.

Transylvania University was formed by the union of Transylvania Seminary and Kentucky Academy, the history of each of which we will trace separately until they are merged into the more general and larger institution, the university proper.

TRANSYLVANIA SEMINARY.

We have seen in connection with the investigation of the early State university system that this school had its origin in the act of the Virginia Assembly of May, 1780, for the conception and passage of which Rev. John Todd, of Virginia, and his nephew, Col. John Todd, of Kentucky, are entitled to lasting credit and honor. This act,[1] which has been quoted at length in connection with the inauguration of the early academies, put the endowment of 8,000 acres of land in the hands of thirteen trustees, including Colonel Todd himself and several other prominent men of Kentucky, then the western frontier county of Virginia, and declared that the seminary should be "erected within the said county as soon as the circumstances of the county and the state of its funds will admit."

No corporate powers were conferred on the trustees mentioned, and not even a name was given to the proposed school. No definite idea was probably entertained of its being opened at an early date, for Virginia was then in the midst of what was to her one of the most disturbing times of the Revolution, and Indian hostilities in Kentucky, while experiencing a temporary lull, were soon to break forth with such violence as to bear down in their course the founder, Colonel Todd[2] himself and other trustees and valuable friends of the enterprise. The matter was, however, not entirely lost sight of, as we find that on July 1, 1780, an inquest of escheat was held near Lexington, Daniel Boone, so famous in the early annals of Kentucky, being one of the jurors, and

[1] Toulmin's Acts of Kentucky, p. 462; Littell's Laws of Kentucky, Vol. III. p. 571; Hening's Statutes at Large of Virginia, Vol. X, p. 288.

[2] Col. John Todd and Col. Stephen Trigg were killed in the disastrous battle of the Blue Licks, fought on August 19, 1782. Col. John Floyd was killed from ambush near Floyd's Station, on April 12, 1783. John May, another trustee, was also killed in a boat on the Ohio River in the early part of 1790.

4,000 acres of the land given to the seminary was condemned and appropriated to its uses. This land, together with the remainder of the original donation, which was condemned later, is described as "as good as any in the country."

Nothing more seems to have been done until May 5, 1783, when another act[1] was passed by the Virginia Assembly, largely, at least, through the influence and efforts of Hon. Caleb Wallace,[2] then a representative in that body from the county of Lincoln, in the District[3] of Kentucky, and later one of the justices of its supreme court when Kentucky became a State. Judge Wallace was perhaps more thoroughly identified with the cause of education, at least higher education, in Kentucky than any other one man before or since his time. We have already noticed somewhat his connection with the founding of Transylvania Seminary, and shall see him later taking an equally prominent part in establishing its rival, Kentucky Academy, and then in uniting the two into Transylvania University.

The preamble of the act of 1783, after quoting the act of 1780 donating public land to the school, gives the reason for its own enactment as follows:

> And whereas it hath been represented to this general assembly that voluntary contributions might be obtained from individuals in aid of the public donation, were the number of said trustees now alive and willing to act, increased, and such powers and privileges granted to them, by an act of incorporation, as are requisite for carrying into effect the intentions of this legislature in the said act more fully recited: Be it therefore enacted, etc.

The act goes on to name as trustees twenty-five men, the most prominent in the district, including Judge Wallace and seven of the trustees under the former act. Their names are worthy of being mentioned on account of their prominence in other matters as well as those of education, embracing as they do future governors, generals, judges of circuit and supreme courts, legislators and prominent lawyers, physicians, and ministers. They are as follows: William Fleming, William Christian, Benjamin Logan, John May, Levi Todd, John Cowan, Edmund Taylor, Thomas Marshall, Samuel McDowell, John Bowman, George Rogers Clarke, John Campbell, Isaac Shelby, David Rice, John Edwards, Caleb Wallace, Walker Daniel, Isaac Cox, Robert Johnson, John Craig, John Mosby, James Speed, Christopher Greenup, John

[1] Toulmin's Acts of Kentucky, pp. 463–467; Littell's Laws of Kentucky, Vol. III, pp. 571–576; Hening's Statutes at Large, Vol. XI, p. 283.

[2] See Whitsitt's Life and Times of Judge Caleb Wallace, especially pp. 122–135; also Bishop's History of the Church in Kentucky for forty years (containing the Memoirs of Rev. David Rice), pp. 96–97.

[3] Kentucky was at first a part of Fincastle County, Va. It was first made a separate county by an act going into operation on December 31, 1776, and by an act going into effect November 1, 1780, was called the District of Kentucky, and was divided into the counties of Jefferson, Fayette, and Lincoln. See Littell's Laws of Kentucky, Vol. I, p. 626.

Crittenden, and Willis Green. The name Transylvania[1] is then for the first time given to the proposed seminary, and it is granted 12,000 acres[2] of other escheated lands in addition to the 8,000 acres already bestowed. The 20,000 acres are also exempted from taxation and the teachers and students from militia duty. The trustees are made by the act a self-perpetuating body on the principle of cooptation and are given in general—

"All the powers and privileges that are enjoyed by the visitors or governors of any college or university within the State." They are also given the right to confer, by diploma signed by the president and five of the trustees, the degree of bachelor or master of arts "upon all such students, if such there be, as the said trustees, with the concurrence of a majority of the professors, shall adjudge to have merited the honor of the seminary by their virtue and erudition," and at the same time confer "any honorary degree which, with the same advice, shall be adjudged to other gentlemen on account of merit."

You will observe that we have here, under the name of a seminary, all the provisions of a college charter; in fact, this very charter, with its powers and privileges not materially changed, as far as can be ascertained, was the one under which a university was afterwards operated.

We have already seen that the seminary, by reason of its plan of endowment and in its purposes, was looked upon as a State institution, but it is also to be noted that most of its chief promoters were Presbyterians, a denomination then and for some time afterwards largely predominant, as an intellectual factor at least, in Kentucky affairs, and quite a large majority of its first active board of trustees, just mentioned above, were members of that church and prominent in its councils. The Presbyterians are undoubtedly entitled to the credit of inaugurating higher education in Kentucky.[3] Transylvania Seminary, the first institution in the State, distinctively one of higher education, owed its origin to their initiative, and was opened under their auspices. In purpose and name it was a State institution, but in organization it was really Presbyterian by reason of its cooptative board of trustees

[1] This name a classical synonym for 'back woods', or frontier, was borrowed from the use of it by Col. Richard Henderson, of North Carolina, and his followers who, in 1775, by the purchase from the Cherokees of the portion of the State between the Kentucky and Cumberland rivers, attempted to set up an independent government in Kentucky, under the name of Transylvania, in defiance of the claims of Virginia, to which they soon had to submit. The use of the name for the school was in one way rather appropriate, as its founder, Colonel Todd, had been a representative in the temporary legislature, organized by Colonel Henderson at Boonsborough in May, 1775. Colonel Todd had come to Kentucky from Virginia just prior to that date. Later in the spring of 1780 he was sent as a delegate from the County of Kentucky to the Virginia Assembly. See Morehead's Boonsborough Address, pp. 34-35 and 79-81.

[2] Davidson tells us, (Presbyterian Church in Kentucky, p. 289), that when Kentucky became an independent State in 1792, she so modified her laws of escheat, in order to encourage settlers, that the Seminary was deprived of this 12,000 acres and was only left the original 8,000 acres.

[3] See Davidson's Presbyterian Church in Kentucky, pp. 314 et seq.

being largely of that denomination. The bad results of this unfortunate union of church and state soon began to appear.

The trustees met, according to the requirements of the charter, on November 10, 1783, "at John Crow's Station, near Danville," which town had lately been made the capital of the district,[1] and was also at that time its intellectual center, and organized with Rev. David Rice, ordinarily called "Father" Rice,[2] the oldest and in some respects the most prominent Presbyterian minister of the western country, as chairman.

Mr. Rice was born in Virginia, in 1733, had graduated from Princeton College, New Jersey, in 1761, and had later studied theology under Rev. John Todd. He had already been among the founders of what is now Hampden-Sidney College, in his native State, and having come to Kentucky in the spring of 1783, at once took a natural interest in the new educational enterprise just starting there. He remained connected with the seminary board until July 18, 1787, during which time he took quite an active part in its affairs. We shall subsequently find him equally active in raising up its rival Kentucky academy. His successor as chairman of the seminary board was Judge Harry Innes,[3] of the district court, who presided over its meetings for several years.

As has been said above, this original grant, as quoted also in the charter of 1783, required the school to be opened as soon as the condition of the country and the state of its funds would admit. We have seen that the extremely unsettled state of affairs in the pioneer district was at first an insurmountable obstacle. It continued to be a hindrance for some time to come, but soon the second of the conditions was the greater difficulty of the two. No funds from the endowment lands were yet available, and no other means were at hand to inaugurate the enterprise. Good lands were abundant and cheap in the district, just then fairly settled, and the seminary lands could consequently neither be sold for much, nor rented, nor leased in such a way as to bring in much immediate income. The policy of the trustees from the beginning was to lease[4] these lands for comparatively long periods at a low rate, trusting to the growth of the country to increase their value and consequent returns. All the board seems to have done at their first meeting was to elect a chairman and appoint a committee to solicit subscriptions of money or property for the enterprise. They

[1] By having been made the seat of the supreme court of the district in 1783.

[2] So called from his fatherly care over the infant Presbyterian churches in the State. At this time he was only about 50 years of age. For sketches of his life see Collins's History of Kentucky, Vol. I, p. 460, and Sprague's Annals of the American Pulpit, Vol. III, p. 248.

[3] Also spelled Innis, but this seems at least the preferable spelling.

[4] The arrangements for the first important lease, Bradford tells us (Notes, p. 438), were made on October 14, 1788, after which date the school began to derive some income from this source, but the returns under the lease system never seem to have been very large.

recognized the imperative need of such a school in a young and rapidly growing community, and so issued their call for aid in its early establishment.

There seems, however, not to have been much response to this call, and what few small subscriptions were received seem to have been mainly contributed by the trustees themselves. The time was not propitious for such an undertaking. The financial trouble and distress due to the close of the Revolution were augmented by troubles with the Indians, the contest then on being mainly that of tomahawk, scalping knife, and rifle, and not of intellectual growth or prowess; moreover, the attention of the people was necessarily largely absorbed in subduing the wilderness and making homes and a livelihood for themselves and their families. Land had to be cleared, roads opened, and other means of communication and civilization prepared.

At a meeting of the board, held at Danville, March 4, 1784, one of the few encouragements received at this period—and quite an important acquisition, as such things were a great luxury in a frontier settlement, where they were rare and hard to obtain, owing to the imperfect facilities for transportation—came in the form of the gift of a small library and some philosophical apparatus from Rev. John Todd, of Virginia, who, although at such a great distance in that day, seems still to have kept a watchful eye over the interests of the infant institution, the original foundation of which he had encouraged, and who showed his spirit in such matters by making the donation "as an encouragement to science." The difficulty of communication at the time is well illustrated by the fact that, although the trustees seem to have made early arrangements to have these articles transported as promptly as possible, they were not received in Kentucky until the spring of 1789. Notwithstanding discouragements and the still unsettled state of the country, the trustees persevered, and at a meeting held on November 4, 1784, resolved to open a grammar school "at or near the residence of Rev. David Rice,[1] the tuition being put at 4 pistoles[2] per year, payable quarterly, and a committee being appointed to provide a suitable person to teach under the direction of the chairman. This committee reported on May 26, 1785,[3] that the school had been conducted at the house of Rev. David Rice since the 1st of the previous February by Rev. James Mitchell, and that Mr. Mitchell had been then employed to

---

[1] Records of the Board of Trustees of Transylvania Seminary.

[2] A pistole was a Spanish coin whose value was about $3.60. Kentucky was at this time more directly connected financially with New Orleans than with the United States.

[3] This and in fact all the other dates of the university's history up to 1818, unless otherwise specified, are taken from the records of the board of trustees. That the committee reported on this day has caused Peter (Transylvania University, p. 28) to give it as the natal day of the institution; and that the school was to be opened "at or near the residence of Rev. David Rice," has caused Davidson and others to make Mr. Rice its first teacher.

teach for another year. So February 1, 1785, is the natal day of Transylvania Seminary, and Rev. James Mitchell was its first teacher. He received the modest salary of £30 ($100)[1] a year. The school was taught in the house of Mr. Rice because no other suitable place, it seems, could be found for it.

Such were the humble beginnings of the first[2] literary institution west of the Alleghany Mountains, an institution which after a comparatively obscure history of a few years was to blaze forth with sudden effulgence and to remain for two generations the highest star of the Western literary firmament. We summarize from Morehead[3]:

> A seminary of learning in a "barbarous neighborhood"—a wilderness still resonant with the war whoops of the savage—chartered in the midst of great political convulsion—organized at a frontier station—on the extreme verge of civilized society! Such were the auspices under which the first literary institution of Kentucky and the West was established.

We have no information as to how many pupils at first attended the school, but there were probably not many. Those were stirring times politically at Danville, where a number of the conventions[4] looking toward the separation of Kentucky from Virginia were held during the time of the location of the seminary there. Courage and fidelity were also then required of both teacher and pupils in staying at their posts, when the war whoop of the Indians was liable to be heard at any time and rifles had to be carried to and from school for protection. Political and other similar matters seem, at least in that community, to have then had by far the largest share of public attention, and the seminary was left to struggle on with difficulty. Mr. Mitchell, of whom we know little, seems to have remained something over a year and then to have returned to North Carolina, from which State he had probably come. About the only definite information[5] we are able to obtain con-

[1] The pound in early days in Kentucky was $3.33⅓, a value which is to be always attached to it throughout this monograph.

[2] The facts clearly establish at least the strong probability, if not the certainty, of the seminary antedating Martin Academy, which subsequently developed into Washington College, Tenn., and has been claimed by Foote (Sketches of North Carolina, p. 311) to be the oldest school in the Mississippi Valley. Foote says Martin Academy was incorporated in 1788; Merriam's Higher Education in Tennessee, p. 227, correctly gives this date as 1783. As a matter of fact, Transylvania Seminary rests directly on the act passed by the Virginia assembly in May, 1783 (Acts of 1783, p. 40), entitled "An act to amend an act entitled an act to vest certain escheated lands in the county of Kentucky in trustees for a public school," and indirectly on the earlier act here mentioned, which was passed in May, 1780 (Hening, X, 287-288). This earlier act vests 8,000 acres of Tory lands in thirteen trustees, who are mentioned, for the benefit of schools. In the Transylvania act of 1783 seven of these thirteen trustees are reappointed. The North Carolina act chartering Martin Academy was passed at the April session, 1783 (Martin's Private Acts of North Carolina, p. 119).

[3] Boonesborough address, p. 81.

[4] Six of the nine conventions held for this purpose occurred between December, 1784, and July, 1788.

[5] Sprague's Annals of the American Pulpit, Vol. III, p. 248.

cerning him is that he married the daughter of the Rev. David Rice. After his departure the existence of the seminary was probably for two or three years only nominal, as no other teacher seems, during that time, to have been employed.

The trustees, if they had ever looked upon Danville as the permanent seat of the school, had soon, probably by reason of the lack of efficient local support in its behalf, changed their ideas in this respect and had, as early as May 26, 1785, begun to discuss its location elsewhere. A committee of the board on June 1, 1786, reported in favor of its being located on the seminary lands 2½ miles south of Lexington. The legislature of Virginia, again appealed to in behalf of the struggling enterprise, passed an act on December 13, 1787,[1] granting to the seminary one-sixth of the surveyor's fees in the district of Kentucky, which by a general law, together with a similar share of these fees throughout the State, had formerly been bestowed upon William and Mary College—an act which might have materially helped the school out of its financial troubles if its provisions had not been so defective as to make it practically inoperative until an additional act of December 20, 1790,[2] made it effective by attaching the proper penalties to its violation.

Meanwhile all efforts at endowment at Danville by private subscription had failed, and the trustees, having continued to discuss the matter of location, finally, on April 17, 1788, resolved to hold their next stated meeting in Lexington, probably partly with the view, as has been noted, of soon locating the seminary on the endowment lands near there, and partly because they thought the school would receive a more favorable public consideration in that town. The celebrated John Filson,[3] then teaching in Lexington, took a considerable interest in the enterprise about this time, and through his articles in the Kentucky Gazette[4] and otherwise was perhaps one influence in causing this action of the trustees. We accordingly find the board meeting in Lexington October 13, 1788, and without finally deciding the question of location, which was discussed, resolving to open the school in that

[1] Toulmin's Acts of Kentucky, p. 136; Littell's Laws of Kentucky, Vol. III, p. 576.

[2] Toulmin's Acts of Kentucky, pp. 136, 137; Littell's Laws of Kentucky, Vol. III, pp. 577, 578. Davidson tells us (Presbyterian Church in Kentucky, p. 289) that this law was repealed by Kentucky in 1802. The writer has not been able to find any such repealing act in any of the early collections he has seen, but has found an act of June 23, 1792 (Acts of 1792–1797, p. 171), which suspended the act of 1790 for one legislative session. It is quite certain that the seminary did not get the benefit of these surveyors' fees for very long nor was its income from them ever very large.

[3] See references to sketches of Filson's life in Chapter I, p. 12.

[4] The Kentucky Gazette was established in Lexington, Ky., by John Bradford and his brother, Fielding Bradford, on August 11, 1787, and was the second oldest newspaper published in the Mississippi Valley, being only antedated a few weeks by the Pittsburg Gazette. A number of bound volumes of the early numbers of the Kentucky Gazette are now in the city library of Lexington, and furnish much valuable information on the public affairs of the time, in which its editor, John Bradford, took an able and prominent part.

town, a convenient property to be rented until suitable buildings were erected on the seminary lands or elsewhere. Two days later they appointed Elias Jones as "professor" in the seminary, at a salary of £100, payable quarterly from March 1, 1789, and made arrangements, if the number of pupils justified it, to have a grammar master at £60, and an usher, also, if needed. A subscription paper was at the same time drawn up to secure building funds.

The response by the Lexington public does not seem, however, to have been at the first much, if any, better than that of the people of Danville; and probably because the revenue from the leased lands—its only source of income at the time—was too small to pay his salary, Mr. Jones seems never to have taught at all in the school, as we find the trustees, on April 15, 1789, resolving to have only a grammar master, assisted by an usher if there were more than fifteen pupils. The arrival at this time of the library and apparatus given by Rev. Mr. Todd seems to have been some encouragement, and it was decided to open the school immediately at some convenient place. This convenient place does not seem to have been easy to find at first, and an advertisement[1] for a teacher, inserted in the Kentucky Gazette, did not even receive a ready response. Mr. Isaac Wilson, who had been for some time master of Lexington grammar school, however soon applied in answer to the advertisement, and after being examined by a committee of the board on May 22, 1789, was employed to teach for six months from June 1, 1789, "at the public schoolhouse adjacent to the Presbyterian meetinghouse, near Lexington."[2] This building was probably the seat of the school of which Mr. Wilson had been for some time master, and the two schools were thus probably united for the time. Mr. Wilson's salary was to be at the rate of £100 per annum, and the tuition rate in the seminary was fixed at £3 per annum.

The new master opened the school at the appointed date, June 1, 1789, which is the opening day of the school in Lexington. He went to work with a will, it seems, making a considerable success, at least locally, with the school, and on April 10, 1790, what may be called the first public college commencement probably occurring in the Mississippi Valley was held in Lexington. The following description of this commencement is taken from the Kentucky Gazette of April 26, 1790:

> Friday, the 10th instant, was appointed for examination of the students of the Transylvania Seminary by the trustees. In the presence of a very respectable audience several elegant speeches were delivered by the boys, and in the evening a tragedy acted, and the whole concluded with a farce. The several masterly strokes of eloquence throughout the performance obtained the general applause, and were acknowledged by an universal clap from all present. The good order and decorum observed throughout the whole, together with the rapid progress of the school in literature, reflects very great honor on the president.

[1] In the issue of April 25, 1789.

[2] From an advertisement in the Kentucky Gazette of June 6, 1789, which speaks of the school as already in operation.

The act of December 20, 1790, besides granting to it the surveyors' fees, gave to the seminary the use of the house it occupied free of rent after January 1, 1791, "so long as the public shall have no use for the same." The needed subscriptions which had been solicited not being forthcoming, loans and even a lottery scheme[1] were resorted to in vain to supply a permanent house for the school. Mr. Wilson had been reelected from time to time, but the number of scholars on April 13, 1791, was reported to have fallen from thirteen to five, probably largely on account of the Indian wars then raging, and as these wars had greatly reduced the income from the surveyors' fees, the tuition was raised from £3 to £4. At the same time Mr. Wilson severed his connection with the school.

On September 1, 1791, Rev. James Moore, a Presbyterian clergyman, lately come to the State from Virginia, succeeded Mr. Wilson as master. The latter probably reestablished Lexington grammar school, or academy, in the house lately occupied by the seminary, for we hear later of overtures from the seminary trustees looking toward its union with Lexington academy, and the seminary seems never to have occupied its former quarters again. Its master, Rev. James Moore, undoubtedly conducted the school for some time in his own house, as is evidenced by certain allowances made to him on various occasions by the trustees in the way of rent. Mr. Moore's salary the first term[2] was £25 and the tuition fees, and the second term £36 and the tuition fees, he being allowed in each case to charge an extra fee "for the Roman and Greek classics." The income from the surveyors' fees and leased lands soon improved somewhat, and the seminary gradually became more prosperous under Mr. Moore, whose salary was made £50 at the beginning of his second year, but the existence of the school was still somewhat precarious and its location still undecided until April 8, 1793, when the offer of the Transylvania Land Company was accepted and the institution permanently located in Lexington.

---

[1] Although the writer has been able to find no such act of Virginia, the records of the trustees show that a scheme of a lottery for raising £500 for the purpose of erecting a building for the seminary was adopted by the board on April 12, 1791, pursuant to an act of the general assembly. There is an advertisement of this lottery in the Kentucky Gazette of April 23, 1791, signed by a committee of seven of the trustees, and containing the following expression of what would now be considered a singular blending of moral ideas: "Since the cultivation of the moral virtues of the heart, as well as the advancement of the knowledge of the rising generation, is an object equally interesting to every good citizen, it is earnestly hoped that this scheme will attract the attention and patronage of the public." A notice in the issue of April 21, 1792, says that the drawings of the first class of the lottery will take place on June 20, 1792. The amount realized from the plan does not seem to have been large.

[2] The college year for many years in the early history of Kentucky was divided into two terms, one beginning in May, the other in November, April and October being vacation months. The stated meetings of the seminary trustees always occurred in these last two months.

This Transylvania Land Company was composed of John Bradford and other prominent and public-spirited citizens of the town, who, having organized themselves in a corporate capacity shortly before that time, on March 27, 1792, purchased a lot[1] (now Gratz Park), upon which a plain two-story brick house had been previously erected, which, on October 10, 1792, they offered to present to the seminary on condition of its permanent location in Lexington. This offer was accepted by the trustees on April 8, 1793, when arrangements were made "to make the house habitable"[2] for the school. Lexington was then rapidly becoming the most important commercial point in the upper Mississippi Valley,[3] a position it was to hold for some time to come, and was therefore a very favorable location for a college or university. The permanent location there of the seminary which was soon to develop into a university made the town for two generations "the literary capital of the West," and helped it to hold the political supremacy of the State for a time. The organization of the Transylvania Land Company was the beginning of a policy of generously fostering the educational enterprises in its midst, in which, as a rule, from that time forward, the town has never faltered. The members of the new company especially took a great interest in the future welfare of the seminary, to whose board of trustees a number of them were soon elected, John Bradford becoming president of that body in 1793 and remaining so for many years.

Mr. Moore was continued at the head of the school, which now at last had a settled home, and the greater prosperity of which, at least financially, is shown by the fact that on October 10, 1793, the master's salary was fixed at £100 per annum, and he was authorized to employ an usher at £60, to teach the "Latin and Greek classics," and an English teacher at a salary of £15, and the tuition in that department which was fixed at £2 10s., the tuition in the classical department being £4. Arrangements were also made to admit, free of tuition, as many as ten orphan boys. The general condition of the institution is shown by the following advertisement taken from the Kentucky Gazette of December 6, 1793, the original spelling being retained:

> The Transylvania Seminary is now well supplied with teachers of natural and moral philosophy, of the mathematics, and of the learned languages. An English teacher is also introduced into the Colledge who teaches Reading, Writing, Arithmetic and the English Grammar.

---

[1] Known as lot No. 6

[2] From the nature of the articles purchased for this purpose, which were locks, hinges, glass, etc., the house was evidently an old one, already on the lot when acquired by the company and not a new one erected after the purchase of the lot by them, as is stated by several writers on the subject. Neither do the records show that the seminary was required to pay for this building, as is also frequently stated. The cost of the house is given as £400.

[3] Espy, in his Tour in Kentucky and Indiana in 1805, p. 8, says that its main street then had much the appearance of Market street in Philadelphia. He adds that his brother, who was then at Transylvania University, was making considerable proficiency "in the dead languages and in general science."

The advertisement concludes with the following statement:

This Seminary is the best seat of education on the Western Waters; and it is to be hoped the time is not far distant when even prejudice itself will not think it necessary to transport our youths to the Atlantic States, to compleat their education.

John Price was the English teacher at this time, but we are not informed as to who the other teacher was besides Mr. Moore. The school had, however, hardly gotten settled in its new home and made a fair start toward prosperity when it experienced the first of the many troubles which it encountered on account of disagreement among the members of its self-perpetuating trustees and the peculiar relation in which it stood to religious denominations, especially the Presbyterians.

This denomination, through whose foresight and energy the school had been mainly founded, was put much more on the defensive and was more sensitive than usual in regard to doctrinal matters on account of the prevalence at that time in Kentucky, especially among her public men,[1] of the French deistical philosophy of the day. This fact is to be constantly borne in mind in considering the attitude of the Presbyterians toward the seminary. They had mainly founded the school, but they never seemed, either then or afterwards, to have attempted to obtain exclusive denominational control over it, which, by reason of their preponderance as an intellectual factor for a long time in the early history of the State, they could probably have been able to accomplish on more than one occasion by the aid of legislative action, as was done in regard to other schools by other denominations.[2] Their prominence in connection with the management and administration of the school for some time seems to have been, on their part, more the natural result of their interest in such matters than of any direct intention to control it. It is probably true, as Davidson tells us, that they voluntarily retired from its board of trustees, and allowed prominent public men to be elected in their places in order to increase the popularity of the institution. It was doubtless in this way that they lost their numerical superiority in the board. They were satisfied with the school and were willing to patronize it as long as it conformed to their ideals of what such a school should be, but when its religious tone or teaching, by reason of other control, became what they considered dangerous, they simply withdrew their patronage and established one that better suited their ideas and aims, one of which was to prepare suitable ministers for the church; and yet they were willing to even take the initiative in coming back again when these difficulties were out of the way. They were also equally prompt to retire again and establish another rival when a similar emergency arose.

[1] Several authorities agree that it was owing to the prevalence of these ideas probably that ministers of the gospel were excluded from public offices under the first and second constitutions of the State, a state of things they considered very deleterious to the interests of education, especially public-school education.

[2] For instance, in the case of Bethel Academy and the Methodist Church.

Mr. Moore had for some reason,[1] which does not appear, become unsatisfactory as master of the seminary, and on February 5, 1794, Rev. Harry Toulmin, a prominent Baptist minister recently come to the State from Virginia, was proposed as his successor. Mr. Toulmin was a personal friend of Thomas Jefferson, by whom he was strongly recommended for the position. He was also a man of ability, and subsequently became secretary of state under Governor Garrard, but he was suspected of Unitarian sentiments and his friendship with Mr. Jefferson was not in his favor, especially in the eyes of the Presbyterians, as on that account he was supposed to be tinctured with French philosophy, or infidelity, as they considered it. His candidacy brought on a contest in the board, perhaps intensified by jealousy between the Baptists and Presbyterians, and although Mr. Toulmin was finally elected on April 7, 1794, the Presbyterian members were greatly dissatisfied with the situation, and most of them resigned, either at once or soon after. Mr. Toulmin's salary per year was to be £100, one-half the tuition fees, and a residence. He was to take office on October 9 following his election, but Mr. Moore resigned two days after that event and Mr. Toulmin was inducted into office on June 30, 1794. The Presbyterians determined at once to establish an institution more distinctively under their own control, to which they could transfer their patronage. Their efforts resulted in the founding of Kentucky Academy, the history of which will mainly engage our attention until the two schools are subsequently united.

KENTUCKY ACADEMY.

This school was established on account of the dissatisfaction of the Presbyterians with the management of Transylvania Seminary, especially with the election of Mr. Toulmin as its master. "Father" Rice, Judge Wallace, and others, prominent in founding Transylvania Seminary, were also leaders in establishing the new school.

The initial step in this enterprise, and one that shows its purposes, was the issue by the presbytery of Transylvania on April 22, 1794, of an address to the people of Kentucky, Cumberland, and the Miami Settlement,[2] proposing to set on foot a grammar school and public seminary, meaning by the latter term a department of collegiate grade, which was to be "under their own patronage" and "might furnish the churches with able and faithful ministers."[3] It was to be under the control of the presbytery in a general way, but was not to be otherwise

[1] This was not probably, as some have stated, because of his leaving the Presbyterian Church at this time on account of his trial sermon not having been sustained by the Presbytery, for the Presbyterians later put him at the head of their own distinctive school, Kentucky Academy.

[2] Cumberland was the country around Nashville, Tenn., then one of the principal centers of population in that State. Miami referred to the settlement on the Miami River, occupying a similar position in Ohio.

[3] Davidson's Presbyterian Church in Kentucky, p. 291.

sectarian. The charter of the school, granted by the State legislature on December 12, 1794,[1] shows its spirit, which is more catholic than sectarian, in the following provisions:

(Sec. 7.) The president of the said academy shall be a minister of the gospel, of the most approved abilities in literature and acquaintance with mankind that may be obtained, and zealously engaged to promote the interest of real and practical religion.

(Sec. 15.) No endeavors shall be used by the president or other teachers to influence the mind of any student, to change his religious tenets, or to embrace those of a different denomination any further than is consistent with the general belief of the gospel system and the practice of vital piety.

So, while not narrow in spirit, Kentucky Academy is the first school in the State to be called denominational, soon to be one of the characteristic features of Kentucky's educational institutions, although it was not strictly so, as it had no denominational name or legal church connection and was really, in organization, one of the State academies, the first one chartered by Kentucky as an independent State. Its charter conformed to the general academy plan with a cooptative board of eighteen trustees, its management as a somewhat distinctively Presbyterian institution being secured by having its trustees largely, if not entirely, Presbyterians, Rev. David Rice, Judge Wallace, Rev. James Blythe, and others, prominent in local Presbyterian circles, being among their number. We shall see Bethel, another of the State academies founded about the same time, also soon coming under a similar denominational control for a time.

The presbytery, soon after issuing its address, appointed a committee of forty-seven as canvassers for funds to inaugurate the proposed institution. These proceeded with vigor, and soon raised, mainly in Kentucky, upwards of £1,000 ($3,333), quite a respectable sum considering the time and the circumstances under which it was raised. In 1795, Revs. David Rice and James Blythe went East as commissioners from the presbytery to the general assembly of the church at Philadelphia, and while there appealed to a larger Presbyterian constituency and to general benevolence. They succeeded in obtaining in the Atlantic States subscriptions amounting to about $10,000[2] to aid in endowing the new educational enterprise. Among other prominent contributors for this object were George Washington, John Adams, and Aaron Burr, the first two contributing $100 each and Burr $50.[3] Washington, in connection with making his contribution, is said to have inquired very carefully in regard to the state of learning and literature in the West, as Kentucky was then called.

[1] Littell's Laws of Kentucky, Vol. I, pp. 228-230.

[2] Davidson's Presbyterian Church in Kentucky, p. 164.

[3] This is as given by Davidson (Presbyterian Church in Kentucky, p. 124) and other authorities. Peter's Pennsylvania University, p. 62, gives one of the original subscription papers, which shows this sum to have been $40. It also shows that, among other prominent public men, Robert Morris gave $100.

The first business meeting of the academy trustees was held on March 11, 1795,[1] when its location was decided upon and arrangements made to erect the necessary buildings. The new school was located at Pisgah, seven miles southwest of Lexington, near the home of Judge Wallace, and had as its initial endowment, as we have seen, about $14,000. Later, on September 15, 1797, it received a small but valuable library and some philosophical apparatus,[2] amounting in all to about £80 in value, through Rev. Dr. Gordon, of London, contributed by himself and other English friends, and under the academy act of February 10, 1798,[3] it was granted 6,000 acres of land by the State.

Its grammar-school department seems to have been opened on October 26, 1795,[4] and had as its first teacher Rev. Andrew Steele. On April 13, 1796, Mr. Steele was succeeded by Rev. James Moore, formerly master or principal of Transylvania Seminary. Mr. Moore was reelected to his former position in Transylvania Seminary on September 23, 1796, and notices in the Kentucky Gazette show that Mr. Steele again took charge of the academy, John Thomson becoming his assistant on October 6, 1797, when the seminary or collegiate department was first arranged to be opened. We know very little of the history of the school, but it seems in the main to have been fairly successful during the period of its existence. The last meeting of its trustees occurred in October, 1798, when the question of its union with Transylvania Seminary was finally decided, and the arrangements looking toward that end completed.

Meanwhile Transylvania Seminary seems to have had somewhat of a similar history under Mr. Toulmin. The funds of the school seem for some reason to have become low again, and so we find that on the day he took the oath of office the previous order of the trustees allowing free scholarships was revoked. Only two teachers were employed during the administration, the assistant teacher for at least most of the time being Jesse Bledsoe, later one of the distinguished law professors of Transylvania University. It is probably true that several of the State academies, especially Salem Academy, at Bardstown,[*] being in various ways situated under somewhat more favorable circumstances, were more highly prosperous about this time than either Transylvania Seminary or Kentucky Academy. The people of most portions of the State, especially that around Lexington, then the commercial and for a time the political center of the State, were too deeply engrossed in the Indian wars of the Northwest, the reform of the criminal stat-

[1] Bishop's Church in Kentucky, p. 97.

[2] Ranck and others mention certain antiquated pieces of apparatus, now in Kentucky University, as being probably parts of this old donation. They probably either belonged to it or to the apparatus given by Colonel Todd, or perhaps to both.

[3] See references to Toulmin and other authorities in Chapter II.

[4] This is according to Bradford (Notes, p. 438) and is probably correct. Davidson says the opening occurred early in 1795, soon after the presbytery had issued its address.

utes, the resolutions of 1798, the free navigation of the Mississippi River, the acquisition of Louisiana, and similar matters to pay very much attention to education. Later the war of 1812 became a matter of all-absorbing interest, in which struggle we have accounts of teachers and scholars, especially in the "old-field" schools, enlisting almost en masse.

Frequent calls for meetings through the columns of the Kentucky Gazette, and the passage of a law by the legislature in 1795[1] making seven members a quorum for all ordinary business, because it seems more would not attend their meetings, show that even the trustees were not very careful in regard to their duties. The course of study in Transylvania Seminary was laid out by a committee of the board early in Mr. Toulmin's administration, probably at his suggestion, and arrangements were made to enlarge the library. It is rather interesting to note the curriculum laid down, as showing the scope of the work then done and the ideas of classification then in use. The following division of subjects is given: Professional—the Greek, Latin, and French languages, and bookkeeping; nonprofessional—geometry, geography, politics, composition, elocution, moral philosophy, astronomy, history, logic, and natural philosophy. Additional library facilities were at this time secured by the foundation, on October 8, 1794, of what is now the city library of Lexington, then first established by a stock company on the share plan and for some time located in the seminary building.

Mr. Toulmin was unanimously reelected at the end of his first year's service, but voluntarily retired on April 4, 1796. In a letter in the Kentucky Gazette, on April 9, 1796, he gives as the principal reason for his withdrawal the smallness of the salary attached to the office, but also intimates that the state of public opinion in regard to the school was not very satisfactory, owing probably to the contest which arose at the time of his first election. Some acts[2] of the legislature passed during his administration, which were calculated to interfere with the powers and rights of the trustees, but which seem never to have been pressed to any definite result, are probably evidences of this dissatisfaction. The financial condition of the school had improved somewhat, as it was arranged on June 10, 1795, to erect a dormitory for it at a cost of £1,073⅓, which amount was derived from the rent of the seminary lands. Soon after his retirement from the seminary Mr. Toulmin became secretary of state under Governor Garrard and was subsequently a federal judge in Alabama.

On September 23, 1796, Rev. James Moore was again called to the head of the seminary, with the same salary as that of his predecessor.

[1] Passed December 21. See Toulmin's Acts of Kentucky, p. 467, and Littell's Laws of Kentucky, Vol. III, pp. 576–577.

[2] One passed November 21, 1795, suspended the trustees from office until the end of that legislative session, and another, passed December 21, 1795, put them under the control of the court in the judicial district in which they met.

The active rivalry between it and Kentucky Academy seems to have ceased as soon as Mr. Toulmin, whose election had caused the separation, had resigned. The members of the two boards most deeply interested in the cause of education, particularly Judge Wallace, seem soon to have thought of the union of the two schools, desiring to build up an institution that might be a credit and honor to the State by combining the two endowments. Moderation and good sense prevailing, this commendable object was at length accomplished after considerable discussion and deliberation. A proposition for the union came from the academy trustees as early as June 3, 1796, and on September 23 of that year was reported on by a committee of the seminary trustees as "for the public good" and "consistent with the laws."[1] On October 10 following, committees of the two boards agreed upon a plan of union practically the same as that subsequently adopted, but for some reason, although it was at first accepted by the seminary board the next day, this was debated and discussed at intervals for over two years, whether on account of the academy trustees insisting, as one of the conditions of union, that the students should be required to attend prayers daily and church service on Sunday does not appear, although this was in the terms proposed by the academy trustees and may have been one of the questions at issue.

Meanwhile, Transylvania Seminary, although apparently growing more prosperous, as is shown by the appointment, on October 10, 1797, at the same time that Mr. Moore was unanimously reelected, of a French teacher at a salary of $50 and the tuition in his department, even made propositions for union to another school in Lexington—Lexington Academy; but finally, on November 2, 1798, the union with Kentucky Academy was definitely agreed upon. This union was, upon joint petition of the two boards drawn up November 3, 1798, and consummated by an act of the State legislature on December 22, 1798.[2] This action was not indorsed by "Father" Rice and some other promoters and friends of Kentucky Academy, who still mistrusted the management of Transylvania Seminary, but was largely brought about by the influence of Judge Wallace, a friend of both schools and of the cause of education in general. It was, as we have seen, only part of a splendid educational plan, of which the academy act of the same date was another part, for the conception of which Judge Wallace is entitled to imperishable honor.

THE UNIVERSITY PROPER.

January 1, 1799, the day on which the act of December 22, 1798, went into effect, may be truly called the natal day of Transylvania University, as the combined institution was called in the act of union. The history of the new university from this time forward may be, in

---

[1] Records of the Board of Trustees of Transylvania Seminary.

[2] Toulmin's Acts of Kentucky, pp. 467–469; Littell's Laws of Kentucky, Vol. II, pp. 234–236.

general, according to Collins, divided into four periods, as follows: (1) That from 1799 to 1818, (2) from 1818 to 1827, (3) from 1827 to 1849, and (4) from 1849 to 1865.

PERIOD FROM 1799 TO 1818.

The joint petition of the two boards to the legislature asking for the act of union is of interest as showing the ideas and purposes had in view in their action. The main clause of its preamble reads as follows:

> That the respective boards of the said trustees, contemplating the many singular advantages to be derived to this remote country from promoting therein a university well endowed and properly conducted, more especially as by this measure only many of our youths can be prevented from going into other countries to complete their education, where they must greatly exhaust their fortunes, and from whence they may probably return with corrupted principles and morals to be the pests and not the ornaments of the community, and further contemplating that the uniting of several of the institutions of learning which have been originated in this country is essential to the speedy attainment of that object; therefore, the said boards of trustees have unanimously resolved and mutually agreed on the following terms of union, which they also consider very desirable in many points of view.[1]

Then follows the plan of union, which will not be quoted at length. It was simply, in effect, an enlargement of the Transylvania Seminary act of 1783, as the laws regulating the seminary were to be those regulating the university, unless altered by the legislature upon joint petition of a majority of its new board of trustees, and the seat of the university was to be Lexington, unless changed by a two-thirds vote of that board. The more distinctive outlines of a university are to be seen in the new charter in the extension somewhat of the already ample powers conferred by the seminary charter, in the arrangement of a broad plan of possible union with other schools, in the system of preparatory schools provided for, as noticed in connection with the history of the early university system, and in the establishment of free scholarships for deserving poor students.

The new institution, by the union of the funds of the academy and seminary, also began to have quite a respectable endowment for the time. Kentucky Academy, according to a report of a committee of its trustees made October 11, 1796,[2] possessed nearly $8,000 in cash, reliable subscriptions, books, and apparatus, besides the 6,000 acres of land later given to it by the State; while Transylvania Seminary had, besides its educational plant in Lexington, 14,000 acres of land, having, as Davidson[3] tells us, secured an additional 6,000 acres under the general academy act of 1798, thus making the combined land endowment, according to various estimates, to be worth from $40,000 to $179,000. He also informs us that the combined chemical and philosophical

---

[1] Records of the Board of Trustees of Transylvania Seminary.

[2] £2,298 14s. 10½d., Records of Trustees of Transylvania Seminary.

[3] Presbyterian Church in Kentucky, p. 296.

apparatus of the new institution was good, and that its library numbered 1,300 volumes.

The legislature had selected, as trustees, the list of twenty-one names submitted to them in the petition, instead of accepting the other alternative proposed, to unite the two old boards and not allow any vacancies to be filled until twenty-one members were left. The new board was made up of eight members selected from each of the old ones, and five others, including Judge Wallace, John Bradford, George Nicholas, James Garrard, and other prominent public men, and was constituted in such a manner as to give the Presbyterians a representation of one-half or more of the whole. The new body was on the same cooptative basis as the old one, and unfortunately some of the old factional spirit seems to have remained among its members.

Rev. James Moore, now an Episcopalian, was continued at the head of the new university as its president, and had associated with him in its faculty Rev. James Blythe, M. D., D.D., and Rev. Robert Stuart, both Presbyterians, the respective chairs of the three being mental philosophy, logic, and belles-lettres, mathematics and natural philosophy, and languages. The president's salary was $500 and certain perquisites, including a residence, while that of the professors was $400 each. At their first meeting under the new régime, on January 8, 1799, the trustees gave the institution the appearance of a real university by appointing Hon. George Nicholas, professor of law and politics, and Drs. Samuel Brown and Frederick Ridgely, professors respectively of chemistry and surgery.[1]

Mr. Nicholas had been prominent in Virginia, especially in the convention that adopted the Federal constitution, and is called by Butler[2] practically the author of the first constitution of Kentucky, to which State he had come shortly before the meeting of its first constitutional convention, and "the most eminent lawyer of his time, whether his learning or his powers of mind be regarded." He began a course of instruction in law in the university to a class of about nineteen students, among whom, it appears, were William T. Barry and others, subsequently celebrated in Kentucky history, but died before the end of the year, the remaining lectures and the examination of his class being taken charge of on August 7 of that year by a committee of the trustees, themselves prominent lawyers.

Dr. Brown is famous as being the first[3] regular medical professor in

[1] The transcript of the minutes of the trustees examined by the writer calls these chairs simply chairs of medicine. They are given in the list as usually stated in most authorities. Peter's Transylvania University, page 77, gives them as chemistry, anatomy, and surgery, and materia medica, midwifery, and practice of physic. It is quite certain that Dr. Ridgely gave lectures on surgery.

[2] History of Kentucky, p. 206.

[3] He was appointed before Dr. Ridgely. Dr. Brown vaccinated as many as 500 people in Lexington and vicinity before any other physician in America would try the experiment.

the West and for his achievements in the introduction of vaccination into America. He was connected with the medical faculty of the university until 1806 and again from 1819 to 1828.

Dr. Ridgely is noted as being the first to deliver medical lectures in the West and as being the preceptor of the celebrated Dr. B. W. Dudley, afterwards so long and successfully connected with the university faculty. Dr. Ridgely lectured about this time to a class of six medical students, but seems to have done so in an individual capacity, as both his appointment and that of Dr. Brown as professors in the university seem to have been, at this early period, merely nominal.

On October 18, 1799, Hon. James Brown, a member of a family then and since very prominent in the history of the State, became Mr. Nicholas's successor as professor of law. This chair for the remainder of this period was occupied for short intervals by Henry Clay, who was elected October 10, 1805; James Munroe, elected October 16, 1807; John Pope, elected March 1, 1814, and John Breckinridge, elected April 18, 1817, all of whom probably lectured more or less.

On November 4, 1799, Rev. James Welch succeeded Rev. Robert Stuart as professor of languages. He held the position until July 17, 1801, when some difficulty with the students caused him to resign, and on July 23 following Alexander McKeehan was elected to the chair. Considerable trouble seems, for some reason, to have been connected with this chair, for we find that, on October 7, 1802, Rev. Andrew Steele, formerly connected with Kentucky Academy, succeeded Mr. McKeehan, and that on November 3, 1803, he was succeeded by James Hamilton, and he in turn, on October 1, 1804, by Ebenezer Sharpe, who was either more fortunate or more efficient than his predecessors, for he held the position until the end of this period.

We know that the number of students in attendance upon the university was not large about the end of this period, and there were, probably, comparatively few[1] during Mr. Moore's presidency. A college course of fairly good compass for the time was, however, maintained, and on April 7, 1802, the first degree granted by the institution, that of A. B., was conferred on Robert R. Barr. On October 6, of the same year, the same degree was conferred on Josiah Stoddard Johnston and Augustine C. Respass. Mr. Johnston subsequently became United States Senator from Louisiana.

For some reason, not apparent, a misunderstanding seems soon to have arisen between Mr. Moore and the trustees, and on October 4, 1804, Dr. Blythe was asked to act as president, while still retaining his professorship, and on November 4 following, Mr. Moore having resigned the presidency, his chair was filled by the appointment of

[1] Davidson tells us that, at the close of the century, there were 45 students in the academic department, 19 law students, and 6 medical students. For further statements in regard to the early attendance, see Peter's Transylvania University, pp. 90-91.

Rev. Robert H. Bishop, A. M., who held the position until 1824.[1] Mr. Moore did not, however, lose his interest in the institution or sever his connection with it entirely, as we find he became a trustee in 1805, and remained one for some time afterwards. He subsequently devoted himself mainly to the work of his church, becoming, in 1809, the first regular rector of Christ's Episcopal Church, in Lexington. He was distinguished for his learning, piety, and courtesy, and had done considerable under the circumstances toward laying the foundation of Transylvania's future prosperity.[2]

Rev. Dr. Blythe remained as acting president of the university until near the end of this period, during which time the institution grew in a sound and healthy, though moderate way. The course of instruction in its academic department was soon brought up to an equality with that of the Eastern colleges, except in the classics, which were then regarded as of somewhat secondary importance in the West, and on October 31, 1812, an extra teacher was added to the faculty of this department in the person of John B. Fouchier, who was made instructor in French.

Dr. Blythe also endeavored to develop the professional departments, especially that of medicine. Dr. Elisha Warfield had already, in 1802, been added to the medical faculty, as yet only prospective, as professor of surgery and midwifery, and in 1805 Rev. James Fishback, M. D., was appointed to the chair of theory and practice of medicine, thus making, with Dr. Brown, who held the chair of chemistry, what may be called the first regular faculty of the department. No teaching was, however, done at this time, and all the professors resigned their chairs in 1806. On April 8, 1809, a more complete faculty was organized, among whom the celebrated Dr. Dudley appears for the first time. The professors and their chairs were as follows: Dr. B. W. Dudley, anatomy and physiology; Dr. Joseph Buchanan, institutes of medicine; Dr. James Overton, materia medica, and Dr. Elisha Warfield, surgery and midwifery. Dr. Dudley remained in this faculty one or two years, but neither he nor any of his colleagues seem to have delivered any lectures at this time.

Another reorganization of the faculty took place on November 11, 1815, when Drs. Thomas Cooper, B. W. Dudley, Coleman Rogers, Samuel Brown, William H. Richardson, and Charles W. Short were elected to chairs.[3] All of these, however, declined except Drs. Dudley and Richardson, the former of whom lectured regularly in his department of surgery, and the latter occassionally in 1816–17, a committee of the trustees reporting to this effect on February 22, 1817, when it is also stated that Dr. Richardson had fifteen or sixteen students in his depart-

[1] He resigned at that time to become president of Miami University, Ohio.

[2] A short sketch of Mr. Moore is to be found in Collins's History of Kentucky, Vol. I, p. 442.

[3] The first names of Drs. Cooper and Rogers are here taken from Peter's Transylvania University, pp. 95-96, where the chairs of all these prospective professors are also given.

ment of midwifery and would lecture regularly in the future. On December 10, 1816, Dr. Daniel Drake was elected professor of materia medica, and on February 28, 1817, Dr. James Overton became professor of theory and practice of medicine and Dr. Blythe was transferred to the chair of chemistry. These, with Drs. Dudley and Richardson, became the first active medical faculty of Transylvania University. They lectured regularly during the session of 1817–18 to a class of about twenty students, and in 1818 the first medical commencement in the Mississippi Valley was held at Lexington, the degree of M. D. being conferred on one candidate, John L. McCullough.

The funds of the institution also improved during this period. The greater part of the original endowment grant of 8,000 acres of land, which had been previously leased for long terms at a low rate, had been sold, about 1812, for $30,000, which was invested in stock of the Bank of Kentucky, and with its increments and the income accruing from other sources, Davidson[1] tells us, made the money endowment of the institution, in 1812, $67,532.

We now begin to find many resolutions passed by the trustees looking toward the erection of a new building, the means for which were to be at least partly obtained by selling a portion of the old campus, which was to be divided by having streets[2] run through it. Steps were also taken with a view of securing "a gentleman of ability and talents" for president. Counter propositions were also made to simply repair the old building and let affairs proceed in much the old way. Rev. Dr. E. Nott, Rev. John B. Romeyne,[3] and finally Rev. Horace Holley, D. D., were successively invited by the trustees to accept the presidency of the university, and then this action was rescinded in favor of retaining Dr. Blythe. There were evidently factions[4] in the board, and strong differences of opinion as to the proper policy to be pursued, rumors of which soon began to reach the public ear, for, as early as December 29, 1815, we hear of a legislative committee being appointed to inquire into the state of the institution, in answer to which action the board issued an address to the public, and on February 3, 1816, appointed a committee to defend the university before the State senate against calumniating reports, and two days later John Pope was employed as counsel for that purpose.

In 1816 the university grounds were ornamented with shrubbery and otherwise greatly improved, and also considerably enlarged through

[1] Presbyterian Church in Kentucky, p. 297; Davidson says the sale of lands occurred about 1806, but the records of the trustees show that the principal sale occurred in 1812.

[2] Mill and Market streets were run through it at this period, and a small strip on the west, cut off by Mill street, sold to Thomas January for $1,000. The running through of a street from east to west and the sale of one-half the campus thus divided was also discussed.

[3] Dr. Nott was then president of Union College, New York, and Rev. John B. Romeyne was a prominent Presbyterian clergyman of New York.

[4] See Davidson's Presbyterian Church in Kentucky, p. 298, for these factions.

the liberality of several friends of the institution, including the celebrated statesman Henry Clay, the Higgins lot, now the western part of the Kentucky University campus, having been acquired in the latter part of this year, partly by donation and partly by purchase. In 1817 the erection of a large and handsome new brick building was begun. It was completed in 1818, was located near the center of the old campus, was three stories in height, and contained thirty rooms. It included, besides the rooms set apart for academic purposes, a dormitory and refectory, with accommodations for a hundred students. Rev. Luther Rice, a prominent Baptist clergyman, had been called to the presidency in March, 1816, and in April, 1817, Philip Lindsley, later and long the distinguished president of the University of Nashville, was elected to the position. These both declined, and on October 25, 1817, Dr. Holley was again balloted for, ineffectually at that time, but on November 25 following he was unanimously elected, at a salary of $2,250[1] per annum, an amount which shows the improved financial condition of the university. After a visit to Lexington, during the following summer, Dr. Holley formally accepted the position.

Dr. Blythe had, on March 23, 1816, after one or two previous resignations which he had been induced to withdraw, finally resigned his professorship, and with it the acting presidency of the university. He had remained at its head for twelve years, during which time it had made considerable progress. He was too exclusive to be popular, but was a diligent and efficient teacher and a man of ability. Collins[2] tells us that he had "native strength of character, prompt decision, and a practical turn which enabled him to acquit himself well in every situation." On February 28, 1817, he was elected professor of chemistry in the medical department of the university, which was then first regularly opened, a position which he retained until 1831. Just prior to his resignation in 1816 the trustees had furnished him with $1,000 for the purchase of apparatus for the chemical department.

On February 3, 1818, occurred what may be called the closing incident of this period of the university's history. On that date, at whose solicitation it does not appear, an act[3] was passed by the legislature removing the old board of trustees and appointing a new one of thirteen members, eight of them being at the time members of the old board, and another, Henry Clay, having been formerly so. The new body was composed of prominent public men of excellent merit, but of

[1] This is the correct amount of his salary at first, and not $3,000, as usually stated. He did receive the latter amount at a later period in his administration. The salary of the professors was $1,000 in 1818, and was later made as much as $1,800 in some cases.

[2] History of Kentucky, Vol. I, p. 463. Another sketch of his life is to be found in Sprague's Annals of the American Pulpit, Vol. III, p. 592.

[3] Acts of 1818, pp. 554-556: Among the thirteen trustees were Henry Clay, Robert Trimble, Edmund Bullock, John T. Mason, jr., Robert Wickliffe, John Pope, John Brown, and Charles Humphreys.

no special religious pretensions or connections. The religious apprehensions of the Presbyterians, especially of the old board, already perhaps considerably aroused by the alleged Socinianism[1] of Dr. Holley, the new president, whose last election had been unanimous, because they had refused to take any part in it, were further intensified by this action which they considered dangerous in its religious tendencies and which they also regarded as illegal,[2] in that it had not been petitioned for by a majority of the trustees, as required by the charter. We shall find these circumstances rather adverse to the interests of the university in raising up against it a strong religious prejudice in the public mind generally and in causing the Presbyterians particularly to be very unfavorably disposed toward the new administration and very much inclined to withdraw their patronage, as we shall soon see them doing. At the same time this act of reorganization had its beneficial effect, as expressed by a committee of the two houses of the legislature in 1827, in taking Transylvania University "into their more immediate protection,"[3] and attempting to make of it more distinctively a State institution and to build it up into a great university under State auspices. The old board, in view of their going out of office, issued, on February 28, 1818, an address on the interests and prospects of the university, the former of which they considered of great public importance, the latter very flattering. This was their last official act.

The attendance during this early part of the institution's history was not large, as the records of the trustees report, on October 18, 1817, that there had been 77 students the past session.[4] The slow growth in the number of students may be partly accounted for by the preoccupation of the people in other matters and by the constant elevation of the standard of scholarship which made entrance more difficult. Hon. Robert Wickliffe, the president of the new board of trustees of 1818, says in a notice in Niles's Register[5] that the college is

[1] This had been noised abroad somewhat at the time of his first election, on November 11, 1815, and was probably the cause of that action being rescinded later, when a committee was appointed to inquire into his character.

[2] The language of the charter and the position taken by previous legislatures certainly gave them good grounds for taking this position. The act of 1783 had merely declared "that the said trustees shall at all times be accountable for their transactions touching any matter or anything relating to said seminary in such manner as the legislature shall direct." The natural inference from this was that they might be removed from office or otherwise punished for malfeasance, but not that their organization could be altered except according to the provisions of the charter itself. This was the construction put upon that charter by the acts of November 21, 1795, and December 21, 1795, which did not reorganize the old board, but merely suspended them from office in the one case and in the other made them accountable for the discharge of their duties to the district court. The position taken by the Presbyterians was at least as tenable as the opposite one, given in Peter's Transylvania University, pp. 22-24.

[3] Davidson's Presbyterian Church in Kentucky, p. 315.

[4] Niles's Register, vol. 23, p. 387, tells us there were 60 students in the academical department in the summer of 1818.

[5] Vol. 15, p. 132.

to give an education "as good as is given in other colleges in the United States." There had been altogether, including honorary degrees, only 22 degrees granted during this period, which may be called a period of substantial though gradual growth and of excellent preparation for future work.

PERIOD FROM 1818 TO 1827.

Dr. Holley's[1] administration, extending from November, 1818, to March, 1827, is by far the most brilliant era of the university's history. The new president aimed to make of Transylvania a genuine university, complete in every college and liberally endowed. He was in many ways admirably fitted for the undertaking. Having graduated at Yale in the class of 1803, when about 22 years of age, he had, after studying law for a while in New York and then abandoning it for the ministry, pursued the study of theology under Dr. Dwight in New Haven, where he had become a Unitarian, not under his preceptor, but from his personal conviction. Since 1809 he had been the pastor of the Hollis Street Unitarian Church of Boston, Mass., where he was greatly beloved and admired. He was a man of engaging manners and of great personal magnetism. Besides, his learning was very wide and his eloquence so stirring as to cause a staid New England audience to burst into noisy applause on the occasion of his delivering a sermon before the Ancient and Honorable Artillery Company of Boston. In Lexington he entertained freely patrons of learning and distinguished strangers, and captivating, as he did, all who came near him, was calculated to interest them in the welfare of the university. This he did in a very successful way in the case of the State legislature and of such public-spirited citizens as Col. James Morrison, Henry Clay, and others.

The circumstances were also favorable for a new era of progress, as the State had just emerged, with great credit to herself, from the war of 1812, which effectually did away with all Indian hostilities in or near it in the future, and the people had now time and opportunity to turn their attention to educational matters, hitherto necessarily much neglected. The State was also now disposed to renew its attention and patronage to the university as the only effective center of higher education in its midst, the academies by this time having proven recognized failures in many cases. This help was greater than ever before, and was now especially timely.

Dr. Holley was formally inaugurated on December 19, 1818, and at once set to work to build up the institution, and proving, in many ways, the man for the place, the university entered upon a career of almost marvelous prosperity, in which the plans of Judge Wallace seemed

[1] For more extended sketches of Dr. Holley, see Collins's History of Kentucky, Vol. II, pp. 217-218, and especially Dr. Charles Caldwell's Discourse on the Genius and Character of Rev. Horace Holley.

about to be realized. The faculty was soon reorganized and enlarged, and men of reputation called to the various chairs, largely through the president's personal influence. Its personnel in October, 1821, was as follows: Academical department: Rev. Horace Holley, A. M., LL. D., president, philology, belles lettres, and mental philosophy; Rev. R. H. Bishop, A. M., natural philosophy and history; J. F. Jenkins, A. B., mathematics; John Roche, A. M., languages; Constantine S. Rafinesque, natural history, botany, and modern languages; J. W. Tibbats and B. O. Peers, tutors. Medical college: Charles Caldwell, M. D., institutes of medicine and materia medica; B. W. Dudley, M. D., anatomy and surgery; Samuel Brown, M. D., theory and practice of physic; W. H. Richardson, M. D., obstetrics and diseases of women and children; James Blythe, M. D., D. D., chemistry. Law school: William T. Barry, professor.

Dr. Daniel Drake was soon added to the medical faculty and Judge Jesse Bledsoe to the law faculty.

Prof. C. S. Rafinesque,[1] who held the chair of natural science in the academic department and of medical botany in the medical department, was connected with the university from 1819 to 1825, and was probably, at the time, the most eminent scientist in America. In 1824 he established, in connection with the university, a botanical garden, which, however, was not a financial success, and was not long kept up. He is the author of a number of scientific works, and although somewhat visionary, did much valuable teaching.

The professional departments especially were developed by Dr. Holley, and the medical college, which had been again suspended in 1818, but was revived in 1819, soon began to hold a prominent rank not only in the West, but in the country at large. Its library, secured by a special visit of Dr. Caldwell to the continent in 1820, was so rare and valuable, many of the books being those of eminent French physicians ruined by the Revolution, as to make it one of the best of its kind in America. The number of students in this department grew from 20 students and 1 graduate in 1817–18 to 281 students and 53 graduates in 1825–26, there being 93 students in 1820–21, 138 in 1821–22, 170 in 1822–23, 200 in 1823–24, and 234 in 1824–25.[2] Its faculty was also unexcelled in the country for their talents and acquirements. We have already noticed Dr. Brown's celebrity in speaking of his nominal connection with the university from 1799 to 1806.

Dr. Caldwell[3] had been formerly a member of the faculty of the University of Pennsylvania, and was very noted both as a physician

[1] For a more extended sketch, see Collins's History of Kentucky, Vol. II, pp. 201–202; also, Life and Writings of Rafinesque, by R. E. Call, M. A., M. Sc., M. D., Louisville, 1895.

[2] There were 241 students in 1826–27, after Dr. Holley's first resignation had been offered.

[3] For fuller sketch, see Collins's History of Kentucky, Vol. II, p. 219; Collins's Sketches of Kentucky, pp. 558–559.

and a teacher. He was connected with the Transylvania medical faculty from 1819 to 1837.

Dr. Drake,[1] long one of the most eminent medical professors in the West, in the medical colleges of Cincinnati and Louisville as well as Lexington, was connected with the Transylvania University faculty from 1823 to 1826, as well as in 1817–18.

Dr. B. W. Dudley,[2] long the most eminent surgeon in the Mississippi Valley, if not in the whole country, famed especially for his operations in lithotomy and upon the eye and cranium, as well as other delicate treatments, was a great teacher as well. An alumnus of Transylvania University and a graduate of the University of Pennsylvania in medicine, he had later pursued the study of his chosen profession for four years in London and Paris. He entered the Transylvania medical faculty regularly in 1817 and remained in it for forty years, contributing in no small measure to its great success by his personal efforts and reputation.

Drs. Richardson and Blythe were also noted as successful teachers in their respective departments.

Dr. Drake tells us, in speaking of this faculty and of the law faculty at this time, "that they were men of brilliant talents and wide reputation, and collectively constituted a greater array of strength and brilliancy than was scarcely ever collected in any institution at one time."[3] Much valuable research and investigation was carried on at the university at this time by its medical faculty, the results of which were made known through the Transylvania Medical Journal, which they then published. This faculty was further strengthened, either during this period or soon after, by the addition of such eminent professors as Drs. John Esten Cooke, L. P. Yandell, H. H. Eaton, and Charles W. Short, most of whom remained connected with it for many years afterwards. For some time to come, with its distinguished corps of professors, its excellent chemical and anatomical apparatus, and its unsurpassed library, it fairly claimed to be the equal of any medical school in the country in equipment, and was only excelled in numbers by the medical department of the University of Pennsylvania.

President Holley not only thus enlarged and strengthened the professional departments, but, as a means toward this end and toward the general building up of the university, was able to induce the legislature and Lexington to contribute[4] to the wants of the institution

---

[1] For fuller sketch, see Collins's History of Kentucky, Vol. II, p. 580; also memoirs of Dr. Drake, by Mansfield. Collins incorrectly says he remained at Transylvania the second time until 1827.

[2] See also Collins's History of Kentucky, Vol. II, p. 218. Dr. Dudley remained connected with the Transylvania medical faculty until 1858. He died in Lexington, January 20, 1870, aged nearly 85 years.

[3] Mansfield's Memoirs, p. 128.

[4] For these various appropriations, see Report of the Superintendent of Public Instruction of Kentucky for 1875–76, pp. 15–16, Appendix; Autobiography of Dr. Charles Caldwell, p. 360; also Acts of 1818–19, pp. 692–693, of 1819–20, p. 952, and of 1822–23, pp. 149–151 and 160–162.

more liberally than ever before. In 1819 the legislature granted to the university the bonus of the Farmers and Mechanics' Bank for two years, amounting to $3,000; in 1820, $5,000 from the State treasury to buy books and apparatus for the medical college; in 1821, one-half the net profits of the Lexington branch of the Bank of the Commonwealth for two years, yielding $20,000, which was, however, only equivalent to $10,000 in specie; in 1822, a lottery privilege of $25,000 for a new medical building, and also 2 per cent of the auction sales in Fayette County for a law library; in 1824, $20,000 from the State treasury. Lexington, in 1820, also gave $6,000 for the equipment of the medical college, and in 1822 citizens of the town contributed about $5,000[1] more. These would be considered rather small donations nowadays to a State educational enterprise, but were quite liberal for the time and circumstances. They were, however, always given against strong opposition in the legislature, and were accompanied by other legislation in some respects adverse to the university.[2] We shall soon find that when the old opposition became strengthened by popular dissatisfaction in regard to the administration of the university, all State appropriations were entirely withdrawn.

Unfortunately all the early donations, instead of being added to the endowment of the institution, had to be used to pay its debts and supply it with books and apparatus. The result was that in 1825 few colleges in the country had better libraries and internal equipment generally than Transylvania University, but there were little means for the institution's future expansion. The attention of benevolently-minded individuals was, however, being attracted to the university by its work under Dr. Holley, as is shown by the bequest of Col. James Morrison,[3] who had been for some time the chairman of its board of trustees and who died on April 23, 1823. This legacy included the gift of $20,000 to endow a professorship,[4] and a residuary estate of about $50,000 to be used to erect a new college building, which was to bear the name of the donor.

Circumstances, as we have seen, were favorable, and as Dr. Holley's objectionable opinions and actions were not generally known for some time, he was able by his great executive ability to build up the institution very rapidly and to make its name known not only in the State, but throughout the country and even in Europe. The governors of the State soon began in their messages to speak of the honor and

---

[1] The exact amount was $4,832.

[2] Caldwell tells us (Autobiography, p. 360) that the failure of the legislature to renew the charter of the Bank of Kentucky, in which its original endowment funds were invested, lost the university about $20,000.

[3] Colonel Morrison was a Pennsylvanian who had come to Kentucky in 1792, where he had acquired large wealth for the time. He was very public spirited and took an interest in other public enterprises besides Transylvania University. For a more complete sketch of his life see Collins's History of Kentucky, Vol. II, p. 196, and Davidson's Presbyterian Church in Kentucky, p. 306 et seq.

[4] Or library by the will, but the trustees chose the professorship.

luster it reflected upon Kentucky, and its graduates soon began to be important factors in the life of the South and West, from which sections most of them came. The relative importance of the university among American colleges during the early part of this period may be shown somewhat by the fact that in March, 1821,[1] it had 282 students, while Yale had 319, Harvard 286, Union 264, Dartmouth 222, and Princeton 150. Of the Transylvania students, 185 were at that time in the academic department.[2]

But Dr. Holley's religious opinions, supposed by many to verge on infidelity, began to be noised abroad, as did also his love of worldly amusement, equally objectionable to many, and, by reason of the prejudice and sectarian animosity of the day, it soon began to arouse criticism and opposition. The Presbyterians had early become alarmed, and soon after his election had again determined to have an institution undoubtedly under their own control, a movement resulting in the founding of Centre College in 1819. The Catholics founded St. Joseph's in the same year and St. Mary's in 1821, and the Methodists Augusta in 1822. The same denominational idea was prominent in the establishment of Cumberland College by the Cumberland Presbyterians in 1827, and later of Georgetown College by the Baptists in 1829 and of Bacon College by the Christians in 1836.

Opposition on the part of the general public, through the press and otherwise, also soon began to manifest itself, and as early as 1824 Professors Barry, Bledsoe, and others, connected with the faculty of the university, deemed it well to issue a pamphlet defending Dr. Holley against unjust calumnies. The former opposition of the legislature also increased in response to the state of public opinion, as was perhaps first shown by the reorganization of the board of trustees in 1821,[3] when four new members were added to its number. Committees of investigation into the condition of the university, which was accused of extravagance, began to be frequently appointed soon after this, and

[1] Statistics from Niles's Register, vol. 29, p. 63. Vol. 31, p. 158, of this work gives the total number of graduates of other colleges for the year 1826 as follows: Harvard, 53; Yale, 100; Princeton, 24; Amherst, 32; Dartmouth 37, and Union 71. The following degrees conferred by Transylvania (taken mainly from the American Journal of Education for 1826, pp. 311-313) will serve for a comparison later in this period; in 1823, 32 A. B.'s (B. L.'s and M. D.'s not given); in 1824, 24 A. B.'s, 16 B. L.'s, and 47 M. D.'s; in 1825, 32 A. B.'s, 16 B. L.'s, and 57 M. D.'s.

[2] The number of students in this department of the university for other years of this period, as obtained from catalogues and other sources, was as follows: 1821-22, 200; 1822-23, 172; 1823-24, 159; 1825-26, 131; 1826-27, 96. Of these, the number in the preparatory classes in each year respectively were 62, 51, 27, 40, and 39. The law students for the period, as far as ascertained, were for 1820-21, 9; for 1821-22, 49; for 1822-23, 44; for 1823-24, 48. The medical students have been given on page 59. The academic students for 1823-24 represented fourteen States and the District of Columbia.

[3] In the act of December 18, 1821, appropriating the profits of the branch Bank of the Commonwealth, in connection with which it was declared that the university was not to depend for the future on State aid.

hindrance rather than help was to be expected in the future from the State.

Discouraged and irritated by the state of public opinion, and harassed by charges which he felt to be unmerited, Dr. Holley, despairing, as he did, of the further enlargement of the university, especially through State aid, felt constrained to resign, offering his resignation at first to take effect in January, 1826. He withdrew this resignation at the solicitation of friends, but on January 18, 1827, finally resigned, to take effect in the following March, greatly to the regret of the majority of the citizens of Lexington, of the trustees, and of the students, a number of the latter leaving the institution upon his retirement. He left Lexington on March 27, 1827, to engage in other educational enterprises in Louisiana, and died of yellow fever on July 31 following, while on his way by sea to New York.

He certainly had done much for the university, as shown by its remarkable growth during his administration. He is, however, not entitled to all the credit for the most brilliant period of the institution's history, for, as we have seen, he was greatly aided by favorable circumstances, which, under any fairly good management, would have caused a considerable expansion in the university's sphere. A great deal of the foundation of its prosperity had been laid under the conservative but careful adminstration of Dr. Blythe. The academic department had been brought up to the proportions of a college, the law department inaugurated, and the medical department fairly started. Much of the success of this last department is to be attributed to the energy and ability of Dr. Dudley, who had already become fully identified with the department in 1815, and was a member of its first regular faculty in 1817. Dr. Drake tells us that the prosperity of the medical school was mainly due "to the public spirit and exertions of Dr. Dudley."[1] Before the advent of the Holley era the institution had already acquired considerable local reputation, and was beginning to attract the favorable attention of the State authorities, how much through the personal influence and efforts of Dr. Blythe we know not. Governor Slaughter, in his message of December 2, 1817, recommended that Transylvania University, which he says "will soon hold an eminent rank among the institutions of learning in the United States," be extended such aid as will place it "on the most respectable footing."

Dr. Holley is, however, entitled to much praise and credit for the institution's success on account of his power of increasing the interest in it of public men like Henry Clay and benevolently-minded men like Colonel Morrison, by reason of his influence with the State authorities, as is evidenced by the favorable tone ot the governors' messages during the greater part of his administration and the legislative appropriations secured during that period, and also for his energy and great executive

[1] Mansfield's Memoirs, p. 128.

ability, as well as his advanced ideas on education. The recommendations contained in his last report to the trustees are quite modern in tone, and are in some respects certainly quite in advance of the ideas then prevalent. He recommended[1] the creation of a regular professorship of modern languages, the increase of the law professorships to four, one of which should treat exclusively of Roman law; the establishment of a gymnasium, the collection of a cabinet of minerals, the foundation of a gallery of fine arts, and a regular arrangement for the establishment of libraries in the different departments, especially that of history and politics. The works to be added to the library were to be largely for the use of advanced students and of the professors, and special attention was to be given in the course to economic science.

Some idea of the growth of the university during this period may be obtained from the increase in size of its general library and the additions to its roll of alumni. The former, as shown by Dr. Holley's last report,[2] had increased from about 1,300 volumes to about 6,500 volumes, and the number of degrees conferred was now 666, instead of 22, as previously. Forty of these were honorary, but the remainder had been obtained by completing a course the standard of which had been constantly elevated. There had been up to this time 327 graduates in the medical department and 41 in the law department.

Dr. Holley was undoubtedly much esteemed by most of those who came in the closest personal contact with him. With all the admirable qualifications for the position he filled, which we have seen him to possess, and with the high rank and recognition he had been able to secure for the university, it seems a great pity that he should not have been able to so conduct himself, and that, too, honorably, as to avoid precipitating a conflict with prejudices and animosities which, however unreasonable they may have appeared to him, he might have known his opposing could not change, but would only further provoke. He was undoubtedly much misjudged and maligned; but it is also true that his own indiscreet words and conduct were responsible to a considerable extent for these actions. Although his motives should not be questioned, yet hardly so much can be said for his judgment.

PERIOD FROM 1827 TO 1849.

We now enter the third period of the university's history, which will witness the adoption by the trustees of a new plan of supporting and building up the institution. Under the act of 1818, and again by that of 1821, which in effect only changed their number, the trustees were to be appointed by the legislature every two years; but by the neglect of this provision it seems that they had been allowed to become, as formerly, practically a self-perpetuating body, who were free to manage the

[1] Caldwell's Memoirs, p. 211.

[2] *Ibid.*, p. 193 et seq.

institution according to their own ideas, which during this period were not materially, at least, interfered with by the legislature. As we have seen, by reason of the adverse condition of public opinion, the university had been virtually abandoned by the State, and was to receive no more State help for nearly thirty years. Without this assistance, upon which it had so long depended, as its own resources were insufficient, it would naturally have had to struggle on in rather a poor way in the future. The trustees therefore sought to bring to it the needed help through partial denominational control, or at least the use of denominational influence and patronage. The institution was placed first under Baptist, then Episcopal, again Presbyterian, and lastly Methodist auspices, prominent ministers of these denominations being successively called to its presidency, in the hope that thereby the support of their church organization might be secured for it.

The control exercised by these denominations was in each case only partial, and their patronage in itself always insufficient. So, in order for it to be at all efficacious, there had to be some outside assistance, and as the State would not furnish this, it came from local sources—from the friends of the university in Lexington and from the town itself. We find soon after the resignation of Dr. Holley a number of its local friends rallying around the institution and subscribing for its maintenance a conditional emergency fund of $3,000 a year, for four years, of which amount about $11,000 seems to have been finally paid in. With this help and the proceeds of the lottery of 1825, and perhaps something from an earlier one of 1804,[1] instituted for the same purpose, the returns from both of which are quite uncertain in amount, a new and spacious medical hall was projected, the corner stone of which was laid with imposing ceremonies on April 26, 1827. This building, which was handsome and well equipped, was completed soon afterwards. It was located where the present city library of Lexington now stands. Prior to its completion the medical lectures were doubtless given in the main college building.

The resignation of Dr. Holley was of course, under the circumstances, a considerable shock to the university. There was an immediate loss of a number of students, and the attendance the next session was naturally considerably decreased, especially in the academic department. Even in the medical department, which was now quite well established and less directly affected by the change of administration, the number of students fell off from 241 to 190 the next year.

The academic faculty,[2] after Dr. Holley's departure, was composed

[1] The Kentucky Gazette for July 10, 1804, contains an advertisement of the "Lexington Medical Lottery," projected to establish a medical college in Transylvania University.

[2] John Everett, A. B., the brother of the celebrated Edward Everett, and Mann Butler, A. M., the historian of Kentucky, were professors, respectively, of ancient languages and mathematics in the university for a part of Dr. Holley's administration.

as follows: John Roche, professor of Greek and Latin; Rev. George T. Chapman, professor of history and antiquity; Rev. B. O. Peers, professor of moral philosophy; and Thomas J. Matthews, professor of mathematics. No new president was at once elected, but it was arranged that the academic department should be managed by its faculty and that Drs. Caldwell, Dudley, and Short, of the medical faculty, should preside in succession on all public occasions.

During the future history of the university the professional departments somewhat overshadow its other parts. They were conducted upon a somewhat independent basis, and being largely self-supporting by reason of their reputation and their celebrated faculties, especially with the aid of the local financial help, which was mainly bestowed upon them, they were in the main prosperous and were not greatly affected by the ups and downs of the literary department. After Dr. Holley had left they maintained themselves fairly well for the immediate future, and there was no reason why the university as a whole should not have continued to succeed, if it had not been abandoned by the State, and indeed, for the time, to a considerable extent, by every one, some public-spirited citizens of Lexington excepted. This now becomes a characteristic feature of its history, especially of its academic department. As it was not sufficiently endowed to be self-supporting, outside assistance or strong local aid was imperative; and when, for any reason, either or both of these were lacking, it lapsed into a condition of inactivity or torpor until it was in some way temporarily revived by a new impetus. This applies especially to the whole period after Dr. Holley's resignation, when regular legislative patronage was withdrawn, but the decline did not show itself for some time after that event.

The first denominational experiment of this period was inaugurated, in June 1828, by the election of Rev. Alva Woods, D. D., of Rhode Island, to the vacant presidency of the university. The reputation of the institution was still considerable in the East, as is shown by the fact that Dr. Woods resigned the presidency of Brown University to accept its presidential chair. He was a Baptist clergyman of some celebrity, being particularly highly respected for his learning and the liberality of his views. He seems to have been a practical matter-of-fact man, who made very good use of the facilities he had at his command and managed to keep the university in a fair state of prosperity during his administration, which lasted about two years.

His practical energy was well shown in connection with the loss of the main building of the university by fire, when temporary quarters

[1] A catalogue of the medical department of the University for 1828 shows that there were, that year, 40 graduates in that department who came from the States of Kentucky, Mississippi, Alabama, Tennessee, South Carolina, Virginia, Louisiana, Michigan, and Ohio. Niles tells us (Register, vol. 37, p. 216) that near the opening of the session of 1828-29 there were 150 students in the medical department and 130 in the college and preparatory classes. A catalogue gives, for 1829-30, 21 law students, 141 academic students, of whom 49 were in the preparatory classes, and 241 medical students who represented 13 States.

were at once secured, and not a single day's exercises were suspended nor a single student left the institution. This great misfortune happened on the night of May 9, 1829, and besides the excellent university building completed in 1818, destroyed the law and societies' libraries and most of the philosophical apparatus. It entailed a loss of about $30,000, exclusive of the insurance, thus practically wiping out all of the original endowment coming from Transylvania Seminary. It of course greatly crippled the university's future usefulness, and the discouragement due to it was probably the cause of Dr. Woods's resignation, in 1830, to accept the presidency of the rising University of Alabama, where he considered he had a more promising field of labor.

There was then an interregnum in the presidency for about three years, during which two events of some importance occurred. Dr. Blythe, so long connected with the university faculty, resigned his chair of chemistry in 1831 to accept the presidency of Hanover College, Indiana.[1] His successor at Transylvania was the celebrated Dr. Robert Peter, so intimately associated with the university's later history, and subsequently with that of Kentucky University and the Agricultural and Mechanical College. Professor Peter came in with the new administration in March, 1833.

The other event referred to above is the erection of the college building provided for from the residuary estate of Col. James Morrison. It was begun during this interregnum and was located on the eastern part of the Higgins lot, acquired by the university in 1816. Afterwards, in 1835, the place of Dr. Blythe's former residence, known as the Blythe lot, now the eastern portion of the Kentucky University campus, was purchased by the trustees, from funds also arising from the Morrison bequest, thus completing a beautiful campus, near the center of which the Morrison College building was located.

The Baptists had now begun to transfer their patronage to their own distinctive institution, founded at Georgetown in 1829, and so another source of assistance for the university was sought after by its trustees, and Rev. B. O. Peers,[2] a prominent Episcopal clergyman, was called to its presidency in 1833.[3] He was a man of high character and advanced views and was one of the many alumni of Transylvania University now rapidly coming forward into public prominence. He had graduated in the class of 1821 and was then a tutor in his alma mater for a time. He later studied theology at Princeton and was for a while

[1] He continued as president of Hanover until 1836, when he resigned on account of bad health. His death occurred in 1842.

[2] For other facts in regard to Rev. B. O. Peers' life, see Collins's History of Kentucky, Vol. I, pp. 442–443. Mr. Peers, besides writing numerous articles for newspapers and magazines, is the author of a small work entitled "Christian Education."

[3] Peter's Transylvania University, pp. 160–161, gives the dates of President Peers' inauguration and resignation as, respectively, 1832 and February 1, 1834, but the appended sketch of Mr. Peers gives these dates as 1833 and 1835, which are given also by a number of other authorities consulted by the writer.

engaged in church work in Alexandria, Va. From conscientious reflections he then decided to enter the profession of teaching and became, in 1827, professor of moral philosophy in Transylvania.

He was one who devoted himself with great enthusiasm and earnestness to whatever he undertook, and having thought deeply and observed widely upon educational problems, was soon quite in advance of his State and even, in some respects, of his country in his ideas and theories. We shall find that he is the virtual founder of the public school system of Kentucky, at least in being the first one who most prominently and successfully agitated the question of its adoption.

On June 1, 1829,[1] he founded in Lexington a Mechanics' Institute on the model of that introduced into Scotland by Dr. John Anderson some thirty years before, but at the time of its establishment quite a new enterprise for this country. In connection with this institute an Apprentices' School was soon opened, in which systematic courses of public lectures were delivered, mainly by professors of Transylvania University. We have in these lectures what appear to be very fair types of modern university extension courses. They are reported to have been quite a success for a time, similar ones being, through their example, instituted at Louisville and other important points in the State, but for some reason are soon lost sight of.

In October, 1830,[2] after severing his connection with the university faculty, he had established in Lexington the Eclectic Institute, in which an attempt was made to put into practical operation, as in the Rensselaer Institute at Troy, New York, the principles of Pestalozzi and Fellenberg. This school was quite successful for a time, but was too advanced for its surroundings and so did not last long. Mr. Peers had associated with himself in its faculty, in 1832, two model educators, Henry A. Griswold and Dr. Robert Peter. He was still in charge of the school when elected to the presidency of Transylvania University. As noted above, Dr. Peter went with him into the university faculty.

Another of President Peers's advanced ideas, quite advanced for the time[3] and quite practical if public opinion had been prepared for it, was to convert Transylvania University into a State normal school, which should have its revenues supplemented by ample State appropriations, and should be put at the head of a State public-school system. This view is clearly expressed in the address delivered at the time of his

---

[1] This date is variously given by different authorities, but the one accepted here is supported in quite an authentic way by Barnard's American Journal of Education, vol. 16, p. 353, and is probably correct.

[2] There is as much variation in regard to this date as in the case of that of the establishment of the Mechanics' Institute, but this seems best authenticated. See Barnard's American Journal of Education, vol. 17, p. 148.

[3] The normal-school idea had at the time been discussed comparatively little even in New England, and the first regular normal school was not opened until July, 1839. (See Gordy's Rise and Growth of the Normal School Idea in the United States, especially pp. 19 and 47.)

inauguration as president of the university. Mr. Peers's ideas seem to have been too advanced for his time and perhaps too for his executive ability, although an extraordinary amount of the latter would probably have been needed to pull the university out of the "Slough of Despond"[1] into which she had then fallen.

The denominational feature of the institution's management appeared more distinctively during this administration in the establishment, in connection with its other departments, of a theological seminary, under the control of the Episcopal Church. The new department was conducted for a comparatively short while after its establishment in 1834, and never had any really organic connection with the university, being really an independent institution[2] temporarily associated with it.

It was during President Peers's term of office that the building erected from the residuary estate of Colonel Morrison, and named in his honor Morrison College, was completed. It was quite a commodious and imposing structure, costing about $40,000, and is still in use, comparatively unaltered, as one of the principal buildings of Kentucky University. It was dedicated with elaborate ceremonies on November 14, 1833, and at the same time President Peers was formally inaugurated, and, after having taken the oath of office prescribed for all Transylvania officers by the original charter,[3] delivered an impressive address on the prospects of the university and the proper aims of such an institution.

In the early part of 1835, when he had begun to see the futility of at least most of his cherished plans in regard to the institution, he resigned its presidency and entered, in the work of his church at Louisville, what he considered wider fields of usefulness. In 1838 he was transferred to other church work in New York City, where he died, in 1842, in the midst of a career promising much for the future. He was noted for his ardent piety, sound learning, and zealous devotion to the cause of general education.

His associates in the academic faculty of Transylvania University at the opening of his administation in 1833,[4] in addition to Dr. Peter, who has been already mentioned, were John Lutz,[5] D. P., professor of mathe-

[1] A catalogue shows us that, in January, 1834, there were only 63 students in the academic department, of whom 31 were in the preparatory classes; at this time, however, the law department had 52 students and the medical department 260, the latter from 15 different States.

[2] This seminary was incorporated by an act of the State legislature approved on February 24, 1834, which stipulates that it is to be conducted entirely without State aid. The American Almanac for 1834 shows that the seminary in that year had three professors and eight students, and that its library then contained 2,000 volumes.

[3] By section 4 of the act of May 5, 1783.

[4] Barnard's American Journal of Education, vol. 27, p. 335.

[5] Prof. Lutz was acting president of the university for a short time during interregnums, both before and after President Peers's administration He held the Morrison professorship, which carried with it the acting presidency under such circumstances.

matics, E. Rosel, professor of languages, and Charles E. Bains, principal of the preparatory department. In 1835 Prof. S. Hebard had taken Professor Lutz's place in the faculty. The medical faculty in 1833 included Doctors Dudley, Caldwell, Cooke, Richardson, Short, and Yandell, and the 260 medical students of that year were from 15 different States, mainly in the Southwest.

A few months[1] after Mr. Peers's resignation as president of the university, he was succeeded, in that position, by Rev. Thomas W. Coit, D. D., who had been a member of the theological faculty then associated with the institution and was a high churchman of some celebrity. President Coit retained his office about three years, which was somewhat longer than the usual presidential term during this period of the university's history.

In January, 1836, an attempt was made to carry out President Peers's idea and convert, by the aid of legislative action, the university into a State normal school, the State contributing $5,000 a year to its support and receiving in return free tuition for 100 State students; but the plan was too advanced for the legislature to then adopt, and we shall see, when about twenty years later another legislature did establish such a school, the idea was still ahead of public opinion and the experiment was destined to be a failure.

President Coit seems to have been an excellent man, but perhaps less energetic than President Peers, and so less able to stem the tide of general decline in the fortunes of the university, which had set in stronger than ever, and which even affected the professional departments, hitherto comparatively vigorous. This depression resulted in 1837 in an attempt, participated in by Drs. Caldwell, Cook, Yandell, and Short, the majority of the medical faculty, and perhaps others, which seems, for a time at least, to have been conducted secretly, to move the medical department bodily to Louisville, which had developed into the largest and most important business center in the State and was considered by them in many ways a more eligible location than Lexington for the school. When this plan became generally known, a storm of local indignation was aroused and the professors who favored the change resigned their chairs, as they may perhaps have done in any event if their views had not been carried out. They were mainly instrumental soon after in establishing at Louisville, on an independent basis, a rival school called the Louisville Medical Institute, which subsequently developed into the medical department of the University of Louisville, but which does not seem, for a time at least, if at all, to have materially injured the medical department of Transylvania University.

[1] The dates given here for the administration of President Coit, 1835 and 1838, are those given by most authorities; Peter's Transylvania University, pp. 161-162, gives them as October, 1834 (inaugurated July, 1835), and September, 1837.

Indeed, the movement was upon the whole really beneficial to Transylvania, as local public opinion was awakened to her condition and needs, and help was brought to her in 1838–39 from the same source and partly in the same manner that it had come several times before. The city of Lexington granted $70,000 to the funds of the institution, while a company of 70 of her citizens, organized in a corporate capacity under the name of the Transylvania Institute, on February 20, 1839, subscribed $35,000 for the same purpose, transferable scholarships carrying with them free tuition being issued to the city and to the subscribers for each $500 contributed. Of the money given by the city, $40,000 was to go to the construction of a new medical college building and $5,000 to equip that with library and apparatus; another $5,000 was for the library of the law department, and the remainder for the endowment of Morrison College. The money raised by the Transylvania Institute also went to Morrison College, part of it being used to erect a new dormitory. After these additions the property of the college was estimated to be worth about $100,000, and its endowment, including the Morrison fund, about $75,000.[1] The medical faculty, which was reorganized on April 29, 1837,[2] also came to the rescue by subscribing $3,000 to purchase a lot for the new medical building and afterwards paying off a debt of about $15,000 remaining on that structure after its completion. The corner stone of this building[3] was laid July 4, 1839, and it was dedicated on November 1, 1840.

The reorganized medical faculty was constituted as follows: B. W. Dudley, M. D., anatomy and surgery; James C. Cross, M. D., institutes of medicine and medical jurisprudence; John Eberle, M. D., theory and practice of medicine; W. H. Richardson, M. D., obstetrics and diseases of women and children; Thomas D. Mitchell, M. D., materia medica and therapeutics; Robert Peter, M. D., chemistry and pharmacy. James M. Bush, M. D., was adjunct professor of anatomy and surgery. He subsequently became Dr. Dudley's successor in that chair, and is hardly less celebrated than his predecessor as a surgeon. Dr. Peter at this time became first connected with the medical department of the university. He was a member of its faculty throughout the remainder of its history, and was for many years its dean or chief executive officer.

This department maintained its former relative standing comparatively well throughout this period. In 1834–35 it had 255 students, while the University of Pennsylvania had 392, and Jefferson Medical College 233. Yale at that time had 64 medical students, and Harvard 82. In 1839 there were 240 students in the medical department of Transyl-

[1] See North American Review, vol. 49, pp. 262–263, which gives the endowment and property at this time and also the use made of the funds of 1838–39.

[2] Collins's History of Kentucky, Vol. I, p. 41.

[3] This, the second medical building of the university, was located on North Broadway street, opposite the southwest corner of the university campus, where the residence of Dr. J. M. Bush subsequently stood.

vania, which up to November, 1838, had had altogether 3,820 students and 1,058 graduates.[1]

The law department of the university was also enlarged in its scope about the time of the reorganization of its medical faculty, and henceforth had three regular professors, while its library, increased by the donation of Lexington, Peter[2] tells us, was the finest of its kind in the West. He also says that it was not surpassed in the country in the ability of its professors and the number of its regular students.

This department had had as a rule only one regular professor since the close of Dr. Holley's administration, but the professors of the school at different times had been such men as John Boyle, Charles Humphreys, and Daniel Mayes, while its attendance had ranked well with that of similar schools throughout the country. In 1834 Transylvania had 1 professor and 36 students in its law department, while Harvard had 2 professors and 32 students; the University of Virginia, 1 professor and 33 students; Yale, 2 professors and 43 students. In 1839, after its reorganization, Transylvania's law school had 71 students, while Harvard had 120, Yale 45, and the University of Virginia 72.

The reorganized Transylvania law faculty[3] was composed of George Robertson, Aaron K. Woolley, and Thomas A. Marshall, men rarely, if ever, excelled in their ability as jurists or as teachers. They remained in charge of the department throughout the remainder of this period, and under them its attendance and reputation were considerably increased.

About the close of President Coit's administration another change in the plan of managing the university was made which marks more emphatically than ever the withdrawal of the State from any attempt at active participation in its management. By an act approved February 16, 1838, the old trustee system was abolished and the institution was put under the temporary management of five trustees appointed by the governor of the State. On February 20, 1839, the governing power of the university was vested in a board of eight trustees, two of whom were to be appointed by the Transylvania Institute, three by the city of Lexington, and three by the State legislature—a system of control which was in the main to be retained throughout the remaining

[1] Peter's Thoughts on Medical Education in America, p. 12.

[2] History of Fayette County, p. 295.

[3] Their chairs, in the order their names are mentioned, were respectively constitutional law, equity, and law of comity; elementary principles of common law; national and commercial law and law of pleading, evidence, and contract.

Of this faculty Hon. George Robertson, LL.D., was on the supreme bench of Kentucky for about sixteen years, during about fifteen of which he was chief justice. He taught in Transylvania for more than twenty years. Hon. Thomas A. Marshall, LL.D., was also a member of the supreme court of the State for over nine years, for over six of which he was chief justice. He taught in Transylvania for about fourteen years subsequent to 1836. Hon. A. K. Woolley was for a time a circuit judge and taught in the university a number of years prior to 1849.

history of the institution, and which gave to its trustees, now largely local, power to manage it themselves or to transfer its management to other parties, as we shall soon see them doing.

The other members of the academic faculty at the time of President Coit's resignation were as follows: Rev. Louis Marshall, D. D., professor of ancient languages; Rev. Robert Davidson, D. D., professor of mental and moral philosophy; Arthur J. Dumont, professor of mathematics; Robert Peter, M. D., professor of natural history and experimental philosophy; and Rev. Charles Crow, principal of the preparatory department. Dr. Marshall[1] became the acting president of the university and remained so until the beginning of the next regular administration.

The trustees now appear to have endeavored to recall to the aid of the institution an old denominational influence. They attempted to conciliate the Presbyterians, then earnestly striving to make the equipment and endowment of Centre College superior to that of Transylvania, by tendering the presidency of the university, Davidson tells us, successively to Dr. J. C. Young, the efficient president of Centre, and then to Drs. L. W. Green and R. J. Breckinridge, other ministers of high standing in the Presbyterian Church. These all declined, and the position was then offered to Rev. Robert Davidson, D. D.,[2] also a prominent Presbyterian clergyman. Dr. Davidson, who accepted the presidency, was a man of considerable reputation, and had already for some time occupied a chair in the university faculty. He was inaugurated as president in November, 1840, probably at the same time that the large and fine new medical building was dedicated.

The attempt to bring back Presbyterian support was, however, in the main, ineffectual, as Centre, the distinctively Presbyterian college, had by this time become too firmly established in the affections of the denomination for the effort to be of much avail. Dr. Davidson early recognized this, and, as he himself tells us, despairing of being able to stem the tide of general depression now setting in again, and hindered in his work by numerous and vexatious embarrassments, resolved to resign, which he did in March, 1842.

His resignation may have been hastened by the consummation of negotiations, begun perhaps before his election, but not leading to any definite result until after he resigned. As early as 1840 the trustees, whether on their own initiative or not does not appear, had made overtures to the general conference of the Methodist Episcopal Church in the United States looking toward the control of the university by that body, which, under the circumstances, they probably considered capable of bringing stronger denominational support to the institution than

[1] Dr. Marshall afterwards, in 1855, became the president of Washington College, now Washington and Lee University, Virginia.

[2] Dr. Davidson is the author of the important work, The History of the Presbyterian Church in Kentucky, a work quoted a number of times in this monograph, especially in this chapter.

even the Presbyterians. At the meeting of this conference, held in Baltimore in May, 1840, the matter was taken up and seven commissioners[1] were appointed from the church at large and the Kentucky conference to consider it and to carry out the transfer if it was deemed desirable.

The directing spirit in this movement was Rev. H. B. Bascom, D. D., LL. D., a leading minister of his denomination, and afterwards, when the division of the church occurred, a bishop of its Southern branch. Dr. Bascom had been, since 1832,[2] a prominent professor in Augusta College, an institution long considered the adopted college of Kentucky Methodism, under whose auspices it had been mainly founded, but he seems to have been conscientious in thinking that that institution was no longer available for the highest and best educational purposes of his denomination, and therefore devoted himself with his accustomed energy, which was very great, to securing the control of Transylvania University for his church. He experienced considerable opposition from the friends of Augusta, whose funds he vainly tried to secure for the new enterprise; but, after considerable negotiation, was able to effect the desired arrangement. Either because he feared an appeal to the legislature on account of the opposition of Augusta, or because he did not believe such action necessary, no legislative sanction was obtained for the transfer, which was made by the trustees on September 21, 1841.

The professional departments still remained on their former basis, the new arrangement applying only to Morrison College, or the academic department, the direct management of which was to be vested in a board of nine curators, to be appointed by the general conference. The curators were to have control of the department in all important respects, such as the nomination of its faculty, the prescription of its course of study, and its internal police and regulation. The church was to be given an additional representation of three members on the board of trustees, which body reserved to itself only a kind of residuary control over the action of the curators. Kentucky conference was to be interested in the institution through a visiting committee of three members to be appointed annually by that body.

The transfer was not regularly ratified by the general conference until its meeting in 1842, but shortly before that event, in the spring of that year, Dr. Bascom became, by the appointment of the conference commissioners, the acting president of the university, and at once, with

[1] For the names of these commissioners see Alexander's Earliest Western Schools of Methodism, p. 372.

[2] This date is given by most authorities as 1831, but appears as in the text in Henkle's Life of Bascom, p. 230, which should, all things considered, be the most authentic. It is given also in Sprague's Annals, Vol. VII, p. 536. Henkle's life of Dr. Bascom is most complete. Comprehensive sketches of his life are also to be found in Sprague's Annals, Vol. VII, pp. 535-536, Collins's History of Kentucky, Vol. I, pp. 453-455, and Smith's History of Kentucky, p. 556.

characteristic vigor, devoted himself to building up the institution. He associated with himself an able faculty, whose personnel, in 1843, not long after the beginning of his administration, was as follows: Rev. H. B. Bascom, D. D., president and professor of mental and moral philosophy; Rev. R. T. P. Allen, A. M., professor of mathematics, natural philosophy, and civil engineering; Rev. B. H. McCown, A. M., professor of ancient languages and literature; Rev. W. H. Anderson, A. M., professor of the English language and literature; Rev. J. L. Kemp, A. M., adjunct professor of mathematics; Rev. Thos. H. Lynch, A. M., adjunct professor of languages; Rev. Wright Merrick, principal junior section preparatory department.

Of this faculty Professor McCown had, like Dr. Bascom, been long a prominent professor at Augusta, and was especially celebrated as a teacher. The faculties of the professional departments of the university were at this time the same as those under the reorganization of 1837, except that Drs. Lothan G. Watson and Leonidas M. Lawson had taken the place of Drs. Eberle and Cross in the medical department.

The new president set to work with energy, and was for a time eminently successful in increasing the patronage of the university, the number of students in its academic department, says Henkle,[1] rising from 20 or 30 at his accession to 281 the second year and 290 the third year of his administration. The professional departments were also well attended.[2] In 1844 Dr. Bascom became the regular president, by the appointment of the curators, who had then been selected for the institution by the general conference of his church. Under his able management it seemed that Transylvania would soon equal if not excel, in numbers at least, her palmiest days. The partial endowment of the chair of English had been accomplished by 1843. Further endowments were proposed and other ambitious and excellent plans, besides procuring new students, were entertained. Disunion in the church, however, soon set in and was a great hindrance to the enterprise.

After the division of 1844–45 had taken place the control of the university passed, in May, 1846, into the hands of the Methodist Episcopal Church South. Dr. Bascom was again elected president, and in order to secure popularity for the institution had men from all the different parts of the church elected to its various chairs, but, on account of the irritation and the divided responsibility still remaining in thedenomination, especially in Kentucky, neither the church nor the South generally increased their support, either in students or funds. So Dr. Bascom, discouraged by the situation and despairing of the

[1] Life of Bascom, p. 278.

[2] Catalogues for the years 1842–1843, 1843–1844, 1846–1847, and 1847–1848, which have been examined, show that the average annual matriculation in the academic department for these years was 240, of whom something over half were in the preparatory classes. The average annual attendance in the medical department for these years was 215, and in the law department, 65. In 1843 13 A. B.'s, 30 B. L.'s, and 59 M. D.'s were conferred.

further enlargement of the institution, resigned in 1849, and soon after steps were taken by his church to abandon the enterprise as a denominational one.

Some idea of the standing of Transylvania University in comparison with other institutions in the country may be obtained from the following statistics of the scholastic year 1842–43: In that year Harvard had 30 instructors and 245 academic students, while Yale had 30 instructors and 410 academic students. Transylvania had 17 instructors and 281 students. A considerable portion of the latter were, however, doing preparatory work. In the same year Transylvania had 75 law students, while Harvard, the only school that exceeded it, had 115. The total number of volumes in the libraries of Harvard and Yale in this year were, respectively, 53,000 and 32,200, while there were 12,242 volumes in the library of the academic department of Transylvania. Collins tells us, in his Sketches,[1] that Transylvania in 1847 had libraries numbering 45,000 volumes, besides which it had a fine medical museum and an extensive assortment of chemical and philosophical apparatus. Its medical school up to January of that year, he tells us, had had more than 1,500 graduates. Published statements[2] of the yearly expenses of attendance at Transylvania at this period show them to have been little less than those of the Eastern colleges; in fact, something more than those of Yale.

PERIOD FROM 1849 TO 1865.

In 1850 the general conference of the Methodist Episcopal Church South turned over the management of the university to its two conferences in Kentucky, Kentucky and Louisville conferences, and they, not deeming its possession of advantage to themselves, turned it over to the trustees, so that the institution fell back to the plan of control established for it in 1839.

Once more practically abandoned by everyone and left to its own slender resources, another season of decline set in in its history, although its collegiate department seems for the next few years to have performed a considerable amount of useful service under the direction of Prof. J. B. Dodd, the mathematician, as acting president, and the professional department continued to have considerable vitality up to the time of the civil war.

In 1850 the plan of the medical department was changed in such a way as to have its sessions held in the spring, instead of the fall and winter, as before, and its faculty took the principal part in establishing, to act in conjunction with it, the Kentucky School of Medicine, in Louisville. This arrangement, however, after having been tried for

---

[1] Sketches of Kentucky, p. 266.

[2] In American Almanac and Repository of Useful Knowledge for 1843. Tuition at Transylvania was $40, while the total college charges were $52, and board, fuel, etc., are estimated at $125 (board, $100). The same figures for Yale are $33, $54, and $110 (board, $70). The charges for fuel, etc., are not given at Harvard, but tuition is $75; total college charges, $93, and board is estimated at from $70 to $90 per year.

TRANSYLVANIA UNIVERSITY IN 1860.

four[1] sessions, does not seem to have been a success, and so, in 1851, the Transylvania school was changed back to a winter session, although an extra spring session was for a time retained. The Kentucky School of Medicine was subsequently continued, in other hands, as another rival institution.

In 1856 the university underwent its last reorganization as a separate institution. We have a return once more to more direct State control and the advent again of the principle of State patronage. The plan formerly advocated by President Peers was also revived, and the university was, by an act of March 10, 1856,[2] converted into a State normal school, especially designed to supply well-trained teachers for the public schools of the State—a much-needed and very commendable object. The school was intended to be an indispensable aid to the common-school system, and the cause of public-school education in Kentucky had never looked brighter than then. This reorganization of the university was doubtless brought about largely through the persistent agitation of the matter and the unremitting efforts in that direction of Rev. Robert J. Breckinridge, D. D., LL. D., State superintendent of public instruction from 1847 to 1853, and an enthusiastic advocate of a State normal school.

Under the new arrangement State regulation was secured by the appointment of a board of trustees composed of the former trustees and the principal State officers. The State was to contribute $12,000 a year to the enterprise, $7,000 of which was to be used to aid deserving teachers unable to properly educate themselves, and $5,000 was to go to the general support of the institution. The grounds and buildings of the university at that time were estimated[3] to be worth about $100,000, and its whole property and funds about $200,000, its income from endowment being a little less than $4,000 annually. The institution was not to be converted into a normal school exclusively, but the normal department was to be made its most prominent feature, while other regular college courses were to be maintained, to which the State teachers were to have free access and thus be enabled to greatly broaden their education.

An excellent president was selected for the new school in the person of Rev. L. W. Green, D. D. President Green resigned the presidency of Hampden-Sidney College to accept the position. He was a former student of Transylvania University, an alumnus of Centre College in its first graduating class in 1824, and was subsequently a professor there before going to Virginia.

---

[1] The period of the trial of this experiment is usually stated as three years, but the university catalogue of 1850 and the announcement of the medical school for 1854 show it to have been four years. There were 92 medical students in 1850 and 53 in 1854 (spring session). In 1850 there were 125 students in the academic department and 35 in the law department.

[2] Collins's History of Kentucky, Vol. I, p. 76.

[3] President Green's inaugural address.

The school was opened auspiciously, with 80 students, on September 7, 1856,[1] and on November 18 following[2] the president was ceremoniously inaugurated under all the old Transylvania forms. The attendance rapidly increased and under the judicious management of President Green excellent progress toward the desired ends was being made, when the legislature, on February 13, 1858, having previously refused for some reason to renew the appropriation for its support, repealed the act establishing the institution. President Green had already despaired of its success, and had resigned in the latter part of 1857. He became the president of Centre College on January 1, 1858.

So, at the end of the two years for which the original appropriation had been made, the normal-school feature of the university was entirely abandoned and the institution reverted to its status prior to the act of 1856. The only reason the writer has seen suggested for the withdrawal of legislative support from the normal school was that the appropriation made in its behalf encroached on the revenue of the public-school fund, from which it seems to have been drawn.

After 1858 the university sunk hopelessly. Its academic department struggled on for a time under Abram Drake, and during the civil war became simply a local grammar school under Prof. J. K. Patterson, the present efficient president of the State College. It lost one of its dormitories in 1860 by fire.

The medical department of the university existed, with varying success, up to the opening of the civil war. Its faculty in 1859 was composed of Drs. E. L. Dudley, S. L. Adams, W. S. Chipley, B. P. Drake, S. M. Letcher, H. M. Skillman, J. M. Bush, and Robert Peter. Its building was for a time used as an army hospital, and was on May 22, 1863, destroyed by a fire, which also consumed practically all its equipment. The school had had, altogether, 6,406 students, of whom 1,854 had graduated.[3] It has never been resurrected since on its old basis, but a department of Kentucky University was for a time maintained under a similar name.

The law department had a somewhat similar history during this period, closing its career at the opening of the war. Judge Robertson remained connected with it most if not all of the time, and its other professors during this period were Madison C. Johnson, George B. Kinkead, and Francis K. Hunt. The last three were later connected with law departments of Kentucky University. Judge Robertson, during his long connection with the school, extending for more than twenty years, had lectured to more than 3,000 young men, 2,000 of whom had graduated.[4]

The libraries and apparatus of all kinds belonging to the university were scattered and much of them destroyed during the war, and its

[1] Collins's History of Kentucky, Vol. I, p. 76.

[2] *Ibid*, Vol. I, p. 77.

[3] *Ibid*, Vol. II, p. 184.

[4] Biographical Sketch of Gov. L. W. Powell, p. 23.

prospects were indeed gloomy near the end of that struggle. The trustees had, in 1863, shortly after the acceptance of the gift to the State from the General Government, made by the Congressional land-grant act of 1862, endeavored to have the institution made the foundation of the agricultural and mechanical college provided for by that act, but the State did not then undertake the establishment of that institution, nor accept the very advantageous offer made by the trustees of the university.

The outlook for the latter institution had not improved in 1864, when Kentucky University, having lost its building at Harrodsburg by fire, was looking for a new location. The trustees of Transylvania, then seeing their opportunity to perpetuate the character and usefulness of Lexington as an educational center, proposed to transfer all its property and funds, amounting at that time to about $100,000 in real estate and $59,000 in endowment, to Kentucky University, on condition of that institution being located in Lexington and fulfilling all the trusts incumbent under the charter of Transylvania University. Their offer was accepted and the union with Kentucky University consummated by the aid of legislative action on January 22, 1865.

While the equity of this transfer of what was largely, at least legally, State property to a denominational institution may be questioned by some, it is certainly true that that property has since been of eminently more educational value to the people of the State at large than it was at the time, or than it seemed likely to be at any time soon. Since January, 1865, Transylvania University has ceased to exist as a separate institution, becoming then a part and parcel of Kentucky University, with the history of which her history has since blended.

The reasons for the failure of Transylvania University, as indicated by the progress of this narrative, are not far afield, but as they are of some special interest, and perhaps in some ways instructive, it may be worth while to recount them somewhat explicitly, as follows:

(1) The initial endowment, as in the case of the early academies, was not sufficient to make the institution self-sustaining, nor had the State sufficiently committed herself to the policy of ample regular appropriations supplementary to the endowment. The State had not assumed moral or pecuniary obligations sufficiently large, nor had she committed herself to a policy of sufficiently liberal support through taxation, either or both of which could be pleaded in behalf of future aid. Unless something of the kind had been done in the early history of the institution through the influence of prominent public men, as was the case later in regard to Jefferson and the University of Virginia, public opinion was not sufficiently strong in its behalf to demand that the university be properly supported.

(2) The institution was never made a distinctively State enterprise, as the State had only a partial control over it, being, as a rule, associated with some form of denominational management, the power of

each being just sufficient to hinder and weaken that of the other. Either power by itself might have built up a great university, but together they could not, as it was impossible for them to cooperate harmoniously. Then, too, each denomination when attempting to operate the institution was hampered by the others, as was later the case in regard to Kentucky University, where another attempt was made to build up a great university with the same union of forces as in the case of Transylvania originally, but with these forces reversed in order.

(3) This lack of proper cooperation, always in the nature of the case more or less necessary, was rendered much more so in the early history of Kentucky by the prevalence in the State, especially among its public men of French deistic ideas, which naturally put the religious bodies more on the defensive and made them more sensitive to what they thought were attacks upon their faith, when probably there was no intention of anything of the kind. This same feeling seems to have led, at least to a considerable extent, to the educational institutions of the State generally taking such a decided denominational character.

(4) By reason of the plan of joint control just described the university was never placed under the direct supervision of the State authorities, who could hold its management responsible and could themselves be called to account. Its board of trustees were in the main, throughout its history, either by law or practice, self-perpetuating, not even having, as a rule, to report their action in any way to any superior officer. The plan of their organization was very similar to that of the early academy boards, and gave, as we have seen in the case of these, great opportunity for the creation and perpetuation of factions among themselves, for the carrying out of schemes, denominational or otherwise, and for irresponsible action generally.

The record of Transylvania University for the two generations it existed is, in many respects, a proud one. Although unusually hampered in its usefulness in many ways, especially by the unfortunate plan of its organization and the state of public opinion on religious and edutional questions—never being largely endowed or regularly supported by either State, denomination, or individuals, and always depending largely on tuition fees for its maintenance—it perhaps accomplished as much, or even more, than any other of the earlier educational institutions of this country in the same period, counting from the foundation of each. The record of growth and expansion during the Holley era may certainly fairly be said never to have been excelled, if equaled, in America in the same length of time until comparatively recent years.

The history of the professional departments was especially brilliant, for a long time almost entirely eclipsing that of any rivals in the West of that day. Its medical faculty, with the celebrated Dr. Dudley at its head for forty years, and at various times including such other men as Caldwell, Cooke, Drake, Short, Yandell, Cross, Bush, and others, was quite generally unsurpassed of its kind in the country. The faculty of its law college, embracing at different times such names as those of Barry, Bledsoe, Boyle, Humphreys, Mayes, Robertson, Marshall, Woolley, and others, was almost, if not quite, as noted.

We have already spoken in a general way of the number of graduates in the various departments. Among the names of these, reaching in number into the thousands, are such men as Josiah Stoddard Johnston, Richard M. Johnson, Jefferson Davis, Dr. B. W. Dudley, Thomas F. Marshall, Richard H. Menifee, John Boyle, James McChord, Dr. Joseph Buchanan, John Rowan, William T. Barry, Jesse Bledsoe, Charles S. Morehead, Elijah Hise, "Duke" Gwinn, Charles A. Wickliffe, Robert H. Bishop, Robert J. Breckinridge, and a host of others, thus described by Collins,[1] "statesmen, jurists, orators, surgeons, divines, among the greatest in the world's history—men of mark in all the professions and callings of business life."

Morehead[2] speaks as follows of the work of the institution:

"An institution which has nursed to maturity the intellect of the Commonwealth, having in the progress of sixty years filled her assemblies with lawgivers, her cabinets with statesmen, her judicial tribunals with ministers of justice, her pulpits with divines, and crowded the professional ranks at home and abroad with ornaments and benefactors to their country."

One or more of these alumni were to be found at the close of the university's history in almost every community of any size in the South and West, where they were principally located, and upon the history of which sections and through them upon that of the whole country they have exerted a great influence.

BIBLIOGRAPHY.

All the works referred to in regard to the early State university system, except Bradford's Laws, Littell and Swigert's Statutes, Spalding's Early Catholic Missions, McMurtrie's Sketches, and the Report of the Commissioners of 1822, also contain some information about Transylvania University. The following additional authorities have been consulted in regard to the facts of the university's history:

Sprague's Annals of the American Pulpit.

Hening's Statutes at Large of Virginia.

Sketches of North Carolina, by Rev. W. H. Foote, D. D., New York, 1846.

A Tour in Ohio, Indiana, and Kentucky in 1805, by Josiah Espy, Cincinnati, 1871.

A History of the Church in Kentucky for Forty Years, Containing the Memoirs of Rev. David Rice, by Robert H. Bishop, Lexington, 1824.

Notes on Kentucky History, by John Bradford, published in the Kentucky Gazette between August 25, 1826, and January 9, 1829.

An address delivered at Boonesborough in Commemoration of the First Settlement of Kentucky, by J. T. Morehead, Frankfort, 1840.

A History of Lexington, Ky., by George W. Ranck, Cincinnati, 1872.

An address to the Public in regard to the Controversy about President Holley, by Professors Barry, Bledsoe, Dudley, and Caldwell, Lexington, 1824.

A Discourse on the Services and Character of Rev. Horace Holley, LL. D. (also called Memoirs), by Charles Caldwell, M. D., Boston, 1828.

[1] History of Kentucky, Vol. II, p. 184.

[2] Boonesborough address, p. 81.

Autobiography of Charles Caldwell, M. D., edited by Harriot W. Warner, Philadelphia, 1855.

Memoirs of the Life and Services of Daniel Drake, M. D., by E. D. Mansfield, LL. D., Cincinnati, 1855.

Memoirs of Rev. Thomas Cleland, D. D., by E. P. Humphrey and Thomas H. Cleland, Cincinnati, 1859.

The Life of Rev. H. B. Bascom, D. D., LL. D., by Rev. M. M. Henkle, Nashville, 1856.

A Scrapbook of Law, Politics, Men, and Times, by George Robertson, LL. D., Lexington, 1855.

A Biographical Sketch of Hon. L. W. Powell, by direction of the General Assembly, Frankfort, 1868.

Thoughts on Medical Education in America, by Robert Peter, M. D., Lexington, 1838.

Thoughts on Public Education in America, by Robert Peter, M. D., Frankfort, 1877.

The Minutes of the Board of Trustees of Transylvania University. These are preserved in the archives of Kentucky University and are quite complete up to February, 1818, after which date they are quite fragmentary.

By-Laws of Transylvania University, Lexington, 1818.

Inaugural Address of President Woods, Lexington, 1828.

Laws of Transylvania University, Lexington, 1829.

The Transylvania Journal of Medicine for October, November, and December, 1831.

Inaugural Address of President Peers, Lexington, 1833.

Extra of the Lexington Intelligencer for April 11, 1837.

Statutes of Transylvania University, Lexington, 1842.

A communication from the Commissioners of Kentucky Conference to the Legislature of Kentucky in reply to a Memorial from the Trustees of Augusta College, Lexington, 1843.

The Transylvania Journal of Medicine for December, 1850.

Inaugural Address of President Green, Frankfort, 1856.

Reports of the State Superintendents of Public Instruction, from 1839 to 1857, and Appendix to the Report of 1875–76.

Niles's Weekly Register, September, 1811, to July, 1849; third edition, 76 volumes, Baltimore, Washington, and Philadelphia, 1816–1849.

The American Almanac and Repository of Useful Knowledge, 1830–1861, 32 volumes, Boston and New York, 1830–1861.

The last two authorities have been consulted mainly for the statistics used, which in the case of Transylvania, have been fully verified by reference to a number of old catalogues. The History of Transylvania University, by Robert Peter, M. D., edited by Johanna Peter, Louisville, 1896, has been carefully examined; but, as this chapter had been practically completed before it was accessible, very little use has been made of it, and what has been made is duly credited in the footnotes.

Chapter IV.

INSTITUTIONS MORE OR LESS DIRECTLY CONNECTED WITH TRANSYLVANIA UNIVERSITY AND OLDER COLLEGES.

KENTUCKY UNIVERSITY, LEXINGTON.

Kentucky University, in the most extensive use of the name, may be said not to have come into existence until the regular ratification, on June 20, 1865, by the board of curators of the previous Kentucky University of the legislative act of February 28, 1865, which completed the arrangements for uniting the older Kentucky University, Transylvania University, and the Agricultural and Mechanical College into one general institution, which was designed to be, and actually was for a time, the most extensive in the history of the State. The Agricultural and Mechanical College was then just being brought into existence, but the former Kentucky University and Transylvania University both had histories extending considerably back of this date, that of the latter, as we have seen, reaching even to the beginnings of Kentucky.

We have traced the history of Transylvania University up to the time of this union and will now take up the other source of the enlarged University, bringing its history up to the same date before beginning the history of the combined institution. The primary origin of the original Kentucky University is to be found in Bacon College, whose history will now for a time engage our attention.

BACON COLLEGE.

This institution is one of the many arising in Kentucky between 1830 and 1840, owing to the desire of the various denominations to possess institutions over which they would have direct control and which would serve their purposes better, as they considered, than Transylvania University, previously the most important educational institution in the State.

The beginnings of the college are to be found in a school opened at Georgetown, Ky., on November 7, 1836,[1] by T. F. Johnson, formerly a professor in Georgetown College, assisted by tutors Mullins and Knight. Its pupils numbered only 50 or 60 at first, but within four months their number had increased to 130. The school was from its inception under

[1] Collins's History of Kentucky, Vol. I, p. 41.

the patronage of the denomination known as Disciples of Christ, or Christians, and had, as a specially fast and valuable friend, Elder John T. Johnson, then a prominent man in that church. Its prosperity soon led its friends to think of enlarging its scope, and so, mainly through the influence of Elder Johnson, a charter was obtained for it on February 23, 1837, which started it on its career as Bacon College, so named in honor of Sir Francis Bacon, and the earliest institution of its grade established by the Christian Church.

It was placed under the control of a board of six trustees, and Walter Scott was selected for its first president. We know comparatively little of the history of the institution while it remained at Georgetown. One fact of some interest in connection with its history while there is, that John B. Bowman, a man to be so prominently connected with the future of the institution, was then one of its students, being among the first to enter its halls. President Scott's connection with the college seems to have been largely nominal, he probably not having entered regularly upon any academic duties, and, after a few months David S. Burnet became the first active president.

The success of the institution at this period does not seem to have been very great, and accordingly, in the summer of 1839, it was removed to Harrodsburg, Ky., as being a more eligible location. Elder Johnson, who was one of its first curators, had especially interested himself about the time of its removal in endeavoring to secure for it an endowment of $100,000, one-half the income of which was to be used to assist deserving poor youths in obtaining an education. He does not seem to have had very much success in carrying out his idea. At the opening of the first session of the college in Harrodsburg, on September 2, 1839, its endowment appears to have been about $20,000, something more than one-half of which was invested in a fairly good building.

It existed for some time at its new location with varying fortune. It maintained a course of high grade and soon gained an excellent reputation, but, as its endowment was insufficient, its success was irregular. Collins tells[1] us that, in 1845–46, there were in attendance upon its classes 113 students, from 9 different States, and that the institution was flourishing in 1847, with 180 students, and yet we find that in 1850 it was suspended and virtually abandoned because of financial difficulties. Various plans had been submitted in vain and many unsuccessful efforts made for its permanent upbuilding, and so its best friends, including its curators, had practically given up all hope for its future. Its history as Bacon College ends with its suspension in 1850, for when it was revived several years later, it appears under a new name and with a character somewhat different.

Its presidents during the period of its existence as Bacon College, with their terms of service, were as follows: Walter Scott, few months in 1837; David S. Burnet, 1837–1839; Samuel Hatch, 1839–40; James

[1] Sketches of Kentucky, p. 114.

Shannon, 1840–1850. Its faculty in 1847, one of its most prosperous periods, was composed as follows: James Shannon, president and professor of intellectual, moral, and political science; Samuel Hatch, professor of chemistry and natural philosophy; Henry H. White, professor of mathematics and civil engineering; George A. Matthews, professor of ancient languages; E. Askew, teacher in the preparatory department. Its library at that time numbered 1,600 volumes.

During its existence the college had had 27 graduates, among whom especially may be mentioned John B. Bowman and H. H. White, both later so prominently connected with its history, Professor White, as we have seen, being already a member of its faculty before its suspension.

THE ORIGINAL KENTUCKY UNIVERSITY.

The failure of Bacon College caused John B. Bowman, then living near Harrodsburg, to reflect upon the consequences due to the loss of the institution and to meditate upon a plan whereby an institution of even greater compass might be erected on the ruins of his alma mater. After mature deliberation he determined, in 1855, to devote himself to the task upon a plan peculiarly his own, and accordingly, in the winter of 1855–56, leaving his own important business affairs, he proceeded to make, in behalf of his design, a house to house canvass of several counties in central Kentucky, where his denomination was particularly strong. His plan was to get the members of his own church, and others interested in educational matters, to contribute in the form of notes in which the payments were made easy, and which, as they were paid, would form an endowment fund, which in time, being invested, would furnish a fixed income for the institution. Scholarship coupons were issued to the subscribers in proportion to the amount subscribed.

Mr. Bowman met with a hearty response in his canvass and was successful, it seems, even beyond his own expectations; but his ideas grew as the funds secured enlarged. In about one hundred and fifty days he secured $150,000, contributed chiefly in small amounts, and given mainly by the farmers of the region, and mostly by members of the Christian Church, although other public-spirited citizens also subscribed.

For the better materialization of his ideas, Mr. Bowman, through the trustees of Bacon College, called a public meeting of the friends and donors of that institution to consult about its reorganization. This meeting occurred at Harrodsburg on May 6, 1857, and was numerously attended, especially from the counties to which the appeal in behalf of the new plan had been principally directed. It was harmonious in spirit and earnest in action, and to it Mr. Bowman presented the report of his canvass and his ideas in regard to the proposed institution. It was not his intention to reestablish Bacon College in its old form, but, as expressed in his own words, to found an "institution more liberal in all its appointments—permanent in its nature—and auxiliary to the cause of sound morality and pure religion in our State,"[1] which was to be made easily accessible to poor young men of the industrial classes.

These plans were heartily approved by the meeting, and a committee of conference appointed to act in conjunction with the trustees of Bacon College in determining what amendments were needed to the charter of the college in order to carry them out. Accordingly, amendments were obtained, by legislative action approved January 15, 1858, investing, with all the property and claims of Bacon College, a new body of curators, representing the various counties contributing to the new enterprise, who were to be not less than thirty in number, and two-thirds of whom must be members of the Christian Church in Kentucky. They were given the corporate power necessary to establish "a first-class university, upon a modern American and Christian basis," under the title of Kentucky University, and were given the right "to grant such literary honors as are usually granted in the best colleges and universities in the United States," the diplomas conferred entitling their possessors "to all the immunities and privileges which by law or usage are allowed to the possessors of diplomas granted by any other college or university in the United States."

The amended charter, with its enlarged provisions, was accepted by the trustees of Bacon College on February 2, 1858, and the new board of curators, at their first meeting on February 4, 1858, adopted the necessary laws and regulations for putting it into operation. They then issued an address to the public on the history, aims, and objects of the institution, in which they called upon its friends to increase the endowment, which they proposed to make at least $500,000, and declared that what had been done was only a small amount of what they hoped to do in the future, their ideas and aims, under Mr. Bowman's inspiration, enlarging as the means for carrying them out increased. Disavowing sectarian purposes and deprecating the multiplicity of sickly and puny institutions throughout the West, not furnished with "the true apparatus of an education," they only proposed to lay, in their day, a foundation upon which future generations might build. All the departments of a genuine university were contemplated, embracing normal and agricultural departments as well as literary and scientific ones.

The beginning of the new Kentucky University is to be found in a preparatory department, to which a normal department was attached, opened in Harrodsburg, on September 21, 1857, under the name of Taylor Academy, William C. Piper being its principal and Joseph B. Myers his assistant. About 80 pupils were present at the opening of this school and 94 were in attendance altogether during its first year. The university proper was first opened on September 19, 1859, with Robert Milligan, A. M., as its first president, who was duly installed two days later.

President Milligan associated with him while the university was at Harrodsburg Robert Richardson, Robert Graham, L. L. Pinkerton,

[1] Minutes of the meeting of the friends and donors of Bacon College, page 7.

H. H. White, and J. H. Neville as professors in the various departments which were, at the time, biblical literature and moral philosophy, mathematics, ancient languages, physical science, belles-lettres, and modern languages, all except the last, which might be substituted for some of the work in mathematics, being required for the degree of A. B. The scientific apparatus of the university, at its opening, was estimated to be worth $10,000, Mr. Bowman having recently raised $5,000 for the purchase of new apparatus. He had also, about the same time, secured conditionally an additional $50,000 for the purchase of Harrodsburg Springs and the erection on that splendid estate of new buildings for the institution. He was, however, disappointed in securing that property.

More than 150 students were present at the opening in 1859, and 194 were in attendance during the year. One hundred and seventy-two were enrolled in 1860–61. The advent of the civil war reduced the matriculation considerably, but it is rather remarkable, considering the circumstances, that during that struggle not a week's exercises of the university were suspended nor a dollar lost from its endowment. In 1862–63 there were only 62 students, but in 1863–64 the number had increased to 100.

The institution was conducted at Harrodsburg until the summer of 1865, having 14 graduates between 1861, the first year since the opening to send out a graduating class, and 1865.

On February 23, 1864, the university building was destroyed by a fire, which also consumed the library and apparatus, and although the next session was continued at Harrodsburg, the institution began to look around for another location and, in September, 1864, received propositions looking toward this object from Covington and Louisville, as well as one from the trustees of Transylvania University. This last offered to transfer the Transylvania University property and funds to Kentucky University, provided the latter should be moved to Lexington and the two institutions consolidated in such a way as to carry out all the Transylvania trusts. This offer was favorably considered and finally accepted by the curators of Kentucky University.

Committees of the two boards had met in Frankfort in January, 1865, to make the final arrangements for the consolidation and to secure the necessary legislative ratification of their action, when the question of making provision for the carrying out of the land grant for agricultural colleges, made by Congress in 1862, came before the legislature, and that body seeming to be unwilling to comply with the conditions imposed, Mr. Bowman, the chairman of the committee of the Kentucky University curators, proposed to make the new college a department of the university in such a way as to fully carry out the intent of the act of Congress in regard to agriculture and the mechanic arts, the university furnishing an experimental farm and the requisite buildings, to cost not less than $100,000, and giving free tuition to 300 State students.

Accordingly a bill to this effect was drawn up, and after an animated discussion in which the principal objection was to the denominational control of a State institution, was passed by a large majority, being approved on February 22, 1865.[1] The union with Transylvania University was accomplished by a bill approved February 28, 1865. These actions were accepted by the curators of the university on June 20, 1865, which may thus be considered as the day on which began

THE ENLARGED KENTUCKY UNIVERSITY.

As soon as the acts of consolidation had been passed, Mr. Bowman went to work with a will to raise the needed extra endowment, a task which he accomplished in less than three months, being able to report his success to that session of the legislature before its adjournment. He not only secured the $100,000 needed for the equipment of the Agricultural and Mechanical College, but raised an additional $30,000 which was repaid to the citizens of Harrodsburg and Mercer County who objected to the removal. In the enlarged Kentucky University the dream of old Transylvania's developing into an institution ranking with the first in the land seemed about to be realized. The consolidated institution had an endowment of at least about $400,000, and property of about $200,000, a library of 15,000 volumes, with ample museums and apparatus, and accommodations considered sufficient for 1,500 students. Three departments of the university, in addition to a preparatory department, were to be opened at once in Lexington; the colleges of the Bible and of law having been added to the previous college of literature, science, and arts. The Agricultural and Mechanical College was to be instituted as soon as the funds from the land scrip donated by Congress were realized, and additional medical, normal, and commercial colleges were contemplated in the near future.

All the professors at Harrodsburg, except Professor Richardson, accompanied President Milligan to Lexington. President Milligan devoted his attention mainly to the College of the Bible, in which he was assisted by John W. McGarvey, A. M. In the College of Arts the faculty had been increased by the addition of John Augustus Williams, A. M., Robert Peter, M. D., J. K. Patterson, A. M., and G. F. Eyraud, their respective chairs being intellectual and moral philosophy, chemistry and experimental philosophy, Latin, and the French language. Of this faculty, besides Dr. Peter, who has been mentioned in another connection, Professors White and Neville were at this time specially noted for their scholarship and teaching ability. The professors in the College of Law were M. C. Johnson, LL. D., W. C. Goodloe, A. M., and R. A. Buckner, A. M., of whom Professor Johnson had already established a reputation as a member of the law faculty of Transylvania University.

The university was first opened in Lexington on October 2, 1865, with

---

[1] Chapter 968, acts of 1865.

about 300 students. During the year 336 students were in attendance altogether, 223 of whom were in the College of Arts, 37 in the College of the Bible, 13 in the College of Law, and 63 in the preparatory department.

By action of the curators on July 17, 1865, the office of regent had been created and Mr. Bowman made the official head of the institution under that title. In 1866, when the Agricultural and Mechanical College was put into operation, the new plan of administration was more fully carried out, the regent looking after the general interests of the university, while the affairs of each college were supervised by its own presiding officer. Under this arrangement President Milligan, the office of president of the university having been abolished, became presiding officer of the College of the Bible, Professor Graham presiding officer of the College of Arts, Professor Johnson presiding officer of the College of Law, Prof. A. R. Milligan principal of the preparatory department, and Professor Williams presiding officer of the new Agricultural and Mechanical College.

This new department was opened on October 1, 1866, Mr. Bowman having that year purchased for its use "Ashland," the home of Henry Clay, and an elegant adjacent tract, "Woodlands," nearer the city, indeed partly within the city limits, paying for the combined magnificent estate, containing 433 acres of unsurpassed beauty and fertility, $130,000. As the land scrip had not yet been sold, the State legislature, by an act of February 10, 1866,[1] granted to the university the loan of $20,000 to put the institution into immediate operation. It occupied temporary quarters the first year, but in 1867 four brick buildings were erected at "Woodlands" for its officers and students, and in 1868 a mechanical building was erected at "Ashland." Its effective organization was largely due to the efforts of Professor Williams, its presiding officer, who, however, remained at its head for only one year, resigning for more congenial work in 1867, when he was succeeded by J. D. Pickett, A. M. In 1869 Professor Pickett was succeeded by Prof. J. K. Patterson, who presided over it during the remainder of its connection with the university. The college had 190 students during its first year and 220 the second year, all of whom were required to labor two hours each day, either on the ornamental grounds, the farm, or later in the shops of the institution, the course otherwise being quite similar to that of the College of Arts, stress being put particularly upon civil engineering, modern languages, and military tactics.

Enlargement also took place in other directions and changes in other departments of the university. In 1867 a commercial college was added by the association with the university of Hollingsworth's Business College, a relation which, while lasting some time, was always more or less nominal, about the only connection being the privilege of attendance upon university classes extended to matriculates of the

[1] Chapter 483, acts of 1866.

business college. In 1870 the preparatory department was discontinued, and in January, 1874, a regular medical department, called the Transylvania Medical College, with seven professors, several of whom, including Dr. Bush, had formerly been connected with the medical department of Transylvania University, was inaugurated. This department was, however, never a very great success, and was soon discontinued.

In 1869 Professor Graham resigned as presiding officer of the College of Arts, and was succeeded in that position by Professor White. Upon his voluntary retirement in 1877 Professor Pickett was elected to the position. The course in this department had been maintained on the original plan, but had been somewhat enlarged, the schools of natural history, history, music, and drawing having been added; the first two were additional requirements for the degree of A. B.

The matriculation of the institution had grown with its enlargement and soon became comparatively quite large. In 1866-67 there were 502 students in all departments; in 1867-68, 650, and in 1868-69, 767. In this last year thirty different States and countries were represented by the students, and only three other educational institutions in the country had a larger matriculation. So it appeared the institution was going to overshadow every rival, at least in the Mississippi Valley. During the next four years its average attendance was about 700, the largest number being 772 in 1869-70.

The university, however, began to be somewhat financially embarrassed about 1873, by reason of some of its stocks failing to pay dividends, owing to the panic of that year. In June, 1875, $40,000 of its endowment fund and $30,000 of its building fund remained uncollected, and it was at that time $37,000 behind with all of its financial obligations. This fact partially accounts for the fact that "a most unhappy issue and strife arose within the official management."[1] Many of the church controlling it considered it too great a burden on the denomination to conduct so extensive an educational enterprise, and thought the union with the Agricultural College, especially, a burden rather than an advantage, a feeling intensified by the comparatively small returns realized from the sale of the land-scrip fund, from which much more had been at first expected. On the other hand, there was a wide-spread dissatisfaction throughout the State against any kind of denominational control of this college, and a belief that it would succeed better on an independent basis, a feeling also, strange as it may seem, strengthened by the same land sale for which many unjustly blamed the university authorities.

This state of the public mind, both within and without the church, combined, as has been noticed, with financial difficulties to some extent, soon destroyed, by producing a lack of confidence in his plans and management, the usefulness in connection with the institution of Mr. Bow-

[1] Smith's History of Kentucky, p. 535.

KENTUCKY UNIVERSITY. THE COLLEGE OF LIBERAL ARTS.

man, who had always been in favor of a comprehensive university, and led to his resignation as regent, that office being abolished by the curators on June 12, 1878.

The condition of public feeling, both within and without the church, had already led to two previous acts, both of which necessarily produced a great change in the organization of the university. In July, 1877, the old College of the Bible had been abrogated and a new one instituted, under its own charter, which in control and administration was entirely independent of the university, and by a legislative act of March 13, 1878,[1] the Agricultural and Mechanical College had also been separated from the institution. This led, in the summer of 1878, to the reorganization of the university upon a more strictly denominational basis, and to its becoming for the future one of the important denominational colleges of the State rather than a comprehensive university, complete in all of its departments, into which Mr. Bowman had labored to develop it.

THE LATER UNIVERSITY.

The completion of the reorganization of 1878 left of the former university really only its College of Liberal Arts, with which was associated a commercial college, as the Colleges of the Bible and of Agriculture and the Mechanic Arts had previously been made independent, the Medical College was already suspended, and the Law College, which had been declining of late, was discontinued the next year.

The new College of the Bible went into operation in the fall of 1878, the old one having continued until the summer of that year. This college and that of Liberal Arts have since, while administratively independent, been conducted in close union, the students of each being freely admitted to the classes of the other, and the management being such otherwise as to practically make them still parts of the same institution. Some notice will now be taken of the history of each of these up to the present time, together with the movements, partly successful and partly not, which have recently been made to put the university again on a somewhat enlarged basis.

THE COLLEGE OF LIBERAL ARTS.

This is the modern title of the older College of Science, Literature, and the Arts, ordinarily called simply the College of Arts. Upon the abolition of the office of regent on June 12, 1878, the office of president of the university was revived, the position carrying with it, ex officio, that of presiding officer of the College of Arts. To this position Prof. H. H. White was at that time elected, and continued to discharge its duties for two years, when, in 1880, he voluntarily retired and was succeeded by Charles Louis Loos, who held the position for seventeen years, during which the university made gratifying progress in many ways.

[1] Chapter 424, Acts of 1878.

During the period of dissatisfaction the attendance of the university had necessarily decreased, there being only 125 students in the College of Arts and the Commercial College combined in 1877-78, but the administrations of Presidents White and Loos soon restored confidence in the future of the institution, and its matriculation has for several years past been almost constantly larger than it ever was as a separate department. The preparatory department, which had been abolished in 1870, was restored in 1878, and has since been maintained as a feeder to the larger institution. It is known as the Academy. The Commercial College, which has remained associated with the university, without, however, in recent years, having its students counted as a part of the institution's matriculation, has had, since 1877, Wilbur R. Smith as its successful president. It has become one of the most important schools of its kind in the South, and annually has large numbers of students from many different States.

The course of instruction in the college of arts has been maintained substantially on its original plan, but some modifications have taken place. Upon the reorganization in 1878 a B. S. course was instituted, in which the school of Greek was not required, as that of modern languages was not in the A. B. course. In 1893 a B. L. course was added, which does not require the schools of Greek and mechanics and astronomy. In 1892 a system of partial electives in the courses of study was inaugurated, which, by allowing the substitution of studies for each other in the several courses, permits a considerable modification of these in accordance with the student's needs and tastes.

The schools of instruction as at present arranged are: Greek language and literature, Latin language and literature, mathematics, mechanics and astronomy, English language and literature, natural science, sacred history and evidences of Christianity, civil history, mental, moral, and political philosophy, and modern languages. Of these, the school of sacred history and evidences of Christianity has recently been especially emphasized, perhaps more so than formerly.

The faculty of the college has in recent years been increased by the addition of two new members. Its equipment was, in 1893-94, materially improved by the erection of a handsome and well-arranged gymnasium, supplied with modern apparatus, at a total cost of something over $10,000. There has otherwise been no material increase in its property or funds since the benefactions raised by Mr. Bowman. Its grounds, buildings, and apparatus of various kinds are now approximately worth $200,000, and its endowment funds are something over the same amount.

Its graduating class has in recent years numbered something over twenty annually. Since sending out its first graduating class in 1861, it conferred, altogether, 310 regular degrees up to and including 1898. Of these, 227 were A. B.; 34, B. S.; 12, B. L.; 32, A. M.; 3, M. S.; and 2, C. E. It also granted 9 honorary A. M.'s and 1 LL. D.

KENTUCKY UNIVERSITY. THE COLLEGE OF THE BIBLE.

Among its alumni a number have made a considerable reputation as teachers, physicians, lawyers, ministers, and in political and literary life. Among the last may be mentioned particularly James Lane Allen.

THE COLLEGE OF THE BIBLE

As has been noted, the first College of the Bible, which was an integral part of the university, was organized upon the removal of the institution to Lexington in 1865, and closed its career in 1878. President Milligan was its first presiding officer, and he and J. W. McGarvey, A. M., were its first professors. Professor Milligan died in 1875, and was succeeded by Prof. Robert Graham, who at that time resigned the presidency of Hocker Female College and returned to the service of the university, he and Professor McGarvey constituting the faculty of the College of the Bible for a considerable period. The first College of the Bible sent out its first graduating class in 1867, and had, during its existence, a total of 65 alumni.

The present College of the Bible was separated from the university in July, 1877, and was placed by its new charter under the control of its own board of trustees, making it a distinct institution, which has, however, since remained closely associated with the university. Under the new arrangement Professor Graham continued as its presiding officer, and he and Professor McGarvey still constituted its faculty, together with one other professor, which in recent years has been I. B. Grubbs, A. M.

The number of matriculates of the college increased considerably after 1878, there being 54 in 1879–80 and 128 in 1887–88. For the last few years the attendance has averaged nearly 150, who have come from as many as twenty different States of the Union and five foreign countries. This necessitated an increase in the faculty in June, 1895, when B. C. Deweese, A. M., was made an additional professor. At the same time Professor Graham, while still retaining his chair, retired from the position of presiding officer, in the duties of which he was succeeded by Professor McGarvey, who is the present executive head of the institution.

The college had, up to this time, had its lecture and recitation rooms in the main university building, but in this year a fine new building was completed for it at a cost of $25,000. It is located on the university grounds and furnishes for the institution excellent class rooms, society halls, a chapel, and a library and reading room. The college has besides the permanent use of three brick buildings on the university campus, which afford boarding accommodations for about 100 of its students. Its library has also of late been considerably enlarged. The institution has a permanent endowment of $5,000 for its library, also a general endowment of about $70,000.

The college, while intended primarily to furnish systematic instruction in the Scriptures both in English and the original tongues and otherwise prepare its students for the special work of the ministry, does not claim to be strictly a professional school, but receives all who wish to extend their knowledge of the Bible, from those who have only a common school education to those who possess a college degree, its courses being so coordinated with those of the college of arts that the former class of students can profitably pursue strictly classical and scientific work at the same time.

The institution has annually a number of students, not candidates for graduation, who only take certain special studies, while it also confers diplomas in two courses made up from the following independent schools of instruction:[1] Sacred history, Christian doctrine and church polity, church history, hermeneutics and exegesis, homiletics, Hebrew language and literature, philosophy, mental, moral and political, Biblical criticism, Hellenistic Greek, vocal music, and elocution. No degrees are granted, but only a diploma of graduation in these courses, which are called, respectively, the classical and English course. The former is only open to college graduates, is three years in length, and includes all the above schools except the last; the latter requires a preliminary training equivalent to a college course to the end of freshman year in mathematics and natural science, and to the end of junior year in English language and literature, and the completion of the first eight of the above schools, except that of philosophy, mental, moral and political, a course extending through four years.

The Kentucky Christian Education Society, an independent organization of the church, assists annually a limited number of deserving students who have not the means to defray all their expenses.

The College of the Bible has in recent years had an average of something over 20 graduates annually. Its total alumni, to 1898 inclusive, are 357, of whom about 60 have graduated in the classical course, the others in the English course. Among the alumni are a number of eminent ministers, a dozen or more college professors, and some prominent editors of religious papers.

RECENT HISTORY OF THE UNIVERSITY AS A WHOLE.

The university as a whole, looked upon as an association of cooperating colleges, has of late years enlarged the scope of its instruction and the sphere of its action in several respects.

In 1890 the College of Liberal Arts and the Commercial College were opened, in all their privileges, to women upon the same terms as men.

In 1892 the College of Law, which had closed in 1879, was revived with Hon. Joseph D. Hunt as its presiding officer, with whom were associated, as other professors, David G. Falconer, John T. Shelby, and John R. Allen. The success of the college was not, however, sufficient to justify its continuation and it was again suspended in 1895.[2]

---

[1] These schools require different times, from a half year to two years, for their completion. A half year's course in Old Testament criticisms has recently been added.

[2] The two colleges of law during their existence had a total of 164 graduates.

In November, 1897, a further extension of the operations of the university was brought about by an arrangement which constituted the Kentucky School of Medicine, located in Louisville, as the medical department of the institution,[1] thus substituting a well-established and vigorous medical college for the former medical department, closed in 1878, and also reestablishing an old connection, as the Kentucky School of Medicine is in a sense a lineal descendant of the medical department of old Transylvania University.

In the the summer of 1897 President Loos, after seventeen years of capable and useful service in the position, resigned the presidency of the university. He, however, still retained his professorship. His successor in the presidential chair of the institution is Rev. R. Lin. Cave, who assumed the executive duties of the institution in September, 1897, shortly before the expansion referred to above. President Cave is an alumnus of the College of the Bible in the class of 1867, and has been mainly engaged in the active work of the ministry of his church since graduation. He has had, however, some special training for his present position in having been for a time the president of Christian University, at Canton, Mo. He has devoted himself, in connection with the university at Lexington, mainly to the work of informing the public, especially his denomination, more fully in regard to its work and getting them interested in its welfare.

The faculty of the medical department will be given in connection with the appended sketch of the Kentucky School of Medicine.

The following is the combined faculty of the colleges of the university located in Lexington: Rev. R. Lin. Cave, president of the university and ex-officio presiding officer of the College of Liberal Arts; Charles Louis Loos, LL. D., professor of the Greek language and literature; John W. McGarvey, A. M., president of the College of the Bible and professor of sacred history and evidences of Christianity; Wilbur R. Smith, presiding officer of the Commercial College; Henry H. White, LL. D., professor emeritus of mathematics and astronomy; Robert Graham, A. M., professor of mental, moral, and political philosophy; Alexander R. Milligan, A. M., professor of the Latin language and literature; Isaiah B. Grubbs, A. M., professor of exegesis, church polity, and church history; Alfred Fairhurst, A. M., professor of natural science; Charles J. Kemper, A. M., professor of the French and German languages and of mechanics and astronomy; Clarence C. Freeman, A. M., professor of the English language and literature; Richard H. Ellett, A. M., professor of mathematics; Walter G. Conley, A. M., professor of sacred history and evidences of Christianity; Benjamin C. Deweese, A. M., professor of Hebrew and homiletics; Mrs. A. R. Bourne, professor of civil history and assistant professor of English.

[1] The connection between the Kentucky School of Medicine and Kentucky University was dissolved in the latter part of the summer of 1898, and the university established a new medical department, also located in Louisville.

There are besides an assistant in the Academy and an instructor in elocution, also a number of other teachers in the Commercial College. Professor White, while having given up the duties of his professorship, still continues a long and honorable service for the institution by acting as its treasurer and librarian.

THE KENTUCKY SCHOOL OF MEDICINE, LOUISVILLE.

As has been mentioned above, this school became, in November, 1897, the medical department of Kentucky University, thus resuming, even more closely than formerly, an old relation, as we have already seen that the medical faculty of Transylvania University, the predecessor of the present Kentucky University, had a large share in founding the Kentucky School of Medicine, and that the two schools were in this way connected for several years. Others were, however, interested in the establishment of the new school, the second of its kind in Louisville. The first steps looking toward its organization were taken in 1847, when a number of the most eminent physicians and other citizens of Louisville petitioned the State legislature for a charter for the enterprise from considerations of public policy as well as in the interests of medical education. For some reason the legislature did not see fit to grant a charter at that session. Another unsuccessful attempt to secure a separate charter was made at the next session, as well as an equally futile one to have the proposed medical school made explicitly the medical department of the Masonic University, then in operation at Lagrange, Ky. Finally, in 1849, the charter of this institution was modified in such a way as to give it university privileges, and under this provision of its charter the Kentucky School of Medicine was opened in the succeeding year.

Just about the time the matter of the charter had been arranged, the sessions of the medical department of Transylvania University were changed from fall and winter to spring, and its faculty were invited, on account of the eminence of their services and their reputation as teachers, by those in Louisville interested in the new school to take part in its organization. They accordingly constituted the main part of its first faculty. The first session of the Kentucky School of Medicine was opened in Louisville on the first Monday in November, 1850, and its initial faculty was composed as follows: Benjamin W. Dudley, M. D., emeritus professor of anatomy and surgery; Robert Peter, M. D., professor of medical chemistry and toxicology; Samuel Annan, M. D., professor of pathology and the practice of medicine; Joshua B. Flint, M. D., professor of the principles and practice of surgery; Ethelbert L. Dudley, M. D., professor of descriptive anatomy and histology; Lewellyn Powell, M. D., professor of obstetrics and diseases of women and children; James M. Bush, M. D., professor of surgical anatomy and operative surgery; Henry M. Bullitt, M. D., professor of physiology and materia medica; Philip Thornberry, M. D., John Bartlett, M. D., demonstrators of anatomy. Of this faculty, Drs. Peter, Annan, E. L. Dudley, and Bush were, with one exception, the medical faculty of Transylvania University at the time, while Drs. Flint, Powell, and Bullitt were additional members from Louisville. Dr. Bullitt was made the first dean of the faculty. Dr. B. W. Dudley's connection with the school, as with Transylvania University at the time, was only nominal. It was originally intended that he should from time to time deliver lectures on special points of surgical doctrine and practice, but it is known that he never delivered any of these. The first quarters of the institution were on the southeast corner of Fifth and Green streets, where an amphitheater capable of seating 400 students had been fitted up, besides a convenient dissecting room and rooms for a library and museum. Dr. Peter had been sent East the previous summer to purchase the apparatus for a complete modern laboratory, and Dr. Bush had been dispatched to Europe, where he had secured an excellent anatomical cabinet.

The original course of the school was the one then generally in vogue in Transylvania and elsewhere, of two courses of lectures, with one year's office study. The sessions at first were four months in length, beginning the first of November.

The institution was fairly prosperous from the start, having 101 students the first year, a number of them being advanced students from Transylvania and elsewhere, of whom 35 were graduated at the end of the session. For the next year, Dr. Annan resigned and Dr. Thomas D. Mitchell, the remaining member of the Transylvania medical faculty of the year before, was made professor of the theory and practice of medicine, Dr. Bullitt taking the chair of physiology and pathology, and E. D. Foree, M. D., of Louisville, becoming professor of materia medica and therapeutics; at the same time Dr. Flint succeeded Dr. Bullitt as dean of the faculty. There were, that session, 110 students and 26 graduates, while the third year there were 101 students and 31 graduates.

In 1854 Drs. Peter, Dudley, Bush, and Mitchell severed their connection with the school, as the Transylvania Medical School at that time resumed its winter sessions; Dr. Powell also resigned, so the faculty of the Kentucky School of Medicine had, as new professors, Drs. Robert J. Breckinridge, Thomas W. Colescatt, J. G. Norwood, John Hardin, and L. M. Lawson, who held the chairs, respectively, of materia medica and clinical surgery, anatomy, chemistry, obstetrics and diseases of women and children, and theory and practice of medicine and clinical medicine. The institution then became entirely an independent school and remained so until its recent connection with Kentucky University, its affairs being managed by a board of seven self-perpetuating regents.

At an early date in its history, the school, in order to secure a better season of the year and better suit the courses of other schools, changed its sessions to the spring, a custom which it has since maintained, and which it was the first institution to follow as a regular policy. The school continued many years in its original location, during which time it continued to grow in public favor. In 1866 an affiliation was formed between it and the medical department of the University of Louisville, a joint faculty of ten professors being appointed from the two faculties; but this connection lasted only about a year, at the end of which each institution resumed its separate existence.

The prosperity of the Kentucky school was such that after a time it was forced to seek larger and better quarters, which were obtained at its present location on Sixth street, between Walnut and Chestnut streets, where its original building was capacious and well adapted to its uses. The institution has put stress upon practical and demonstrative teaching and early had, as a part of its equipment, a dispensary to furnish the desired clinical advantages. In 1890 laboratories of histology, pathology, and bacteriology were added to the previous laboratories of chemistry, of materia medica and pharmacy, and of anatomy, and at the same time the ample museum was refitted. Since then clinical and surgical laboratories have been established. In 1894, in order to further enlarge the clinical advantages of the school, its faculty had erected, in connection with the college building, a large auxiliary hospital at a cost of $50,000. This building is a credit to the city and its founders. It is fitted throughout with modern appliances and its appointments are in every way commodious and elegant.

The graduation requirements of the institution have, in recent years, been brought up to those of the foremost medical schools of the country. In 1892 a preliminary matriculation examination and a three-years' course of lectures were required of all students entering that year, and in 1895 the regular matriculation requirements and lecture courses of four years of the Association of American Medical Colleges were made essential to graduation. The sessions of the school now extended six months, from January 1 of each year.

The course of instruction is that of a modern progressive institution, and embraces the following departments: Anatomy, chemistry, physiology, materia medica, therapeutics, physical diagnosis, medicine and clinical medicine, diseases of children, nervous diseases, hygiene, obstetrics, gynecology and abdominal surgery, operative gynecology, surgery and clinical surgery, ophthalmology and otology, venereal and skin diseases, dental surgery, medical jurisprudence, and medical physics.

The popularity of the school is attested by its large annual matriculation, which has not been largely reduced by the additional requirements for graduation recently instituted. In 1889, 263 students were in attendance upon its classes; in 1891 their number had increased to 411, and in 1892 to 504, these last representing 34 States and Territories of the United States and 6 other countries. The average matriculation for the past two years has been 338. There were 104 graduates in 1889, 155 in 1891, and 188 in 1894. The average for the past two years has been 79. The school had educated, altogether, something over 5,000 physicians up to 1898, inclusive. Its graduates are scattered throughout the States and Territories, and many of them have won prominence and distinction in practice and teaching in all parts of the country. Besides these already mentioned and the present faculty of the institution, the following prominent physicians have, among others, at different times been connected with its faculty for longer or shorter periods: T. G. Richardson, Middleton Goldsmith, A. B. Cook, G. W. Bayless, J. M. Bodine, N. B. Marshall, C. W. Wright, L. J. Frazee, George J. Cook, and J. A. Ireland.

The following are the present regular professors in the school:

Samuel E. Woody, A. M., M. D., professor of chemistry, public hygiene, and diseases of children; William H. Wathen, M. D., LL. D., professor of obstetrics, abdominal surgery, and gynecology; Martin F. Coomes, A. M., M. D., professor of physiology, and clinical lecturer on ophthalmology and laryngology; Clinton W. Kelly, M. D., C. M., professor of anatomy and clinical medicine; Henry Orendorf, M. D., professor of materia medica and therapeutics, and clinical lecturer on genito-urinary, venereal, and skin diseases; Joseph M. Mathews, M. D., professor of surgery, and clinical lecturer on diseases of the rectum; James M. Holloway, A. M., M. D., professor of surgery and clinical surgery; Joseph B. Marvin, B. S., M. D., professor of medicine and clinical medicine; William L. Rodman, A. M., M. D., professor of surgery and clinical surgery; Carl Weidner, M. D., associate professor of medicine, and director in the laboratory of histology and pathology; Louis Frank, M. D., professor of bacteriology, and director in the laboratory of bacteriology; W. T. St. Clair, A. M., professor of medical Latin; Harry Gault Brownell, B. S., professor of medical physics; David W. Fairleigh, B. L., professor of medical jurisprudence.

The faculty also contains 4 lecturers on special subjects, 3 directors of laboratories, and 15 assistants in the various departments. Dr. Wathen was for many years its dean, but was succeeded in 1895 by Dr. Woody, who is the present executive officer of the institution.

BIBLIOGRAPHY.

Collins's Sketches

Collins's, Smith's, and Perrin, Battle and Kniffen's histories.

Biographical Encyclopedia of Kentucky.

Peter's Fayette County.

Reports of the Superintendent of Public Instruction.

Barnard's American Journal of Education.

Acts of the Legislature.

Home and School, an educational magazine published at Louisville, Ky., for some time after 1872.

The Biography of Elder John T. Johnson, by John Rogers, Cincinnati, 1861.

Minutes of a Meeting of the Friends and Donors of Bacon College at Harrodsburg, Ky., May 6, 1857. Harrodsburg, 1857

The Statutes and Laws of Kentucky University, Harrodsburg, 1858.

Inaugural Address of Robert Milligan, A. M., as president of Kentucky University, Louisville, 1859.

Annual Report of the Executive Committee of Kentucky University, Cincinnati, 1863.

Charter, Statutes, and Laws of Kentucky University, Lexington, 1866.

Regulations for the Government of the Cadets of the Agricultural and Mechanical College, Lexington, 1867.

Report of the Agricultural and Mechanical College to the Governor of Kentucky, by J. B. Bowman, Regent, Frankfort, 1869.

The Annual Report of the Treasurer of Kentucky University, with a financial history from 1855 to 1871, Lexington, 1871.

Report of the Board of Visitors of the Agricultural and Mechanical College of Kentucky, Frankfort, 1873.

A Centennial Exhibit of Education in Kentucky, by H. A. M. Henderson, Frankfort, 1876.

The History of the Ohio Falls Cities and their Counties, by L. A. Williams & Co., 2 vols., Cleveland, 1882.

Newspaper Sketch of the Kentucky School of Medicine, by Dr. J. A. Ouchterlony (date uncertain).

THE AGRICULTURAL AND MECHANICAL COLLEGE—LEXINGTON.

The foundation of this institution, ordinarily called the State College simply, is due to the act of Congress of July 2, 1862, which granted to each State of the Union that would provide colleges for the benefit of agriculture and the mechanic arts a donation of 30,000 acres of land for each of its Representatives in the National Legislature. Section 4 of this act requires that the leading object of such colleges—

> Shall be, without excluding other scientific and classical studies, and including military tactics, to teach such branches of learning as are related to agriculture and the mechanic arts in such manner as the legislatures of the States may respectively describe, in order to promote the liberal and practical education of the industrial classes in the several pursuits and professions of life.

This donation amounted, in the case of Kentucky, to 330,000 acres of land, and was formally accepted by the State legislature on January 27, 1863. The act provided, however, that the State should furnish an experimental farm, proper buildings, and a suitable equipment otherwise for the new college, and as Kentucky was at the time, owing to the civil war, in quite a depressed condition financially, some difficulty was experienced in getting her legislature to make the needed direct appropriation for putting the institution into operation. Proposals for bids for its location were arranged for, but none were offered during the next two years that were considered sufficiently advantageous to be accepted.

It is probably because the proposition carried with it no experimental farm that the excellent proposal of the trustees of Transylvania University to make the property and funds of that venerable institution the basis for the new one was not taken advantage of. The buildings, grounds, and apparatus of the university at that time were estimated

AGRICULTURAL AND MECHANICAL COLLEGE OF KENTUCKY—MAIN BUILDING.

AGRICULTURAL AND MECHANICAL COLLEGE OF KENTUCKY—EXPERIMENT STATION BUILDING.

to be worth $100,000 or more, while its endowment was about $65,000 in bonds and $5,000 in cash. This would have furnished a splendid foundation for the Agricultural and Mechanical College, one for which it had to wait years afterwards before acquiring in its own right. It was this difficulty in securing the proper equipment, besides the advantages of the offer itself, which made the legislature as a body, in January, 1865, quite willing to turn over the inauguration of the enterprise to Kentucky University upon the terms then proposed by Mr. Bowman, its founder.

We have seen, in connection with the history of that institution, what were the terms of that offer and how it was accepted by the act of February 22, 1865, and the new college opened, under the auspices of the university, on October 1, 1866, a loan of $20,000 having been made by an act of February 10, 1866, in order to put it into immediate operation without depending on the returns from the sale of the Government land scrip. This sale was authorized by an act of February 28, 1865,[1] and occurred some time after that date. The land was disposed of for 50 cents an acre, thus realizing a fund of $165,000, which was invested in State bonds, bearing 6 per cent interest, the returns from which for a considerable time were the principal income of the institution. The comparatively small amount obtained from the land endowment caused much dissatisfaction throughout the State, especially among the friends of Kentucky University, and was, as has been noted, one of the causes operating to separate the college from the university. If any are to be specially blamed in this connection they are those, both within and without the denomination controlling the university, who by their clamors for the early inauguration of the new college, caused those in whose hands the matter had been placed to be perhaps rather hasty in disposing of the college lands. Kentucky did quite as well with this endowment as some States who were equally hasty in realizing on it, although other States handled their scrip more judiciously and were thus able to obtain much more from it. When the Agricultural and Mechanical College was first put in operation, on the splendid estate provided for it by Mr. Bowman, its faculty was constituted as follows: John Aug. Williams, presiding officer and professor of mental and moral philosophy; H. H. White, professor of mathematics and astronomy; Robert Peter, professor of chemistry and experimental philosophy; James K. Patterson, professor of Latin, political economy, and history; Alexander Winchell, professor of geology and natural history; Joseph D. Pickett, professor of the English language and literature; William E. Arnold, professor of military tactics. Besides these there were six instructors, a farm superintendent, and two stewards.

The original course of instruction in the institution embraced the ten schools of philosophy, English language and literature, mathe-

[1] Chapter 1174, acts of 1865.

matics, chemistry and experimental philosophy, natural history, history, modern languages, civil engineering and mining, military tactics, and fine arts. In addition to this, practical work was required of all students for two hours a day on the ornamental grounds, the farm, or in the mechanical shops after these had been established in 1868, a number of students being assisted financially by being paid for extra labor on the farm.

We have seen that the college was, for a time, quite successful, having as many as 300 students in 1869-70; but the connection with Kentucky University, for the reasons already given, soon proved unsatisfactory to all parties, the number of students having, in 1877-78, declined to 78; so, by an act of March 13, 1878, the legislature, which had reserved such a right over the control of the land-endowment fund, as well as the right of inspection through a board of six visitors appointed by the governor, separated the college from the university, the act to take effect July 1, 1878, from which date the former became an independent institution. The college up to this time had had two other presiding officers besides Professor Williams, who had directed it the first year and largely organized its course. He had been succeeded in 1867 by Professor Pickett, and he in 1869 by Professor Patterson. It had sent out its first graduating class of one member in 1869, and had had altogether during this period of its history 12 graduates.

The act separating the institution from Kentucky University, which the legislature looked upon as having made a loyal attempt to fulfill its pledges to the college, but had failed, owing to adverse circumstances, appointed for the latter a commission, composed of the lieutenant-governor and one member from each of the ten Congressional districts of the State, whose duties were threefold: (1) To arrange for continuing the operation of the institution until the next session of the legislature; (2) to decide upon its permanent location at that place in the State which would, all things considered, offer the greatest inducements; (3) to prepare a plan for its reorganization in regard to departments of instruction, and other important particulars.

The first of these objects was accomplished by an arrangement, entered into on July 5, 1878, between the commission and a committee of the board of curators of Kentucky University, by which the college was to still occupy its former grounds and buildings until July 1, 1880, and was to have the use of 100 acres of the experimental farm, together with one acre additional for every student it had over 100, the institutions meanwhile acting in harmony as previously and mutually opening their courses to each other's students. The board of visitors, composed of six representative public men to whom the direct management of the institution had been committed for the next two years, after organizing on July 12, 1878, elected a new faculty of seven members, composed mainly, if not entirely, of members of the former faculty, with Prof. J. K. Patterson, who had been at the head of the institution for the past nine years, as its president, thus putting the college in running order for the next two years.

In accordance with the terms of the Congressional land grant, the commission made agriculture and the mechanic arts, as also military tactics, obligatory in the course of instruction, but, in regard to other departments a wide discretion was given to the trustees of the college. An advanced course in agricultural chemistry and other subjects were at once added to the curriculum, which, according to the recommendations made, was to be wide in scope and to be conducted on a university and not simply a college basis. The putting of the institution on this basis was not, however, to be hurried, but was to be carried out as its means would permit. Kentucky University had for several years been unable, by reason of financial embarrassment, to carry out the intention of Congress in regard to agriculture and the mechanic arts, as its experimental farm had been used only to aid students and its expensive machine shops had for some time been closed. The college only attempted to give the scientific basis of instruction in these departments, waiting for greater resources before instituting practical operations.

After having made these preliminary arrangements the commission, in accordance with its instructions, had advertised for bids for the permanent location of the college to be reported to the next session of the legislature, and at a meeting on August 14, 1879, recommended that of Lexington and Fayette County as offering the best and greatest inducements. Lexington, in order to secure the location of the institution permanently in its midst, proposed to give the city park of 52 acres, lying within the limits of the city and valued at $250,000, as a site and $30,000 in bonds for building purposes, which was to be supplemented by $20,000 in bonds given for buildings or land by Fayette County.[1] This offer was accepted, and the college so located by an act of the legislature approved February 6, 1880.[2]

Meanwhile the institution had made a fair start toward its future prosperity. Its first session under the new auspices was opened on September 7, 1878, and during the year 118 students were in attendance, an advance of 50 per cent over the previous year's attendance. The college also closed the year with some cash in the treasury, although its agricultural produce for the year had not been realized on and considerable had been paid out for student labor. During its second year its attendance reached 137.

By a legislative act of March 4, 1880,[3] the institution was granted a liberal charter, conferring upon it full collegiate powers, and putting it under direct State control, by having its management committed to a

[1] The donation of Lexington was authorized by a legislative act approved January 31, 1880 (chapter 49, acts of 1880), and that of Fayette County by an act approved January 24, 1880 (acts of 1880, chapter 71).

[2] Chapter 157, acts of 1880.

[3] Chapter 350, acts of 1880.

body of twelve trustees, appointed by the governor and confirmed by the senate every four years, with the governor as an additional ex officio member. A clause provided for the addition of four other members elected by the alumni of the college from among themselves whenever their number should reach 100. This last provision was abrogated by an act of May 9, 1893, which placed the control of the institution in the hands of fifteen trustees, one-third of them appointed every two years by the governor, who, with the president of the college, is also an ex officio member.

The original charter provided free tuition for 4 students from each of the 100 legislative districts of the State. An amendment of April 23, 1880,[1] did a great service to the cause of public education in the State by establishing a normal department which, as declared by section 7 of the act, is "designed more particularly, but not exclusively, to qualify teachers for common and other schools," and was also to furnish free tuition to 4 students from each legislative district who are preparing themselves for teaching. To further increase and make efficient the endowment of the institution, an additional amendment of April 29, 1880,[2] imposed a regular tax of one-half cent on each $100 of the property of the white citizens of the State, thus making a very material and much needed addition to the scant income derived from the land-scrip fund. This tax yielded in 1880, the first year it was levied, about $17,000 and now furnishes an income of about $33,000 a year.

The history of the college from the time of its permanent location, when it received its endowment from Lexington and had the income from a State tax added to its former revenue of about $10,000 a year, has been one of constant and regular growth and expansion, which have been further extended by the increased income derived from the Hatch bill of 1887 and the Morrill bill of 1890.

In 1880 its faculty was enlarged and its course of instruction extended. Its faculty as then constituted was composed as follows: James K. Patterson, president and professor of history and metaphysics; Robert Peter, professor of chemistry and experimental philosophy; John H. Neville, professor of Latin and Greek; John Shackleford, professor of English; J. G. White, professor of mathematics and astronomy; A. R. Crandall, professor of natural history and mechanics; R. J. Howell, U. S. A., professor of civil engineering and military science; F. M. Helveti, professor of French and German; W. A. Kellerman, professor of agriculture, horticulture, and economic botany; Maurice Kirby, principal of the normal school; T. C. H. Vance, principal of the commercial department; W. K. Patterson, principal of the preparatory department; A. M. Peter, adjunct professor of chemistry and natural history; John Patterson, assistant professor of Latin; David A. King,

[1] Chap. 1094, acts of 1880. Under this act, as female teachers were admitted as well as male teachers, the institution became coeducational and has since so remained in all departments.

[2] Chap. 1315, acts of 1880.

instructor in practical mechanics; J. L. McClellan and M. L. Pence, assistants in the preparatory department.

The course of instruction as laid down in the regulations of the board of trustees, adopted in final form on June 30, 1882, was divided into twenty-one departments, besides a preparatory department, all of which, except those relating to commercial education, are included in the present curriculum of the college, with its fifteen departments, which will be enumerated later.[1] Instruction in bookkeeping, commercial law, and phonography were originally included in the regular curriculum, but in 1889 an arrangement was made by an association with Orcutt's Short Hand and Commercial Institute to furnish college students desiring it free instruction in these departments in that institution. A similar arrangement, which continued until quite recently, was later made with Lexington Business College; but commercial education is now looked upon by the institution as professional, and is not made a part of its curriculum.

When the agreement made by the commission of 1878 and Kentucky University expired on July 1, 1880, the college, seeing its new quarters could not be prepared for it for some time, rented its former buildings and grounds from the university and continued in its old location for nearly two years longer. The corner stone of a fine new main building, constructed of brick with stone trimmings, with accommodations for 600 students in the way of chapel, lecture rooms, etc., was laid with appropriate ceremonies on October 28, 1880. This building was completed and occupied as a new home for the institution on February 15, 1882. About the same time a brick residence for the president and a brick dormitory, with accommodations for 90 students, were erected. Meanwhile the matriculation continued to increase, there being 234 students in attendance in 1880–81.

The work of the college in its new home soon began to show that expansion which has since been characteristic of it. In the latter part of 1885 the first important step in realizing the special aims of the institution was taken by the organization of the agricultural experiment station. Prof. M. A. Scovell, its present efficient director, was then placed at its head, and in 1886 the station began work as a State enterprise, it having been reorganized and named the Kentucky Experiment Station by the legislature in that year. Its twofold work of making experiments in scientific agriculture and making their results known to those interested by the publication of frequent bulletins was able to be still further increased and enlarged by the passage by Congress, on March 2, 1887, of what is ordinarily known as the Hatch bill, from its author, which appropriates annually $15,000 to similar stations in each State throughout the country. The board of control of the

[1] The degree courses provided in 1880 were a classical and a scientific course of four years each, leading to the degrees of A. B. and B. S., with A. M. and M. S. conferred after an additional year's study. There was also a general course of four years not leading to a degree.

Kentucky station, as at present organized, is composed of three of the college trustees, together with the president of the college and the director of the station as ex-officio members. The provisions of the Hatch bill were accepted by the legislature on February 20, 1888,[1] and an experimental farm of 48½ acres, situated near the college campus, was soon purchased and equipped with suitable buildings. The chief building for the station is located on the campus. It is a handsome and well-planned structure, costing, with its equipment, about $20,000, and was completed in August, 1889. All commercial fertilizers sold in the State are required by State law to be analyzed and inspected by the station. This so far has been a means of some income, besides furnishing valuable information to the agricultural community. The staff of the station contains, in addition to the director, two chemists, an entomologist and botanist, a horticulturist, a meteorologist, a superintendent of field experiments, and a dairyman.

The development of the other leading object for which the college was established has had a similar, although somewhat more recent, history. A course in practical mechanics was first offered in 1889, but no regular mechanical department was organized until two years later. Meanwhile the revenue of the institution and its ability to carry out its purposes in this direction were materially increased by what is commonly known as the Morrill bill, of June 23, 1890, which granted to each of the agricultural and mechanical colleges in the different States an appropriation of $15,000 for the year 1890, which was to be increased each year by $1,000 until it reached $25,000 annually. A regular department of mechanical engineering was organized in the Kentucky State College in June, 1891, when the chair of mechanical engineering was established and the professor appointed. A new mechanical building was soon begun and was completed and occupied in January, 1892. It is commodious and specially well adapted to its purposes and has an equipment second to none south of the Ohio River, the estimated value of the building and apparatus being about $60,000. The building contains, besides three recitation rooms and three offices, two drawing rooms, a wood pattern shop, two boiler rooms, a wash room, a tool room, an engine room, two machine shops—one for working wood, the other metal—a foundry, a blacksmith shop, and two large rooms devoted to experimental engineering.

The addition of the normal school in 1880 and the recent enlargement of the means of instruction in the special departments of the college, to which we have just been referring, have led to a corresponding expansion in its courses of study, courses in pedagogy, in agriculture, in civil engineering, and in mechanical engineering, having been added to those already in operation, so as to make the present curriculum quite broad in scope as well as special in character. The former scientific course has recently been subdivided into mathematical, biological, and

[1] Chapter 208, acts of 1888.

chemical courses, all scientific in character, but each emphasizing especially the science indicated by its name. The equipment of the departments of biology, physiology, geology, botany, chemistry, and physics has become quite complete for work and illustration, the apparatus of those departments being estimated to be worth something over $20,000.

The facilities for instruction in these departments were largely improved in 1897 by the erection of a new natural science building. This is a three-story brick structure and is modern in all its appointments, costing, with its electric-lighting and steam-heating apparatus, $20,000. The entire third floor of this building is given up to the proper display of a recent valuable acquisition to the scientific apparatus of the college, consisting of the collection of minerals and other products of the State, collected by the State geological survey and for many years deposited in the capitol at Frankfort. This collection is now in charge of the State inspector of mines, who by an act of the legislature of 1898 was attached to the staff of the State college and had his office and the geological collection moved to Lexington. This collection will constitute a valuable scientific museum for the future.

The libraries of the different departments of the college, especially the scientific departments, have of late been considerably enlarged and now contain the standard authorities needed for reference in each case. The plan of having special libraries has been adopted rather than having one large general collection.

The approximate value of the entire college property is $475,000. The income of the institution, including the experiment station, is about $80,000 annually. The following is an exhibit of the revenue between July 1, 1896, and July 1, 1897:

College proper:	
State taxes	$32,429.32
Federal fund of 1890	18,810.00
Students' fees	1,428.57
From other sources	498.91
Total	53,166.80
Experiment station:	
Federal fund of 1887	$15,000.00
Fertilizers	3,240.00
Farm	1,280.43
Other sources	132.70
Total	19,653.13

To the college income, besides the above items, is to be added $8,464.50 annually coming from its share of the Federal fund of 1862, from which no revenue is given above, because the former State bonds had expired in 1896 and no new revenue was derived from this source until September, 1897, on new bonds issued by the legislature of 1896.[1] The Federal

[1] The legislature of this year gave to the State Normal School at Frankfort its share, 14½ per cent, of the Federal fund of 1862, which made the share of the State college $141,075, which bears 6 per cent interest annually.

fund of 1890 also increases $1,000 each year until the year 1900, 85½ per cent of which will go to this institution.

The course of instruction in the college as at present constituted is composed of the following departments: History, political economy, and metaphysics; botany, horticulture, and agriculture; the English languages and literature; military science; chemistry; mathematics and astronomy; modern languages; Greek and Latin; pedagogy, or the normal school; civil engineering; mechanical engineering; anatomy and physiology; geology, zoology, and physics.

The college offers six degree courses of four years each, leading respectively to the degrees of bachelor of science, bachelor of arts, bachelor of agriculture, bachelor of civil engineering, bachelor of mechanical engineering, and bachelor of pedagogy. The degree of master is also conferred in the first five of these departments, upon an additional year's regular study and the presentation of an acceptable thesis in the principal department of study. In certain departments special courses, not leading to a degree, are arranged to suit the needs of a particular class of students. In agriculture a short course has been lately inaugurated for scientific instruction in the most practical part of agriculture, which may be attended by farmers during their leisure season. In pedagogy, besides the regular degree course, there are special State-diploma, State-certificate, and county-certificate courses, designed to meet the needs of certain classes of teachers, especially in the State public schools. In the course in mechanical engineering a choice of one of three lines of work—mechanical engineering proper, chemical engineering, or electrical engineering—is allowed in the last two years of the course.

The academy courses are preparatory to those of the college and are two years in length. There are two of them—the scientific, agricultural, and engineering course and the classical and normal course. The college has recently arranged for a more general preparation of its students throughout the State by the recognition of a number of private and public high schools as accredited schools, whose courses are coordinated with those of the college, and whose students are received upon certificate into certain classes of the institution.

The matriculation of the college has in a general way kept pace with expansion in other ways. Within five years after the occupancy of the new building its students had risen in number to 309, and for the past five years they have averaged 390, of whom an average of about 90 have been in the normal school and about 100 in the academy. There were in 1897–98 432 students in all departments. The general financial depression has not, as in many other institutions, decreased the attendance, which has kept up well, and in the numbers in the college classes especially has shown a marked enlargement, the average in these for the past two years being about 100 more than in the three years previous.

The accommodations for students were materially increased about 1890 by the addition of a new dormitory with rooms for 50 students. The legislative act of May 6, 1893, in addition to changing the plan of managing the institution, as already noted, made the appointments of beneficiary pupils in the normal school four from each county of the State, instead of each legislative district, as before, and besides furnishing free tuition to all beneficiary students, grants them free traveling expenses to and from Lexington to their homes after they have honorably sustained themselves for one year as matriculates. In order to bring the benefits of the college within the reach of as many as possible, the tuition fees for other students are made very moderate and a number of poor students are given work on the college farm for several hours each day, for which they are paid from 6 to 10 cents an hour.

The college has had an average of about 19 graduates each year for the past five years, and its total alumni in all of its regular courses to 1898, inclusive, are 190. Several of these are members of its present faculty and others occupy important positions in teaching and other professions. Among them may be mentioned particularly T. V. Munson, of Texas, who is considered the highest authority in the United States on the subject of vine culture. In recognition of his services in introducing the American stocks upon which to graft the French vines, he received from the Government of France the decoration of the Legion of Honor.

The faculty of the institution, including the nine instructors in the various departments, is at present composed of twenty-four members, nearly four times as many as at the time of the reorganization in 1878. The regular professors, with their chairs, are as follows: James Kennedy Patterson, Ph. D., LL. D., F. S. A., president, professor of history, political economy, and metaphysics; John Shackleford, A. M., vice-president, professor of English and logic; James Garrard White, A. M., professor of mathematics and astronomy; John Henry Neville, A. M., professor of Greek and Latin; Walter Kennedy Patterson, A. M., principal of the academy; Joseph Hoeing Kastle, Ph. D., professor of chemistry; Rurie Neville Roark, Ph. D., principal of the normal school; Joseph William Pryor, M. D., professor of anatomy and physiology; Frederic Paul Anderson, M. E., professor of mechanical engineering; James Poyntz Nelson, C. E., M. E., professor of civil engineering; Clarence Wentworth Mathews, B. S., professor of botany, horticulture, and agriculture; Arthur McQuiston Miller, A. M., professor of geology and zoology; Merry Lewis Pence, M. S., professor of physics; Samuel Miller Swigert, captain Second Cavalry, U. S. A., commandant and professor of military science; Paul Wernicke, professor of modern languages.

Two venerable and able members of the faculty died in 1894, Dr. Robert Peter and Prof. F. M. Helveti. Dr. Peter, of whom mention has been made elsewhere, had had a distinguished career and was noted for his high character and eminent worth. He had entered the faculty of the college in 1878 and had retired from the active duties of his professorship in 1887, on account of the infirmities of age. Professor Helveti had been professor of modern languages in the institution from 1869 until the time of his death. He was universally respected and was an accomplished and faithful teacher.

The career of steady and uniform prosperity which the State College of Kentucky has experienced since 1878 has been due in large measure to the able and energetic management of President Patterson, who has been at its head almost from its incipiency. In his hands it is probable, as much of the work of the institution is already on a university basis, that it will become before long a university in name as well as in fact.

BIBLIOGRAPHY

Report of the Agricultural and Mechanical College for 1878-79, Frankfort, 1879.

Biennial Report of the Board of Visitors for 1878-1880, Frankfort, 1880.

An address before the Commission on the Agricultural and Mechanical College by J. K. Patterson, Ph. D., Frankfort, 1882.

Regulations of the Agricultural and Mechanical College adopted June, 1882, Frankfort, 1882.

Peter's History of Fayette County.

Legislation, Federal and State, in relation to the Agricultural and Mechanical College of Kentucky and Regulations Governing the same, compiled by George B. Kinkead, Lexington, 1890.

Biennial Reports of the Board of Trustees.

Reports of the State Superintendent of Public Instruction.

Acts of the State legislature.

CENTRE COLLEGE, DANVILLE.

Centre College has had a continuous history under its present title since 1819, and is therefore the oldest college in Kentucky with a continuous name and corporate existence. It dates back in conception even to the beginnings of Transylvania Seminary, with which institution its continuity appears, in a sense, in the fact that Governor Isaac Shelby, the president of its first board of trustees, was also a member of the Transylvania Seminary board of 1783. It may, however, be looked upon as the more direct successor of Kentucky Academy, for it was founded by the same religious denomination, and the reasons for its establishment—dissatisfaction with the religious status of Transylvania University and the plan of its management—were practically identical with those that operated in separating Kentucky Academy from Transylvania Seminary. That this succession was felt explicitly by its founders is shown by the effort made by them to secure the return of the Kentucky Academy endowment from Transylvania University.

The Presbyterian members of the Transylvania University board of trustees had already become acquainted with Dr. Holley's religious

CENTRE COLLEGE—MAIN BUILDING.

opinions even prior to his final election as president of the university in November, 1817, at which time a number of them had resigned, while others retired soon afterwards or were removed from the board by the reorganization of February, 1818. These and other members of the denomination, fearful of what they considered the irreligious influences then surrounding the university, especially those emanating from Dr. Holley's ideas, resolved to have an institution of their own whose religious atmosphere would be what they desired, and where the young men of the church who were preparing for the work of the ministry might be educated free from contaminating influences.

Accordingly, in October, 1818, under the leadership largely, it seems, of Rev. Samuel K. Nelson, who may be called, before any other one man, the founder of the college, steps were taken by the synod of Kentucky looking toward the organization of the new institution. The legislature of the State was soon petitioned for a charter for the enterprise, but, although this was granted, it was refused—Davidson thinks mainly because of the influence of Transylvania University, which did not want competition—to the church upon the terms they desired. This charter, which bears the date of January 21, 1819,[1] located the institution under its present name "in or near the town of Danville," granted to it the funds of Danville Academy, and placed it under the control of a self-perpetuating board of nineteen trustees, largely composed of prominent public men of that portion of the State, with ex-Governor Shelby as their chairman. Instead of placing it under the management of their synod, as the Presbyterians wished, the legislature, on the ground, it seems, that such action would be, in effect, uniting church and state, made it in organization a State institution, and, instead of the charter making provision for religious or theological instruction, section 4 explicitly declares that "no religious doctrines peculiar to any one sect of Christians shall be inculcated by any professor in said college."

A committee of canvassers had been appointed by the synod at the time that body petitioned for the charter, and a considerable endowment had been raised for the new college, but the Presbyterians refused to endow it under the conditions imposed, these funds, for the present, being held subject to the orders of the synod, and so the institution went into operation under a board of trustees which was not exclusively Presbyterian and many of whose members were only interested in the matter as a general educational enterprise. Presbyterian influence

[1] Acts of 1818-19, pp. 618-621. The trustees named in the act were Isaac Shelby, John Boyle, William Owsley, Thomas Montgomery, Samuel M'Kee, William Craig, Thomas Cleland, Barnabas McHenry, Samuel K. Nelson, Nathan H. Hall, Joshua Fry, James Birney, Joshua Barbee, James Barbour, Daniel G. Cowan, John Bowman, Ephraim McDowell, Jeremiah Briscoe, and Jeremiah Fisher. In locating the institution in Danville the act was again following in the steps of Transylvania Seminary, but there has never been any occasion to remove the college for lack of local support, as was the case with the seminary.

seems, however, to have been predominant in its affairs from the start, through the prominence of members of that church in its councils, and the denomination had a moral, if not a legal, control of the institution in this way.

Soon after the charter was obtained the trustees, through their chairman, in order to disarm opposition, especially that of Transylvania University, issued an address[1] to the public in which it was declared that the college would not inculcate any denominational tenets, that its main intention "was to supplement the work of the declining academies," and that its object was not to injure the university, but rather to aid it by a generous rivalry.

Immediately after the charter was secured in 1819 a modest building was erected in Danville, mainly from local contributions, and in 1820 Rev. James McChord was chosen as the first president of the new college. He, however, never served in that capacity, having died the year of his election after he had probably declined the proffered honor. Rev. Samuel Finley was then temporary president for two years, during which, by an act of December 18, 1821,[2] which shows the institution was looked upon at that time as to some extent a State enterprise, the legislature aided the struggling undertaking by giving to it, for two years, one-third the profits of the branch Bank of the Commonwealth at Harrodsburg, to be used for purchasing a library and a scientific apparatus. The amount secured from this source appears to have been about $6,000, which at the time must have been quite a help to the new school, although, as we shall see, it was not permanently retained.

On July 23, 1822, Rev. Jeremiah Chamberlain, D. D.,[3] became the first regular president of the college. Dr. Chamberlain was a man of learning, ability, and piety, and by the vigorous cooperation of several philanthropic individuals brought the institution out of its incipient state, placing it on a firm basis and filling its halls with students. The professors who assisted Dr. Chamberlain at the opening of his administration were John Dailey, professor of mathematics, and Redmond Dougherty, professor of the Latin and Greek languages. During this administration, the first graduating class was sent out by the institution in 1824, one of the two graduates being L. W. Green, afterwards prominently connected with the history of his alma mater.

[1] The substance of this address is given by Professor Chenault in Smith's History of Kentucky, p. 704.

[2] This was part of the act which established the first public-school fund of Kentucky.

[3] A sketch of Dr. Chamberlain is to be found in Sprague's Annals, Vol. IV, pp. 591–592, and also in the general catalogue of Centre College for 1890, p. 5. In the latter account it is said he was born in Pennsylvania in 1794, graduated at Dickinson College in that State in 1814, and at Princeton Seminary, New Jersey, in 1817. He was then engaged in the active work of the ministry until he became the president of Centre. He is described as "a man of marked ability, of strong intellectual power, of great public spirit." Various dates are given in different accounts as the beginning and end of his administration at Centre, but those given in the text seem best verified.

President Chamberlain resigned on September 26, 1826, to become the president of Jackson College, Louisiana. He was later instrumental in founding Oakland College, Mississippi. While at Centre he did much toward giving that institution an impetus toward its future career. He and Rev. Thomas Cleland were largely instrumental in obtaining the new charter of 1824, of which mention will now be made.

In October, 1823, the synod of Kentucky, which was thoroughly aroused, as Davidson[1] tells us, by the theological views expressed by Dr. Holley, in the previous April, upon the occasion of the funeral of Col. James Morrison, the benefactor of Transylvania University, determined to establish without delay such an institution as they desired, where what they considered proper Biblical instruction could be given. They appointed nine trustees, who were empowered to confer, at the end of the month, with the trustees of Centre College, with a view to its reorganization on a new basis, with or without a charter. The desired arrangement was harmoniously made and a charter applied for, which was finally obtained, the bill being carried through the lower house of the legislature, as related by Davidson,[2] against the violent opposition of Transylvania University and other denominational institutions of the State, mainly by the telling, by Col. James Davidson, one of the friends of the enterprise, of a humorous anecdote which disarmed the opposition.

This amended charter was granted on January 27, 1824,[3] and gives as the reason for its enactment that the funds of the college were low and it needed the endowment which the synod proposed to give to it. That body was to endow the institution with $20,000, the agreement going into effect as soon as $5,000 should be paid in. The number of trustees then in office was to be retained until, by death, resignation, or otherwise, their number should be reduced to eleven.[4] The former character of the institution, as to some extent a State enterprise, was removed by the requirement that the money previously received from the Harrodsburg branch of the Bank of the Commonwealth should be paid over to the State Institution for the Education of the Deaf and Dumb, recently located in Danville. The funds bestowed upon the institution were also to be restored to the synod if its charter was altered or repealed without the consent of that body. The powers and privileges of the college by its amended charter were very wide in their character and scope, so much so that no extra provisions needed to be added for the operation of a university. A medical department was

[1] Presbyterian Church in Kentucky, p. 303.

[2] Presbyterian Church in Kentucky, pp. 313, 314.

[3] Acts of 1824–25, pp. 63–64.

[4] The number of trustees is, however, still retained as nineteen, one-third of whom (seven in one year, of course) are elected each year by the synod of Kentucky. It is usually stated that when the synod had paid in $5,000 it should have the power to elect three trustees each year until all the original ones were replaced; but the act of 1824 contains no such provision, at least in the collection examined.

operated under it in Louisville for a while after 1833, and the present law school of the institution also finds the warrant for its existence in the same instrument.

Six solicitors were appointed at the same time the trustees were, in 1823, to further increase the endowment funds already in the hands of the synod. These do not seem to have been able, for some reason, to push this work very rapidly or successfully, as the whole of the needed $20,000 was not secured and paid over until 1830, at which date Centre may be said to have become strictly a denominational college, the Presbyterians finally having an institution they could really call their own after a struggle of fifty years, counting from the date of the first incorporation of Transylvania Seminary in the establishment of which they had taken so prominent a part.

About the time of the granting of the amended charter an unsuccessful attempt was made, through a memorial to the legislature, to secure the return of the funds brought to Transylvania University by Kentucky Academy at the time of their consolidation and largely contributed by Presbyterians in Kentucky and the Eastern States, the amount of money, books, and other apparatus at the time of the union being estimated at $7,662,[1] besides which there were 6,000 acres of land. The $20,000 raised to secure the control of Centre for the church was all contributed by the denomination in Kentucky, except about $1,000, which came from New England. A large share of the whole amount was contributed by Danville and its vicinity.

After Dr. Chamberlain resigned in 1826, Rev. David C. Proctor, D. D., was acting president of the college until Rev. Gideon Blackburn, D. D., was elected the next president in 1827.[2]

That Dr. Blackburn was a man of enterprise and perseverance is illustrated by his successful effort in paying his own expenses through Dickinson College, Pennsylvania. He was a man of the people and enthusiastic in whatever he undertook. He was also noted for his popular eloquence, and has been called[3] "one of the most eloquent divines of the West." He seems to have been more of an orator than a profound scholar or strong administrator, but was popular with his students, as was shown by several of them leaving the institution in 1830, when he resigned its presidency under circumstances which caused his friends to think he had been unjustly treated by the trustees.

This probably partially accounts for the fact that there were, at the end of that year, in the college only 33 students, including those in the

[1] Davidson's Presbyterian Church in Kentucky, p. 314.

[2] This date is given in a recent catalogue sketch as 1828, but all other authorities examined give 1827. A short sketch of Dr. Blackburn is to be found in Sprague's Annals, Vol. IV, p. 46, and the general catalogue of Centre College for 1890, p. 6. He was born in Virginia in 1772, and was licensed to preach in 1792. He had engaged mainly in the work of the pastorate before becoming president of Centre. After he left Danville he was instrumental in founding a theological seminary at Carlinsville, Ill. He died in 1838.

[3] Collins's Sketches of Kentucky, p. 137.

preparatory department. It was during Dr. Blackburn's administration, in 1828, that a projected theological department modeled on the plan of the seminary at Princeton, N. J., with three professors and a proposed endowment of $20,000, was attached to the college by the synod of Kentucky. A fund of $2,000 was actually raised and the department opened with one professor, Rev. James K. Burch, on October 14, 1828, but trouble in securing the remainder of the endowment caused it to be abandoned in 1831. The funds already raised subsequently went to Danville Theological Seminary.

In connection more particularly with this department, another experiment was also made by the college in the purchase, about 1830, of an industrial farm, intended primarily to assist candidates for the ministry not financially able to educate themselves by furnishing them the opportunity of remunerative labor for two hours a day. The benefits of the enterprise were opened to all the students in 1833, but it appears not to have been a financial success, like other experiments of the same kind made about the same time by other institutions in the State, and so was soon abandoned.

For many years during the early history of Centre its faculty was composed of only two professors and a grammar-school teacher. The number of students during this period varied from 50 to 110 annually, a very large proportion of whom only took a partial or irregular course. Up to the end of Dr. Blackburn's administration there had been 25 graduates.

Dr. Blackburn's successor in the presidency was Rev. John C. Young, D. D., who assumed the duties of the position on October 26, 1830, and continued to discharge them with great acceptability and success until his death on June 23, 1857, doing during this time more than any other one man before or since to establish the prestige of Centre among Kentucky colleges.

Dr. Young, after attending Columbia College, New York, for a time, had graduated in 1823, when just about 20 years of age, at Dickinson College, Pennsylvania, then under the presidency of the celebrated Dr. John M. Mason. He was then for two years a tutor in Princeton College, New Jersey, and later studied theology in Princeton Seminary for four years. He came to Kentucky in 1828 as the pastor of the McChord Presbyterian Church in Lexington, and it was from this popular pastorate that he was called to the presidency of Centre College. He was eminently fitted for this position, being young, energetic, capable, and prudent, while he was also a forcible and effective speaker and a born teacher.

The affairs of the college, however, seemed in a bad way at his accession. A number of its students had left dissatisfied with the treatment of Dr. Blackburn, and the institution was also without funds. About $36,000 had been raised for the institution up to this time, but this had all been expended in buildings, books, and other apparatus, or for the support of the faculty and other purposes, and so affairs looked rather discouraging, but the circumstances were not real hindrances to a man like Dr. Young. The time was, moreover, somewhat propitious, as Transylvania University had materially lost her prestige, and the confidence of the public in her had been greatly shattered, so that this, the principal source of competition at the time, was no longer to be greatly feared.

Dr. Young's many excellent qualities soon made him a favorite with people, church, and students, and so the attendance was soon largely increased and new members were added to the faculty. This body had been composed in 1830, besides Dr. Young, of James Buchanan, professor of mathematics; Alvin G. Smith, professor of chemistry, and William R. Thompson, professor of the Latin and Greek languages. In 1833[1] the faculty was constituted as follows: Rev. John C. Young, A. M., president and professor of logic and moral philosophy; James M. Buchanan, A. M., professor of mathematics; Rev. William L. Breckinridge, A. M., professor of ancient languages; Lewis W. Green, A. M., professor of belles-lettres and political economy; Luke Munsell, M. D., professor of chemistry, mineralogy, and natural philosophy; Rev. Joseph Huber, professor of modern languages; William Y. Allen and Henry G. Cumings, grammar-school tutors. Tuition was at that time[2] $30 per annum and the estimated yearly expenses of a student from $80 to $100, the usual price of board being $1.50 a week.

Contributions to the endowment also soon began to come in, Dr. Young's own congregation in Danville leading in this movement. In 1835 about $12,000 was received for this purpose from New York, but the total endowment of the institution in 1839 was only about $16,000,[3] and for the first nine years of Dr. Young's administration the college was mainly supported by tuition fees. During this time, however, the institution was establishing for itself a reputation for sound learning, and the intellectual and oratorical gifts of its president and professors were placing them and it in the front ranks of the intellectual advancement of the day. Not only had the number of students increased, but the ratio of those who were taking a regular course was becoming much greater, and classes respectable in size and attainments were soon being graduated, there being 5 graduates in 1832, 9 in 1833, 11 in 1837, 15 in 1838, and 12 in 1839.

It was during this period, on December 1, 1833, that a medical college, called the Medical Institute, was opened in Louisville under the charter of the college. There seems, however, to have been very little real connection between the two institutions, and whatever there was was soon dissolved, the Medical Institute, which never seems to have amounted to much, being absorbed in 1837 by a new institution, under

[1] American Almanac and Repository of Useful Knowledge for 1834.

[2] The college had then a two-story brick building and also a refectory and dormitory, a library of 1,600 volumes, and a good chemical and philosophical apparatus.

[3] Barbour's Alumni Address, p. 13.

the same name, which subsequently developed into the Medical Department of the University of Louisville.

It was also about the close of this same period that the increasing reputation of Centre led the trustees of Transylvania University to offer the presidency of that institution to Dr. Young, in the hope that some of the tide of popular favor might be turned in their direction.

The schism in the Presbyterian Church in 1838 between the old and new schools injured Centre considerably, as did also, to some extent, the agitation, about this time, in the State in favor of the emancipation of its slaves, with which movement the college, especially through Dr. Young, who was a prominent advocate of the movement, had become to some extent identified. In regard to both these questions, however, its faculty took the position they deemed to be right without regard to the consequences.

The period between 1840 and 1853 is one of especial growth in the history of the college. Notwithstanding strenuous efforts in its behalf, the institution had often been crippled in its work for lack of funds prior to 1840, but in that year its own imperative needs and the recent munificent donations bestowed upon Transylvania University by Lexington and the Transylvania Institute spurred up the Synod of Kentucky to take more active measures in raising an endowment for the college, which it was intended to make not less than $100,000. This movement soon made favorable progress, but meanwhile the expansion in matriculation more than kept pace with it until, in 1846, the expenses of the institution were again greater than its income, while, at the same time, an additional new professorship was urgently needed. To meet this situation, a special effort was made, which was soon almost completely successful in raising the desired amount.

Collins tells us in his Sketches[1] that the income of the college in 1846 was $3,000 a year, and that its library then had about 5,000 volumes, many of them rare and valuable. Its course of instruction, he says, then differed but little from that of the older colleges of the country, being equal to them in classics and mathematics, and while somewhat inferior in natural science, owing to the lack of equal facilities, stronger in the mental and moral sciences. At this time an increased endowment was especially desired in order to enlarge the sphere of work in natural science. We find that in 1849 the income of the college had increased to $4,000 a year, and that its course is soon announced in its catalogue as the equal of any in the land.

The importance of the institution, which had been constantly increasing for a number of years, was still further added to, in 1853, by the establishment of Danville Theological Seminary, which, being under the auspices of the whole church and being operated in close harmony with the college, necessarily enlarged the prestige of the latter materially.

[1] Sketches of Kentucky, p. 206.

Throughout this period and the remainder of Dr. Young's administration the number of students and the size of the graduating classes continued to grow. In 1851 there were 201 students, who were from fifteen States and Territories of the Union and one other country, and in 1855 seventeen States and one foreign country were represented by 220 students. In the last scholastic year of his administration there were 225 students and 47 graduates, the average number of graduates for several years past having been about 30.[1] The whole number of graduates in 1857 was about 500, located mainly in the South and West, where they were to be found in every State and Territory.

Dr. Young died in the prime of life, greatly beloved and lamented, and his loss was considered a great blow to the college for which he had done so much. Besides this, his great life work, and his labors in behalf of emancipation, he had done much, in conjunction with Rev. B. O. Peers and others, in behalf of the cause of public school education in Kentucky. The other regular members of the faculty at the time of his death were: Ormond Beatty, A. M., professor of physics and chemistry; Rev. Alfred Ryors, D. D., professor of mathematics; Rev. James Matthews, A. M., professor of English literature and of the Latin language, and Rev. Jacob Cooper, Ph. D., professor of the Greek language and literature.

Dr. Young's successor in the presidency was Rev. L. W. Green, D. D., the outlines of whose previous career have been given in connection with the history of Transylvania University, of which he was president at the time of his election to the presidency of Centre, on August 6, 1857. As already noted, he was an alumnus of the institution, having been a member of its first graduating class, that of 1824, and had taught in his alma mater for a time in his earlier educational career. Dr. Green entered upon the duties of his new office on January 1, 1858, and, like his predecessor, also died in office, on May 20, 1863. Dr. Green was a worthy successor of Dr. Young, and the prosperity of the college continued until interrupted by the advent of the civil war. There were 253 students in attendance in 1859–60, and in 1861 the endowment of the college was reported as $109,398.

In 1858 an agent was appointed by the synod to secure funds for a new building and additional equipment. By 1861 $50,000 had been raised for this purpose, but the uncertainty of affairs, due to the coming on of the war, led to the erection of the building being postponed. At the same time, $5,000 was given for a library building by Mr. David A. Sayre, of Lexington, the founder of Sayre Institute. This building was completed and occupied in 1862, being named Sayre Hall, in honor of the principal donor.

During this administration more emphasis than formerly was put upon the scientific departments, and the foundations were laid of what has since developed into a regular bachelor of science course. For a considerable time, students devoting their main attention to these

[1] There were 29 graduates in 1853, 31 in 1854, 24 in 1855, and 27 in 1856.

departments were special scientific students, who did not receive a regular degree.

The operations of the college were only interrupted for a few days occasionally by the civil war, and its funds during that period were not materially decreased, although its matriculation, of course, was. In 1862–63 there were only 105 students altogether. Upon Dr. Green's death, in May, 1863, Rev. William L. Breckinridge, D. D., was elected to the vacant presidency. He had already been for a while professor of ancient languages at Centre, and had for the past four years been the president of Oakland College, Mississippi. He entered upon the duties of his position at Danville on October 18, 1863, and served until his resignation on October 16, 1868.

Dr. Breckinridge stood high in the councils of his church, and while perhaps more noted as a preacher and pastor than as an educator, was a wise and capable executive head for the college. His administration fell during the difficult times of the latter part of the war, and the even more troublous period, to one in his position, of the reconstruction era. His difficulties were especially complicated by the contention between the two synods of Kentucky, after the disruption of the original synod in 1866, as to which should have the right to control the college by electing its board of trustees. This contest occurred mainly during the next administration, but was begun in 1867. It, of course, led to a continuation of the small matriculation brought about by the war. The average attendance during this period was only from one-third to one-half what it had been prior to the war.

When Dr. Breckinridge resigned in October, 1868, Ormond Beatty, LL. D., became president pro tem., acting in this capacity until September 1, 1870, when he was elected president, a position held by him until September, 1888. Dr. Beatty was an alumnus of the college in the class of 1835, and had been teaching in it all his life, having been appointed its professor of natural science just prior to his graduation, when he was only twenty years old. He had accepted the position on the condition that he might spend a year at Yale College in additional preparation before assuming its duties. He held that chair until 1847, when he was transferred to the chair of mathematics, but in 1852 he again resumed his old chair. At his election as president in 1870, he took charge of the department of metaphysics. He had been prominently connected with the work of his church in various capacities and was a man of ability and of great equableness of temper, besides being a speaker of force and clearness. Under his administration several progressive steps in the history of the college occurred.

In the first place a fine new building was erected, mainly from the funds collected for this purpose before the war. It was completed and dedicated on June 26, 1872. At the same time Dr. Beatty was formally inaugurated as president.[1] It was quite a handsome structure, costing

[1] The requisite majority of trustees had not been present when Dr. Beatty was first elected in 1870, and so his election was confirmed at this time and his formal inauguration took place.

about $60,000, and was considered the finest of its kind in the State at the time.

In addition to the new building, new books and apparatus were also added to the equipment of the institution. The Scott museum of natural history was begun at this time. The faculty was also increased in numbers and the scope and sphere of its work generally enlarged. Its regular professors in 1872, with their departments of instruction, were as follows: Ormond Beatty, A. M., LL. D., president and professor of metaphysics and political science; Rev. John L. McKee, D. D., vice president and professor of moral philosophy; Rev. James C. Randolph, A. M., professor of mathematics; Jason W. Chenault, A. M., Ph. D., professor of the Latin language and rhetoric; Salvator De Soto, A. M., professor of Greek and modern languages; John C. Fales, A. M., professor of physical and natural science.

Since the occupation of the new building the old one has been converted into a dormitory for students, especially intended for those who wish to live in an inexpensive way.

The difficulty about the future control of the college was also permanently settled. After various unsuccessful efforts had been made to heal the schism, unite the parts in support of the institution, or divide its funds, the legislature and the courts—circuit, appellate, and United States district—were invoked, all of which tribunals gave the college to the original synod, commonly called that of the Northern Presbyterian Church in contradistinction to the newer body, the Southern Presbyterian Church, as being the party in control and as having steadfastly adhered to the original General Assembly. The final decision in the matter was reached in 1873.

The institution had then begun to regain some of its former vigor, but had hardly started on its new career of prosperity before it was overtaken by what was apparently a new adversity, in the form of the robbery of about $60,000 of its bonds, on March 10, 1873, from the vaults of the Falls City Tobacco Bank of Louisville, Ky. This amount was nearly two-thirds of its productive endowment at the time and it seemed that the college would either have to suspend entirely for a time or greatly curtail its work for the future. Its friends, however, rallied to its aid, and in the end it was really strengthened by the catastrophe. When Dr. McKee, its vice-president, announced its condition[1] to his congregation, at Danville, $6,000 was raised in its behalf in a very short while, and $6,000 more was subscribed in the vicinity in the next few days. Largely through the efforts of Dr. McKee subscriptions and promised legacies, amounting to more than $100,000, were soon secured, and, as all but about $20,000 of the stolen bonds were ultimately recovered, the institution was really placed in a much better financial condition than before—its endowment by 1885 having been nearly

[1] On March 23, 1873, when it was thought the college would have to suspend in June if $50,000 was not raised towards its endowment (Collins's History of Kentucky, Vol. I, p. 246).

doubled—and continued to enlarge its work rather than curtail it, as had been feared would be necessary.

It was during this period that a regular course leading to the degree of bachelor of science was instituted, while an elective course quite similar to that formerly taken by scientific students was also added to the former curriculum.

The funds given at this time, as at other periods, were mainly given in hundreds of small donations, but among the most prominent contributors were Samuel Laird, who gave about $12,000; Caldwell Campbell, L. L. Warren, and B. F. Avery, who gave over $10,000 each; while Dr. John Scott contributed $10,000, A. M. January, $5,000 or over, Mrs. M. A. Wilson, $5,000 or more, and many others $1,000 each.

Dr. Beatty, owing to advancing years and failing health, first tendered his resignation as president of the college to its board of trustees on June 15, 1886. He again tendered it on November 30, 1886, at which time it was accepted, to take effect upon the qualification of his successor. The selection of his successor did not take place, however, until June 19, 1888, when, after various unsuccessful efforts to secure a president, Rev. William C. Young, D. D., the son of the distinguished former president, Dr. John C. Young, was unanimously elected to the position. Dr. Beatty retained his professorship until his death, on June 24, 1890, after a long career of faithful and able services to his alma mater and the interests of education in general.

Dr. W. C. Young promptly accepted the presidency upon his election and entered upon the duties of his office at the opening of the next scholastic year, on September 5, 1888. He had graduated from Centre in the class of 1859, when about seventeen years old; had taught, traveled, and studied for the next three years, and had then entered Danville Theological Seminary, from which he graduated in 1865. He then engaged principally in the successful work of various pastorates of his church until, upon the general desire of the Synod of Kentucky and, in some sense, of the whole Presbyterian Church, he accepted the presidency of Centre College. He was a man of an agreeable personality, was a fine scholar, an able minister, and made an admirable college president.

His administration was one of general enlargement in almost all directions, Dr. Young's efforts in this direction being seconded by old and new friends of the institution. Funds for this purpose soon began to be contributed, a considerable part of the contributions coming from the East, and by 1891 the endowment had been increased by $100,000. In that year three new professorships were added to the faculty, and a splendid new gymnasium was added to the equipment of the college, largely through the liberality of Judge A. P. Humphrey and Hon. St. John Boyle, of Louisville, alumni of the institution. The library of Dr. Beatty, and also a large portion of that of Rev. S. D. Burchard, of New York City, another alumnus, were also added, by bequest, to the college library, thus increased to 6,000 volumes, while an effort on the part of other alumni to endow a chair of English named in honor of Dr. John C. Young was partly successful. In 1894 a beautiful new library building, with space in its alcoves for more than 20,000 volumes, and an attractive and commodious reading room attached, was erected. It still bears the name of Sayre Hall, in honor of the donor of the original building.

In October of 1894 a new law school, with three professors, was attached to the college. J. Proctor Knott, LL. D., a man prominent in both Kentucky and national public affairs, and who had been connected with the faculty for the past three years as professor of civics and economics, was made dean of the new department, in the instruction of which he is assisted by Robert P. Jacobs, LL. D., and John W. Yerkes, A. M., LL. B. Their respective chairs are: Institutes of law, constitutional law, pleading and evidence, domestic relations and contracts; equity, jurisprudence, mercantile law, real and personal property and wills; and corporations, criminal law and procedure, insurance, agency, and torts. These titles indicate the scope of the curriculum, which leads to the degree of bachelor of law. The course of instruction covers two years and is designed to fit students for the practice of their profession in any part of the country. Matriculates of the school can attend lectures and recitations in other departments of the college without additional expense.

The attendance upon this department since its organization has been very gratifying and seems to be such as to guarantee its permanency for the future. More recently a new chair of physics and chemistry has been established, which shares with the chair of geology and biology the work of the previous chair of natural science. The scientific apparatus of the college has also been improved in such a way as to furnish it with well-equipped laboratories and an excellent museum for work and illustration. By 1896 the invested funds of the institution had become about $265,000, about $125,000 having been added in the previous eight years. Its annual income from all sources was then about $23,000, whereas in 1887 it had been about $9,000.

The matriculation of the college had meanwhile increased in a manner corresponding with the expansion in other directions. At the beginning of Dr. Young's administration the annual attendance had been about 175 each year, of whom about 100 had been in the collegiate department. In 1895–96, the last full year of his presidency, there were 208 students in the collegiate classes, while there were 20 law students and about 75 others in the academy. The graduating classes about 1888 averaged 15. In 1895–96 the class numbered 40. During this period students had at one time been in attendance from sixteen of the States and Territories and one foreign country.

On September 16, 1896, President Young died suddenly while in the active discharge of his duties, being cut off, like his honored father, in the prime of life and in the midst of a career of usefulness. His administration had been a pronounced success, as during it the number of students had been largely increased, a law department auspiciously organized, and the income of the institution more than doubled, while about $20,000 had been spent for new buildings and the scientific apparatus of the institution had also been much enlarged.

For about two years after Dr. Young's death, while negotiations for securing a new president were being conducted, Prof. J. C. Fales, as the senior member of the faculty, or dean, was the acting president of the college, Dr. McKee, who had served the institution so long and well, especially in the matter of securing its endowment during Dr. Beatty's administration, declining the new responsibility and retiring from the faculty at the end of the first of these years. At that time Rev. W. H. Johnson, M. A., became professor of logic and psychology. A lecturer on criminal law and an instructor in elocution were also added to the corps of instruction.

The institution also continued to advance in other ways. Its library especially was increased by the gift of 1,000 volumes from the library of its late president, Dr. Young, by an additional donation from the library of Dr. Burchard, and by a collection of 3,000 volumes of new and modern works presented to the institution by the Memorial Presbyterian Church of Philadelphia, Pa., through its pastor, Rev. S. A. Mutchmore, D. D., an alumnus of the college, which is to form the nucleus of a collection to be called "The S. A. Mutchmore Library." These additions, together with the purchase of standard works from time to time, have augmented the present college library to about 12,000 volumes, besides which the two literary societies connected with the institution have combined libraries of about 3,500 volumes. Among other improvements contemplated by the college are a new academy building, a new scientific building, and an alumni commencement hall, and the probabilities are that these will soon be secured.

Centre College is one of the few larger and more important institutions in the State which has not adopted coeducation, now a pretty generally accepted policy throughout educational circles in Kentucky. The institution considers that, at least for the present, it has a sufficiently large field for it to carry out its work in the old historic way. This position appears to be abundantly maintained by its large matriculation from year to year, which, although it has not been quite so large as formerly for the past two years, has sustained itself well in comparison with other educational institutions generally in the State and throughout the country.

In June, 1898, a new president for the institution was secured in the person of Rev. William C. Roberts, D. D., LL. D., S. T. D., who was born in Wales in 1832, graduated at Princeton College, New Jersey, in 1855 and at Princeton Seminary in 1858. Since the latter date he has been mainly engaged in the pastorate of various Presbyterian churches, and has served two terms, from 1881 to 1886 and from 1893 to 1898, as corresponding secretary of the board of home missions of his church, in which he has always held a prominent position. He should be well fitted to carry out the traditions of the college over which he has been called to preside, which has always been noted for its high moral tone and its devotion to sound learning.

No institution in Kentucky has a more distinguished body of alumni than Centre College; in fact, few colleges in the country have a greater number of graduates distinguished in political life especially, the profession of the law and that of the ministry being those most largely followed by Centre alumni. Once or twice in the past seventeen years there have been more old students of Centre in both Houses of Congress than of any other college in the country except Yale University. The following statement, taken substantially from the catalogue of the college for 1897–98, will perhaps best show the number and attainments of Centre's graduates:

The entire number of its alumni at the present time is over 1,200. Among these are more than 330 lawyers, about 225 ministers of the gospel, and more than 100 physicians, and the remainder are found in various professions and callings. Among the alumni are many, both of the living and the dead, who have greatly distinguished themselves in their respective professions, and have attained the highest positions of honor and trust, especially throughout the South and West, where they reside, or where they did reside while they lived.

Centre College has educated 24 college presidents, 41 college professors, 26 representatives in Congress, 5 United States Senators, 7 governors of States, 2 Vice-Presidents of the United States, 1 justice of the United States Supreme Court, 38 circuit judges, State and national, 48 editors, 4 or 5 ministers to foreign countries, and many others occupying positions of trust and responsibility in other fields.

The course of instruction in the collegiate department of the institution is at present divided into thirteen departments, as follows: Biblical studies, moral philosophy and history, evidences of Christianity and logic, metaphysics, civics and economics, geology and biology, physics and chemistry, mathematics, Greek, Latin, English, modern languages, and hygiene and physical training. There are two regular courses, that of bachelor of arts and that of bachelor of science,[1] the latter substituting certain natural sciences for Greek. In the junior and senior years of these courses considerable specialization is allowed by the choice of so many hours' work a week among a group of elective studies. There is, besides, an elective course of two years, not leading to a degree, for students desiring to take special subjects, in which practically the only requirement is that the student be properly qualified to pursue with success the subjects taken and that the amount of work done be equal to the work of one of the regular courses.

An academy, with a course of two years specially arranged to prepare students for the college classes, is attached to the institution and

[1] In each of these courses, as usual, the master's degree is granted upon the satisfactory completion of an additional year's work and the presentation of an acceptable thesis.

KENTUCKY WESLEYAN COLLEGE, WINCHESTER.

has been from the beginning. It is under the control of the college and its students are enumerated as a part of the college matriculation, but it has really been operated as a separate institution for over fifty years.

The following are the regular professors of the college faculty, besides whom there are connected with the institution a lecturer, three instructors, and a principal and assistant of the academy: Rev. William C. Roberts, D. D., LL. D., S. T. D., president, professor of moral philosophy and history; John Cilley Fales, A. M., F. G. S. A., professor of geology and biology, and librarian; Alfred Brierley Nelson, A. M., M. D., professor of mathematics; John W. Redd, A. M., professor of Greek language and literature, secretary of faculty; Samuel Robertson Cheek, A. M., professor of Latin language and literature; James Proctor Knott, LL. D., professor of law, civics, and economics; Robert Powell Jacobs, LL. D., professor of law; John Watson Yerkes, A. M., LL. B., professor of law; Richard Oakley Stilwell, M. E., professor of physics and chemistry; Frederick Houk Law, M. A., professor of English language and literature; Rev. William Hallock Johnson, M. A., professor of logic and psychology.

BIBLIOGRAPHY.

Collins's Sketches, Collins's, Shaler's, Smith's, and Perrin, Battle, and Kniffen's histories. The last is especially valuable, as it contains a sketch of the college, written by President Beatty.

Davidson's Presbyterian Church in Kentucky.

The Biographical Encyclopedia of Kentucky.

Henderson's Centennial Exhibit.

Acts of the State legislature.

Cleland's Memoirs

Sprague's Annals.

Barnard's American Journal of Education.

Niles's Register.

The American Almanac.

A Memoir of Sylvester Scovel, D. D., by James Wood, D. D., New Albany, 1851.

A History of Mercer and Boyle counties, by Maria T. Daviess, weekly articles in the Harrodsburg Democrat from January 30, 1885, to November 20, 1885.

KENTUCKY WESLEYAN COLLEGE, WINCHESTER.

Although Kentucky Wesleyan College has been in operation as a college only since 1866, yet, in conception and as a representative college of Kentucky Methodism, it dates back even to the planning of Bethel Academy in 1790, as the institution is, in a sense, a continuation of the three older institutions, Bethel Academy, Augusta College, and Transylvania University, while under the control of the Methodist Episcopal Church. As President Pearce expresses it,[1] "The journeying ark of educational purpose of the church fathers in Kentucky found rest for a time," first at Bethel—then truly in a western wilderness—then at Augusta, then at Lexington, then at Millersburg, and finally at Winchester on the one hand, and Nashville, Tenn., on the other, for Van-

[1] Inaugural address, p. 23.

derbilt University is the adopted institution of Louisville Conference, the western portion of old Kentucky Conference of the Methodist Episcopal Church. This continuity of history is typified, both in the case of Kentucky Wesleyan, and Vanderbilt, by some of the bricks from the walls of old Bethel Academy having been built into the walls of the main building of each of these institutions.

In regard to the strictly Kentucky branch of this educational movement, we have already traced the history of the sojourn at Lexington, in connection with the history of Transylvania University. A sketch of Bethel and Augusta will be reserved for a later date, and our attention for the present will be confined to the principal events connected with the career of Kentucky Wesleyan College at its two locations, Millersburg and Winchester.

AT MILLERSBURG.

The Methodist Episcopal Church was rent asunder not long before the final decline, in 1849, of Augusta College, its originally adopted educational institution in Kentucky, and its abandonment, at the same time, of Transylvania University, both of which events were doubtless hastened by the disruption. Neither branch of the denomination in Kentucky undertook any other educational enterprise at once. The Methodist Episcopal Church South, however, which was then, more so than now, much the larger of the two branches of the original organization in the State, soon began to consider plans to supply its educational needs, which developed into the founding of Kentucky Wesleyan College at Millersburg.

Rev. Daniel Stevenson, D. D., of whom we shall hear more in connection with the history of Union College and the State public-school system, in 1856 or earlier caused Kentucky Conference of that church to pass a resolution favoring the location of a college in the town within its limits offering the greatest inducements, but Rev. T. P. Shellman is the one most prominent in bringing about the immediate organization of the institution.

In September, 1857, while presiding elder of the Covington district, Mr. Shellman had set to work to establish a male and female conference school somewhere in his district. By seeking for propositions from different towns, he induced Millersburg to undertake the building of a house for the proposed school, the idea at the time being to engraft it upon the school already being conducted there by Dr. George S. Savage, which had outgrown its building. A number of other people had become interested in the enterprise, principally through Mr. Shellman, and $7,500 having been subscribed by citizens of the town, in the summer of 1858 a building committee, which had been appointed for the institution and consisted of Dr. A. G. Stitt, Mr. Alex. S. Miller, and Mr. William Nunn, purchased grounds just outside the northern limits of the town and laid the foundations of a large building for the institute, as the school was to be called.

When conference met in Millersburg, in September of that year, it caught, as it were, more strongly than ever the spirit of education then in the air there, and its committee on education, of which Dr. Stevenson was a member, proposed to the stockholders of the institute that, if they would enlarge the building and present it to the Conference, that body would endow the institution with $100,000, and make it a male college. This offer was promptly accepted by the stockholders, most of whom doubled their subscriptions in order to aid in carrying it out. The grounds, incomplete foundations, and all the funds of the institute were at once turned over to the representatives of the Conference for the new college, which was intended to be of high grade and was to be under the patronage of the church, the purpose in view in its foundation being "the promotion of literature, science, morality, and religion."[1]

The corner stone of the main building of the intended institution was laid, with impressive ceremonies, during that session of the Conference, Bishop Kavanaugh and others delivering addresses. Under the supervision of the former building committee, which was continued in office, the building was soon again under way, although it was not entirely completed for about two years. It cost when complete $30,000, and could furnish excellent accommodations for from 150 to 200 students.

The session of conference which projected the new institution also appointed an agent to secure subscriptions and donations for its support. By the autumn of 1859, $57,000 in cash and good notes had been secured for this purpose, and, as the success of the enterprise seemed assured, on January 12, 1860, a charter was secured for the college, placing it under the control of a board of education composed of twelve members, half lay and half clerical, one-third of whom were to be chosen each year by the conference. To these were given by the charter all the usual corporate and academic powers and privileges needed to conduct an institution of liberal culture. The first board had as members Rev. W. C. Dandy, Rev. Daniel Stevenson, Rev. J. H. Linn, Rev. J. W. Cunningham, Rev. J. C. Harrion, Rev. Robert Hiner, David Thornton, Moreau Brown, Hiram Shaw, B. P. Tevis, William Nunn, and A. G. Stitt. The name Kentucky Wesleyan University was first adopted for the institution, but Kentucky Wesleyan College has since been substituted.

A high school was opened in the autumn of 1859 in the town hall of Millersburg, as the college building was then not ready for occupancy, under Prof. A. G. Murphey, for a number of years subsequently a member of the faculty of Kentucky Wesleyan and Millersburg Female colleges and the present president of Logan Female College. It was expected to add a collegiate department soon, but as the civil war came on this did not take place until 1866. Professor Murphey taught until April, 1862, when he resigned on account of bad health, and the school was closed temporarily. Professor Murphey during this time

[1] Perrin's History of Bourbon, Scott, Harrison, and Nicholas counties, page 128.

had as assistant teachers Benjamin Ashbrook, J. F. Neal, John W. Craig, and Joseph T. Onten, there being one assistant the first year, two the second, and three the third. Seventy-five pupils were in attendance the first year and 100 the second, over 30 of the latter being from a distance. The attendance was fair during the third year, as up to that time it had not been largely, at least locally, affected by the war. On December 5, 1860, the school had been moved to its new building, some of the rooms of which had then been completed.

In October, 1863, the school was reopened by Prof. T. J. Dodd, who had been elected principal by conference in the previous September. Professor Dodd was assisted by his brother, Virginius Dodd, and remained in charge until the middle of the next scholastic year, when he resigned, the second year being finished out by Rev. Duke Slouns, upon the appointment of conference. Rev. H. W. Abbett and Rev. S. L. Robertson were then joint principals of the school for a year.

In September, 1865, most of the first board of education having resigned, a new board then appointed, after deciding that the funds on hand justified it, determined to open the collegiate department at an early date. After considerable canvassing, in the spring and summer of 1866, Rev. Charles Taylor, A. M., M. D., was selected by them as the first president of the college, under whom the institution was regularly opened in the autumn of that year. Since that time Kentucky Wesleyan College has had a continuous existence.

The college faculty, as announced in its first annual catalogue, was constituted as follows: Rev. Charles Taylor, A. M., M. D., president, also professor of mental and moral philosophy and evidences of revealed religion; A. G. Murphey, A. M., professor of logic and English literature and adjunct professor of natural sciences; Rev. H. W. Abbett, A. M., professor of the Latin and Greek languages and literatures; Charles H. Theiss, A. M., professor of mathematics and natural sciences. Theological department: Rev. S. L. Robertson, professor of Hebrew and Biblical literature. President Taylor remained in office until 1870, when he resigned. The first year of his administration there were 90 students in attendance and the last year 144, the latter being the largest matriculation the college has had until comparatively recent years. Classical and scientific courses of instruction were instituted from the beginning, and in 1868 the first bachelor of science degree was conferred. In 1869, 2 A. B.'s were granted, and in 1870 5 A. B.'s and 2 B. S.'s.

Dr. Taylor's successor in the presidency of the college was Rev. B. Arbogast. About the beginning of his administration the West Virginia Conference was invited by the Kentucky Conference to become part owner of the college and give it their patronage. They contributed a small amount toward building a dormitory, and for a number of years were given two representatives on the board of education. These have, however, recently been replaced by two members selected from the alumni of the college. The name board of curators has also been substituted for that of board of education.

In June, 1872, President Arbogast, by reason of the pressure of other engagements, resigned, and was succeeded by Prof. John Darby, A. M., Ph. D., who had been professor of natural science in the college for two years already, and a teacher of advanced reputation for nearly forty. Professor Darby resigned the presidency in 1875, and Rev. T. J. Dodd, D. D., was then elected to the position. President Dodd, however, left the institution at the end of a year to accept a professorship in Vanderbilt University, then newly established. Rev. W. H. Anderson, D. D., then became president of Kentucky Wesleyan, which position he retained for three years.

During President Anderson's administration the course of instruction was modified to some extent, the previous scientific course being lengthened somewhat and a course leading to the degree of bachelor of philosophy instituted. The college also received by gift the valuable herbarium and scientific library of Professor Darby. There were at this period 5 teachers and a maximum of about 90 students in the institution, the average attendance being considerably below this number. Since 1870 there had been from two to six graduates each year, and in the nine years 22 A. B.'s, 11 B. S.'s, and 1 Ph. B. had been conferred.

Upon the resignation of President Anderson, in 1879, D. W. Batson, A. M., an alumnus of the college in the class of 1874, and since then its professor of mathematics, was put at the head of the institution. President Batson was quite a young man at the time of his appointment, and had associated with him a faculty also of young men, mainly alumni of the institution. He was, however, thoroughly interested in his work and soon succeeded, with the cooperation of his colleagues, in restoring the institution to something of its early prosperity, its average attendance being almost doubled within the first two years after his election. He was the presiding officer of the college up to 1894, with the exception of the scholastic year 1883–84, when Rev. Alexander Redd, A. M., was president.

During these fifteen years several events of importance took place in the history of the college. In 1884, the valuable library of Bishop Kavanaugh and also that of Rev. S. L. Robertson were donated to the college. These, together with its previous nucleus, formed the foundation of a good collection for the future, the lack of which had previously been much felt, for while the institution had always maintained a high standard in its courses and had kept itself well supplied with apparatus, in the department of natural science especially, its educational equipment in other respects, outside of a fairly good building, had not been of the first order.

President Batson was able to keep up the matriculation fairly well and the college prospered, but its enlargement in the future was not hopeful and its work was much crippled for lack of sufficient funds.

The original endowment was never large, the productive funds, in 1882, only aggregating about $32,000,[1] and although several agents had at different times been appointed to solicit further means, they had been able to accomplish little or nothing. The endowment the college did have was also much less effective than it would otherwise have been, because it had been secured on the basis of allowing a free scholarship for comparatively small amounts contributed.

Owing to this state of affairs, the board of education, in September, 1886, presented to the conference a plan arranging that proposals be invited from any and all places in the bounds of the conference looking toward the future relocation of the college, in order that it might secure the largest facilities and the most favorable conditions. Conference at once appointed a commission to receive, examine, and accept or reject any such proposal. This commission, on July 12, 1887, voted to accept the offer of the citizens of Winchester and Clark County, who had that summer agreed to present to the institution a campus of eight acres of ground lying within the corporate limits of Winchester and $42,000 in cash for new buildings and general equipment. This decision was afterward ratified by the board of education and by the conference, and the college was removed to Winchester, where it was first opened on September 3, 1890, since which time it has entered upon a new era. During the period from 1879 to 1890 there had been from 3 to 9 graduates each year and the following regular degrees had been granted: 35 A. B.'s, 15 B. S.'s, 5 Ph. B.'s, and 2 A. M.'s.

AT WINCHESTER.

As its building at its new location was not ready for occupancy at the time of the removal, the college occupied temporary quarters in a private residence in 1890-91, when it had 4 regular professors and 122 students were matriculated.

The new main building was sufficiently completed to be occupied in the autumn of 1891. It is a handsome structure, built of brick with stone trimmings, and is very complete in its appointments, having fifteen rooms, all commodious and arranged with reference to the most approved methods in educational work. In 1891-92 a new professor was added to the faculty, the work in the scientific department especially being further subdivided and specialized. At the end of this year the character of work done by the institution was further enlarged by the introduction of coeducation, young women being admitted to its course upon the same terms as young men. About the same time, or soon after, a special English course of two years, a business course of one year, and a common-school teacher's course of one year were added to the previous curriculum for those who could only attend for a limited time and were not candidates for a degree, an instructor in shorthand and typewriting being then added to the faculty.

[1] Perrin's History of Bourbon, Scott, Harrison, and Nicholas counties, p. 129.

While its matriculation was somewhat larger than before, the operations of the college were considerably embarrassed and its prospects hindered during its first four years at Winchester by the litigation in which it was involved through those who were opposed to its removal from Millersburg, and who appealed to the courts against that step. This contest was finally settled in 1894 by a decision in favor of the present location, a result which has materially conduced to the subsequent prosperity of the institution. In this year, also, Mr. Batson retired from the presidency, after fifteen years' faithful and efficient service in that position. He has since continued to be one of the members of the regular faculty.

In 1894-95 Prof. B. T. Spencer was chairman of the faculty, the next regular president, Rev. E. H. Pearce, D. D., being elected in the latter part of the year. President Pearce was formally installed on June 4, 1895, and entered auspiciously upon his administration. The college has since made a distinct advance. During the first year of his term the main building was finished and newly furnished throughout at a cost of $8,000, while extensive additions were made to the apparatus in the departments of chemistry and physics. Soon after this a hall in the main building set apart as a gymnasium was equipped with the latest and best appliances for physical exercise.

The most marked enlargement of late has been in the founding of preparatory schools, under the control of the college, in different parts of the Kentucky Conference. Besides the preparatory department connected with the college in Winchester and another operated in the old building at Millersburg, three others have been established at Campton, Burnside, and London, important points in the eastern part of the State. Campton Academy was opened on January 1, 1896; Burnside Academy on September 1, 1896, and the academy at London, called Bennett Memorial Academy, in September, 1897.

These schools make quarterly reports to the college, of whose faculty their principals are considered members, and prepare students for the sophomore class. They are also training schools for teachers for the portion of the State in which they are located. They all have excellent buildings, for the erection and equipment of which about $30,000 has recently been contributed by friends of the college, part of it by the Woman's Home Missionary Society. New dormitories for the academies at Campton and Burnside have recently been projected, and arrangements are now in progress for the erection of a new $10,000 dormitory on the college campus at Winchester. Material additions to the endowment of the college have also been made in the last three years, and plans are now under way which it is hoped will cause its property and funds, now about $100,000 in value, to reach $250,000 in the next five years.

In 1895 the faculty was enlarged by the addition of special lecturers on church history, on the Bible, and on civics, and in 1896 an instructor in elocution was appointed. The matriculation of the institution has also recently increased, there being 154 students in the college proper in 1894–95 and a total of 448 in college and academies together in 1897–98. The number of graduates has increased in like manner, nineteen degrees having been conferred in the last three years.

Kentucky Wesleyan College has always been able to maintain an able faculty, and its standard of classical and scientific education has been high. It has consequently occupied a worthy place among similar institutions of learning in the State, and has turned out many well-equipped graduates who have taken an honorable rank in the various professions and callings of life, the ministry being more largely represented than any other profession. Its students have recently maintained an excellent standing in eastern institutions, where they have gone to pursue special and advanced work. The total number of graduates up to 1898, inclusive, is 169, of whom about 30 have entered the ministry, about 25 the law, quite a number teaching, while medicine and other vocations are well represented. Many of those who spent a time at the college, but took no degrees, are occupying important places in church and state.

The curriculum of the institution is divided into the following schools of instruction: Latin, Greek, German, French, English, mathematics, chemistry and biology, physics and astronomy, history and political science, psychology and ethics, theistic and Christian evidences, Bible study, bookkeeping and commercial science, and shorthand and typewriting. The completion of eleven out of the first twelve of these schools leads to the two regular degrees of bachelor of arts[1] and bachelor of science, the former requiring the school of Greek, while the latter substitutes German and French for Greek. There are also the special courses already indicated and an academic or preparatory course of three years in length. The present faculty, in addition to the principals of the various preparatory schools, two instructors in elocution and in shorthand and typewriting, respectively, and two special lecturers, the one on Bible history and literature, and the other on civics, has the following regular professors and officers: Rev. E. H. Pearce, A. M., D. D. president and professor of psychology and ethics; D. W. Batson, A. M., professor of natural science; B. T. Spencer, A. M., professor of Greek and instructor in German; W. H. Garnett, Ph. D., Abram Megowan professor of mathematics and instructor in French; Marvin West, A. M., professor of Latin and history.

BIBLIOGRAPHY.

Collins's and Smith's histories, Henderson's Centennial Exhibit.

A History of Bourbon, Scott, Harrison, and Nicholas Counties, by W. H. Perrin, Chicago, 1882 (contains a sketch of the college by President Batson).

A Manuscript History of Kentucky Wesleyan College, by Rev John Jay Dickey.

Installation exercises and inaugural of E. H. Pearce, D. D., as president of Kentucky Wesleyan College, Winchester, 1895.

[1] The degree of A. M. is conferred on bachelors of arts who pursue some literary profession for three years and present a satisfactory thesis.

ST. MARY'S COLLEGE—FRONT VIEW OF MAIN BUILDING.

ST. MARY'S COLLEGE, MARION COUNTY.

St. Mary's is the oldest and most important Catholic male college now in existence in Kentucky, and is one of the oldest, if not the oldest, of its kind in the Mississippi Valley. It had its own beginning in 1821 and in a way now has a right to have the date of its origin made about two years earlier, as it was in 1890 made in a sense the legal successor of St. Joseph's College at Bardstown, Ky., its older and in some respects more celebrated colleague, whose history will be sketched in another chapter. There we shall find that the foundation of St. Joseph's was largely due to the efforts of Rev. G. A. M. Elder; St. Mary's, in a still more eminent degree, owes its existence to the self-sacrificing exertions and the energy of one man, Rev. William Byrne, and it is rather remarkable that these two men should have been ordained to the priesthood in their church at the same time, a ceremony which occurred in the cathedral at Bardstown, Ky., on September 18, 1819.[1]

Father Byrne was born in Ireland in 1780. His talents were not brilliant nor his education extended, but he was noted for his industry and application. He had not the means of obtaining an advanced education in early life, but after coming to America had studied for a time at St. Mary's College, Emmittsburg, Md., where he held the position of prefect of discipline. On coming to Kentucky and seeing the pressing need of educational institutions, he determined to found, to meet the needs of the hour, a school for boys similar to the school for girls lately established at Loretto.

He set to work with his characteristic energy, only waiting long enough to obtain the bishop's permission. Without money or anyone specially to help him, he purchased a farm in Marion County about 5 miles from where Lebanon now stands, which had been occupied for a time by the Sisters of Loretto, and which Rev. Charles Nerinckx had secured in 1820 for the purpose of founding a new Christian brotherhood devoted to the education of boys and had named St. Mary's. This Father Byrne obtained possession of in 1821 by means of funds partly raised by subscription, and here he first opened a school, called St. Mary's Seminary, in the early spring of that year in an old stone distillery fitted up with rough furniture partly made by his own hand.

The school soon became popular and so increased in numbers as to speedily outgrow its old quarters. For the accommodation of its patrons, who were then mainly the farmers of the neighborhood, its tuition fees were largely paid in produce, which Father Byrne partly converted into money and partly exchanged for labor, and by this means soon paid for the farm, and by 1825 had erected a modest new building at a cost of $4,000.

Unfortunately just as this structure was nearing completion, and while Father Byrne was in Louisville completing arrangements for that

[1] Allen's History of Kentucky, p. 173.

purpose, it was burned, but was reerected within a few months under the personal supervision and partly by the labor of its founder. The school was peculiarly unfortunate in this respect, as hardly had the debt incurred by the first fire been paid and the wing of an additional building nearly completed when it, too, was destroyed by fire; but—

> Nothing daunted, Father Byrne rebuilt the burnt edifice on an enlarged plan, and in a few years was able by patient industry and rigid economy to pay all its debts and to place the institution on a firm and enduring foundation.[1]

That he was able to do this entirely from tuition fees at the very moderate rate of $6 per session is a high tribute to his financial management and to the popularity of the seminary. This popularity was due largely to its cheap tuition, its good discipline, and excellent teaching. There were early in its history 120 students in its classes and its numbers during Father Byrne's administration are said to have been all that its limited quarters could accommodate, and students had to apply a whole year in advance in order to secure admission. During the first twelve years of its existence it educated, either completely or partially, at least 1,200 youths, among whom may especially be mentioned Martin J. Spalding, subsequently archbishop of Baltimore, who was its professor of mathematics at 14 years of age, two years before his graduation, and was famous for his solution of difficult mathematical problems.

Never was an institution, for the same length of time, more completely the work of one man, as Father Byrne was not only its financial stay, but he was much more.

> He formed himself the teachers who were to aid him in carrying on the work of the college. He originated everything. He was president, chief disciplinarian, principal professor, procurator, missionary, everything at the same time.[2]

He was greatly assisted in the work of instruction by the advanced students, who in their turn became teachers.

The spirit in which all his efforts had been put forth is well shown by the fact that when negotiations were begun in 1830 looking toward the transfer of the institution to the control of the order of Jesuits he cheerfully acceded to their assuming possession, because he saw that other colleges were beginning to offer superior advantages and he considered the Jesuits, by reason of their greater resources and higher scholarship, better calculated than he to conduct the seminary successfully. These negotiations were completed in the latter part of 1831,[3] but, by request, Father Byrne remained at the head of the school, Fathers Gilles, Lagouais, and McGuire being associated with him in 1832 in its management. Father Byrne died of cholera in 1833, and then the Jesuits took exclusive control of the institution.

---

[1] Spalding's Early Catholic Missions, p. 267.

[2] Spalding's Life and Times of Bishop Flaget, p. 300.

[3] This date is usually given as 1832, but extracts from the private papers of the Jesuits, furnished by President Fehrenbach, show it to have been 1831.

The seminary was opened under their supervision in September, 1833, and had as its new president Rev. Peter Chazelle, S. J., who was a native of France, and a man of great energy and perseverance. The institution was then regularly organized as a college and President Chazelle was assisted by a faculty composed of Fathers Nicholas Petit, Thomas Legouais, Vital Gilles, Simon Fouche, and Evremond Harrissart, all Frenchmen and men of high literary education and pronounced ability. Under the new order of things pupils came in from all directions, and the prospects for the future were bright, but the session of 1833-34 was hardly well begun before the fire fiend descended upon the institution for the third time and sent many of the students to their homes by destroying the main building. This was, however, restored within a single month, and not long afterwards, from the revenue arising from increased patronage, another wing was added.

In 1836 the faculty of the institution was much strengthened by the addition of Fathers William G. Murphy and Nicholas Point, who came over from the provincial headquarters of the order at Lyons, France, having been sent for by President Chazelle. Father Murphy was at first the college professor of English literature, and was noted for his accomplishments in that department. On January 21, 1837,[1] mainly through his influence and that of Rev. Robert Abel, a charter for the institution was obtained from the State legislature which conferred upon it all of the usual collegiate powers and privileges. In this year also the faculty was further enlarged by the arrival of Fathers Augustus Thebaud and Peter Lebreton.

In 1839 Father Murphy succeeded Father Chazelle as president of the college, and Father William Larkin, a man of great natural gifts and of profound and varied learning, joined the corps of professors. Father Murphy continued at the head of the institution during the remainder of the period of Jesuit control, which extended to 1846. During this period the prosperity of the college was uninterrupted. It not only continued to flourish, but soon grew in such a way that its patronage was only restricted by the limited capacity of its buildings, which, being situated in the country, had to furnish boarding, as well as educational accommodations.

Students during this era came from all parts of the United States, the West Indies, Mexico, and even South America. In 1836 and for several years later the reputation of the fathers attracted students from many of the most influential families of Kentucky and the surrounding States, most of whom were Protestants, that element largely predominating at this time in the history of the institution. In addition to those already mentioned as having come over from France to join the faculty, Fathers De Luynes and Gockeln came out later, so that in 1842 the teaching body of the institution was a very able one.

One feature of the history of the college during this period is that, according to a rule established by Father Byrne and continued during

[1] Collins's History of Kentucky, Vol. I, p. 41.

the Jesuit era, every student was required to work on the college farm for one day a week. This farm, which was an important adjunct to the institution in the way of furnishing food products and additional revenue, had been enlarged, in 1838, by the purchase of an adjoining estate so as to accommodate the increased number of students. The authorities seem to have been quite successful in getting the students to cheerfully comply with this regulation, as well as to perform such other tasks as looking after the tallow candles, with which, at that time, the college study-hall was lighted.

The commencement exercises of this era were attractive events for the surrounding country. Original dramas, written by Father Chazelle, or some other member of the faculty, were usually performed, and in order to accommodate the visitors the exercises were usually held in the open air, a suitable spot having been chosen in the primeval forest, where a stage, adorned with drapery and appropriate scenery, was erected on the rising slope, in front of which temporary seats, covering a whole acre or more of ground, were arranged for the vast audience. In 1846, owing to some misunderstanding with the local diocesan authorities, the Jesuits left St. Mary's for what they considered wider fields of usefulness at St. John's College, Fordham, N. Y., their departure being widely regretted by the friends of St. Mary's.

Before this time every State in the South and West had become represented in the catalogue of that college, and she had sent out a number of alumni, scattered all over that region especially. Many of these have since risen to prominence in various professions and callings in life, among them being governors, Congressmen, circuit judges, writers of merit, and others of reputation in other fields.

When the Jesuits left St. Mary's, in 1846, the institution was again turned over to the secular clergy, under the supervision of the bishop of the diocese. We are informed[1] that at that time its buildings were extensive and handsome and its library contained 5,000 volumes, while its faculty numbered 8 instructors and its enrollment was 125 students. The secular clergy took charge in 1847, and under their management the college was successful and useful for twenty-two years.

The following is the list of the presidents of the institution from 1847 to 1869, with their terms of office: Rev. Julian Delaune, 1847–1849; Rev. John McGuire, 1849–1851; Rev. John B. Hutchins, 1851–1853; Rev. Francis Lawler, 1853–1856;[2] Rev. P. J. Lavialle, 1856–1865; Rev. A. Viala, 1865–1869. The following is a similar list for the same period of the vice-presidents of the institution, who had a considerable share in its management: Rev. Francis Lawler, 1849–1853; Rev. Michael Coghlan, 1853–1855; Rev. Edmund Driscoll, 1855–56;

[1] Collins's Sketches of Kentucky, p. 426.

[2] Father Hutchins was again president in the latter part of 1855–56, when he took the place of Father Lawler.

Rev. Joseph H. Elder, 1856–57;[1] Rev. A. Viala, 1857–1865; Rev. T. J. Disney, 1865–1869.

Of the presidential administrations of this era, that of President Hutchins is especially noteworthy, because the college was under him again put on a sound financial footing. Among the alumni of this period, at least one rose to the dignity of a bishop in his church, and others obtained repute in other vocations. In 1869, on account of financial embarrassment it was found necessary to close the time-honored institution for two years; during this period its lands were leased to a farmer of the neighborhood.

This gloom in the history of the college was, however, soon dispelled and a new era for it began when, in September, 1871, upon the invitation of the Right Rev. William G. McClosky, bishop of Louisville, it was reopened by a new and vigorous teaching order, the Fathers of the Resurrection,[2] under the leadership of Rev. Louis Elena, C. R., D. D. Father Elena was assisted by a select corps of lay, secular, and religous officers, and remained at the head of the institution until 1873, during which time repairs and improvements were made on the buildings and grounds, and all the former rights and privileges of the institution were confirmed under the new order of things by an amendment to the charter, secured in 1872.

In 1873, one of the most successful presidents in the history of the college came into office in the person of Rev. David Fennessy, C. R., who held the position continuously for twenty-four years, with the exception of a period of two years. Under his management the standard of discipline and scholarship was raised and his well-chosen corps of professors, together with his own prestige as a scholar and educator soon attracted patronage and gained the confidence of the people of Kentucky especially.

The history of the college during and since his administration has been one of substantial improvement and expansion. The course of instruction was developed until, in 1879, it included a classical course of five years in length, together with a scientific course of four years and a commercial course of three years, in addition to a preparatory department. In 1882 a military department was added, with a regular professor of military tactics, and in 1883 a professor of music was attached to the faculty. There had been up to this time, since 1873, an average matriculation of about 100 students, and the number of teachers and other officers connected with the institution had been about 13 each year.

In 1884 a fine new building was completed, which furnished much better and larger accommodations for students, whose numbers have since increased considerably. In order to put the institution on a solid

[1] Father Elder only held the office for a part of the year 1856–57, being succeeded early in 1857 by Father Viala.

[2] This is a religious order of the Catholic Church one of whose chief objects is the imparting of education, intellectual and moral.

financial basis and to insure its incorporation into his order, Father Fennessy succeeded in obtaining from the Bishop of Louisville a deed in fee simple to the college property, the management of which was vested in a corporation of his own choosing, composed of five self-perpetuating trustees; he also secured the recognition of St. Mary's as the official Catholic college of the diocese. This was accomplished in August, 1890, when, by the action of the Bishop, St. Joseph's College, at Bardstown, was closed for a period of twenty years in order that St. Mary's might have the proper opportunity for its development, as these colleges were so situated as necessarily to draw their students largely from the same limited field, by which each was thus hindering the progress of the other.

In connection with the new arrangement, the curriculum of St. Mary's was strengthened, the classical course being made six years in length, and otherwise enlarged. Additions were also made to the library and scientific apparatus, and other steps taken to make the institution rank with the first Catholic colleges of the land. In conducting its educational work its corps of teachers and officers are selected by its president, who is in turn appointed by the superior-general of the teaching order which controls the institution.

In 1893 other improvements were made in the college property, all of its buildings being renovated and their interior equipped with modern appliances, while an additional mansard story was placed upon each of the three main buildings. In the fall of this year an adjoining farm was also purchased and added to the college farm, which now contains about 450 acres of first-rate land. By a recent decision[1] of the supreme court of the State this and all the other property of the college, without limit, is exempted from taxation. In 1893 Father Fennessy retired from his office on account of bad health, and Rev. John L. Steffan, C. R., D. D., Ph. D., became president. In the fall of 1895, however, Father Fennessy recovered his health and again resumed his position at the head of the institution, where he remained for about two years longer, resigning finally in July, 1897.

From 1871 to 1897 the following were vice-presidents of the college for the terms indicated by the appended dates: Rev. D. Fennessy, C. R., D. D., 1871-1873; Rev. R. De Carolis, C. R., 1873-1879; Rev. A. Vaghi, C. R., 1879-80; Rev. V. T. Lanciotti, C. R., 1880-1886; Rev. John Fehrenbach, C. R., D. D., Ph. D., 1886-1897.

When Father Fennessy retired from the presidency in 1897, Father Fehrenbach became his successor. At the same time Rev. John Koskinski, C. R., became vice-president.

Father Fehrenbach was born in Berlin, Ontario, in 1857 and graduated at St. Jerome College in that place. He subsequently received the degrees of Ph. D. and D. D. from the Roman University, Rome,

[1] Case of the Commonwealth of Kentucky *v.* Loretto Literary and Benevolent Institution, and Same *v.* St. Mary's College.

Italy. He had been vice-president of the college since 1886, and being a man of great practical ability and business tact had ably assisted the successful efforts of President Fennessy to build up the institution and put it on a higher and more enduring basis.

There is therefore good reason to believe that the prosperity of the college will not only continue but enlarge under his administration as president. In fact some progressive steps have already been taken. In the summer of 1897 a frame gymnasium was erected on the college campus, and in November of that year a collection of mineralogical specimens and Indian relics numbering several hundred was purchased for the institution. In that year also, in order to suit the depressed financial condition of the country and bring the benefits of the institution within the reach of as many as possible, the prices of board and tuition were very materially reduced.

The college has no endowment, but depends for its support and its progress in material equipment entirely upon tuition fees. That it has been able from this source, in the last few years, to not only maintain itself but to expand considerably is an evidence of its success. Situated as it is, its chances for future growth may not be very flattering, owing to the depressed condition of the agricultural classes of the South, from which its patronage is mainly drawn, but it is probable that it will more than hold its own under its present management. The property of the college is at present estimated to be worth about $65,000, and its library contains about 5,000 volumes. Its matriculation as regards distribution is largely confined to the South. In the last twenty-four years there have been one or two classical graduates and five or six commercial graduates each year. The whole number of graduates during this period is 151, of whom 26 have taken the degree of A. B. and 12 that of B. S. A number of these have taken prominent positions in political, legal, medical, business, and clerical circles.

The curriculum of the institution as at present arranged embraces three courses of study: The commercial, extending over three years, and including, besides instruction in bookkeeping and kindred subjects, the elements of a good English education, in which only a certificate is granted; the scientific or mathematical, which includes additional instruction in English, mathematics, and the natural sciences, extends over four years, and leads to the degree of B. S.; the classical, in which the classics, English, philosophy, and modern languages are the principal features, which extends over six years and leads to the degree of A. B. The degree of A. M. is conferred upon Bachelors of Arts who study an additional year at the college or attain recognized standing in one of the higher professions. There is also a preparatory department and there are besides supplementary studies in the fine arts, elocution, military drill, and gymnastics.

The faculty of the institution is composed of men who have made the education of youth their life work, this being the principal object of the order to which they belong. As at present constituted its members are as follows: Rev. John Fehrenbach, C. R., Ph. D., D. D., mental philosophy, modern languages; Rev. John Koskinski, C. R., classics, elocution, algebra; Rev. Michael Jaglowitz, C. R., classics, history; Rev. E. M. Crane, A. M., higher English, history, classics; T. A. Schalder, A. M., natural sciences, mathematics; J. M. Cooney, A. M., English, mathematics, bookkeeping. There are also assistant teachers in bookkeeping and shorthand, in music and drawing, in penmanship, and in United States history and geography. Rev. Michael Jaglowitz, besides being one of the professors, also holds the position of disciplinarian, an officer with important functions.

BIBLIOGRAPHY.

Collins's Sketches, Collins's and Perrin, Battle and Kniffen's histories; Henderson's Centennial Exhibit; Spalding's Early Missions.

A History of Kentucky, by William B. Allen, Louisville, 1872.

Sketches of the Life, Times, and Character of Bishop Flaget, by Right Rev. M. J. Spalding, Louisville, 1852.

The Life of Rev. Charles Nerinckx, by Rev. C. P. Maes; Cincinnati, 1880.

A Centenary of Catholicity in America, by B. J. Webb; Louisville, 1884.

Extracts from the Jesuits' Private Papers, furnished by President Fehrenbach.

THE HISTORY OF GEORGETOWN COLLEGE, OF GEORGETOWN, KY.

By J. WILLIAM BLACK, Ph. D.[1]

EARLY HISTORY.

Georgetown College is located in Georgetown, Ky., which is on the northern rim of the famous "Blue-grass" region. It is a convenient and delightful location for the college. The climate is good, the country fertile and beautiful, the railroad facilities excellent, the town convenient to large centers, being only 12 miles north of Lexington and about 50 miles south of Cincinnati. The social environment of the college student is all that could be desired.

THE TOWN.

The town itself, though it has not grown to large size, is an old and historic one, and bears the proud title, "Belle of the Blue Grass." It is said to be the site of the first permanent settlement north of the Kentucky River, for as early as November, 1775, one John McClelland and a few pioneers came down the Ohio River from Pittsburg, wandered about in northeastern Kentucky, and finally located here. The attraction was a big spring, near which the first cabin was erected, and which received the name of the "Royal Spring." This spring, since called "Big Spring," is one of the features of the town to this day. In 1790, by act of the legislature of Virginia, the name of "Georgetown," in honor of the first President, was given to the settlement which had grown up about this spot.

[1] Professor of history and political economy, Colby College; formerly professor of history and political science *pro tempore* (1891-92) in Georgetown College, Kentucky.

LIBRARY
OF THE
UNIVERSITY
OF
CALIFORNIA

THE COLLEGE.

The founding of the college dates from January 15, 1829. It was the first collegiate institution of the Baptists south and west of the Alleghanies to receive a charter, and the fifth in order among the Baptist colleges established in the United States. In this new and sparsely settled country there was much pioneer work to be done by this institution and its sister colleges of the South and West, many of which were founded during this era of westward expansion.

The college was incorporated by the legislature of Kentucky under the name of the Kentucky Baptist Education Society. The charter in its original form, including also the names of the first board of trustees, is as follows:

THE CHARTER OF THE KENTUCKY BAPTIST EDUCATION SOCIETY, GRANTED JANUARY, 1829.

AN ACT to incorporate the trustees of the Kentucky Baptist Education Society.

Be it enacted by the general assembly of the Commonwealth of Kentucky, That Alva Woods, Silas M. Noel, Jeremiah Vardeman, John Bryce, David Thurman, Gabriel Slaughter, Joel Scott, Peter Mason, Thomas P. Dudley, Peter C. Buck, Jephthah Dudley, Benjamin Tyler, George W. Nichols, Gurdon Gates, Ryland T. Dillard, Benjamin Davis, William Johnson, Samuel M'Kay, Thomas Smith, C. Van Buskirk, James Ford, and Cyrus Wingate shall be, and are hereby, constituted a body politic and corporate, to be known and designated by the name and style of "The Trustees of the Kentucky Baptist Education Society," and by that name shall have perpetual succession and a common seal, with power to change and alter the same at pleasure; and, as a body corporate, shall be authorized to exercise all the powers, privileges, and rights which are exercised by the trustees of any academy of learning in the State; but that the property of said corporation shall be subject to taxation, except the college buildings and five acres of ground around the same; and on the death, resignation, or other disqualification of any of the said trustees or their successors in office a majority of two-thirds of the trustees remaining in office may fill such vacancies, and the person or persons so appointed shall be vested with the same powers and privileges as those named in this act, and by the name and style and denomination of "The Trustees of the Kentucky Baptist Education Society" may sue and be sued, plead and be impleaded, defend and be defended, in any court of law and equity in this State.

SEC. 2. *Be it further enacted*, That it shall and may be lawful for the said trustees and their successors in office, and that are hereby invested with full power and authority in their corporate capacity, to purchase, or receive by donation, demise, or bequest any lands, tenements, hereditaments, monies, rents, goods, and chattels, and to hold the same, by the name aforesaid, to them and their successors forever for the use and benefit of said institution, and according to the intention of the donor or donors of any such lands, tenements, hereditaments, monies, rents, goods, and chattels, and not otherwise, and to sell, transfer, and convey the same, under the seal of said corporation, unless prohibited by the terms of any such donation.

SEC. 3. *Be it further enacted*, That it shall and may be lawful for the trustees aforesaid, and their successors in office, to appoint, out of their own body, a chairman or president,[1] and a majority of the trustees shall at all times constitute a quorum to do business and may make such by-laws, rules, and ordinances necessary for the proper government of said institution as shall not be repugnant to the Constitution and laws of the United States or laws of this State. The said president and trustees shall also have power at all times to select and appoint such officers, teachers, tutors, and professors for the management of said institution as they may think necessary, to fix their salaries and prescribe their duties, to fix and prescribe the terms upon which students may be admitted into said institution, and for any misconduct in any officer, teacher, or professor to dismiss such person from office and appoint another or others in their stead.

SEC. 4. The said president and trustees shall keep a record of their proceedings in a book or books, to be provided for that purpose, and may, if they deem it neces-

[1] The Rev. Silas M. Noel was chosen first president of the board of trustees.

sary, appoint a clerk to record their proceedings and prescribe his duties. It shall be the duty of the said president and trustees, and their successors, to have recorded in the office of the county court of the county where the said institution may be located the names of the trustees thereof hereby appointed and the names of such as shall hereafter be appointed in their stead.

SEC. 5. *Be it enacted*, That within 60 days from the passage of this act the trustees aforesaid shall meet in Lexington and enter upon the duties assigned them by this act, not less than a majority of two-thirds being competent thereto: *Provided, however*, That the real and personal estate acquired by the said corporation shall at no one time exceed the yearly rent or value of 50,000 dollars.

SEC. 6. *Be it enacted*, That full power is reserved to the general assembly to repeal or modify the privileges hereby granted.[1]

In December 22, 1798, the Rittenhouse Academy was founded in Georgetown, and endowed by the State with 6,000 acres of the public lands of Kentucky. A building was erected on the site of the present academy of Georgetown College, which occupies a spot 50 yards to the west of Recitation Hall. In 1829, when the college was organizing, the trustees of Rittenhouse Academy, by the authority of the legislature of the Commonwealth, transferred all the property of the academy, real and personal, to the trustees of the Kentucky Baptist Education Society for the benefit of Georgetown College.

At the same time Issachar Pawling, a man not of great wealth but of generous impulses, a good Baptist and a friend of higher education, gave the founding of the college a great impetus by placing at the disposal of the newly created board of trustees a fund of $20,000. Pawling deserves much of the credit that attaches to his memory as the real founder of the college at Georgetown, and the trustees have fittingly recognized their obligation to this noble benefactor by naming one of their largest buildings Pawling Hall.

To this endowment fund of Pawling's there was added immediately a contribution of $6,000 from the citizens of Georgetown, which had been subscribed by them for the purpose of securing the location of the college in their midst.

On September 2, 1829, Rev. William Staughton, D. D., of Columbian College, Washington D. C., was chosen the first president of Georgetown College, but unfortunately he died suddenly on December 12, 1829, while in the midst of preparations to proceed to his new field of labor. After this misfortune the trustees met with some difficulty in their efforts to find a suitable man for the newly created institution.

Stephen Chaplin, D. D., likewise of Washington, was next called to the presidency in January, 1830, but he declined. The third choice then fell upon Irah Chase, D. D., president of the Newton Theological Institute, Massachusetts. President Chase went to Georgetown, looked over the field, and declined the call. The fourth effort of the trustees proved successful, and on June 21, 1830, Dr. Joel S. Bacon, of Newton

[1] By an act of the Kentucky legislature dated January 23, 1840, the number of trustees was reduced to thirteen, with the further provision that a majority of this number should constitute a quorum. By a later act (January 28, 1841) this first proviso was repealed, the number of trustees was increased to twenty-four, and the quorum for business was fixed at eight.

Center, Mass., was elected president. He had previously been chosen professor of languages, May 4, 1830, and had accompanied Dr. Chase to Georgetown to assume his new duties.

When Dr. Chase decided to decline the call to the presidency, he strongly recommended Bacon, and the trustees acted favorably upon his advice. Thus President Bacon, the fourth to be chosen, was the first to enter actively upon the duties of the presidency of Georgetown College.

Meanwhile, however, the college had begun without a head, for in accordance with a resolution of the board the doors had been opened and instruction begun on January 11, 1830, the faculty at the opening consisting of but two officers, a principal of the preparatory department and a professor of mathematics.

Charles O'Harra was the first principal of the preparatory department and the instructor of the 43 pupils who entered at the opening. In the college a mathematical class was formed with 15 students, and, under the instruction of Thornton F. Johnson, of Virgina, the professor of mathematics, and the first member of the college faculty chosen by the board of trustees. Indeed, the intention of the board was to create manifold duties for the first college officer, if we are to judge by the full title of his chair, which reads: "Professor of mathematics, natural and experimental philosophy, and the French language."

A professor of languages—presumably the classical languages—a Mr. Ruggles, of Columbian College, Washington, was also invited to Georgetown, but he declined. Joel S. Bacon was then chosen to the chair, and later was elected president, as already explained. The salary of the members of the faculty was fixed at $800 each; the salary of the president at $1,500, and the latter's chair was to be known as the "Pawling Chair,"[1] in honor of the first benefactor of the college.

The college plant at the opening consisted of one small unpretentious structure, the former Rittenhouse Academy building; lots, valued at $6,000, for a campus—the gift of Georgetown citizens—and the $20,000 endowment fund contributed by Pawling.

The college year was divided into two sessions irrespective of vacations, which were somewhat irregular at first, one continuing from March 20 to September 20, the other from September 20 to March 20. It was also further provided that during the first or summer term the hours of study should be from 8 to 12 a.m. and from 2 to 6 p.m., and in the latter from 8 to 12 a.m. and from 1 to 4 p.m., and a curious regulation required the professors and tutors to remain in their lecture rooms during these hours, and prohibited the student from leaving the college inclosure without the permission of his professor. Tuition fees in the college department were fixed at $25 per annum; in the preparatory department at from $12 to $20, according to the studies taken.

[1] The title of the president's chair was changed at a later time, as noted elsewhere, and it is now known as the "R. M. Dudley Memorial Chair."

The purpose of the college, as stated in its prospectus, was "to impart the lights of education to pious indigent applicants of the Baptist order who are desirous of embarking in the ministry." Pawling had made his donation to the college with the proviso that it be used for the support and education of indigent young ministerial students. He was now persuaded to incorporate the gift unconditionally with the general funds of the college, in return for which the trustees offered to grant free tuition to young men studying for the ministry. The policy then agreed upon has prevailed to this day, and free tuition has always been granted this class of students.

The college closed its first session June 11, 1830, to open again July 26, 1830. On the latter day Rev. Joel S. Bacon, the first active president of the college, delivered his inaugural address in the Methodist Church in Georgetown. The number of students was now about 60, equally divided between the college and the academy. A library of 500 volumes had been added, and a small assortment of maps, charts, globes, physical and chemical apparatus.

Several new appointments on the staff of the college faculty were now made, and at the opening of the next spring session, April 18, 1831, the faculty had its full complement for the first time. It was as follows: Rev. Joel Smith Bacon, A. M., president; Rev. N. N. Whiting, A. M., professor of languages;[1] Thornton F. Johnson, esq., professor of mathematics, etc.; Samuel D. Hatch, M. D., professor of chemistry; Mr. F. E. Frebuchet, of France, professor of French language; William Craig, A. M., tutor in the college proper; William F. Nelson, A. B., principal of preparatory department (the academy).

The college was by this time fairly well organized and the work proceeded with more system. Two courses were provided—a full college course of eight sessions, which would correspond approximately to the modern four-year classical course, was offered, and the degree of bachelor of arts conferred upon those completing it; besides this an English course of six sessions (three years) was also offered and an English diploma conferred upon those completing the latter course.

Provision was also made for the granting of certificates of scholarship to those who desired them for work done in any department.

Three recitations were given daily for five days in the week and one recitation on Saturday. Speaking and composition were required weekly and examinations were held in all studies at the close of each session, and all candidates for degrees or diplomas were required to take the same bill of fare in their respective courses. Two breaks or vacations in the college year were now provided, one beginning the first Monday in March and continuing six weeks; the other beginning on the third Thursday in September and continuing until the third Monday in October. The third Wednesday in September was com-

[1] Resigned shortly after his appointment and was succeeded by George W. Eaton, A. M.

mencement day. Tuition fees continued the same. The estimated annual expenses of the student for board, washing, lodging, fuel, and lights were $75, making the total average expenditure for the college year $100. For the preparatory students the charges were slightly less, the tuition for those taking classical studies being $20 a year; for those taking an English course, $15. There was also an additional charge of $1 for fuel used in the winter season.

Dr. Bacon remained president of the college about two years. Lack of funds and controversies over the management of the property made his administration a trying one, and he felt obliged to retire from the presidency. From 1832 until 1836 the college was without a head, being managed as a private institution under the leadership of the professor of mathematics, Thornton F. Johnson. In the latter year the Rev. B. F. Farnsworth was chosen president and held the office for a few months. He made an earnest though unsuccessful attempt to place the institution on a sound financial basis and resigned the same year (1836).

In October, 1838, Rev. Rockwood Giddings, D. D., of Shelbyville, Ky., became president. His term was limited to one year, his death occurring October 29, 1839, but it was long enough to demonstrate that he was the most successful administrator that had yet presided over the affairs of the college. Dr. Giddings was very active during his short administration. Though he never entered upon the work of the class room, he performed a more important service to the college in securing harmony among the trustees in the management of the institution. He also made a strenuous and successful effort to increase the endowment fund, and secured subscriptions amounting to about $100,000, a large portion of which, however, was not paid in, owing to the subsequent financial distress which affected the whole country and prevented many of the friends of the college from meeting their pledges. Furthermore, through the aggressive efforts of President Giddings, the main college building, which still occupies the center of the campus and is now known as "Recitation Hall," was begun and completed from the Giddings endowment. This was the first college building erected by the trustees of the Kentucky Baptist Education Society, the college exercises having been conducted hitherto in the old Rittenhouse Academy building and in rented quarters.

After an interval of a few months Dr. Howard Malcolm became the successor of Dr. Giddings. The choice was a fortunate one for two reasons—in the first, he had the qualifications necessary to carry forward the movements so auspiciously begun by his predecessor, and, secondly, he remained in the office long enough—a period of ten years—to leave upon it the impress of his personality and to secure an efficient organization of the work, the general lines of which have remained to this day. Dr. Malcolm's service rounded out the second decade of the history of the college. In 1850, the year of the great compromise on slavery, Dr. Malcolm retired from the presidency, impelled largely by the arising of political conditions about him with which he was not in full sympathy, and was succeeded by the Rev. Dr. J. L. Reynolds, of South Carolina. At the end of two years Dr. Reynolds retired for domestic reasons and gave place to the Rev. Dr. Duncan R. Campbell.

During President Reynolds's administration an important change was made in the charter of the college. By act of November 25, 1851, it was "enacted that each individual who since January 1, 1840, has donated to the Kentucky Baptist Education Society $100, or shall do so in the future, shall be and are hereby constituted a body politic and corporate, to be known and designated by the name and style of the Kentucky Baptist Education Society, and by that name shall have perpetual succession, and a common seal, with power to change and alter said seal at pleasure." Power was also given to this body "to carry out" such measures as would promote the interests of Georgetown College and the cause of college education.

It was further provided also that business meetings of this new corporation should be held annually in Georgetown during commencement week; that 25 members of the society should constitute a quorum for business at the annual meetings, 20 sufficing for called meetings during the interval between commencements; that this corporation should make such by-laws, rules, etc., and elect such officers as were necessary to carry into effect the provisions of the act; and further provided also that the society should have the sole power to appoint trustees of the Kentucky Baptist Education Society, and that henceforth the following method of choosing the trustees should prevail: "They" (the members of the society) "shall, at the first annual meeting, choose all the trustees aforesaid, dividing as equally as practicable the whole number into four classes, one of which classes shall be appointed for a term of one year, another for two years, a third for three years, and a fourth for four years. At each subsequent annual meeting said corporation shall nominate, etc., for a term of four years persons to fill vacancies of class whose term of office shall expire, etc., at said meetings, or fill vacancies in any class for unexpired terms. If said corporation fail to fill vacancies, then the trustees of Kentucky Baptist Education Society are empowered to fill vacancies by a two-thirds vote." The trustees were to report the condition of the college at the annual meetings of the society.[1]

This act of 1851 changed fundamentally the governing machinery of the college, for instead of a close corporation of 24 trustees, a permanent and self-perpetuating body, there is substituted in its stead the Kentucky Baptist Education Society, which is now more than a mere corporate title, and which becomes an active and growing body of

[1] A few changes were made in this act by a subsequent act of January 10, 1863, but these changes were repealed in a repealing act of January 19, 1866, thus leaving the act of 1851 intact and in force to-day as the constitution for the government of the college.

friends of the college, who are entitled to membership in return for a gift of $100 or more to the endowment of Georgetown College. This body selects the trustees, who in turn select the president and faculty and manage the general business affairs of the institution. Conversely, also, the trustees are responsible to the Kentucky Baptist Education Society. It is expected that at least three-fourths of the trustees shall be active members of regular Baptist churches. Such a method of incorporation and organization as the foregoing is unique, and it has the advantage of attracting support to the college and of giving all who have contributed to its existence and maintenance a share in its direction.

President Campbell entered upon the duties of his office in 1853, and the year and event were highly auspicious for the fortunes of the college, for the new president proved to be one of the most energetic, tactful, and efficient executives Georgetown ever had.

He saw at once the imperative need of an enlarged endowment fund and set himself without delay to the task. Of the "Giddings Fund," less than half of which had been collected, only $10,000 remained, the rest having been absorbed in the completion of the main college building and the enlargement of the campus. The result of President Campbell's laborious efforts was a subscription list of $100,000 for the endowment of the college. Of this amount one-half was collected and invested by the trustees. The rest, carried along for a number of years in the form of personal bonds and pledges,[1] was swallowed up in the civil war, which carried down with it many a Southern institution and brought financial ruin to many a home. Misfortune thus rendered many donors unable to meet their obligations, and the college was obliged to cancel them.

Notwithstanding these severe losses, however, Georgetown College was more fortunate in its investments than many of its contemporaries, and there is abundant evidence of the good management of its affairs in the fact that of the $50,000 of the Campbell fund which had been collected and invested, scarcely any portion of this amount was impaired by the war. This fund was the chief bulwark and support of the college during the trying period following the civil war.

Dr. Campbell died suddenly in 1865, and was succeeded by the Rev. Nathaniel Macon Crawford, who resigned in 1871, owing to ill health, and who, in turn, was followed in September of that year by the Rev. Basil Manly, jr. D. D. Dr. Manly was a native of Alabama, a graduate of the University of Alabama in 1843 and of Princeton Theological Seminary in 1847. He was called to the presidency of Georgetown from his chair in the Southern Baptist Theological Seminary of Louisville, which he had occupied since the foundation of the latter institu-

[1] Many subscribers were permitted to retain the principal, provided they paid the annual interest on the amounts of their subscriptions. This proved an unfortunate arrangement for the college, as in many instances the financial failures of donors caused heavy losses of both interest and principal.

tion. President Manly continued in the office of president until 1879, when he resigned to accept again his old professorship in the Southern Baptist Theological Seminary at Louisville. The faculty numbered eight in the time of Dr. Manly.[1]

During these last two administrations no general efforts were made to increase the endowment of the college, owing to the danger of conflict with efforts that were being made to raise a fund of $300,000 for the Southern Baptist Theological Seminary at Louisville. After the civil war there was a marked falling off in the number of students in attendance at the college, and this decline was attributed by President Manly to several causes; first, the inpoverishment of many families by the war prevented them from giving their sons a collegiate education; secondly, because of the narrowing of the field of the college, which had formerly extended to the Gulf and beyond the Mississippi River in view of the appearance of new rivals in the field, like the new Baptist institution, Bethel College at Russellville, in Western Kentucky, and the efforts of many Southern States in restoring and extending the efficiency of their colleges and schools through public as well as private beneficence.

One or two efforts to supply needs of the college are worthy of note. One of these was the attempt to endow a professorship to be known as the "Student's chair," and toward which some $8,000 was collected through the zeal of Prof. J. J. Rucker, assisted by some of the alumni;[2] and the other, the enlargement of the students dormitory, Pawling Hall, by the erection of a large wing forming a new front to the old building. This improvement was completed in 1879. It involved an expense of $7,000, the amount being raised by President Manly in cooperation with Mrs. James F. Robinson and Mrs. D. Thomas, of Georgetown.

Rev. Richard M. Dudley, D. D., was the successor of Manly. Dr. Dudley was born in Madison County, Ky., September 1, 1838, and was descended from a line of Kentucky preachers. He graduated from Georgetown College in 1860. He then entered the Baptist ministry, and in 1880 was elected president of his alma mater, being the first alumnus to attain that distinction. He remained president until his death, January 5, 1893, a period of thirteen years, and bears the distinction of having served a longer term than any other president of the college; but his fame rests upon a more substantial foundation than this. The college now entered upon a new era. The endowment fund[3]

---

[1] Basil Manly, jr. D. D., president and professor of English literature; Danford Thomas, A. M., Greek; J. E. Farnam, LL. D., physical science; J. J. Rucker, A. M., mathematics; J. N. Bradley, A. M., Latin; R. M. Dudley, D. D., history and modern languages (1872-76); Rev. H. McDonald, D. D., professor of systematic and pastoral theology [The Western Baptist Theological Institute Foundation]; L. V. Ware, A. M., principal of the academy.

[2] For a further account of this effort and its success, see page 151.

[3] An account of this fund, together with the purposes for which the different foundations were intended, will be found elsewhere. (See pp. 149-152.)

was tripled, new professorships were created, new courses were added to the curriculum, the number of students increased, and coeducation was adopted. The new buildings recently erected were the results of efforts inaugurated by him. Indeed President Dudley's connection with the college was so long and so recent that the college is to-day largely as he left it, and in the description of its present resources and activities, which follows this historical sketch, many of the traces of his handiwork may be seen. After the death of President Dudley in January, 1893, the next choice of the trustees fell upon the Rev. Augustus Cleveland Davidson, D. D., of Covington, Ky., a graduate of the college in the class of 1871. After a six years' service, President Davidson resigned (August, 1898), and Prof. Arthur Yager was chosen chairman of the faculty during the interregnum. Up to the present time (April, 1899), so far as the writer knows, the trustees have not yet selected a president, and the college is therefore temporarily without a head. The college has now completed seventy years of its existence, and during that interval has had eleven presidents, whose average length of term is something over six years.

ENDOWMENT.

At the close of President Manly's administration (1879) the property of the college consisted of real estate, estimated at $75,000, and invested funds of about $80,000.

During the term of Dr. Dudley, and through his untiring efforts, the endowment fund was largely increased until it amounted to $225,000. To this amount might also be added some $25,000 in notes and personal pledges, which remain as yet uncollected. Again, with the addition of some $65,000 or $70,000 which the college received during the administration of President Davidson, a portion of which represents the fulfillment of promises made to Dr. Dudley, the endowment fund now approximates the sum of $300,000.

The chief specific funds and bequests which were given to the college during the past twelve years, and which form a considerable part of the total endowment, together with the purposes for which they were designed, are as follows:

First. The McCalla-Galloway fund, consisting of a bequest, in 1888, of $15,000 by Maj. F. C. McCalla, and of about $13,600 by W. B. Galloway, esq., both of Scott County, and uncle and nephew. By a combination of the two bequests the trustees established a special professorship, calling it the "McCalla-Galloway professorship of natural sciences;" but in 1892 transferred this professorship to the chair of mathematics.

Second. The Bostwick fund. This is a fund of $25,000 in railroad bonds, with annual interest at 5 per cent, given in January, 1889, by Mr. J. A. Bostwick, of New York. This fund is "to be held by the college in perpetuity and the income to be used for current expenses, or as the board of trustees may annually direct." It was an original condition of this gift that the college should raise $100,000 from other sources, but Mr. Bostwick made his contribution before this condition was entirely fulfilled.

Third. The Macklin fund of $8,000, bequeathed by A. W. Macklin, of Franklin County, Ky. The interest is used to aid poor young men studying for the gospel ministry in obtaining a liberal education.

Fourth. The Newton memorial. Miss Mary J. Newton, of Daviess County, Ky., who died in December, 1892, made provision in her will for several bequests of property to Georgetown College. While the matter still remains unsettled, it is probable that these bequests will realize a sum in the neighborhood of $15,000. A portion of this amount, $5,000, is designated as a memorial to her father, Col. William Newton, and the income of the fund is to be used for the library of the college.

Fifth. The Pratt memorial. This memorial consists of an interest in an undivided property in Birmingham, Ala., of an estimated value of $5,000, which was conveyed to the trustees of the Kentucky Baptist Education Society by the late Rev. William M. Pratt, D. D., of Louisville, president of the board from 1886 to 1896. This property is to be sold and permanently invested, the principal to remain in perpetuity and the income only to be used for the benefit of the scientific apparatus of the college.

Sixth. The Western Theological Institute fund. This fund was acquired by Georgetown College in the following way: The Western Baptist Theological Institute was founded and located in Covington, Ky., in 1840. According to a provision of the charter, the trustees were chosen about equally from Ohio and Kentucky. The new institution was well under way by 1845, and enjoyed considerable prosperity until 1852. About this time disagreements among the trustees over the slavery question wrecked its fortunes, and in 1855, the Northern and Southern elements being irreconcilable, the board of trustees decided to sell the property of the institute, amounting to about $200,000, and divide the proceeds equally between the two sets of claimants.[1] The portion given to the South was transferred by the Kentucky trustees to Georgetown College and used at first for the maintenance of a professorship of theology in the college.

In 1877 the Southern Baptist Theological Seminary moved to Louisville from Greenville, S. C., and shortly after the idea of maintaining a theological foundation at Georgetown was abandoned and the proceeds of the fund were used for a number of years for the support of the

[1] Power was granted the trustees for this purpose in a special act of the Kentucky legislature, approved January 28, 1854. The act also further provided that a majority of the trustees residing south of the Ohio River should have the right to change the location of the Western Baptist Theological Institute from Covington to Georgetown.

president's chair. Though devoted to the exclusive use of Georgetown College, this fund was managed until June, 1891, by a separate board known as the trustees of the Western Theological Institute, a large proportion of whom were also trustees of the college. In that year the fund was formally transferred to the trustees of the Kentucky Baptist Educational Association and the former body ceased to exist. The fund received from the trustees of the Western Baptist Theological Institute, owing to a shrinkage in investments, now amounts to but $40,000.

Seventh. The fund of the Students' Association of Georgetown College, which now amounts to about $22,000. In 1874 Prof. J. J. Rucker started a fund to endow a chair of history and political science and to be known as the students' chair. An association was formed and incorporated by the Commonwealth of Kentucky under the title of The Students' Association of Georgetown College. It was essentially an alumni organization, and the proviso was made that anyone could become a member by subscribing to the capital stock of the association, which was fixed at $20 per share. The alumni subscribed generously until $15,000 in all were raised. This was accomplished by September 1, 1875. But the fund, being deemed insufficient for the purpose intended, was then allowed to accumulate at compound interest until it reached $22,000. In 1884 the trustees appointed Arthur Yager, Ph. D., a graduate of Georgetown College and of the Johns Hopkins University, professor of history and political science, and in 1885-86 the income of the fund of the students' association was used for the first time to pay the salary of the holder of the students' chair. This endowment fund is still managed separately by the students' association, which holds annual meetings during commencement week of each year.

Eighth. The college reading-room fund. President Dudley and his wife, before the death of the former, contributed $2,000 as a foundation for a reading room. The interest of this fund is expended for the maintenance of a file of current American and European periodicals.

Ninth. The Galloway scholarships, a gift of $4,400 (1888) in the will of William B. Galloway, of Scott County, Ky., a trustee of the college and one of the founders of the McCalla-Galloway professorship. This fund is used for the education of indigent students from Scott County, and out of the income five annual scholarships are provided. In case the number of applications for these scholarships exceeds five they are awarded as the result of competitive examinations to the five highest candidates.

Tenth. The Maria Atherton-Farnam chair of natural science. This foundation dates from 1893 and is due to the liberality of Mr. John M. Atherton, of Louisville, Ky., a wealthy and liberal alumnus of the college. The amount of Mr. Atherton's gift was $30,000, and it is a joint memorial created by him in memory of his wife and his father-in-law, the late Prof. J. E. Farnam, LL. D., who occupied this chair from 1839 to 1887. His successor and the present holder of the chair is Prof. John Foster Eastwood, Ph. D., a graduate of the University of Michigan.

Eleventh. The Dudley memorial fund, amounting to $25,000 ($5,000 of this amount being given also by Mr. John M. Atherton). This fund, the raising of which is now being completed, is a tribute from friends and alumni of the college to the memory of the late President Richard M. Dudley. The fund will serve as a partial endowment, at least, of the president's chair.

Besides the above-mentioned bequests, various other gifts of small sums have been made from time to time to the general endowment fund of the college. The proceeds are securely invested in the following securities: $100,000 in mortgage loans (yielding 7 per cent interest), $25,000 in railroad bonds, and the balance, for the most part, in bank stocks. These funds are exempted from all taxes in accordance with the provisions of the general statutes of the Commonwealth of Kentucky.

BUILDINGS, GROUNDS, AND EQUIPMENT.

The campus is situated on high ground in the south end of the town, and covers about 15 acres. Upon it are located the principal college buildings.

In the center of the group and fronting toward the north stands the main building, the first to be erected in the time of President Giddings (1839). It is a large structure built of brick, and the architectural effect is plain and heavy, the front being ornamented with six massive brick pillars surmounted by Ionic capitals, a type of architecture so frequently met with in the public buildings and private residences of the South.

This building until a few years ago contained the chapel, the library, and 5 class rooms, in which all of the college recitations were held. Since the erection of the new chapel and library building it has been devoted entirely to recitation purposes, and is now called Recitation Hall.

On the east end of the campus, and next in point of seniority, is Pawling Hall. This is one of the men's dormitories and has accommodations for 60 students. It is a T-shaped building, the rear or older portion having been built some thirty-five years ago, while the front or newer part was constructed in 1879 at a cost of $7,000. This improvement more than doubled the capacity of the old hall and made it architecturally much more attractive than formerly. The seminary building, within 200 yards of the campus and surrounded by 5 acres of recreation grounds, is also now used as a dormitory for men, and has a capacity of 75. The occupants of both halls are organized in clubs, with officers and a matron in each, who supervise the management of the halls. In this way prudence and economy are studied, as is seen in the statement that the average expense per student, including room rent, is not more

GEORGETOWN COLLEGE—RECITATION HALL (FACING NORTH).

than $9 per month. This is an exceedingly small outlay for the value received. Each student is expected to furnish his own room, and at the end of his college course is at liberty to dispose of his effects to the next occupant upon terms that are mutually agreeable.

The dormitory for the women is known as Rucker Hall, named by the trustees in honor of Prof. J. J. Rucker, LL. D., who for so many years presided over the Georgetown Female Seminary and successfully advocated the adoption of coeducation by the trustees of the college. This building was erected in 1895 at a cost of $30,000. It is commodious, having accommodations for 100 students, and is thoroughly modern in its appointments and comforts.

Unlike the men's dormitories, the rooms in Rucker Hall are all furnished and the rates are somewhat higher, the board and room rent being $160 per year. All young women in attendance upon the college and having homes away from Georgetown are expected to live at Rucker Hall. The hall is under the care of a matron and assistant.

The handsomest and most modern hall on the campus is the New College Building, erected in 1893, at a cost of $35,000, on a site close to and just east of Recitation Hall. It is constructed of brick, with stone base and trimmings, is nicely finished in its interior, with all modern conveniences, is well arranged for the purposes intended, and from the standpoint of architecture and utility is the gem of the campus. In this building are the chapel, library and Dudley reading room, gymnasium, museum, and the two men's literary societies, all of which have commodious and well-arranged quarters. The chapel has a seating capacity of 500 persons.

The library now numbers some 12,000 volumes. A large portion of this collection is made up of gifts of Baptist ministers and other friends of the college from time to time, and the library is well provided with treatises on theology. There is a file of the Baptist Chronicle and also partial files of several old Kentucky denominational and secular newspapers. For a long time there was no fund for the maintenance of the library, and in consequence it was entirely dependent for its growth on the benevolence of friends of the college. Quite recently this deficiency has been partially supplied, and the income of the Newton and Dudley funds, which is about $500 annually, is now used in the purchase of additions for the library and for the maintenance of a file of American and European periodicals in the R. M. Dudley reading room, which is a part of the library. The post of librarian is filled at present by the professor of history and political science, Dr. Arthur Yager, who also has an assistant librarian to aid him in the discharge of the clerical duties of the office.

The museum contains nearly 7,000 specimens, representing the different fields of mineralogy, geology, anthropology, and natural history, all of which have been contributed at various times by generous friends.

The college is also equipped in its laboratories with scientific apparatus valued at $2,000.

The gymnasium, which occupies a part of this building, has an area of 50 by 70 feet and a height of 26. The equipment is excellent. Twelve feet from the floor is a gallery and running track, and in the basement there are a swimming pool, baths, and 124 lockers. Regular exercise in the gymnasium is now required of all students. Within a few hundred yards of the gymnasium is the new athletic field and quarter-mile running track.

In the addition to the above buildings should be mentioned also the Academy Building, standing about 150 feet to the west of Recitation Hall, a small, severely plain brick building, in which is housed the preparatory department. This was the successor of the old Rittenhouse Academy Building, and was erected shortly after the building of Recitation Hall.

Opposite the south side of the campus is another lot of 5 acres belonging to the college, and upon which the trustees erected in 1890 a home for the president. This house is large, modern in type, and is built of brick. It cost $7,000, and was first occupied by the late Dr. R. M. Dudley.

COEDUCATION.

The history of coeducation at Georgetown College is closely connected with that of the Georgetown Female Seminary. As early as 1846 Professor Farnum, who came to Georgetown College with President Giddings in 1839, on grounds hard by the college campus, established a seminary for young ladies. This institution was conducted successfully by him until 1865, when fire destroyed the seminary building. The school was abandoned for a time, but in 1869 was reorganized, this time under the control of the governing body of the college—the trustees of the Kentucky Baptist Education Society. Prof. J. J. Rucker, of the chair of mathematics and physics in the college, became the principal of the seminary. A new building was erected, and for this and the 5 acres of recreation grounds surrounding the seminary the principal paid to the college an annual rental of $600.

On June 10, 1885, the trustees of the college passed a resolution providing for the admission of young ladies from the seminary to classes in the college, and providing further that the college work thus accomplished by them should be fully recognized in the degrees conferred upon them in the seminary by authority of the board. The board was carefully feeling its way, testing public opinion, and had no reason to be discouraged at the results of its experiment. Professor Rucker himself was an ardent champion of coeducation in the college, and frequently urged the trend of modern higher education in that direction. There was but one more step needed. This was taken April 12, 1892, when the board appointed a committee to consider the question of making "a new adjustment of the existing relations of the college and seminary." President Dudley was the chairman of this committee, and on June 7 following presented its report. The report was as follows:

Your committee would recommend that in government and instruction Georgetown Female Seminary be turned over to the faculty of Georgetown College, and that so far as they may be prepared for the college classes, the young ladies shall be admitted to these classes and be taught by the college professors.

We would recommend that upon all the young ladies who may complete a course of study leading up to any one of the degrees which the college confers, such degree shall be conferred, whether it be B. S., B. A., or M. A. Further, that to any young lady who may complete the studies a certificate of proficiency shall be given.

We would recommend that the boarding department of the Female Seminary, together with the departments of art and music, be left in the hands of Prof. J. J. Rucker for another year, and subject entirely to his control.

We would recommend that, not later than the 1st day of May, 1893, the president of the college, after consultation with the faculty, shall make a report to a called meeting of the trustees of the Kentucky Baptist Education Society of the practical working of this new plan of conducting the institutions jointly, and, if so recommended by the faculty of Georgetown College, the formal consolidation of the two institutions shall be promulged in the college catalogue of 1892–93, and the names of the young men and young ladies shall appear together as students of Georgetown College. If at the end of the session of 1892–93 it is desired to make a new arrangement for the music, art, and boarding departments of the seminary, there will be ample time for so doing.

Coeducation in the college was now an accomplished fact, for the experiment met with unqualified success, and such was the report of the president before a special meeting of the board of trustees held February 13, 1893. In the college catalogue of 1892–93 the names of the men and women appear together for the first time and on an equal footing in all respects. In the course of a year the departments of music and art were likewise absorbed by the college, and with the building of the new women's dormitory, Rucker Hall, in 1894, and the conversion of the seminary building into a dormitory for men, as described elsewhere, the work of consolidation was complete.

COURSES OF INSTRUCTION.

The curriculum is now arranged upon the group system. There are three courses leading to the degree of bachelor of arts, as follows: The classical course, the modern language course, and the English historical course. Besides these there are two other courses leading to the degree of bachelor of science—the mathematical scientific course and the English scientific course; and two courses leading to the degree of bachelor of letters—the belles-lettres musical course and the belles-lettres course. Of these seven courses, all except the last require four years' work; the last but three years.

The last two courses are not so severe as the first five and are provided for those who desire to devote their attention to musical studies, the modern languages, and a few other branches in the field of general culture.

The degree of master of arts is conferred upon those who complete one year's work of four recitations daily in addition to the full requirements of any of the A. B. courses.

The scheme of courses and degrees now offered at Georgetown College (1898) is as follows:

Synopsis of courses and degrees.

Courses.	First year.	Second year.	Third year.	Fourth year.	Degree.
Classical course..	Junior English, junior Latin, junior Greek, junior mathematics.	Senior Latin, senior Greek, intermediate mathematics.	Senior English, chemistry and biology, history, physiology ½.	Psychology, etc., ethics and logic, physics, political science, Bible and evidences of Christianity.	A. B.
Modern language course.	Junior English, junior Latin, junior mathematics, junior French.	Senior Latin, intermediate mathematics, senior French, physiology ½.	Senior English, chemistry and biology, history, junior German.	Psychology, etc., political science, Bible and evidences of Christianity, senior German, physics ½.	A. B.
English, historical course.	Junior Latin, junior English mathematics.	Intermediate English, senior Latin, intermediate mathematics, history.	Senior English, senior mathematics, political science, chemistry ½, physics ½.	Literary criticism, American history, psychology, ethics, etc., Bible and evidences of Christianity.	A. B.
Mathematical, scientific course.	Junior English, junior mathematics, French or German, chemistry and biology.	Intermediate English, intermediate mathematics, French or German, chemistry and bioloygy.	Senior English, senior mathematics, history, geology and physiology.	Psychology, etc., political science, physics and mechanics.	B. S.
English, scientific course.	Junior English, junior mathematics, chemistry and biology.	Intermediate English, intermediate mathematics, history, chemistry and biology.	Senior English, political science, physics and mechanics, geology and physiology.	Literary criticism, American history, psychology, ethics, etc., Bible and evidences of Christianity.	B. S.
Belles lettres, musical course.	Junior English, junior French or German, music.	Junior mathematics, senior French or German, music.	Senior English, chemistry and biology, music.	History, political science, music.	B. L.
Belles lettres course.	Junior English, junior mathematics, junior French or German.	Intermediate English, intermediate mathematics, history, senior French or German.	Senior English, political science, psychology, ethics, etc., physiology and geology.	....	B. L.
One year of work additional to any of the A. B. courses					A. M.

The present curriculum, given above, has only been in force during the past three years. Prior to that time there were simply two general courses; one a classical course, leading to the degree of A. B.; the other a scientific course and inferior to the first, which led to the degree of B. S. Each of these courses required four years of study. As indicating the scope of these courses, we find in an early catalogue the following statement:[1]

> Any one passing satisfactory examinations in English, physical science, mathematics, history and political economy, and mental and moral philosophy is entitled to the degree of bachelor of sciences. One who, in addition to these, has accomplished the Latin and Greek courses (first, second, and third years), is entitled to the degree of bachelor of arts. * * * The student who, in addition to courses required for the A. B. degree, will accomplish the French and German languages, shall receive the degree of master of arts.

Students aspiring to the A. M. degree were advised to take two additional years, making six in all.

It was further provided also that anyone who wished might elect such courses as he desired without reference to the completion of a course leading to a degree, and upon finishing the full course in any department would receive a certificate of "proficiency" in that department. This feature of the college work, together with the grouping of the studies by departments with a prescribed course in each department, dates from the beginning of President Manly's administration. Dr. Manly was a firm believer in the elective or free system, and sought to open the curriculum to those who could not contemplate a full college course.

Among the recent improvements in the curriculum we note the raising of the requirements for the degree of B. S., making them equivalent to those of the A. B. course.

The recent expansion of the courses of study and the enlargement of the faculty account for the increased facilities of the college and the greater variety of options now afforded the student. The establishment of a department of history and political science in 1885 and a department of English language and literature in 1897 have greatly enriched the curriculum. Besides, there should be mentioned also the addition of a year's study in the Bible and Christian evidences to the president's chair. Excellent courses in French and German are now given, covering two years, of four hours per week, in each language. The trustees have as yet not created a modern-language department, and we find the rather unique combination of German with the chair of Greek and of French with the Latin chair.

Besides the regular courses leading to the above-mentioned degrees, there are other departments of study which have recently been established in the college and have enlarged the elective opportunities of the student, viz:

The School of Music, established in 1894, which is now in charge of a director and faculty of six, and in 1897–98 had an enrollment of 70 students.

---

[1] Catalogue of Georgetown College, 1889–90, page 21.

The Department of Military Science and Tactics, which was created in 1894 and is under the direction of Capt. P. M. B. Travis, of the Eleventh United States Infantry. Military drill is required three times a week of all students, except of seniors and others who have special and sufficient reasons for exemption. All students enrolled for military drill are required to wear a regulation cadet-gray uniform.

The Normal Department, under the direction of a principal and an assistant. This department was created in the winter of 1895. Its object is to provide a course for those who desire to fit themselves for positions in the public schools of Kentucky, and also for those teachers who desire to perfect themselves in matters and methods of study. The normal course begins on January 24, and continues for sixteen weeks, with six working days each week. The studies include those that are required by law for county and State certificates, while some attention is given to pedagogy and laboratory work in the physical sciences. Tuition is free, save the matriculation fee of $5, and college classes and the other activities of college life are freely opened to this class of students. Success has attended the introduction of this department. The first session (January, 1895) opened with a class of twenty-two teachers. The number in 1898 was fourteen.

There is also an art department and a department of public speaking and reading, each in charge of one instructor, and the work in each is elective and the charges extra.

There is also a practical business course, covering one year's work, and including studies in business arithmetic, commercial law, bookkeeping, and stenography.

THE ACADEMY.

The academy is as old as the college and is the preparatory department of the latter. In fact, it is a part of the college, under the management of the same trustees and the same faculty. It is a large and direct feeder, and a considerable portion of the college students have had a part, if not all, of their preparatory training here. The academy faculty includes a principal, an associate principal, and three assistants.

The curriculum is divided into five grades, covering in all five years, beginning in the first grade with arithmetic, mental and practical; elementary grammar, geography, history, reading, spelling, and penmanship, and concluding in the fifth grade with the the following studies: Higher arithmetic and algebra, grammar and rhetoric, Latin (second year), Greek (second year), and physical geography. After this the academy graduates are ready for admission to college.

AFFILIATED SCHOOLS.

In 1896 the trustees of the Kentucky Baptist Education Society acquired Middleburg Academy, Middleburg, Casey County, Ky., and have since adjusted the course of study so as to fit students for Georgetown College.

Bardstown Male and Female Institute, of Bardstown, Ky., has within the past year also been recognized as an affiliated school, and, as in the case of the students from the two academies previously mentioned, its graduates are admitted to the college without examination.

ADMISSIONS.

The requirements for admission to the college are not severe, and in this particular there is room for improvement. However, it is but fair to say that this is typical of educational conditions in the South, where there is great need of building up the work of secondary education and a sharper and better differentiation as well as coordination of work between the fitting school and the college.

In the last catalogue we find nothing on the subject of "admission to college," though in an earlier issue we do find these statements: "Candidates for admission to the junior Latin or Greek (freshman work in the classical course) must sustain an examination in the preparatory department. * * * For admission to any class in the college a fair acquaintance with the English grammar, geography, and arithmetic is required." * * *

EXCERPTS FROM THE COLLEGE LAWS.

Attendance at the college chapel every morning at 9 o'clock is compulsory; likewise attendance upon the Sunday services of some one of the churches is required, and one of the formalities at the Monday chapel is the calling of the roll to determine whether or not this requirement has been met.

Students must obtain the approbation of the faculty in the choice of a boarding house.

No student will be permitted to be absent from his rooms after 7 o'clock at night, without leave, except to attend church or the voluntary societies connected with the college.

No student shall attend any exhibition of an immoral tendency or frequent any barroom or tippling house.

No student will be permitted to enter upon the grounds or premises of other persons so as to molest or injure property, or to associate with idle or vicious company, or to engage in a frolic of a noisy, disorderly, or immoral nature.

No student shall carry about him deadly weapons, or take any part in a duel, on pain of immediate expulsion.

Parents and guardians who live at a distance are requested to appoint someone to act as fiscal guardian of their children and wards at the college.

Ministerial students are instructed without charge for tuition.

No young minister should think of leaving home for college until he has received a fair common-school education [a piece of excellent advice too often unheeded].

Such a student will not be retained any longer than he evinces true piety and encouraging improvement in his studies, and, as tuition is gratis, a note of obligation to refund, with interest, the amount of tuition received shall be taken each session, which shall be in force only when the deportment shall disappoint or where the ministry shall be abandoned or made subordinate to some secular pursuit.

For Sunday and all public occasions the young ladies are required to wear uniforms of substantial inexpensive material, suitable to the seasons, but for school purposes they are requested to wear simple clothing.

The object of this requirement is to prevent unnecessary ostentation and display on the part of some who might be blessed with more abundant means than others of their classmates and perhaps with an admixture of bad taste. Such a bad ethical example would offend the dictates of common sense. No such requirement, however, is exacted of the men.

THE LITERARY SOCIETIES.

In accordance with the traditions of the South, and of Kentucky in particular, a great deal of attention is paid by the students to the art of public speaking and debate. The college is proud of her three societies, the Tau Theta Kappa, the Ciceronian, and the Euepian, the first two for the men, the last for the women of the college.

The Tau Theta Kappa and the Ciceronian are rival societies and each has a large and well-furnished hall in the new college building. Both were organized about the same time, in 1839, in rooms of the old Rittenhouse Academy building. In the newer academy building, erected in its place, quarters were provided for each of these societies, and here they remained until 1894, when they moved into the new college building. They have meetings once a week, and the programme, which is practically the same as that adhered to from the foundation of these societies, is as follows: Oration, declamation, debate, reading, criticism, and oracle. The societies are incorporated, and during the commencement season confer diplomas upon their graduating members. They own a small amount of personal property, the most important part of which is the library and the banner of the society. Each of them has a well-selected library of about 4,000 volumes, and these collections serve as important adjuncts to the college library, and in some respects are superior to the latter. These societies have now a membership of 80. Each holds occasionally public exercises and once a year a public declamatory contest and in addition contributes three contestants to the primary oratorical contest in the spring, from whom (six in all) an orator is chosen to represent the college in the intercollegiate contest held in Lexington, Ky.

The Euepian Society is similar in many particulars to the men's societies. It was organized in January, 1871, in the old Georgetown Female Seminary, its object being cultivation by debates, essays, recitations, selections, criticisms, etc., and a good deal of attention is now given to literary studies of well-known authors. Meetings were held regularly in the chapel of the old seminary building until 1896, when the society moved into the quarters provided for it in the new Rucker Hall. The society was incorporated June 11, 1895, under the laws of Kentucky and a charter granted, and since that time has, like the men's societies, conferred diplomas upon its graduates during commencement time. Their library now numbers about 350 volumes.

These societies are on friendly terms with one another. Between the men's societies, however, there is always considerable rivalry for prestige. At the opening of the academic year there is active "campaigning" for recruits among the new students by both societies and at times the contest waxes warm. This over, the best of relations usually prevail. There are no fraternities or secret societies at Georgetown.

THE INTERCOLLEGIATE ORATORICAL ASSOCIATION OF KENTUCKY.

The greatest event of the academic year, from the point of view of the student, is the intercollegiate oratorical contest. The association was organized in 1888 and now embraces five Kentucky colleges, as follows: Georgetown, Centre College, State College, Kentucky University, and Central University. Each college sends one representative to this contest, which occurs on the first Friday in April. Lexington is the meeting ground, though the plan was formerly to alternate between the different institutions. The greatest enthusiasm is exhibited at these contests, comparing favorably with the display of enthusiasm shown over great athletic victories in many an Eastern college, and the winning orator is awarded a handsome medal, which is a source of lifelong pride.

There have been eleven of these contests in all, Georgetown having won three[1] of them and holding second place, next to Centre College, the winner of four.

There are other activities at Georgetown College, for the promotion of which there are various organizations. It will suffice, perhaps, to mention the college Young Men's Christian Association, which, in addition to the regular religious exercises in the college, also conducts a city mission work, and the athletic association, for the general direction of the various athletic sports and games, and which every student is expected to join, otherwise he is excluded from the privilege of engaging in athletics.

COLLEGE PUBLICATIONS.

The first college catalogue was published in 1846, and every year since then a catalogue has been issued with the exception of the first two years of the war—1861–62 and 1862–63. At intervals of five years the college issues also a general catalogue containing complete lists of the trustees, professors, and graduates of Georgetown College. There are no annually published president's or trustees' reports or statements.

In 1850 the Ciceronian Literary Society began the issue of the first student publication, called the Ciceronian Magazine, a monthly of 40 pages, and the first of its kind in the West. This publication was continued for six years, when it was stopped for lack of support. In

[1] The winners of these contests are as follows: In the contest of 1891, J. Macklin Stevenson, '92; in the contest of 1895, James Madison Shelburne, '97; in the contest of 1897, Will P. Stuart, '97.

March, 1857, the Georgetown College Magazine appeared as a successor, with the joint support of the two societies.

After a few years it was abandoned, but revived again in 1885, continued for two years longer, and was then finally discontinued. Recently, however (January, 1896), a new college journal has appeared under the title of the Georgetonian. This publication is conducted by the three literary societies in cooperation with the faculty, and is still in existence. In 1898 appeared the first college annual, Belle of the Blue, the joint product of the three literary societies and of the Y. M. C. A.

OFFICERS OF THE COLLEGE.

Georgetown College has had since its foundation 11 presidents and 90 professors and tutors on its rolls. Some of the latter gave the greater parts of their lives to faithful work in this institution, notably Professor Farnam, who served the college in the chair of natural science from 1839 to 1887; Prof. Danford Thomas, who occupied the chair of Greek and Latin from 1838 to 1882, and Prof. J. J. Rucker, who, as professor of mathematics and astronomy, began his career in Georgetown College in 1855, served as principal of the seminary from 1869 until 1892, and is still in active service, his chair at present being mathematics and physics.

The roster of the present faculty (June, 1898), together with their departments, is as follows:

Augustus Cleveland Davidson, D. D., president[1] (R. M. Dudley memorial chair), professor of psychology, ethics, logic, and Christian evidences; James Jefferson Rucker, LL. D. (the McCalla-Galloway professorship), professor of mathematics and physics; Arthur Yager, Ph. D.[2] (the students' chair), professor of history and political science; John Foster Eastwood, Ph. D. (the Maria Atherton-Farnam chair of natural science), professor of chemistry and biology; Joseph Edward Harry, Ph. D., professor of Greek and German; John Calvin Metcalf, A. M., professor of English language and literature; David Edgar Fogle, A. M., professor of Latin and French; Capt. P. M. B. Travis, (West Point), (Eleventh United States Infantry), military science and tactics.

Music department: Charles Edward Hills, director; Miss Elise Dorst, voice and physical culture; Miss Corneille Overstreet, piano and theory; Miss Willanna Smith, violin; Miss Jennie Garnett, piano; Miss Birdie Ewing, piano and organ.

The academy: Stonewall Jackson Pulliam, A. M., principal; Miss Rowena Athelia Pollard, associate principal; Miss Eugenia Pulliam, assistant; Miss Margaret Hackley, assistant; Miss Sallie Ann Tarleton, assistant.

Normal department: Alvus Lemuel Rhoton, principal; W. Marion Smith, assistant.

---

[1] Resigned August, 1898. [2] At present acting as chairman of the faculty.

Art department: Miss Kate Wilson.

Public speaking and reading: Miss Mary S. Hamilton.

Officers: The president, superintendent of college property; Arthur Yager, librarian and secretary of faculty; James Kirtley Nunnelley, assistant librarian; J. E. Harry, director of gymnasium; Rev. W. B. Crampton, general agent.

THE BOARD OF TRUSTEES.

The board of trustees consists of twenty-four members. Each member is elected for a term of four years, and one-fourth of the entire number retire at the end of each year and are eligible to reelection. The officers of the board are a president, a recording secretary, and a treasurer. Beside these, there are two important committees: (1) the executive committee of eight, made up of the three officers of the board, the president of the college, and four other trustees (the chairman of this committee is the president of the board, ex officio), and (2) the board of ministerial education, a committee of four under the chairmanship of the president of the college.

During its entire history the college has been served by 108 different trustees,[1] and the board has had 8 presidents. The presidents of the board, with their terms of office, are as follows: (1) Silas M. Noel, Frankfort, Ky., 1829 to (unknown);[2] Elder Thomas P. Dudley, Lexington, Ky. (unknown) to 1838; (3) Roger Quarles, esq.,[2] 1838 to 1856; (4) R. M. Ewing, M. D.,[2] 1856 to 1864; (5) Governor James F. Robinson, Georgetown, Ky., 1864 to 1881; (6) D. A. Chenault, esq., Richmond, Ky., 1881 to 1886; (7) William M. Pratt, D. D., Louisville, Ky., 1886 to 1896; (8) John A. Lewis, M. D., Georgetown, Ky., 1896 to ——.

Judge George V. Payne, A. B., of Georgetown, has faithfully and efficiently served as treasurer of the college since 1873, and is the present holder of that office. Upon him falls a large share of the responsibility for the investment and care of the college funds, and in turn he merits a considerable share of the credit for the success with which these trusts have been administered during the past twenty-six years.

GRADUATES.

The graduates of the college now number 537. Among these names we find all walks of life represented, and many who have distinguished themselves in the pulpit, press, and the bar, and have become eminent in the public service of the country. In the legislature, in Congress, in the judiciary, and in the diplomatic service are found alumni of Georgetown. The number of students enrolled during the history of the college is much larger than is indicated by the number of gradu-

[1] A list of the trustees will be found in the last (fourth) general catalogue of Georgetown College (1895), pp. 55–57.

[2] Records lost or incomplete.

ates, as a large number left college before the senior year, but there is no means of knowing the exact number, as a considerable portion of the early records were accidentally destroyed by fire.

The catalogue of 1897–98 shows a total enrollment of 357 students in college, academy, and normal department. Of these, 179 are in college, 14 in the normal course, and the rest in the academy. Of the total number 225 are men and 132 are women.

Kentucky is represented by 320 students, the remaining 37 being drawn from 14 other States.

The academic year is divided into two terms. The first term begins on the first Tuesday in September, the second term on the fourth Tuesday in January, and closes with commencement day on the second Wednesday in June.

COMMENCEMENT.

The chief events of commencement week are the baccalaureate sermon by the president, in the college chapel, on the Sunday (at 10 a. m.) preceding the second Wednesday in June. This is followed in the evening by the sermon before the Young Men's Christian Association, usually preached by some distinguished alumnus.

On Monday evening occurs the annual address before the literary societies. The address of 1898 was given by President B. L. Whitman, D. D., of Columbian University, Washington, D. C.

On Tuesday afternoon the board of trustees meets, and at a later hour the Woman's Association of Georgetown College (organized in 1897). At 5 p. m., the same afternoon, the Kentucky Baptist Education Society meets for the election of trustees and other business. At night an address is delivered before the students' association..

On Wednesday, commencement day, college degrees and honors are awarded at the morning exercises; in the afternoon the literary societies confer diplomas upon their respective graduating members, and at night occurs the president's levee, with which the exercises of commencement week are always concluded.

At Georgetown there is no class day, which forms so marked a feature of the commencement festivities in many of our American colleges.

THE OUTLOOK.

The immediate outlook for Georgetown College is highly encouraging. In its past achievements and in the character of its graduates is found inspiration for the future. The increase in the attendance of students, the expansion of the courses of study, the recent growth in the endowment, the new buildings and enlarged faculty, and better facilities generally, all these are signs of progress. The college has more than held its own in comparison with the efforts of its contemporaries and rivals. Kentucky is well endowed with institutions of learning. Only 12 miles from Georgetown, at Lexington, are two vigorous competitors, Kentucky University and the State College, and within a range of 40 miles are two strong rivals in Centre College, at Danville, and Central University, at Richmond. Each of these, to be sure, has in a limited degree its peculiar constituency, and yet they are all laborers in the same field.

Georgetown has many needs and is doing what it can to supply them. A general agent of the college, the Rev. W. B. Crumpton, is kept constantly in the field, and his work is twofold: First, presenting the claims of the college to prospective students; and, second, securing financial aid for the work. The agent is also at present cooperating with another organization of the college, formed only two years ago, the Woman's Association of Georgetown College, in the effort to raise a fund of $50,000 from the women of Kentucky to create the woman's endowment. The object of this fund is "to help poor girls in securing an education."

In conclusion, it would be only fitting to record the sentiment of the trustees expressive of the confident faith of these officers in their trust:

> To Him to whom it was consecrated by our fathers in the beginning, and whose blessing has ever attended it, we commend it for the future.

BIBLIOGRAPHY.

J. H. Spencer, History of Kentucky Baptists. 2 volumes, 1885. See especially Vol. I, 599-761; II, 41.

The Baptist Chronicle, 1830, passim.

Collins's History of Kentucky, 2 volumes, 1874, II, 698.

Basil Manly, jr., The Past and Future of Georgetown College, a commencement address delivered at the fiftieth anniversary of the college, June 21, 1879, by the president. (Privately printed.)

H. Marshall, History of Kentucky, 2 volumes, 1824.

William B. Allen, History of Kentucky, 1872.

Chapter V.

OTHER MALE AND COEDUCATIONAL INSTITUTIONS.

KENTUCKY MILITARY INSTITUTE, LYNDON.

The foundation and a large part of the subsequent success of Kentucky Military Institute are due to Col. R. T. P. Allen, who graduated with honor at West Point in 1834, and served with credit in the Regular Army of the United States until the end of the campaign of 1836-37 against the Seminole Indians, when he retired to private life. In 1838, he became professor of mathematics and civil engineering in Alleghany College, Meadville, Pa., which position he resigned, in 1841, to accept a similar chair in Transylvania University, at Lexington, Ky., then under the presidency of Dr. Bascom, of the Methodist Episcopal Church, of which Colonel Allen had, by that time, become a regular clergyman.

While holding his chair in the university at Lexington Colonel Allen conceived the idea of founding a high-grade school, in which military training should be a prominent feature. Accordingly, having resigned his professorship, he in 1845, with the cooperation of citizens of the community, established the Kentucky Military Institute, which was located at Farmdale, 6 miles from Frankfort, Ky., on the site of old Franklin Springs, a noted health resort since the early history of the State.

The school was opened in the fall of 1845, and 30 cadets were in attendance during its first session. During the second session the matriculation increased to 40, and in the course of this year, on January 20, 1847, an act of incorporation for the enterprise was secured from the legislature of the State, according to the terms of which the institution was placed under the direction and control of a board of visitors appointed by the governor of the State, who is, ex officio, inspector of the institute. The superintendent, faculty, and cadets are constituted a quasi military corps, the officers being commissioned under the seal of the Commonwealth and being responsible to the board of visitors for the faithful performance of their prescribed duties. The institution has always been really a private enterprise, its only relation to the State being that the latter furnishes its military equipment and assumes supervision over its military organization.

Colonel Allen was connected with the management of the school from its foundation until 1874, except that he severed his relation with it in 1848 for a short time, and again from 1854 to 1865, during which time he was at first engaged in educational enterprises in Texas, and later served in the Confederate army with distinguished gallantry as a colonel of infantry.

During the early history of the school Col. E. W. Morgan, also a graduate of West Point and an educator of reputation, was associated with Colonel Allen in the institution, being joint proprietor from 1851 to 1854 and becoming sole proprietor in 1855. Colonel Morgan was a valuable coadjutor of Colonel Allen, and conducted the institution with success himself until the opening of the civil war in 1861, when most of the cadets left to join the armies, mainly that of the South, from which section they chiefly came, and the school was closed until 1865, at which time Colonel Morgan severed his connection with it. He subsequently became professor of engineering and architecture in Lehigh University, Pa.

Two courses of good compass had been early inaugurated by the management of the institution; one, in which ancient languages was prominent, leading to the degree of A. B.; and the other, in which mathematics was the principal feature, leading to the degree of C. E. The school was quite successful during this early period of its history, its students rising in number to 150 in 1851 and numbering 154 just prior to the war. The first graduating class of 4 members was sent out in 1851, and for the next ten years from 8 to 21 were graduated each year, the total number of graduates up to 1861 inclusive being 144. The alumni of the institution took a prominent part and secured a high position in the civil war, as it furnished in that struggle two major-generals, three brigadier-generals, and a number of colonels and officers of lesser rank. Since its students were mainly from the South, the majority of them naturally espoused the cause of that section.

In 1865 Colonel Allen again took charge of the institute, which soon had a larger attendance than ever before in its history, there being 166 students in 1866-67 and 177 in 1867-68. The success of the school continued under Colonel Allen's management until 1874, when he decided to retire from the profession of teaching, in which he considered he had earned a well-merited rest. He had certainly discharged with credit his duties as a minister of the gospel, as a soldier, and as an educator.

He was succeeded in the superintendency of the school by his son, Col. R. D. Allen, who had graduated from the institute in 1852, and, after engaging in other educational enterprises, had, since 1866, been associated with his father in the institute faculty. He remained as superintendent of the school until 1887, when, after an interval of a year, he was succeeded in the position by Col. D. F. Boyd, LL.D., a graduate of the University of Virginia and a teacher of many years' experience. Under these superintendents commercial and normal courses were added to the previous curriculum, and the institution was otherwise kept abreast of the demands of the time. It was upon the whole fairly prosperous, but on account of the competition of endowed schools and the financial stringency gradually became less so until 1893, when Colonel Boyd resigned and the school was suspended for a time.

In 1896 Col. C. W. Fowler, recognizing that there was still a field for such an institution in its distinctively military character and government and its endeavor as far as possible to suit the needs of each individual student, secured the removal of the institute—charter, equipment, and all—to Lyndon, 9 miles from Louisville, Ky., considered in many ways a more eligible location than the old one.

Colonel Fowler is an alumnus of the institution, having been a member of the class of 1878, subsequent to which he had been for several years connected with its faculty. For the past six years he had been superintendent of the Kentucky Training School at Mount Sterling, Ky. He became the superintendent of the Kentucky Military Institute on September 1, 1896, when it was opened in its new quarters.

The new situation and external equipment of the school may perhaps be best described by the following quotation from its catalogue for 1897:

> The buildings comprise the fine, old Ormsby mansion, a substantial brick structure, besides two smaller frame buildings and a gymnasium and drill hall; these buildings are situated in a beautiful blue-grass lawn of about 4 acres, shaded with towering forest trees and evergreen pines. * * * It is so perfectly adapted for school purposes that it could scarcely be improved upon if built to order.

The dormitories connected with the institution furnish accommodations for 80 students.

Under the present management the former college courses have been retained and enlarged by the institution of a scientific course which substitutes modern for ancient languages and the addition of such new features as manual training. For those who are not candidates for a degree there is a practical course of three years in which science is emphasized, and a commercial course of two years. There is also a preparatory course of one year.

It is aimed to have the educational methods used suited, as much as possible, to the needs of each cadet, and to this end it is expected to have the attendance limited to not more than 100 students, probably less. The matriculation so far has been fully as good as, or better than, it was during the corresponding period subsequent to the original foundation. Two degrees have been conferred each year under the new management. The present faculty has 5 regular professors, 4 special lecturers, and 1 cadet assistant.

The institute has been one of the leading military schools of the South. Fifteen States were at times, under the administration of the

SOUTH KENTUCKY COLLEGE—MAIN BUILDING.

elder Colonel Allen, represented in its matriculation, and its graduates and matriculates are to be found in every Southern and in many of the Central and Western States. Up to 1878 its total number of matriculates had been 3,049, and of graduates 242. Up to 1893, a period of forty-eight years, it had an average matriculation of about 100 cadets, making its total enrollment to date about 5,000. Its graduates now number about 400 and have, many of them, taken an honorable rank in other professions besides that of arms. Up to 1878, 50 of them were known to have become lawyers, 21 physicians, 11 teachers, 9 civil engineers, and 5 clergymen.

BIBLIOGRAPHY.

Perrin, Battle, and Kniffen's History of Kentucky.

A Short History of Franklin County, by C. E. James, Frankfort, 1876.

Biographical Sketches and Information of Interest to Professors, Alumni, and ex-Cadets of the K. M. I., by Maj. R. H. Wildberger, Frankfort, 1878.

SOUTH KENTUCKY COLLEGE, HOPKINSVILLE.

This institution was intended primarily for the education of women only, and was conducted as an exclusively female college for a number of years. Its original charter was obtained from the State legislature in February, 1849, and places it under the management of nine trustees, who are empowered—

> To make all such rules and ordinances necessary for the government of said institution as shall not be repugnant to the constitution and laws of the United States and of this State.

The design of its founders was to make it undenominational, but positively Christian, and the Bible was from its beginning given a prominent place among its text-books

Its incorporators and those mainly instrumental in its establishment were John M. Barnes, Henry J. Stites, Benjamin S. Campbell, John B. Knight, W. F. Bernhard, Robert L. Waddell, Jacob Torian, Isaac H. Caldwell, and W. A. Edmonds. These trustees were identified with the Church of the Disciples, or Christian Church, and the college has since remained under the patronage of that denomination.

The college was located by its charter in Hopkinsville, and was first opened there in the autumn of 1849, with John M. Barnes as its first president. Mr. Barnes died in 1851 and was succeeded in the presidential chair of the institution by Enos Campbell, under whose administration it became necessary to erect new buildings in order to accommodate the increased patronage. To obtain the necessary funds, agents appointed by the board of trustees made an appeal to the church and the friends of the college generally. The liberal response given to these efforts resulted in the raising of about $30,000, which was expended for additional grounds and a new building, the latter costing $25,000. The grounds constitute the present campus of 12 acres, situated on a beautiful elevation overlooking the town from the east and splendidly shaded by native forest trees. The new building was completed in 1858.

The patronage of the institution continued to enlarge in its new quarters, and its prosperity was uninterrupted until the spring of 1862, when its work was suspended for several months by the military occupation of Hopkinsville incident to the civil war, its buildings being used during this interval by the Confederate troops as a hospital. At this time President Campbell severed his connection with the institution.

The college was, however, reopened in September, 1862, under J. W. Goss as president. Mr. Goss was succeeded in 1870 by T. A. Crenshaw, who remained at the head of the institution until 1876, when R. C. Cave became president and remained so until 1881. Under the direction of these executive officers the college steadily regained its former prosperity, its attendance being such as to make it more than self-sustaining and to allow considerable improvements in its equipment. In 1876 the faculty was composed of five members and there was an enrollment of 115 students, which seems to have been about the average matriculation during this period of its history.

Its students at this time represented a number of the Southern and Western States, and its list of graduates was large. Many of these became successful teachers, and together with the other alumnæ began to make the institution favorably known, particularly throughout the denomination under whose auspices it was being conducted. That body, however, especially the portion of it located in southern Kentucky, desired a college where its sons as well as its daughters could be educated, and in recognition of this demand the trustees of South Kentucky College, at a meeting held on November 24, 1879, resolved to take steps to put that institution on a different and broader basis. The aim was to so enlarge the faculty and so extend the course of study and raise the standard of scholarship as to make them equivalent to those required in first-class male colleges, and then make the institution fully coeducational. Accordingly the necessary amendment to the charter was secured early in 1881, which provides "for the instruction of the students therein in the arts and sciences and in all necessary, useful, and ornamental branches of a thorough and liberal education such as are taught in the best colleges."

At a meeting of the trustees, held on February 7, 1881, it was determined, in order to make the course of instruction as broad as possible, not only to continue the former departments of music and art, and to conduct, in addition to a preparatory course of one year, a classical course of four years and a scientific course of three years, but also to add a normal course of two years, a commercial course of one year, an agricultural course of two years, a ladies' course of two years, and an elementary course in international, constitutional, and commercial law of one year. Certificates were to be conferred in all these courses, except the classical, scientific, and ladies' courses, in which the usual degrees of A. B., B. S., and M. E. L. were to be granted.

The college was opened under its amended charter as a coeducational institution on the first Monday in September, 1881. President Cave remained at its head under the new order of things. He was assisted in the work of instruction by a faculty which, besides additional instructors in music, art, and domestic economy was, including the president, constituted as follows: R. C. Cave, M. A., president and professor of the English language and literature, philosophy, and logic; S. R. Crumbaugh, M. A., C. E., LL. B., professor of mathematics, mechanics, and astronomy; M. L. Lipscomb, M. A., professor of Latin and Greek; H. T. Suddarth, M. A., professor of pedagogics, commerce, and assistant in English; G. H. Fracker, M. A., professor of natural science and agriculture; R. T. Steinhagen, professor of music, modern languages, and history; J. A. Young, M. D., professor of zoology, anatomy, and physiology; Hon. J. W. McPherson, professor of international, constitutional, and commercial law.

The institution had at the time acquired the foundation of a good reference library and had ample scientific apparatus for all ordinary uses. In 1881-82 there were 121 students enrolled, 69 of whom were females, and, at the end of the year, there were five graduates in the scientific course, nine in the ladies' course, three in the normal course, and four in the commercial course. In the next year, for some reason, the matriculation declined to 89 altogether, with four graduates in the ladies' course and eight in the commercial course. At the end of this year President Cave resigned and was succeeded by B. C. Deweese, M. A., who, however, seems to have remained in the presidential office only a few months, being succeeded early in the next scholastic year by S. R. Crumbaugh, M. A., LL. D., by the beginning of whose administration the courses in law and agriculture had been dropped and the scientific course lengthened to four years.

Soon after the assumption of his office by President Crumbaugh, considerable improvements were made in the college property in various ways, and its affairs were in an auspicious condition when, on February 4, 1884, its prosperity was apparently blighted by a fire which destroyed its main building, with a loss of several thousand dollars above the sum for which the structure was insured.

The exercises of the institution were suspended until the next September, but its trustees met the next day after the fire and resolved to rebuild at once. Funds were raised, through the energy of President Crumbaugh and other friends of the college, and a new building, in every way handsomer and better adapted to its purposes than the old one, was ready for occupancy by the 1st of the following July. This building, which is now in use, is a fine brick structure, three stories in height, with a front 108 feet wide, and two wings, one of them 120 feet and the other 90 feet deep. It afforded considerably larger accommodations than had before been enjoyed.

At the opening of the next year the faculty of the institution was enlarged and the scope of its instruction considerably widened, a military department being attached to it, a course in civil engineering and one leading to the degree of bachelor of letters instituted, and the preparatory course extended to three years. Its patronage also was soon much increased, there being 170 matriculates in 1885–86, so that it seemed to be benefited rather than injured by the apparent calamity which had befallen it. President Crumbaugh remained in charge of the institution until 1887, there being 168 students the last year of his administration. He remained as a member of the faculty for some time after his resignation as president.

His successor in that position was James E. Scobey, M. A., who had been vice-president of the faculty during the previous administration. President Scobey remained in office for three years, during which the average attendance had considerably decreased, but the number of students going forward to a degree considerably increased, the number of degrees conferred during his administration being quite equal to if not more than all that had been granted before since 1881. In 1890 President Scobey resigned and A. C. Kuykendall, M. A., became his successor as executive head of the institution, a position which he also retained for three years, retiring from its duties in 1893, when Prof. J. W. Hardy was elected to the position. Professor Kuykendall has since remained one of the prominent professors of the institution.

Professor Hardy was not only president, but financial agent as well. An appeal being made at the opening of his administration to secure a better equipment and an endowment for the college, sufficient funds were soon raised to erect, at a cost of $10,000, McCarty Hall, a well-arranged and commodious dormitory with accommodations for 30 young men, besides a large society hall. Within the next two years something over $10,000 was contributed for other purposes, $6,000 of which forms the beginning of the first endowment of the institution, for it had previously depended entirely on tuition fees for its support and advancement. During President Hardy's administration the average annual matriculation was about 160, a considerable advance over that of several years previous.

In 1897, upon Professor Hardy's resignation, Prof. S. S. Woolwine, for a number of years past prominently connected with various educational enterprises in Tennessee, was elected president of the college. The single year Professor Woolwine has presided over the institution has witnessed the increase of its matriculation to 186, the largest since 1881, and probably the largest in the history of the institution. These students were from seven different States; 98 of them were young men and 88 young women, which is a reversal of the ratio in the numbers of the two sexes during most years since coeducation was introduced. The present faculty is composed of ten members, one of whom—Prof. R. T. Steinhagen—has been a successful teacher in the institution for seventeen years or more.

PRESIDENT'S HOUSE.
N. LONG HALL.

MAIN BUILDING.

BETHEL COLLEGE, RUSSELLVILLE.

The average number of graduates from the college in recent years has been about 8, who have been about equally distributed among the three principal courses leading to the degrees of bachelor of arts, bachelor of science, and bachelor of letters. A number of the graduates of the institution have attained success in the different learned professions, especially in that of teaching.

The present course is divided into the departments of ancient languages, mathematics, science, mental and moral philosophy, English, modern languages, normal instruction, Bible instruction, commercial instruction, and elocution and oratory. It is arranged in the three courses indicated above, the basis of each of which, respectively, is ancient languages, modern languages, and English. The first two extend through four years each and the last three years. Besides these, there is a teachers' course of two years, a commercial course of one year, and excellent opportunities are offered in music and art. Certificates are granted in these departments. There is also a preparatory course of one year. The degree of M. A. is conferred upon those who have completed the classical course and have spent one year in post-graduate work at the college or two years in literary work elsewhere.

South Kentucky College has done a valuable educational work for many years practically without endowment. If its friends will only rally around it and furnish it the means for which it is now appealing, its permanency will be assured and its usefulness greatly enlarged for the future.

BIBLIOGRAPHY.

This sketch is based mainly on a sketch of the college contained in the catalogue of 1881-82, the facts of which have been confirmed and enlarged by reference to other catalogues, to reports of the Commissioner of Education, and to Henderson's Centennial Exhibits, as well as by other facts furnished by President Darby and Dr. James A. Young, of Hopkinsville. Use has also been made of a sketch in A History of Christian County, by W. H. Perrin, Chicago, 1882.

BETHEL COLLEGE, RUSSELLVILLE.

The want of an institution to supply the educational needs of the church in the southern and western portions of the State had long been felt by the Baptists of Kentucky, and the question of its establishment had been somewhat discussed, especially at the general association held in October, 1848. The preliminary steps for the actual organization of such an institution were, however, taken by Bethel Association at its meeting in Hopkinsville, Ky., in September, 1849, when Rev. Samuel Baker, D. D., as chairman of the committee on education appointed at the previous session of that body, reported in favor of establishing, "at some eligible point within the bounds of the association and under its name, an academic institution, something inferior to a college or university and superior to the ordinary common and primary schools,"[1] the aim of the contemplated school at that time being

[1] Russellville Ledger for April 25, 1896.

to prepare students for the colleges of the church and to furnish the elements of a good English education to others who had not the desire or opportunity to pursue an extended course of study.

In response to this report, a resolution was adopted by the association that the churches should be requested to send delegates to a meeting appointed to be held at Keysburg, Ky., on November 14, 1849, in order that arrangements might be made to locate the school and to raise funds for its establishment. A committee to secure a charter for the proposed school and to look after other matters pertaining to its organization was also appointed. Rev. John P. Campbell, one of the most zealous promoters of the enterprise, was chairman of this committee, and was ably assisted in the advocacy of the undertaking by Rev. R. Anderson, Rev. Robert Williams, Rev. R. A. Nixon, and Rev. J. M. Pendleton, who, with him, may be mentioned as among those mainly instrumental in pushing forward the educational movement. This committee, through its financial agent, Rev. W. I. Morton, raised $3,500 in subscriptions for the proposed school by the next meeting of the association at Russellville,[1] Ky., in 1850, when that body decided to locate the institution in Russellville, and appointed its first board of trustees, with Judge E. M. Ewing as chairman and Rev. J. M. Pendleton as secretary.

The first official act of this board, and one fraught with importance to the school, was the appointment of N. Long as its financial agent, thus early associating with the enterprise a man who became one of its firmest friends and strongest supporters; one who was ever ready to promote its welfare without emolument to himself, which he always refused. His energetic efforts soon led to the palpable result of securing, chiefly in Logan County, about $8,000 in addition to the amount already subscribed, and in March, 1851, he purchased for $3,300, as the seat of the institution, 40 acres of land adjoining Russellville, on which, by the authority of the board of trustees, in October, 1851, he contracted for the erection of the present main building of Bethel College, which was to cost when complete about $15,000. This building was erected, principally in 1852, on a substantial and commodious plan, under Mr. Long's personal supervision, but the funds already raised were only sufficient, besides paying for the grounds, to put it under roof, at a cost of about $10,000, and not to complete or furnish it.

So further help was needed to push the enterprise to a success. This help was found in the person of Rev. B. T. Blewett, A. M.,[2] who, in June, 1853, was elected as the first principal of the school and also as agent to collect funds and superintend the completion of the building. He came from Georgetown College, then the educational center of the Baptist Church in Kentucky, where he had been principal of the preparatory department for six years, since taking his degree in 1847. He

[1] Hopkinsville and Keysburg were also competitors for the location.

[2] Most accounts of the history of the college spell this name Blewitt but Blewett is undoubtedly the correct spelling.

was a worthy coadjutor of Mr. Long, both in self-sacrificing efforts and energy in behalf of the school and these two men may be preeminently called the founders of Bethel High School, out of which subsequently grew Bethel College.

BETHEL HIGH SCHOOL.

Mr. Blewett at once gave his personal note for $6,000 to insure the early completion of the building erected by Mr. Long and took the field, already thought to be quite fully canvassed for that purpose and in which there was considerable competition from other church educational enterprises, to raise the needed amount. By twelve months' work, laboring almost day and night, without allowing his ardor to be dampened or his energy checked by seemingly adverse circumstances, Mr. Blewett succeeded in having the building finished and furnished, at a cost of $8,000, being able by advancing much of this amount out of his own means, to have this accomplished by January 1, 1854.

As a result of these efforts, Bethel High School was first opened on January 3, 1854, Mr. Blewett, with one assistant teacher, constituting its first faculty. The first assistant teacher was George L. Hayes. A charter was secured for the school on March 9, 1854, and during its first session 25 students were in attendance. The salary of the assistant, however, absorbed all the fees paid by these, and so the principal received nothing for his services, as indeed seems to have been the case for eighteen months after he accepted the position.

Moreover, his own funds were now exhausted, and so affairs looked quite gloomy in the summer of 1854; but not despairing, he again took the field to solicit funds and students, and although he did not secure much of the former, the attendance was considerably increased the second term. The debt, however, pressed heavily upon the school, and Mr. Blewett was severely taxed for a time to keep it going. Meanwhile, its excellent corps of teachers, which was maintained notwithstanding the desperate condition of its affairs, was adding to its reputation and attracting a well-paying patronage, which soon relieved its pressing financial embarrassment. By September, 1855, it had three[1] teachers besides the principal and an enrollment of 125 students, and its general prosperity began to attract a wider notice.

The favorable consideration it was receiving at the hands of the public caused its friends to become more ambitious in their aims, and accordingly, under the instructions of Bethel Association, its trustees applied to the State legislature for a charter converting it into a college. This instrument, which was secured on March 6, 1856, changed the name of the institution to Bethel College, and conferred upon it powers sufficient not only for the operation of a college, but of a university as well, if it should ever aspire higher. By the terms of its

[1] These teachers were Fred B. Downs, A. Maasberg, Ph. D., and H. H. Skinner. A preparatory class was also in charge of Colby A. Smith, A. B.

charter the control of the institution was placed in the hands of "The Green River Baptist Educational Society," where it remained for many years.

BETHEL COLLEGE.

The new college was opened in the autumn of 1856 and had, as its first faculty, in addition to President Blewett, Augustus Maasberg, Ph. D., professor of languages; C. D. Lawrence, professor of mathematics, and David Hardy, jr., principal of the preparatory department. In 1857 H. H. Lummis was added as professor of chemistry.

One hundred and fifty students were enrolled the first year, but the condition of the institution at the time is well shown by the following quotation, in which it is said Mr. Blewett had been made president of "a college without endowment, library, apparatus, or any other appliance, except a good building, a good number of students, and a good working faculty."[1] So the prospects under the new order of things were not very bright and President Blewett had almost, if not quite, as great a struggle to maintain the college as the high school during its first years, in both of which attempts it is said he would have several times given up in despair had it not been for the hopefulness and encouragement of his wife, who inspired him to renewed exertions.

The reputation of the school had aroused a favorable public sentiment in its behalf, but no one realized more fully than President Blewett that tuition fees alone could not be depended upon to sustain an efficient faculty and equip the institution with all the educational apparatus needed for successful work. He accordingly again made an appeal to the church in behalf of an endowment for the college, in which action he was efficiently supported by its trustees, that body resolving, in 1856, to endeavor to secure $15,000, and, in 1857, raising that amount to $30,000.

The beginning of the good things to come occurred in this latter year, when H. Q. Ewing, then president of the board of trustees, gave to the institution an unconditional donation of $10,000 in cash and an additional one of $10,000 in real estate, conditioned upon $30,000 more being added to its fund from other sources. In the following year his father, Judge E. M. Ewing, the first president of the trustees of Bethel High School, contributed, under like conditions, $3,000 in money and 80 acres of valuable land,[2] situated near Chicago, Ill. President Blewett succeeded in securing about $3,000 from other sources, so that by July 4, 1859, the larger amount at which the trustees had aimed was more than obtained. Judge Ewing and his son also, about this time, donated a part of the library of Hon. Presley Ewing, containing about 2,000 volumes, which formed the foundation of the present library of the institution. The proceeds of the gifts of the Ewings, by resolution

[1] Barnard's American Journal of Education, vol. 5, p. 431.

[2] This land was considered to be worth $4,000 when it was given, but half of it was sold in 1891 for $14,000.

of the board of trustees, adopted on June 14, 1859, were set apart to the chair of mental and moral philosophy, which is named in their honor. The funds secured by that time had placed the college on a more substantial basis, and one of its special aims began to be more definitely realized. One of its chief objects originally had been to educate more fully young men preparing for the Baptist ministry, and since its organization from 10 to 20 of these students had been in its classes, but in 1860, to meet the needs of these more fully, a professorship of biblical and pastoral theology was established. This department was soon suspended by the civil war, but was revived again, a special charter being secured for it on January 22, 1868, and was maintained until 1877, when the location of the Southern Baptist Theological Seminary in Louisville, Ky., made its maintenance no longer necessary or advisable. The occupant of this chair during the period of its existence was Rev. W. W. Gardner, D. D., who was a valuable laborer in behalf of the college during its early struggles.

Under President Blewett's successful management the college, with its full and able faculty, continued eminently prosperous until May 1861, when, owing to the excitement due to the opening of the civil war, it was closed and remained so for something over two years, during which time its buildings were used for army hospital purposes for several months by the Confederate troops. At the time of its suspension there were 150 students in attendance, and we are informed [1] that its cash endowment was then $40,000, while its property was valued at more than twice that amount.

President Blewett resigned his office in the summer of 1861. He subsequently taught successfully at other places in Kentucky and in Missouri, but was not again connected with the management of Bethel College. His services to that institution in its early days can hardly be overestimated. He, in connection with Mr. Long, mainly secured its funds and besides he had all the labor of its early organization. Spencer [2] well describes his efforts in saying that—

> He raised the money, taught his regular classes, exercised discipline, brought his students into the college, planted the ornamental trees on the lawn with his own hands, and directed the minutiæ of a thousand nameless transactions necessary to the conduct of a growing institution of learning.

The college had sent out its first graduating class of two members in 1857, one of whom was Rev. C. P. Shields, A. M., who was, until recently, for a number of years its professor of Latin and Greek. The class of 1858 had 12 members, and there were altogether 22 alumni during the antebellum period of the institution's history, among whom, besides Professor Shields, were James H. Fuqua, A. M., and Leslie Waggener, A. M., LL. D., since prominently connected with the corps of instruction and administration of their alma mater and other institutions.

[1] History of the Baptists of Kentucky, p. 727. [2] *Ibid*, p. 739.

During the suspension of the college its old friend Mr. Long continued his valuable services to it by carefully husbanding its financial resources, so that it was more fortunate than most other institutions similarly situated in coming out of the civil war not only with its funds unimpaired, but even increased, as these in 1865 had become over $50,000.

In September, 1863, the college was reopened under Rev. George Hunt as president. Mr. Hunt successfully accomplished the difficult undertaking of reorganizing the institution under very unpropitious circumstances and of arousing something of the old-time interest in its behalf. He left it on a good working basis when he resigned in 1864, and was succeeded by J. W. Rust, A. M.

Professor Rust is noted in educational matters, particularly for his able management of the affairs of Bethel Female College, at Hopkinsville, Ky., for many years, both before and after this time, but his administration of Bethel College, lasting about three and a half years, was also a prosperous one in the history of that institution, which, soon after the beginning of his term of office, began to almost equal its best days prior to the civil war. Failing health, however, compelled President Rust to resign on February 1, 1868. He was a man of practical judgment and of tireless energy, and did much to increase the attendance and reputation of the college.

Upon Professor Rust's resignation Noah K. Davis, LL.D., the author of works in mental and moral philosophy which evidence profound thought and scholarship, was elected to the presidency, a position which he held for about five years, during which several progressive events in the history of the college happened. In the fall of 1868 its curriculum was arranged substantially as at present in scope and in plan. This plan, generally known throughout the South as the University of Virginia plan, consisted in the arrangement of the course of study into independent schools, which might be pursued by anyone prepared to profit by them, there being no regular division of the students into college classes nor any fixed time for the completion of the curriculum, students being graduated when they completed the requisite number of schools for the degree which they sought. The number of schools[1] established at this time was eight, of which six had to be completed for the student to obtain the degree of bachelor of arts. The high standard of scholarship required by this course has since been consistently maintained by the institution.

Substantial additions were also made to the endowment and equipment during this period. In 1870 the chair of English was endowed by N. Long, the early benefactor of the college, and in the same year the chair of natural sciences was endowed by the Norton brothers,

[1]These schools were Latin, Greek, English, natural science, philosophy, mathematics, the Bible, and theology. The first six were required for the degree of A. B., the only one given at the time.

G. W. Norton and W. F. Norton, of Louisville, Ky., and Ecstein Norton, of New York City. These chairs have been named after the donors. In 1872 a president's house was erected, at a cost of $7,000, the means for which were largely secured through Mr. Long, and in this year a fund of $8,000, given in 1870 to aid students for the ministry, particularly, by Mr. James Enlow, of Christian County, Ky., first became available. The funds of the institution were then $85,000 and its property at least that much more, while there were 110 students in the college classes proper.

In 1873 President Davis resigned to accept the position he still holds, the chair of moral philosophy in the University of Virginia, and the executive affairs of the college were intrusted to Prof. Leslie Waggener, an alumnus of the college in the class of 1860 and connected with its faculty since 1866, having in 1870 become its professor of English language and literature, a department of education to which he was one of the first teachers of the country to devote his attention as a specialty. Professor Waggener conducted the affairs of the institution with usefulness and acceptability, as chairman of the faculty, until 1877 when he was regularly elected president, a position held by him until 1883.

Among the changes and improvements occurring during his term of office may be mentioned the inauguration of the bachelor of science course in 1875, the degree being conferred on candidates who had completed successfully the schools of English, philosophy, mathematics, and natural science; the usual time required to obtain this degree seems to have been at first three years, but the the course was soon strengthened so as to require four years as required in the bachelor of arts course. A school of modern languages was added to the previous curriculum, and has since been made an important feature of the scientific course.

In 1876–77 N. Long Hall, designed to provide a college home and board at reasonable rates for deserving students who chose to avail themselves of its advantages, was erected, at a cost of $20,000, mainly through the efforts of him in whose honor it is named and largely from funds contributed by him. It will furnish accommodations for about 100 students and has been found a valuable adjunct to the work of the college. This was the last of Mr. Long's important personal benefactions to the institution, but he still continued to give to it valuable services, remaining as president of its board of trustees until his death in 1887, a position held by him since 1879, while he had been a member of that body for thirty years. Besides devoting largely of his time and means to Bethel College he had contributed liberally to Georgetown College, Kentucky; Richmond College, Virginia, and the Baptist Theological Seminary, in Louisville, Ky.

In the last year of President Waggener's administration the college gymnasium, which had been erected in connection with N. Long Hall, was equipped with the latest appliances for physical exercise, through the liberality of Capt. J. B. Briggs, of Russellville. President Waggener resigned in June, 1883, to accept the chair of English literature in the University of Texas, where he became chairman of the faculty, a position held by him until 1895, when he was elected president. He died in the discharge of its duties in 1896.

The other members of the faculty of Bethel at the time of the resignation of President Waggener were James H. Fuqua, A. M., professor of ancient languages; John P. Fruit, A. M., professor of English and modern languages; R. E. Binford, A. M., professor of mathematics; Rev. W. S. Ryland, D. D., professor of natural science, and J. C. Vick, A. B., principal of the preparatory department. Professor Fuqua at that time assumed the duties of the chair of philosophy and became chairman of the faculty. The executive affairs of the institution were managed by him in this capacity for the next four years, during which the patronage of the college was considerably increased. In 1887 Professor Fuqua asked to be relieved of executive duties and Rev. W. S. Ryland, D. D., became his successor as chairman of the faculty. Professor Fuqua still retained his connection with the institution and became at that time its professor of mathematics.

Dr. Ryland, besides having been a member of the college faculty since 1880, had since his graduation at Richmond College, Virginia, and Rochester Theological Seminary, New York, taught in several other institutions in Mississippi and Kentucky, and had been president of the Baptist Female College at Lexington, Ky., from 1877 to 1880. His training and temperament were such as to make him an excellent presiding officer for Bethel. After being chairman of the faculty for two years, he was, in 1889, regularly elected president, and continued to hold the office until June, 1898, thus completing a longer term of service than any other incumbent of the position.

The history of the institution during his administration was one of uniform growth and expansion in almost all directions. In 1887–88 there were 127 students in the college, then a considerably larger number than usual. These increased in 1890–91 to 180, in 1892–93 to 207, and in 1894–95 to 213, the largest number yet enrolled, the matriculation during this period more than once representing as many as eight of the Southern and Western States. The size of the graduating classes increased in a corresponding ratio. In 1891 there were 8 graduates; in 1893, 11; in 1896, 22.

In 1890 a regular professorship of modern languages was established and improvements, amounting to several thousand dollars, made upon the college property. In this year, also, in order to cure a legal defect in the charter, and also because the organization of the educational society, in whose charge the institution had originally been placed, had been allowed to become dissolved through neglect, an amendment to the charter was secured, making the board of trustees self-perpetuating, but requiring that four-fifths of them must be members in good standing of some Baptist church.

In 1892 a school of the Bible, for practical instruction in the Scriptures, was added to the curriculum, and a valuable and handsome addition was made to the equipment and educational facilities of the institution by the gift, for library purposes, from the heirs of N. Long and G. W. Norton, of the Southern Bank building, the original cost of which was $30,000, on condition that a fund of $5,000 for increasing the library should be raised, a condition speedily complied with, as about half the amount needed was subscribed at the commencement of that year, when the conditional donation of the building was announced. The donation of this building, which is conveniently located and well suited to its new purposes, was largely due to the efforts and influence of Capt. J. B. Briggs, of Russellville, who thus became for a second time a contributor to the means of the institution. Among other important donors to the library and its funds have been Mrs. Olive C. Walton, of Allensville, Ky.; Miss Mary Newton, of Daviess County, Ky., and Ecstein Norton, of New York City.

In 1896 the course of instruction was again enlarged and the faculty increased by the creation of a new school of history and the election of a professor of history. In this year also the facilities in the scientific department were much improved by the enlargement of the chemical laboratory and the purchase of new apparatus, a fund for laboratory purposes being at that time contributed by the Norton Brothers, the former benefactors of the college. In 1897, while the former scope of instruction was maintained, the schools of instruction being Latin, Greek, mathematics, natural science, English, philosophy, modern languages, history, and the Bible, the course of study was remodeled in such a way as to divide the students, according to progress, into the usual college classes and a new bachelor of letters course was instituted, in which English and modern languages take the place of Greek in the classical course, the former scientific course, in which the natural sciences and modern languages predominate, also being retained, thus making three regular degree courses, leading respectively to the degrees of bachelor of letters, bachelor of arts, and bachelor of science.[1] At the same time[2] the powers of the president of the college, in regard to the personnel of the faculty and the scholastic and disciplinary affairs of the institution generally, were much enlarged over what they had formerly been.

During President Ryland's administration the endowment of the institution was somewhat expanded. Besides the gifts mentioned above for special purposes, in 1891 one-half of the real estate near

[1] The degree of master is conferred in each of these courses upon an additional year's study.

[2] At this time also all honorary degrees were abolished and all honorary distinctions, except such as are usual in connection with the commencement exercises.

Chicago, given by Judge Ewing in 1858, was sold for $44,000, the remainder being held at a greatly increased value, while, in 1895, Dr. John H. Spencer, the author and a former student of the college, donated $6,000 to its funds, and in recent years Mr. William Price, of Logan County, Ky., has given $3,500 to be used to aid poor students who are candidates for the ministry in the Baptist Church. The income from the Enlow fund, now amounting to about $8,500, and originally intended as part of an endowment for the theological department, has been used for the same purpose since that department was discontinued. The real estate and invested funds of the institution have now accumulated to about $240,000. In addition to the improvements and growth, which have been noted, Dr. Ryland's services to the college were also valuable in upholding and raising the general tone and esprit de corps of the institution.

Upon President Ryland's resignation, in June, 1898, Rev. E. S. Alderman, D. D., was elected president. Dr. Alderman is a graduate of Wake Forest College, North Carolina (1883), and of the full course in the Southern Baptist Theological Seminary, Louisville, Ky. (1886), having, since the latter date, been the pastor of several churches in North Carolina and Kentucky. He should be well fitted to uphold the well-established reputation of Bethel.

The matriculation of the college during the past two years has, owing to various circumstances, been considerably decreased, but there is no reason why, in the near future, it should not be larger than ever before. Under the new order of administration, established in 1897, several of the former members of the faculty resigned and new professors, mainly young men, were elected in their places. Upon the election of President Alderman one of these, Prof. James H. Fuqua, for four years the chairman of the faculty and otherwise long and favorably known in connection with the history of the institution, resumed his connection with it. Under the present arrangement the academic, or preparatory, department has been separated from the college proper, while the duties of the chair of modern languages and mathematics have been divided, and those of the chair of history distributed among the other professors. The college faculty, as now constituted, is as follows: Rev. Edward Sinclair Alderman, D. D., president, and Ewing professor of philosophy; Sidney Ernest Bradshaw, A. B., N. Long professor of English; William Edward Farrar, A. B., professor of Latin and Greek; Edgar Ezekiel De Cou, M. S., professor of mathematics and German; William B. Wilson, M. S., Norton professor of natural sciences; James Henry Fuqua, Sr., A. M., professor of mathematics and French.

One hundred and ninety-eight degrees, for work done in regular courses, have been granted by Bethel College since its resumption in 1863. These, with the 22 degrees conferred before the civil war, make the total number to 1898, inclusive, 220, of which 39 have been bachelors of science and 2 masters of arts. The others have been bachelors

LADIES' HALL. CHAPEL. LINCOLN HALL.

BEREA COLLEGE—ACROSS THE CAMPUS.

of arts. Of the alumni a number have distinguished themselves in the learned professions, more largely in teaching and the ministry than in any others.

BIBLIOGRAPHY.

A History of the Baptists of Kentucky, by J. H. Spencer, Cincinnati, 1885.
The Baptist Encyclopedia, by William Cathcart, Philadelphia, 1881.
Various newspaper sketches and other facts, furnished by President Ryland.
Collins's and Smith's histories; The Biographical Encyclopedia of Kentucky; Henderson's Centennial Exhibits; Barnard's Journal of Education.

BEREA COLLEGE, BEREA.

The chief founder of Berea College is Rev. John G. Fee, for it was largely through his influence and efforts that the school was first established, being, as it is, the direct outgrowth of the antislavery agitation in which he was engaged in eastern Kentucky.

Mr. Fee is a native of Kentucky and was educated at Augusta College. He later studied theology at Lane Theological Seminary, and while there, after much deliberation, adopted the tenets of the abolitionists. He labored for two years in the Presbyterian ministry in eastern Kentucky, but at the end of that time withdrew from that church because he was not in accord with it on the slavery question. He then labored for eight years[1] in that section, organizing antislavery churches, and finally, in 1854, upon the invitation of Cassius M. Clay, the great Kentucky abolitionist, established Berea Church in the southern part of Madison County, Ky., around which as a center Berea College has since grown up. Mr. Fee became the pastor of Berea Church in 1855, a position from the active duties of which he has only recently retired, and still lives to watch over the interests of the institution growing out of that church and of whose board of trustees he is yet a member.

For many years during his early labors he was largely supported in his work by the American Missionary Association, and so this society may, in a sense, be called a co-founder of the school, although it has never had any direct share in the management of the institution. It, however, paid the larger part of Mr. Fee's salary for thirty-four years, and also that of other teachers connected with the school at different times, and, in many ways, encouraged the enterprise.

The school out of which Berea College has since developed was established as a necessary means of sustaining Mr. Fee's antislavery agitation, and was first opened in the early part of 1855. Its first teachers were William E. Lincoln and Otis B. Waters, who came from Oberlin College, Ohio, of which institution Berea may, in a way, be considered an offshoot, since half or more of all its teachers up to the present time have been educated there. Mr. Waters remained at Berea

[1] Mr. Fee began preaching in Lewis and Bracken counties in 1845. He first preached at Berea in 1853, the year before his establishment of the church there.

for two years and Mr. Lincoln a short while longer, and, in the early part of 1858, the third teacher, also from Oberlin, Rev. J. A. R. Rogers, arrived.

Professor Rogers may be called the first principal of the school, and was destined to have more to do with shaping its future than perhaps any other one man except Mr. Fee. He opened a school in a small, rude building prepared for it soon after his arrival, with his wife as an assistant teacher. There were at first only 15 pupils, but before the end of the term the energy and enthusiasm of the new principal had brought the enrollment up to 96, and at the commencement held at that time subscriptions were raised to build an addition to the schoolhouse.

During the next term, beginning in September, 1858, Professor Rogers was assisted by Mr. and Mrs. John G. Hanson, and the reputation of the school, notwithstanding its distinctively antislavery character and sentiments, attracted the patronage even of slaveholding parents. A considerable number of these, however, withdrew their children at the end of the session on account of the expression of a sentiment, in connection with a discussion in one of the school literary societies, in favor of the admission of colored students should they apply. The school, however, continued under the same teachers until closed, as we shall see, by the excitement due to the opening events of the civil war, especially the John Brown raid.

Meanwhile steps had been taken to enlarge the scope of the enterprise, and, on September 7, 1858, a number of the friends of the school met at the residence of Mr. Fee to organize a college board of trustees and prepare a constitution for the incorporation of an institution of that grade. A constitution was then drawn up by a committee of which Professor Rogers was chairman, which, after considerable discussion among the friends of the undertaking, was finally adopted, substantially in its original form, in July, 1859. The general character of this instrument and the nature of the institution it proposed to call into existence may be seen from the following clauses.

This college shall be under an influence strictly Christian, and, as such, opposed to sectarianism, slaveholding, caste, and every other wrong institution or practice.[1]

The object of this college shall be to furnish the facilities for a thorough education to all persons of good moral character, at the least possible expense to the same, and all the inducements and facilities for manual labor which can reasonably be supplied by the board of trustees shall be offered to the students.[2]

At the time of the adoption of the constitution a board of trustees, composed of Rev. John G. Fee, Rev. J. S. Davis, Rev. George Candee, John Burnham, John Smith, William Stapp, Jacob Emrick, T. J. Renfro, John G. Hanson, and Rev. J. A. R. Rogers, was organized and steps taken to secure, under the general statutes of the State, a charter for the proposed college. Four of the trustees had already purchased, at

[1] Prudential Committee History, p. 18. [2] Ibid.

their own risk, for $1,800, as a desirable site for the proposed institution, a tract of land containing more than 100 acres, about 45 acres of which, beautifully situated and shaded with forest oaks, constitute the campus upon which the present buildings of the college are located. Mr. Fee had gone east to secure funds to pay for this property, and otherwise inaugurate the work. The John Brown raid occurred just at this time and caused the enterprise to be abandoned for some time.

The school had already aroused considerable opposition in the State, on account of its pronounced antislavery sentiments and its attitude on the race question, and its friends, especially Mr. Fee, had suffered harsh treatment on several occasions from the rougher elements of the community, led by those opposed to abolitionism. So the John Brown raid, which really frightened the South generally as to the dangers of slave insurrections, led to an organized effort to suppress the institution. A large county convention held in Richmond, Ky., appointed a committee of sixty-five men, many of them wealthy and honorable, to see that it was removed from the State, which "was accomplished with as much dignity and decorum as is consistent with such an enterprise."[1] On December 23, 1859, this committee notified Professor Rogers and ten others, including Mr. Fee, that they must leave the State in ten days. As the governor, when appealed to, informed them that, owing to the state of public opinion, he could not guarantee them protection, they thought it best to leave the State temporarily, and accordingly departed with their families, numbering about forty persons. So the school was closed for the time being, without having been fully inaugurated as a college.

In 1865 the friends of the institution returned, the board of trustees was reorganized, a charter for a college obtained under a general law of the State, and it was reopened as Berea College, the teachers at that time being Professor Rogers and wife, together with W. W. Wheeler and wife. Soon 75 or more students were in attendance, but when in the early part of 1866 3 colored youths applied for admission and were, in accordance with the terms of the college constitution, received, on this account half of the other students left. The places of these were, however, soon more than supplied, mainly by additional colored pupils, who, with other students, came in such large numbers in 1866-67 that temporary buildings had to be constructed for their accommodation. Within three years the school was more than twice as large as before, having in 1869 301 students and 7 teachers. Up to this time, as no students of advanced grade were in attendance, only normal and college preparatory classes were maintained, and Professor Rogers, who remained at the head of the institution, retained the title of principal.

In July, 1868, E. H. Fairchild, an alumnus of Oberlin and a man of ripe scholarship and varied educational experience, was called to the

[1] Special Report of Bureau of Education for 1886 on New Orleans Exposition, p. 230.

presidency of the institution. He assumed the duties of the position in April, 1869, in which year a regular college class of 5 members was first organized, and the school may be said to have started on its career as a real college. President Fairchild remained at its head for twenty years, during which he labored assiduously and successfully in its behalf. Professor Rogers long remained a prominent member of its faculty and is still a valued friend and trustee of the institution. John G. Hanson is another of its early teachers and promoters who, with Mr. Fee and Professor Rogers, has had an important share in its later success and prosperity.

The institution soon made marked progress under President Fairchild's able management. In the first year of his administration Howard Hall, a commodious frame dormitory for young men, was erected by the Freedmen's Bureau at a cost of $18,000, and in 1870-71 Ladies' Hall, a large and elegant brick building with all the modern improvements, costing, with its equipments, $50,000, was added for the accommodation of young ladies, the policy of Berea, like that of her foster mother, Oberlin, having been coeducational from the beginning.

The aim of the institution has been especially to reach two classes of students, which its record and location put it in a particularly favorable position to attract. These are the poorer white people of the eastern part of the State and the colored element of the other portion. It was Berea's strategic position, thus on the border of what are commonly known as the mountain and blue-grass sections of the State, that first suggested it to Mr. Fee, through General Clay, as a favorable point for the promulgation of his antislavery ideas and has since given its college a particularly fine opportunity to reach the classes just mentioned. The institution has also, especially in recent years, attracted many students from the Northern States. As the advantages of many of its students have been very limited, the college has been compelled to sustain all departments of instruction from primary to collegiate. Besides regular classical and literary college courses, it has maintained a normal course, for one of its special offices has been to prepare teachers for the public schools of the State, especially the colored public schools, where well-qualified teachers have been much needed. It also, according to the terms of its original constitution, endeavors to place its advantages within the reach of as many as possible by making its tuition fees and rates for board quite moderate and by furnishing all the opportunities it can for students to support themselves by manual labor. At least for a considerable portion of its history its affairs have been so managed that less than $100 a year would pay all a student's expenses except clothing, and this small amount might be considerably reduced by laboring in shop or kitchen.

Largely because of the poverty of its students, who are not able to remain to complete their courses, the attendance upon its college classes has not been large, but the matriculation in other departments has as a rule been excellent, often more than could be well accommodated by the means at command. The attendance had regularly increased since 1869, until in 1881-82 there were 15 teachers and 402 students, 12 States of the Union having been represented as early as 1872.

The course of instruction, as originally outlined in 1869, included a classical course of four years, a ladies' course of three years, and a normal course of two years, besides preparatory, academic, intermediate, and primary departments. In 1873 the ladies' course was extended to four years, and a special normal course of three years was instituted. In that year the institution sent out its first graduating class of 4 members.

As, according to its policy, its own income from tuition was very small, the college was, during its early years, largely, it is even yet partially, supported by annual contributions from friends, mainly in the North. It soon, however, began to acquire something in the way of permanent endowment. By 1876 this amounted to $24,000,[1] and at that time its grounds and buildings were valued at $100,000, and its library contained 1,000 volumes. In 1881-82 the endowment was increased by about $50,000, $30,000 of which was given by C. F. Dike, of Illinois, and C. F. Hammond, of New York. In this year also the complement of scientific apparatus having been improved, the previous ladies' course was changed into a scientific one leading to a regular degree.

The growth of the institution continued steadily during the remainder of President Fairchild's administration, which terminated with his death on October 2, 1889. In 1883-84 new buildings for the lower departments and a new frame chapel, the latter costing $9,000, were added to the college equipment, and in 1887 Lincoln Hall, a large and superb new brick recitation building, costing about $32,000, was erected through the liberality of Roswell Smith, of New York City, assisted by S. D. Warren, of Boston, Mass. The college then had nine buildings, worth $112,000, its endowment approximated $100,000, its library contained over 4,000 volumes, its faculty 18 members, and its students represented 19 States. Its annual deficit[2] had, however, grown with its expansion, and was then $8,000 a year.

Its students had not only increased in numbers, but more of them were in the higher departments. The average ratio of the white to colored students during this period of the institution's history was about 1 to 2. Since 1873 from 3 to 4 graduates had been sent out each year, and at the time of President Fairchild's death there were 44 alumni, 28 in the classical and 16 in the scientific course, 31 of whom were white and 13 colored, the former having been able, as a rule, to remain in college longer and so complete their course in a larger ratio.

---

[1] Only $19,000 of this, however, was then productive.

[2] The amount its expenses exceeded its income, which had to be secured in contributions each year.

Of the graduates up to this time, two-fifths had chosen teaching as a profession, and nearly as many had entered the ministry. President Fairchild left the institution with a greatly enlarged equipment, and had gathered for it an endowment, estimated at $100,000, not all of which, however, was yet productive. This endowment had been mainly given by Northern persons who had become interested in the institution, only a few thousand dollars of it having come from Kentucky.

In 1890, Rev. William B. Stewart, D. D., became Mr. Fairchild's successor in the presidency of the institution. During President Stewart's administration, extending through two years, a Bible department for prospective candidates for the ministry, which has since been discontinued, was instituted, and a course leading to the degree of Bachelor of Philosophy was added to the previous college courses leading to the degrees of Bachelor of Arts and Bachelor of Science. A system of elective studies was also introduced into the collegiate department, especially in the classical and philosophical courses.

In 1892, President Stewart resigned and the presidency of the college, which had been tendered to Rev. William G. Frost, Ph. D., D. D., just prior to President Fairchild's death but had then been declined for personal reasons, was again offered to him and was accepted at this time, the new president entering upon his duties in the summer of that year. Dr. Frost is a graduate of Oberlin in the class of 1876; he afterwards studied for some time at Harvard and other institutions in this country, and then abroad. He had already become known as a popular and vigorous teacher, the author of scholarly text-books, an earnest and effective preacher, and a lyceum lecturer of considerable repute.

Under his administration, notwithstanding the general financial distress throughout the country, the work of the college has steadily progressed. The matriculation increased 40 per cent during the first year of his term of office, in which a course leading to the degree of Bachelor of Letters was substituted for the previous scientific one and a newly organized normal course, designed to bring the institution into closer touch with the public schools of the State, was established, while a new "Model Home" was erected for training in domestic industry. In 1894–95, a fine new manual training building was erected, largely by the labor of the students themselves. In this there are the usual machine shops for the working of wood and metal while a printing office is attached and arrangements have been made for the introduction of other forms of productive industry. The completion of this building marked the addition of about $50,000 to the college equipment during the previous thirteen years, and made the educational plant of the institution consist of eleven buildings, estimated to be worth $130,000.

In the last three years several small buildings have been erected to accommodate the increased attendance, among them a dormitory, furnishing rooms for about 20 young men, given by A. P. Nichols, of Haverhill, Mass. A new department of horticulture and biology, including forestry, has also been created, the aim being to make this an important feature, and thus, as President Frost expresses it, "bring down the great arm of science to help the poor."[1] Within the present summer a new building for the practical scientific departments of the institution has been partially completed. The complement of apparatus in these departments is now quite good, while the college library has increased to about 13,000 volumes, and bookbinding has been added to the list of productive industries. All these make the educational facilities offered at Berea among the best to be found in the State.

The college has not for several years been aided by the American Missionary Association or any other benevolent society, but has depended on the income from its endowment, the small amount received from student fees, and the contributions of those interested in its work. With the growing wants of the institution, the amount annually required from this last source has of late been about $12,000. To meet this constantly recurring deficit, which is likely to increase rather than diminish, the friends of the institution have lately endeavored to increase its endowment by $200,000. The practical beginning of this movement was made at the commencement of June, 1895, when Dr. D. K. Pearsons, of Chicago, Ill., pledged himself to give $50,000 to the college funds if an additional $150,000 should be raised. An earnest effort was at once inaugurated to fulfill the conditions of this generous donation, the students of the college themselves contributing several thousand dollars for this purpose. The effort has since been zealously prosecuted and, despite the stringency of financial affairs, seems likely to be soon crowned with success, as by the middle of the present summer $85,000 of the conditional amount had been subscribed.

The annual matriculation of the institution has continued to increase during President Frost's administration, reaching 597 in all departments in 1896-97, and approximating 700 in the year just closed. Among the students of late have been a number from various Northern States, as many as 12 States of that section having recently contributed matriculates. In 1896-97 21 States of the Union were represented by the whole student body. For a number of years past the ratio of white to colored students has been constantly increasing, until now the former are considerably in the majority in the institution.

Berea has maintained a high standard of scholarship, which, combined with the limited means of most of her students, has made her college classes small and her number of graduates each year few. The usual number of graduates annually since 1873 has been three or four, except in the last two years, during which there have been about twelve graduated each year. The number of alumni at present approximates 100. Of these several have distinguished themselves in teaching, journalism, and the ministry, as also in political and business life.

The course of instruction in the collegiate department is divided into

[1] Personal letter of March 19, 1898.

the departments of English, history, political science, philosophy, pedagogics, evidences of Christianity, physics and astronomy, chemistry and mineralogy, biology, geology, mathematics, Latin language and literature, Greek language and literature, German, and Bible and Christian religion. The usual combinations of these subjects lead to the three degree courses, of four years each, already indicated. considerable latitude being allowed in the shaping of one's course by the choice of elective studies, which may be substituted for others usual in each course. There are also an academic or preparatory department, with a four years' course of instruction; a normal department, with a three years' course, with model primary, intermediate, and grammar schools, extending through six years, attached; a department of industry, including manual training, printing, horticulture, and domestic science; a department of music, drawing, and painting, and a business school. A diploma is conferred for the successful completion of the courses in the normal department and the department of music, while a certificate is granted in like manner in the business school.

The faculty of the collegiate, academic. and normal departments was, in June, 1898, constituted as follows: Rev. William Goodell Frost, Ph. D., president, professor of mental and moral philosophy, and lecturer on education; Rev. John Gregg Fee, A. M., lecturer on evidences of Christianity and Biblical literature, emeritus; Le Vant Dodge, A. M., professor of political science and acting professor of mathematics, registrar; Rev. Bruce Samuel Hunting, A. M., principal of preparatory department and professor of Latin; Alwin Ethelstan Todd, A. M., professor of natural sciences, librarian; Silas Cheever Mason, M. S., acting professor of horticulture and biology; Rev. Henry Mixter Penniman, professor of Christian evidences; Miss Josephine A. Robinson, A. B., principal of the ladies' department and instructor in mathematics; Miss Katharine Gilbert, A. M., instructor in English, German, and French; Ernest Green Dodge, A. M., acting professor of Greek and instructor in mathematics; Edward Brice Evans, A. B., instructor in history and Latin; Mrs. Eliza H. Yocum, A. M., instructor in methods of teaching and dean of the normal department. This faculty has been much strengthened during the present summer by the addition of George T. Fairchild, LL. D., who is an educator of repute, recently connected with the Kansas State Agricultural College, and is, at Berea, to occupy the chair of English, and also to become vice-president of the college. Besides the faculty just enumerated, the adjunct departments of music and industry and the model and commercial schools employ 15 other teachers and instructors, making the total educational corps to include 28 teachers.

The plan upon which Berea is conducted in regard to the races is not indorsed by a very large proportion of the citizens of the State in which it is located, but these have, as a rule, long ago ceased to exercise even antipathy toward the institution, which, on its part, proceeds upon what it considers its own special mission without any spirit of condemnation for those who think and do differently. There is no doubt that the institution has done a great educational work for classes in Kentucky especially who, at least until the present, would otherwise have been much neglected and among whom there is yet much to be done. It has accomplished much in the way of furnishing well-equipped teachers for the colored schools throughout the South, and its departments of manual training and productive industry, upon which it is now putting emphasis, are calculated especially to do much for the colored race in the future.

BIBLIOGRAPHY.

Berea College, an interesting history, published by the approval of the prudential committee (of the board of trustees), Cincinnati, 1883.

Special report of the United States Bureau of Education on educational exhibits and conventions at the New Orleans Exposition, Washington, 1886, contains a sketch of the college by President Fairchild.

The sketch of the college has been based mainly on the above two authorities, but use has also been made of Collins's and Perrin, Battle and Kniffen's histories, Henderson's Centennial Exhibits, and Barnard's Journal of Education, as well as the other sources of information, the use of which is taken for granted.

LYNNLAND MALE AND FEMALE INSTITUTE, GLENDALE.

This institution, although bearing the name of institute, is entitled to a place in this monograph by reason of its work being of a grade equal to that of many other schools of the State which bear more pretentious titles. The school arose from a local demand for higher education and had its origin in an association of well-to do farmers of the vicinity of Glendale, Hardin County, who about the early part of 1866 organized themselves into a stock company for the promotion of education in their midst and subscribed a sufficient amount to purchase an eligible location of something over 100 acres adjacent to the Louisville and Nashville Railroad and to erect on it a large and imposing building. This structure is situated in the midst of a beautiful campus of 10 acres, shaded with native oaks, and cost about $28,000, including its equipment, which embraced quite a good complement, for the time, of chemical and philosophical apparatus. Among those who may be mentioned as mainly instrumental in promoting the enterprise were T. J. Jeffries, William Sprigg, Samuel Sprigg, Henry Sprigg, and J. R. Gaither, who composed its first board of trustees.

The institution was first opened, under the name of Lynnland Institute, in the autumn of 1866, and had Rev. Mr. Colson as its first principal. The views of its projectors soon enlarged, and in 1867 they secured a charter for the institute, conferring upon it all the usual collegiate powers and privileges. It had been originally intended primarily to meet a local educational want in the neighborhood in which it was situated and has always maintained somewhat of a local character, although frequently drawing many students from other parts of the

State and elsewhere. It has never been put on a distinctively denominational basis, but has since its foundation been conducted in a general way under the auspices of Salem Baptist Association.

In the fall of 1868 Gen. W. F. Perry, who has been prominent in educational circles in Alabama and Kentucky, both before and since, took Rev. Mr. Colson's place as executive head of the institution and thus became its first president under its college charter which then went into operation. President Perry had associated with him in the various departments a faculty of six teachers, under whom a course of instruction embracing preparatory, academic, and collegiate departments was instituted. In order to properly prepare its own students for the work of its higher classes, and to meet the needs of the community in which it is located, the institute has always found it necessary to maintain a preparatory department and even, for part of the time during its history, a primary department. Regular college courses leading to the degrees of bachelor of arts and bachelor of science were conducted during President Perry's administration. This lasted eleven years, and during that time the reputation of the school throughout the State grew to be considerable.

Its annual matriculation during this period varied from about 75 to 160, and its graduates numbered about 75, some of whom have become prominent in the various professions, especially that of teaching. The institution was coeducational from the beginning, being thus among the first schools of the State to try this educational experiment. Its standard of scholarship was always high, but it was not a financial success at the time, and so went into the hands of a receiver in 1879, at which time General Perry resigned its presidency.

It was then closed for several years and its building was partially used as a residence. In 1889 its property, which had been acquired by one of its former trustees, was purchased by Professors E. W. Elrod and E. W. White, who for several years had as co-principals been successfully conducting Liberty College, at Glasgow, Ky., then an exclusive female college. In like manner in the autumn of that year Lynnland was reopened by them as an institution for young ladies only, although still under the same charter and bearing the same title.

The course of instruction under the new order of things included departments of music and art, as well as of English history, mental and moral philosophy, mathematics, Latin, modern languages, and natural science, different combinations of which led, as formerly, to the degree of bachelor of arts and bachelor of science. Five other teachers were associated with the principals in the work of teaching, and during the first year of their administration 54 pupils were in attendance, two of whom were graduated at the end of the year. In the following year the attendance increased so that additional boarding accommodations had to be provided, while the graduating class had three members. During the next session an additional building was erected, so that 50

CENTRAL UNIVERSITY—MAIN BUILDING.

boarders could be accommodated, and about $2,000 was spent in enlarging and modernizing the scientific apparatus of the institution. For the next three years the annual matriculation was about 60, and 11 students were graduated. The standard of scholarship and the reputation of the institution were good in comparison with similar institutions throughout the State, but, for a second time, owing it seems to the panic of 1893, it was not a financial success, and in 1895 had to be relinquished by Professors Elrod and White, who have since been connected with Georgetown College, Kentucky. The property was then purchased by Prof. W. B. Gwynn, who took charge in 1895 and has since conducted the institution, having changed it back to its original coeducational basis, as is shown by its present title. At the opening of his administration considerable improvements were made in the buildings and equipment of the institute generally, and during the first year 63 students were matriculated. The faculty at the time and since has been composed of six teachers. The attendance has recently risen to 80. During the three years, respectively, Professors G. H. Watts, Jacob Fisher, and Thomas A. Binford have been vice-presidents. The course of instruction has been retained substantially as it was formerly, and the graduates for this period number 7. The institution seems to be making good and substantial progress and to have excellent prospects for the future.

BIBLIOGRAPHY.

The facts of the earlier history of the institute have been furnished by President Perry. Its later history has been compiled almost entirely from catalogues.

CENTRAL UNIVERSITY, RICHMOND.

Central University is composed of a college of philosophy, letters, and science, a college of law, and a preparatory school located in Richmond, Ky., a college of medicine and a college of dentistry located in Louisville, Ky., and three preparatory and training schools located in other parts of the State. As the principal executive office of the institution is situated in Richmond, that place is considered more especially as the seat of the university. It is, in organization, one of the youngest candidates for public favor among the institutions for higher education in Kentucky, but in a comparatively short while has won a right to stand beside the older colleges of the State in rank and influence. It is also, in the extensive use of the term, at least, more nearly a real university than any other institution in the State, having more coordinate departments than any other school has or has had, except Kentucky University for a short period in its early history.

Central University was established under the auspices and is now, in a sense, under the control of the Kentucky synod of the Southern Presbyterian Church, and is historically the outgrowth of the educational spirit of the Presbyterians of Kentucky, which was shown in the original foundation of Transylvania Seminary and later of Kentucky

Academy and then of Centre College, of the last of which, as its name implies, Central University is both a continuation and a sister institution, standing in the same relation to the Southern Presbyterian Church as the older college does to the original denominational organization in the State.

The foundation of the university is the result of two simultaneous movements, the participants in each of which recognized independently of each other the need of such an institution to serve the object they had in view. The first of these was a church movement, originating within the State synod of the Southern Presbyterian Church. It began after the conference held at Lexington in November, 1870, between representatives of that body and of Kentucky synod of the Presbyterian Church, ordinarily called in contradistinction the Northern Presbyterian Church, in regard to the question of the adjustment of the property rights of the two bodies in Centre College, had proved barren of results in reaching any agreement which would give the synod of the Southern church any share in the management of that institution. The Southern synod accordingly determined to establish a college of similar compass under its own control, and at its next meeting in November, 1871, resolutions were passed upon motion of Dr. Stuart Robinson, of Louisville, looking toward the immediate endowment and equipment of such an institution. The synod at first only aimed to establish a denominational college of similar rank and scope with Centre, but under the influence of the other movement just referred to, which occurred at the same time, was induced to enlarge its plans.

This second movement arose from the conviction of a number of cultured men that there was a need in the State of a broad and comprehensive university which, while not put on a sectarian basis, should be conducted under Christian auspices. This feeling was voiced by an enthusiastic convention, composed mainly of Centre College alumni, held in Lexington on May 7 and 8, 1872, which organized itself into a permanent alumni association, and memorialized synod, about to meet in the same place, in reference to the immediate establishment of such an institution under its patronage, promising an earnest cooperation in the design, enthusiasm in behalf of which was shown by the prompt subscription by the members of the convention of $50,000 toward an endowment fund. The memorial of the convention shows its spirit by the following statement, among others:

> It is the sense of this convention that steps be taken to at once establish on a broad and liberal basis an institution of the highest order under the auspices of the synod of Kentucky, and thus carry out the earnest wishes of the fathers as demonstrated by the establishment of Centre College, now lost to this church.[1]

It was also proposed that the new institution should be conducted under the joint control of the synod and the association.

---

[1] Catalogue of 1894-95, p. 4.

This plan was generously responded to by the synod, and on May 8 a joint committee was appointed by the two bodies to prepare a plan and charter carrying out this combined system of government for the projected institution, to take measures to secure for it a desirable location, and to arrange for and prosecute its endowment, which it was proposed should not be less than $150,000 before the university should be opened, while it was aimed to make it at least $500,000.

Among those who may be mentioned beside Dr. Robinson as taking a prominent part in pushing forward the enterprise, either as members of the association or the synod, were Rev. Daniel Breck, D. D., Rev. R. Douglas, D. D., Rev. J. V. Logan, D. D., Rev. L. H. Blanton, D. D., Hon. T. W. Bullitt, Col. Bennett H. Young, and Joseph Chambers, esq.

The enthusiasm for the undertaking on the part of the two cooperating organizations was vigorous from the beginning, as shown by the liberal subscriptions made by their members for its endowment, which with that secured by the committee soon exceeded $100,000. A charter, which had been drawn up by the committee, was also adopted by both bodies, and was approved by the State legislature on March 3, 1873. This instrument provided for the inauguration, with full powers, of all the departments of a university, arranging for the opening of a college of philosophy, letters, and science, on the model of the best universities, in conjunction with which as many as six preparatory, or fitting, schools might be established in different portions of the State, and also stating that the institution shall provide for the establishment, "as soon as it may be done with advantage, of a department of law and a department of medicine. It shall also afford every facility for the establishment by the synod of Kentucky of a department of theology, either of itself or in conjunction with any of its co-synods or its assembly."[1]

The university in its origin was thus only denominational in the sense that its proposed theological department was to be controlled as just indicated, and the power of appointing its professor of ethics was to be vested in the synod of Kentucky. The donors of its endowment, who, under the name of the Alumni Association of Central University, were to elect their successors from among the alumni of the institution, as these came forth, or from such of its liberal benefactors as they might select, really owned and directed it, as by them was appointed a board of five trustees, elected for ten years, who looked after its funds, and a board of seven curators, one elected each year, to whom the direct management of its affairs in other respects was intrusted. This oversight, peculiar to the institution, gave all the safeguards that are to be found in ecclesiastical supervision and control, and at the same time guarded against the tendencies to sectarianism incident to such direction under its ordinary forms.

By an act of April 17, 1884, the old board of trustees and curators

---

[1] Section 7 of charter of 1873.

was done away with and the governing body of the institution was made to consist of a chancellor and fifteen curators, two-thirds of the latter being required to be members of the alumni association and three of them being elected each year by the synod. This has made the institution somewhat more denominational, but not materially so, as the essential principle of the former arrangement, which is calculated to inspire confidence and arouse favor on the part of the public generally, has been retained. At the same time the additional beneficial effect has followed of causing the synod to take more interest in the institution and to further its progress more materially, as has been shown by the gifts since received from that source to the endowment.

The internal organization of the institution is also somewhat peculiar. It is composed of independent colleges, with a president at the head of each who directs its special work. The chief executive officer of the whole university is a chancellor, who, under the general direction and control of the curators, is charged with the general supervision of its affairs, both financial and educational, and thus imparts unity of aim and purpose to the entire organization. One of the chief functions of the chancellor is to look after the enlargement of the endowment of the institution.

The first preliminary step looking toward the opening of the university took place on April 29, 1873, when its incorporators met in Louisville and effected a permanent organization, after which it was arranged to settle the question of the location of the institution through a vote of the alumni association and others who had subscribed to its funds. In this way it was first located, on May 13 of that year, at Anchorage, near Louisville, and a temporary organization of the institution took place at Louisville on May 29 following. This selection was afterwards revoked by the same body that made it, and new bids having been solicited, on November 11, 1873, it was permanently organized at Richmond, which place was finally decided upon as its permanent seat. That town had offered, as an inducement to secure the institution, $101,355,[1] which, together with the subscriptions already secured, made a total of $220,000 provided at that time to furnish an equipment and endowment for the institution.

This was regarded as only the beginning of the endowment proposed, but was considered sufficient to justify the inauguration of the enterprise, waiting for the future to develop more fully the aims in view. Accordingly, the board of curators, at a meeting held in Richmond on December 30, 1873, unanimously resolved to open the colleges of philosophy, letters and science, and of law, and a first-class preparatory school in the following September. An appropriation was made for purchasing a suitable campus, and $30,000 was set apart for the construction of the main college building; spacious and beautiful grounds

[1] Collins's History of Kentucky, Vol. I, p. 246r. Bardstown and Paris were also strong competitors for the location.

adjoining the town and lying in a square nearly one-fourth of a mile to the side were soon secured, and a large and handsome brick building four stories in height, and containing a commodious chapel, a library, laboratories, and lecture rooms, erected.

In this fine new structure the university was opened on September 22, 1874. Rev. Stuart Robinson, D. D., had been made its chancellor at first, and Rev. R. L. Breck, D. D., vice-chancellor and active endowment agent; but Dr. Robinson soon retired from the chancellorship, the duties of which from the beginning seem to have been discharged by Dr. Breck. The first president of the college of philosophy, letters, and science was Rev. J. W. Pratt, D. D., the faculty of this department, as announced in its first annual catalogue, being constituted as follows: Rev. J. W. Pratt, D. D., president and professor of the English language and literature and oratory; Rev. L. G. Barbour, A. M., professor of pure and applied mathematics and astronomy; W. G. Richardson, A. M., professor of Latin and French; Rev. J. V. Logan, A. M., professor of logic and biblical literature and the synod's professor of ethics; Rev. R. L. Breck, D. D.,[1] professor of psychology and political science; J. Alston Cabell, C. E., M. E., B. S., professor of physics; Hugh A. Moran, A. B., lecturer on history and mythology; W. M. Willson, A. M., professor of Greek; A. N. Gordon, B. P., adjunct professor of mathematics, and B. Harrison Waddell, A. M., professor of German and adjunct professor of ancient languages.

The law college had a faculty of three professors, with C. F. Burnham, LL. D., as president. Just prior to the opening of these departments the medical college of the university was organized in Louisville, under the name of the Hospital College of Medicine, and its first preliminary term opened there on September 7, 1874. It had a faculty of nine professors and several assistants, its first president being E. D. Foree, M. D., and its first dean William Bolling, M. D. This department and the college of dentistry, which has since been added as a new department to the university, have been located in Louisville, particularly on account of the superior clinical advantages offered by a large city. The history of these colleges will be reserved for a subsequent portion of this article, our attention being confined for the present to the general history of the university, and particularly of those departments of it located at Richmond.

DEVELOPMENT OF THE RICHMOND DEPARTMENTS.

During the first session of the college of philosophy, letters, and science, 117 students were in attendance, 36 of whom were in the collegiate department. A regular college course was inaugurated from the beginning. It contained the nine departments of Latin, Greek, ethics, evidences of Christianity and logic, metaphysics and political economy,

[1] Dr. Breck at this time held a chair as well as discharged the duties of the chancellorship, an arrangement not now in operation.

mathematics, English language and literature, physics and chemistry, mineralogy and geology, and modern languages, the completion of the last five of which led to the degree of bachelor of science, while all but the last were required for the degree of bachelor of arts. The college had at its opening a good supply of scientific apparatus and a library of nearly 1,000 volumes. Its annual matriculation during the early years of its history was fairly well sustained, being usually about 100, and its first graduating class of five bachelors of arts and one bachelor of science was sent out in 1877.

Owing to the relation, already mentioned, in which the chancellor stands to the institution, a large part of the responsibility of its management naturally falls on him, and upon him in a great measure depends its success. A large share of the subsequent prosperity of Central University has been due to the earnest, self-sacrificing efforts of its first active chancellor, Dr. Breck, who, although comparatively young, had become a recognized leader of his church in Kentucky, and was a man of strong convictions and unwavering courage. He threw himself with all the enthusiasm of his nature into the work of organizing and equipping the institution, and to him are its foundations largely due. "To his zeal, efficiency, energy, and weight, more than to any other man's, Central University is indebted for its establishment."[1] He even sacrificed his health in its service and on that account was soon compelled to sever his connection with it.

The institution then for a time experienced dark days. Owing to the general financial stringency of the period of its foundation, trouble had been experienced in collecting the subscriptions to its funds, and its affairs otherwise looked so gloomy that Dr. Pratt resigned the presidency of the college of letters, and its law college, which had opened propitiously, was compelled to suspend for lack of sufficient support. Many friends of the university had begun to despair of its success, when, in looking for a desirable chancellor, the attention of the board of curators was drawn to the qualifications of a man comparatively young but known as an efficient pastor, possessing energy, ability, and varied scholarship, as well as enthusiasm in the cause of education.

This man, Rev. L. H. Blanton, D. D., was selected in 1880 as Dr. Breck's successor in the chancellorship of the university, and with his accession to office in the summer of that year a new era dawned upon the institution. Dr. Blanton, being a man of great executive ability, with an intuitive knowledge of men, and broad and liberal views of college administration, besides being prudent in financial matters and practical in his business plans, has built wisely upon the foundations laid by Dr. Breck. His energy and hopefulness soon so dispelled the atmosphere of doubt and discouragement hanging over the institution that men of liberal means began to pour their contributions into its endowment fund and in a short time its prominence and

[1] Green's Historic Families of Kentucky, p. 214.

future prosperity were completely assured. All of his efforts to advance the interests of the university were ably assisted by Rev. J. V. Logan, D. D., who had formerly been the synod's professor of ethics in its faculty, but had been elected to the presidency of its college of philosophy, letters, and science at the time of Dr. Blanton's accession to its chancellorship. These officers have since retained their respective positions and have efficiently cooperated in the successful management of the institution in whose foundation they had both taken an active interest.

During the first year of the new administration the number of students considerably increased and about $40,000 was added to the endowment; during the second year the new endowment fund, which synod proposed to make $100,000, was raised to half that amount, while the matriculation was enlarged from 109, in the preceding year, to 149. The history of the institution has since been one of improvement and enlargement in many directions.

Although the completion of the endowment proposed by synod had to be suspended in 1883, on account of the general financial stringency, the movement has since continued and much more than the amount then had in view has been obtained. In the early part of 1886, within sixty days, contributions aggregating about $100,000 were made by a few generous friends of the institution in Kentucky, while in 1890 $30,000 more was received, and in 1895 $10,000. These gifts, together with the additions that had been made to its general equipment, made the total value of the property and funds of the university in April, 1896, approximate $325,000. As will be noticed elsewhere, recent enlargements of the equipment have since taken place. A new plan of endowment has also recently been adopted, as a beginning of which one subscription of $8,500 has already been made.

Among the larger contributors to the different funds of the university since 1880 have been Mr. and Mrs. S. P. Walters, $30,000; Hon. H. W. McBrayer, $30,000; Mr. Orville Ford, $20,000; Hon. D. C. Collins, $12,000; Mr. A. J. Alexander, $30,000; Mrs. Mary R. Kinkead, $10,000; Mrs. John McClintock, $5,000; Mrs. Mary J. Lyons, $5,000; Col. Bennett H. Young, $10,000; Mr. William T. Grant, $10,000, and Hon. W. N. Haldeman, $10,000. The Walters professorship of applied mathematics, the McBrayer professorship of the Bible and Christian evidences, the Ford professorship of English and modern languages, the Alexander professorship of philosophy, the Mary R. Kinkead memorial, the McClintock memorial, and the Lyons lectureship have been named in honor of those who mainly or wholly endowed them.

The different contributions which have been mentioned have mainly become part of the productive endowment, but from this and other sources during this period material additions have been made both to the buildings and educational apparatus of the university. A plan was inaugurated in connection with the celebration of the centennial[1]

[1] This centennial was celebrated at Harrodsburg in October, 1883.

of the establishment of Presbyterianism in Kentucky by the synod of the Southern Presbyterian Church, in accordance with which the ladies of that church in the State raised a fund from which was constructed on the university campus, as a fitting memorial of that event, Memorial Hall. This building, which will furnish accommodations for over 50 young men, and cost, with its furniture, $20,000, was completed in September, 1883, and is intended to furnish to deserving students a comfortable college home at a very moderate cost. In that year also the institution received by bequest a valuable contribution to its equipment in the form of the library of the late Rev. R. W. Landis, D. D., of Danville, Ky., which contained about 3,000 volumes. In 1890 a handsome new building was erected for the preparatory department, in connection with which a hall was equipped with the best modern gymnastic apparatus. In 1892 the complement of apparatus in physics and chemistry was materially increased, and in 1898 Mr. C. C. Cooper, of Dayton, Ky., presented to the university museum a valuable collection of typical fossils. The previous means provided for physical training had not proven sufficient to meet the enlarged needs of the institution, and during the present summer, through the liberality of two generous ladies of Richmond, a fine new gymnasium is being constructed, which will furnish splendid facilities in that line for some time to come.

With the growth of its endowment and equipment a similar expansion has taken place in the scope and character of the work done by the institution, new departments and new courses of instruction having been added from time to time, and so its position as a true university more fully attained. In 1887 a college of dentistry was established in Louisville as a new department, and in 1891 a provisional class in theology was instituted, and the collection of an endowment begun looking toward the opening of a college of theology. This latter department will not, however, now probably be added to the university, as its need was supplied by the establishment of Louisville Presbyterian Theological Seminary in 1893, in the foundation of which the officers and friends of the university took a prominent part. Between 1891 and 1896 three new preparatory schools were attached to the institution in different parts of the State, and in 1897 a new college of law was opened in Richmond. These, as well as the college of dentistry, will be noticed later, as we shall confine our attention for the present to improvements which have been made in the curriculum of the college of philosophy, letters, and science.

The previous additions to the endowment allowed two new members to be added to the faculty in 1882, when a beginning was made in raising the standard of scholarship, which has gone on until it has reached the level of that of the older institutions of the State. In 1884 the scientific course was strengthened and brought up to a level with the classical course by having all the departments of instruction added to the former, except Latin and Greek, while part of the department of natural science was made optional in the latter. In 1886 large contributions to the endowment enabled the faculty to widen the curriculum and introduce a system of partial electives into the junior and senior classes, which enabled the student to shape his course more in accordance with his special needs and tastes. The increase of the endowment having continued, new departments of instruction were instituted and two new members added to the faculty, one in 1891 and another in 1892, the department of natural science having been previously subdivided and its work more specialized, while in 1891 a new course leading to the degree of bachelor of letters was established. It substitutes modern languages, English, and history for the Greek and part of the mathematics and science of the bachelor of arts course. This gives the institution three regular degree courses,[1] in each of which the master's degree may be obtained by an additional year of regular study at the university and the preparation of an acceptable thesis in some special field of research.

In 1893 a new department of military science and tactics, regarded, aside from the useful information it imparts, as a valuable auxiliary to physical development and to discipline, completed the present curriculum, which is composed of the departments of Latin, Greek, mathematics, physics and astronomy, English language and literature, modern languages, philosophy, history and political science, chemistry, biology and geology, commercial science, the Bible and Christian evidences, and military science and tactics. The preparatory department attached to the college has a course of four years, especially designed to fit students for one of the college courses.

The annual matriculation of the university has kept pace well with its progress in other respects. The number of students in attendance upon the college of philosophy uniformly increased until 217 were members of its various classes in 1891–92. The average matriculation for the past six years in this department has approximated 200, as many as nine states having recently been represented at one time, and has not been reduced as much as that of several other institutions of similar grade in the State. The matriculation of all the departments of the university as a whole has steadily risen during this period, reaching a total of 807 in 1895–96, of 859 in 1896–97, and of 978 in 1897–98.

The proportion of students in the higher classes of the college of philosophy has, in late years, been very materially increased and the size of the graduating classes in that department has accordingly enlarged. From 6 to 15 graduates have been sent out by the college every year since 1880, until in 1897–98 the graduating class numbered 25 regular degree students, the largest in the history of the institution.

[1] Diplomas are conferred in each department, the requisite number of these leading to a degree. Special students are also allowed to take courses for which they have the proper preparation.

There have been altogether in the different degree courses of the college 224 graduates, of whom 134 have taken the degree of A. B., 69 that of B. S., and 21 that of B. L. Many of these have entered the different learned professions, especially the ministry and teaching, and in the comparatively short period since the foundation of the institution have won an honorable position in their chosen fields of labor.

The board of curators in 1896, in accordance with the ideas now largely prevailing in Kentucky, opened the privileges of the institution to young ladies from Madison County,[1] about 12 of whom were in attendance in 1896–97 and about 15 in 1897–98. On March 10, 1898, having deemed the experiment a success, the board, by resolution, threw the doors of the college fully open to young women upon the same terms as to young men, thus making the institution fully coeducational.

The following constitute the corps of administration and instruction in the college of philosophy, letters, and science, an assistant in each of the departments of elocution, the classics, chemistry, history, and mathematics not being enumerated: L. H. Blanton, D. D., chancellor; J. V. Logan, D. D., LL. D., president, synod's professor of ethics and evidences, and professor of psychology and logic; L. G. Barbour, D. D., LL. D., professor of history and Bible; J. T. Akers, Ph. D., Ford professor of English language and literature, and professor of modern languages; C. G. Crooks, M. A., Walters professor of mathematics; Robert M. Parks, Ph. D., professor of chemistry; A. Wilkes Smith, D. D. S., M. D., professor of physiology; Gordon Paxton, M. A., professor of Latin; Lieut. S. P. Vestal, U. S. A., professor of military science and tactics; Edwin L. Green, Ph. D., professor of Greek; J. H. Chandler, B. L., adjunct professor of English.

COLLEGE OF LAW.

As already noted, this new department, or rather an old department revived, was attached to the university in 1897. It is located in Richmond and is operated in conjunction with the college of philosophy, letters, and science, to whose classes its matriculates have access without additional expense. The college was opened on October 1, 1897, and had 12 students during its first year. It has an able faculty of three members, with William Chenault, LL. D., as its executive head. Professor Chenault was for a number of years a professor in the law department of the University of Louisville, as well as dean of the institution, and is known as one of the leading teachers of law in the South and West.

The methods of instruction in the college are by recitation, lecture, and case study, combined with frequent quizzes and reviews in the different studies of the course, the whole being illustrated and enforced by a moot court, which meets regularly. It is aimed to give

[1] The county in which Richmond is situated.

the student both a theoretical and practical knowledge of the law and to fit him directly for practice. The course of instruction extends over two years and embraces all the subjects usually pursued in the best law schools of the country. It leads to the degree of bachelor of laws. A number of lectures upon special topics are given, in addition to the regular course, by distinguished members of the Kentucky bar. The following constitute the regular members of the present faculty: William Chenault, LL. D., president, professor of elementary law, pleading, commercial law, real property, and criminal law; J. V. Logan, LL. D., professor of political science and civics; R. W. Miller, A. B., LL. B., professor of contracts, torts, evidence, equity and corporations.

UNIVERSITY HIGH SCHOOLS.

One of the most prominent features in the history of the development of the university during the past seven years has been the establishment, in conjunction with it, of three new high schools in different portions of the State, which have proven important auxiliaries to its work. Its charter, as before mentioned, provides for the foundation of six such schools, but only one, the preparatory school at Richmond, instituted at the opening of the university, had been established up to 1891. In that year a second one, known as Jackson Collegiate Institute, was opened at Jackson, while in 1892 a third, named Hardin Collegiate Institute, was established at Elizabethtown, and in 1896 a fourth, called Middlesboro University School, at Middlesboro.

These schools are not intended merely as preparatory schools to the university, but are also to furnish a good well rounded English education to such as can pursue their education no further, and especially to furnish well-trained teachers for the public schools of the State. So, in addition to a regular high-school course of four years extending to the junior year of the college of philosophy of the university, they each have special commercial and normal courses and the usual ornamental departments. The schools at Jackson and Middlesboro especially are so situated in the eastern part of the State as to be able to perform an important public service in furnishing teachers for a section hitherto much neglected educationally, a work upon which the older of these schools particularly has already entered with great success.

The worth of this institution was especially recognized in 1897 by the liberal gift, in addition to her previous annual contribution to its support, of $5,000 by Mrs. S. P. Lees, of New York City, a native of Kentucky, for a new building, while Mrs. N. F. McCormick, of Chicago, Ill., generously added $5,000 to establish a department of manual training. Both donations were made on the condition of an equal amount for the same purpose being raised within the State, which was done, and a splendid new building, with an excellent equipment for manual training, was opened in September, 1897. In honor of these donations the school has since been called the S. P. Lees Collegiate Institute, and the department of manual training the N. F. McCormick School of Manual Training. Hardin Collegiate Institute and Middlesboro University School also have excellent buildings and general equipment, all three of the schools having dormitories for students. All are also coeducational. The S. P. Lees Collegiate Institute has had since its foundation an annual average matriculation of about 200 students. Its present faculty contains 8 teachers. The corresponding figures for Hardin Collegiate Institute are 60 and 5, and for Middlesboro University School 75 and 5. Their respective principals are J. M. Moore, A. M.; Rice Miller, A. B., and James R. Sterrett, B. S.

THE MEDICAL DEPARTMENT OF THE UNIVERSITY—THE HOSPITAL COLLEGE OF MEDICINE—LOUISVILLE.

We have seen that this department of the university was opened in Louisville in the same year the college of philosophy was organized in Richmond. The medical department was from the first located at its present situation, on Chestnut street, opposite the city hospital, and was called the Hospital College of Medicine. The preliminary session of the institution was opened on September 7, 1874, and its first faculty was composed of the following regular professors, besides whom there were five assistants and demonstrators: E. D. Foree, LL. D., M. D.; Frank C. Wilson, A. B., M. D.; William H. Bolling, M. D.; John T. Williams, A. M., M. D.; James M. Holloway, A. M., M. D.; William Bailey, A. M., M. D.; John J. Speed, A. M., M. D.; John A. Larrabee, M. D., and Dudley S. Reynolds, A. M., M. D. Dr. Foree was president of the faculty and Dr. Bolling its dean.

The building provided for the institution at its opening was quite a comfortable and convenient one, while the course of instruction was the two years' course then usual in medical colleges. A modern tone was, however, given to this course at the end of the first session by the abandonment of the time-honored thesis as a requisite for graduation and the substitution of written examinations, in which a high general average was required. The beginnings of a fine museum collection were at once laid, and clinical exercises and laboratory instruction were from the first made a prominent part of the regular curriculum.

One hundred and three students, representing 22 States of the Union and 2 foreign countries, many of whom were advanced students from other institutions, were in attendance the first session, and at its close the degree of M. D. was conferred upon 57 of these. The classes of the institution throughout its history until the last few years have been comparatively small, varying in number from 49 to 153 up to 1894, but they have for the most part been composed of young men of good preliminary education, and the college, by reason of its requirements, has taken and maintained a high rank among similar institutions, in the South and West particularly.

Its methods have been progressive in every way. Since 1879 espe-

CENTRAL UNIVERSITY. THE HOSPITAL COLLEGE OF MEDICINE, LOUISVILLE.

cially a strict compliance with its graduation requirements of the completion of a two years' lecture course of similar scope to its own, with one year's preliminary study, has been enforced by it, and since then it has been among the foremost medical schools of the South in raising its standard. Under the old system of appointments to positions on the resident staff of the city hospital of Louisville by competitive examination, the institution from the very first held its own—in fact, more than did so—in competition with the older medical colleges of the city, often holding all four of the appointments then offered by the hospital.

The equipment of the institution has always been kept up with the demands of modern medical education. In 1878 the McClure cabinet of rare and valuable specimens was purchased for it and added to its museum, which was thus made quite ample. Its cabinet of materia medica was at that time also quite complete, and its dissecting room was early made one of the finest in the West. At the beginning of the session of 1881-82 a laboratory for the study of general pathology and hygiene was equipped, and a laboratory for investigation in bacteriology was also inaugurated as a part of the regular curriculum, the latter being presided over by the professor of pathology and hygiene, assisted by competent demonstrators.

At the conclusion of the session of 1881-82 it was considered, for various reasons, more desirable to have a considerable portion of the annual session in the spring and summer and, accordingly, the next session was opened at the beginning of the next year, a practice which has since been retained, the sessions beginning on January 1 of each year. After this change a fall polyclinical course for advanced students and practitioners of medicine was maintained for a number of years, but has lately been discontinued.

For the session of 1887 a standard preliminary educational qualification, embracing the branches of a good English education was exacted of all matriculants. While this had the effect of keeping the attendance comparatively small for a considerable time, it finally resulted in the gradual increase in numbers of students possessed of all the necessary educational training to fit them for an intelligent comprehension of the technology of medicine.

The college has shared in all the organized movements of the profession to advance the standard of medical education throughout the country. It took part in the convention of medical colleges in Philadelphia in 1876, and was active in its interest in the organization of the Association of American Medical Colleges in Chicago in 1877. It was represented at the revival of that association in Nashville in 1890 and at its full reorganization in Washington in 1891. At both of these last two conventions it earnestly supported the establishment in all the institutions of the country of a graded course of instruction extending through three annual sessions of not less than six months each as a requirement for graduation. As an evidence of its own position in this matter, the Hospital College in 1890 inaugurated such a course, with full requirements for its session of 1891, being the first medical college in the South to do so, its preliminary educational requirements being at the same time also advanced. The institution has since taken a prominent part in the councils of the Association and has conformed fully to the latter's advanced requirements in all respects, instituting in 1895, for new students entering at that time, the standard course of four annual sessions, which must include at least two sessions in dissection and in chemical instruction, and at least one course of instruction in the laboratories of chemistry, histology, pathology, bacteriology, and surgery.

The equipment of the college, both in the way of buildings and apparatus of all kinds, has also been kept up to the demands of the times. In 1886, in order to meet enlarged needs and to make more elaborate arrangements for laboratory and clinical instruction, new buildings were erected and the conveniences of the institution greatly amplified. It was at this time that quarters were prepared for the new College of Dentistry, which was inaugurated in conjunction with the Hospital College in January, 1887. The accommodations then prepared were, however, soon insufficient for the two institutions, and so, in 1893, a fine new modern four-story brick and stone building was constructed for them, which was formally opened on January 2, 1894. It is one of the most complete and ample of its kind in the country and furnished enlarged facilities in every way for the medical college, having commodious laboratories of histology, microscopy, and practical surgery, in addition to those already possessed by the institution, besides affording excellent quarters for lecture and recitation rooms, as well as for the library and museum. It also offered greater opportunities for clinical instruction, as the dispensary connected with the college was at that time greatly enlarged and its service more thoroughly systematized.

In 1896, in order to further increase the facilities for clinical instruction and to furnish students hospital experience and training, a fine new hospital, a three-story brick and stone structure of handsome design, known as the Gray Street Infirmary, was erected, adjoining the college. It was opened January 1, 1897, and contains four wards, two for white and two for colored patients, male and female, with numerous private rooms for special and surgical cases, and is built after the most approved methods of hospital construction, with all the modern appointments. With all its appliances it furnishes clinical advantages probably unsurpassed by any similar institution in this country.

The annual matriculation of the college has largely increased in recent years and is now among the largest in the South, its average for the past four years having been considerably over 200 regular students, besides a number of others taking special courses. About 30 per cent of its students come from the States of Kentucky, Indiana, Illinois, and Tennessee. The remainder are from the South and West, largely, although there are a great many from the Eastern States and some from foreign countries. Several times in recent years more States and countries have been represented by its matriculates than at its opening. Its graduating classes have also gradually increased in size, until that of 1898 numbered 135, the largest in the history of the institution. The total number of graduates to 1898, inclusive, is 996, among whom are many prominent practitioners in all branches of the medical profession in different parts of the country.

The methods of instruction in the institution embrace the blending of didactic lectures, laboratory work, quizzes, dissections, demonstrations, and careful clinical teaching by the professors and the chiefs of the different clinics. The present curriculum includes the departments of anatomy, physiology and hygiene, materia medica and therapeutics, chemistry, principles and practice of medicine, surgery, diseases of the chest, obstetrics, gynecology and abdominal surgery, diseases of children, ophthalmology and otology, diseases of the eye, ear, nose, and throat, diseases of the skin, genito-urinary diseases, and medical jurisprudence.

The following are the present regular professors of the college, in addition to whom its faculty contains twenty-three clinical professors, lecturers, and demonstrators in the various departments: John A. Larrabee, M. D., president, professor of obstetrics and diseases of children; Dudley S. Reynolds, A. M., M. D., professor of ophthalmology, otology, and medical jurisprudence; Frank C. Wilson, A. B., M. D., professor of diseases of the chest and physical diagnosis; Samuel G. Dabney, M. D., professor of physiology and hygiene; Philip F. Barbour, A. B., M. D., professor of medical chemistry and toxicology; Thomas Hunt Stucky, M. D., Ph. D., professor of principles and practice of medicine and clinical medicine; John Edwin Hays, A. M., M. D., professor of anatomy and dermatology; H. Horace Grant, A. M., M. D., professor of the principles and practice of surgery and clinical surgery; Lewis S. McMurtry, A. M., M. D., professor of gynecology; P. Richard Taylor, M. D., dean, professor of materia medica and therapeutics.

The following have been the executive officers of the institution since its foundation: Presidents—E. D. Foree, LL. D., M. D., 1874–1882; William Bailey, A. M., M. D., 1882–1885; William H. Bolling, M. D., 1885–1891; Dudley S. Reynolds, A. M., M. D., 1891–1893; John A. Larrabee, M. D., 1893 to present. Deans—William H. Bolling, M. D., 1874–1885; J. Lewis Howe, Ph. D., M. D., F. C. S., 1885–1894; P. Richard Taylor, M. D., 1894 to present.

THE DENTAL DEPARTMENT OF THE UNIVERSITY—LOUISVILLE COLLEGE OF DENTISTRY, LOUISVILLE.

The establishment of this department of Central University at Louisville in 1887 has already been mentioned. The new college was organized in 1886, but, holding its sessions at the same time as those of the

Hospital College of Medicine, was not opened until January 20, 1887. It occupied the building erected for the two colleges in 1886, but had entirely separate lecture rooms, laboratories, halls, and infirmary from the medical college, as it has since had in the later building of 1893. The two departments, however, to the advantage of both professors and students, being thus contiguous, are operated in close conjunction, several members of their faculties being identical, and the students of each having access to the courses of the other without additional expense, and being able to take an extra degree in one after completing the course in the other, with the saving of at least a year's time.

The original faculty of the College of Dentistry was composed of the following regular professors in addition to three demonstrators: A. Wilkes Smith, M. D., D. D. S., professor of oral and dental surgery and operative dentistry; Charles G. Edwards, D. D. S., professor of prosthetic and clinical dentistry; A. M. Cartledge, M. D., professor of surgery; Dudley S. Reynolds, A. M., M. D., professor of pathology and hygiene; Frank C. Wilson, A. B., M. D., professor of the principles and practice of medicine; Samuel G. Dabney, M. D., professor of physiology and histology; John A. Larrabee, M. D., professor of materia medica and therapeutics; Cornelius Skinner, M. D., professor of anatomy; J. Lewis Howe, Ph. D., M. D., F. C. S., professor of medical chemistry and toxicology.

Dr. Smith was the president of this faculty and Dr. Howe its dean.

The course of instruction originally inaugurated was the usual two years' lecture course for sessions of five months then in vogue throughout this country. Seventeen students, a considerable proportion of whom had pursued dental studies in other institutions, were in attendance the first session, and at its close the degree of doctor of dentistry was conferred on 11 candidates. The matriculation increased to 22 the second year, 45 the third year, and 72 the fourth year, while there were 4 graduates in 1888, 13 in 1889, 12 in 1890, and 26 in 1891. The students had up to this time represented altogether as many as twenty States of the Union and two foreign countries.

The college has always taken a decided stand in favor of the advancement of dental education throughout the country. It became at the end of its first session a member of the National Association of Dental Faculties, and has since continued an earnest participant in the promotion of the objects of that organization. In 1890, in conformity with the requirements of that body, it advanced its standard of graduation so as to require the completion of three annual sessions of not less than six months each, in two of which dissection must have been pursued. A preliminary entrance requirement embracing the elements of a good English education was also established.

The longer period required for graduation and the general financial distress reduced the matriculation somewhat for a short while after 1890, but the attendance soon again enlarged, and it was found necessary, in conjunction with the erection of the new building for the medical college in 1893, to prepare new accommodations for the college of dentistry. The additional quarters prepared for the latter in the new building, opened on January 2, 1894, were second to none of any similar institution, at least in the South or West, in size, beauty, and convenience, and furnished a complete modern equipment in the way of didactic and clinical lecture amphitheaters, chemical and dental laboratories, dissecting rooms, infirmary, and other necessary departments.

The growth of the institution was, however, so rapid that additional accommodations were necessary, and in 1896 a commodious and handsome new infirmary and hospital, containing a spacious clinical amphitheater and provided with every modern convenience for operations in both general and oral surgery, was erected in the rear of the main building. The attendance of the session of 1897 was so large as to even task the capacity of the new buildings at once, and additional provision had to be made in the way of operative clinic rooms for the session of 1898.

The increase in matriculation during the past seven years has been very pronounced. The average annual attendance during that time has been 125, and in 1898 172 regular students were in attendance upon the various classes of the college. As in the case of the medical college, about 30 per cent of the matriculates of the College of Dentistry come from the States of Kentucky, Indiana, Tennessee, and Illinois, but the remainder represent all the other States of the Union and several foreign countries. At one time in recent years as many as twenty-six States of the United States and two other countries have been represented by its students. The enlargement of the graduating class has also corresponded well with that of the general student body, the number of graduates having increased from 6 in 1893 to 49 in 1898. The total number of alumni to 1898 inclusive is 259.

The aim of the course of instruction of the institution is to thoroughly equip the student with that knowledge, both theoretical and practical, which will enable him to practice his profession with eminent success. To this end he is required not only to pursue those studies directly pertaining to dentistry, but other collateral branches, especially of medicine, which will broaden his knowledge and furnish him a better scientific foundation. He takes the same course of elementary instruction as the medical student, the graded course in anatomy, physiology, chemistry, materia medica and therapeutics, histology, pathology, and bacteriology, and in the principles of medicine, surgery, and hygiene. The close conjunction in which the College of Dentistry and the Hospital College of Medicine are operated especially facilitates this broad plan.

In the dental college, as in the medical, the scientific and practical go hand in hand, lectures and clinics being always combined; a knowledge of the course pursued is also exacted by frequent quizzes and practical tests of various kinds. The course of instruction in the college of dentistry, besides the departments already mentioned, includes those of operative dentistry, oral surgery, and dental pathology, prosthetic dentistry and crown and bridge work, orthodentia, technics and anæsthesia, and dental jurisprudence.

The following are the regular professors of the present faculty, which body also includes thirteen lecturers, assistants, and clinical instructors: A. Wilkes Smith, D. D. S., M. D., emeritus professor of oral and dental surgery; Henry Bryant Tileston, D. D. S., president, professor of operative dentistry, dental materia medica and therapeutics, and dental histology; Edward M. Kettig, M. D., D. D. S., professor of oral surgery and dental pathology; Winfield Scott Smith, D. D. S., professor of prosthetic dentistry, crown and bridge work; William Edward Grant, D. D. S., professor of orthodontia, technics, and anæsthesia; Samuel G. Dabney, M. D., professor of physiology and hygiene; John Edwin Hayes, A. M., M. D., professor of anatomy; H. Horace Grant, A. M., M. D., professor of surgery; P. Richard Taylor, M. D., dean, professor of materia medica and therapeutics; Philip F. Barbour, A. B., M. D., professor of chemistry and metallurgy.

The executive officers of the college since its foundation have been as follows: Presidents, A. Wilkes Smith, M. D., D. D. S., 1887-1892. Francis Peabody, D. D. S., 1892-1897. H. B. Tileston, D. D. S., 1897 to present. Deans: J. Lewis Howe, Ph. D., M. D., F. C. S., 1887-1894. P. Richard Taylor, M. D., 1894 to present.

BIBLIOGRAPHY.

Historic Families of Kentucky, by Thomas Marshall Green, Cincinnati, 1889.

Collins's and Smith's History, Home and School (Vol. III), Henderson's Centennial Exhibit.

CLINTON COLLEGE, CLINTON.

Clinton College proposes to furnish a good, substantial education for young men and young women at as moderate expense as possible. The institution is Baptist in management, being conducted under the patronage of West Union Baptist Association. Its original establishment is due to the lack of facilities for higher education in the western part of Kentucky, at the time of its foundation, when good schools were few and the public school system, in the inefficient form in which it then existed, was entirely inadequate to the educational demands of a section fast becoming thickly populated.

The one who first realized most sensibly the need of the college and first agitated the question of its establishment, which he took an active part in bringing about, was Rev. Willis White, ordinarily called in his portion of the State, Father White, who may, more than anyone else, be called the father of the institution.

Mr. White was a highly respected Baptist clergyman, who had entered the ministry of his church in western Kentucky in 1834 and had labored in that capacity many years with great acceptability. Just subsequent to the civil war he became county superintendent of public schools of Hickman County, and it was while in the discharge of the duties of that office that he realized more fully than ever how wholly insufficient were the schools of that section to supply the needs of its people. About 1871 he began to agitate the subject of founding an institution, which would at least partially meet pressing educational demands, and to travel and solicit funds for its equipment.

In this way the money was secured for the erection of the first building of Clinton Female College, which was begun in 1873. The beautiful campus of 8 acres upon which this building is located was donated to the institution by Mr. Robert Moore. The funds raised by Father White were not large, and the cost of the first building, which was not completed for some time after it was begun, was about $7,000.

As its original name implies, the school was at first exclusively for young ladies. It was organized under the general corporation laws of the State and is controlled by a board of seven trustees, each of whom is required to be a member in good and regular standing of some Baptist church. The college is empowered by its charter to confer the usual college degrees, but has chosen, until quite recently, to grant diplomas, but not regular degrees. Its original curriculum embraced all grades of instruction from primary to collegiate, the latter being intended at first to give only a good English education. The classics and other departments were soon added, so that its course was before long quite equal to that of many other institutions in the State, which grant regular collegiate degrees. Its curriculum was early divided into classical and scientific courses.

The school was first opened in September, 1874, before its own building was ready for occupancy, and was conducted for a time in the Baptist Church[1] in Clinton. It had only 15 pupils at the beginning. Its original faculty was Prof. T. N. Wells and Miss Amanda M. Hicks. Some assistance was given in the teaching of the first session by the wife and daughter of Professor Wells. The institution soon occupied its own building, although still somewhat incomplete, and before the end of the year had an enrollment of 45 students. The attendance had increased to 60 matriculates in 1875–76, when there were three regular teachers and the property of the college was estimated to be worth $15,000, while its equipment of scientific apparatus was good.

In the autumn of 1876 young men were for the first time admitted as students, and the institution has since remained fully coeducational, having dropped the word female from its name. In 1879 a course especially designed for teachers and also one in commercial science were added to the previous curriculum and the enrollment for the year rose

---

[1] This is according to the catalogue of 1894–95. The sketch by Rev. Mr. Bailey says it was opened in its own unfinished building and that by Miss Hicks says its building was complete at the opening.

to 150. Professor Wells continued as president of the college for six years, during which the institution sent out 12 graduates, 5 in the scientific and 7 in the classical course, the first class, that of 1878, having been composed of two graduates in the scientific course.

Upon the resignation of Professor Wells, in 1880, he was succeeded in the presidency of the college by Miss Hicks, who had been connected with the institution from its inception. She held the position for fourteen years, and is the one who largely built up the college to what it is to-day. Her success is conceded by all to be due to her own strong and forceful personality, as she had to struggle heroically against the lack of endowment and against prejudice. The school, under her able management, gradually expanded in its equipment, faculty, and courses, as well as in the number of its students, until it soon began to compare favorably with other institutions of higher education in the State.

Miss Hicks was a graduate of the Oswego (N. Y.) Normal School and a teacher of fine talents. The faculty she gathered about her were also well trained and efficient instructors. In 1881-82 there were 6 teachers and an attendance of 200 students, which is perhaps the largest matriculation the college has ever had, but a much larger proportion of its students have in recent years been members of its higher classes. The work had so outgrown itself in 1883 that an addition had to be made to the main building.

The American Baptist Educational Society cooperated with Miss Hicks in her work, and about 1889 appointed an agent to endeavor to secure an endowment for the college. Not much success seems to have been obtained for this laudable purpose, but enough means were realized to complete in 1890 a boarding cottage with accommodations for 40 young ladies, while an additional member had been added to the faculty. Upon the completion of the young ladies' boarding cottage Miss S. A. Fairfield became associated with Miss Hicks in the management of the institution, and so remained until the end of the latter's administration.

Deacon Joseph Cook, of Cambridge, Mass., who had given $5,000 for the building of the boarding cottage and who died in the winter of 1891, was induced, through Miss Hicks's influence and that of a lifelong friend of hers living in Cambridge, to bequeath to the college a sum amounting to between $25,000 and $35,000, the larger portion of which has been paid over to the institution and is now invested as a permanent endowment. In 1892 the college received a considerable collection of valuable books from the library of the Rev. Mr. Leonard, a Baptist minister of Ohio, lately deceased.

In May, 1894, Miss Hicks found it necessary for personal reasons to sever her connection with the institution to which in different capacities she had devoted twenty years of self-sacrificing labor. Besides the additions to its equipment and the foundation of its endowment which have been mentioned, she had accumulated for it a library of 1,200 volumes, and, above all, had established for it a high standard of scholarship and imparted to it throughout a high moral tone. The graduating class at times during the last years of her administration contained as many as 12 members, and the total number of graduates for the period was about 50.

Upon Miss Hicks's retirement Rev. E. K. Chandler, D. D., of Rhode Island, who had been for twenty years the pastor of various Baptist churches in the East—the last seven years of the time at Cambridge, Mass.—was elected as her successor in the presidency of the college. At the beginning of his administration considerable improvements were made in the grounds and buildings of the institution and material additions to its scientific apparatus also took place. In 1895 Prof. J. N. Robinson, an alumnus of Bethel College, Kentucky, and a teacher with a number of years of successful experience, was associated with President Chandler in the faculty as its business manager and financial agent.

President Chandler resigned in 1896, since which time there have been several changes in the presidency of the institution. Rev. A. S. Petty, D. D., first became president, but only retained the office for a few months, when he was succeeded by Rev. G. W. Riley, who held the position until the present summer, when A. F. Williams, A. M., was elected president. Professor Williams has been for several years the vice president of Bethel College, Russellville, Ky., and by his training should be well fitted to make a success of his present position.

The students of Clinton come mainly from western Kentucky, northwestern Tennessee, and southeastern Missouri. The average matriculation annually for the past few years has been about 150. The number of graduates each year of late has averaged about 6. The total number of graduates since the first class was sent out in 1878 is about 90, who are about equally divided between the sexes. Of these graduates several have become successful teachers and lawyers, while others occupy prominent Baptist pulpits. To meet local needs the college still maintains all grades of instruction from primary to a collegiate course of four years. Its preparatory department has a course extending through three years, while the regular classical and scientific college courses[1] extend through four years each. It has also a department of music and a teachers' training course, to prepare for teaching in the public schools. The present faculty has seven members.

[1] The schools of instruction leading to these courses are Latin and Greek, modern languages, English, history, mathematics, mental and moral philosophy, and natural science, in each of which a diploma is granted. In the scientific course certain portions of the schools of natural science and modern languages are substituted for Greek in the classical course.

BIBLIOGRAPHY.

Facts furnished by President Chandler have formed the basis of this sketch, particularly for its early history. The facts thus obtained have been supplemented by information obtained from catalogues, from a short sketch in the Clinton Democrat, by Rev. B. B. Bailey, one in the Baptist Gleaner, by Miss A. M. Hicks, and from Henderson's Centennial Exhibit.

LIBERTY COLLEGE, GLASGOW.

Liberty College is the outgrowth of the interest and enterprise manifested in the cause of higher education by the citizens of Glasgow, Ky., and of the Baptists of Liberty Association, from which body it receives its name. The one principally instrumental in its foundation is Rev. N. G. Terry, still a member of its board of regents, who was for a number of years in charge of Allen Lodge Female College, a local institution situated at Glasgow, of which in a sense Liberty College may beconsidered a development. While engaged in conducting it, Mr. Terry, about 1872, conceived the idea that the scope and character of the educational work then being done in the community could be enlarged by having Liberty Association of the Baptist Church found, under its own control, a higher and better institution. Accordingly he drew up a preamble and set of resolutions looking toward that end, which he was instrumental in having the association adopt at its next regular annual meeting.

Among other generous promoters and warm friends of the enterprise in Glasgow and elsewhere may be mentioned ex-Governor P. H. Leslie, Major Cheek, Hon. S. E. Jones, and Rev. Basil Manly, D. D., then president of Georgetown College, Kentucky. Dr. Manly drafted the charter for the proposed institution, and it was largely through his influence that it was passed by the State legislature in 1873. According to this instrument, the college was to be managed by a board of 16 regents or trustees, elected, two each year after the first year, by the association after which it was named. It was also granted all the usual collegiate powers and privileges.

After its legal basis was thus secured it was decided to locate the institution in that town within the bounds of the association which should offer the greatest inducements. Accordingly a contest of liberality arose, in which Smith's Grove, Cave City, and Glasgow participated, the latter securing the college by furnishing a subscription of about $12,000. Additional funds were soon raised, an admirable site purchased, and a handsome brick building, partly two stories and partly three stories in height, with a front of 140 feet and a depth of 80 feet, erected at a cost of about $25,000. This structure, which was completed in 1875, is well adapted for its uses and contains, in addition to its excellent rooms for educational purposes, accommodations for 40 boarding pupils. The institution was at first designed only for young ladies and was conducted for many years as an exclu-

LIBERTY COLLEGE.

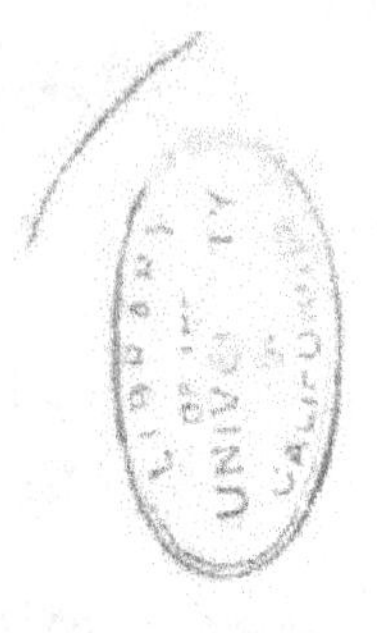

sively female college. Its course as first established was that usually pursued in female colleges at the time.

Upon the completion of its building its presidency was at first tendered to its chief founder, Rev. N. G. Terry, but on his declining the position the board of regents elected as the first president of the college James H. Fuqua, A. M., an alumnus of Bethel College in 1858 and already a teacher of mark, who has subsequently been prominent in the educational history of the State, as a professor for many years in his alma mater, and for a time chairman of its faculty. President Fuqua took charge of Liberty College at its opening in September, 1875, and remained at its head for five years, during which it seems to have been quite prosperous. It sent out its first graduating class of 4 members in 1878 and had 18 other alumnæ during the remaining two years of this administration. President Fuqua resigned in 1880 to accept a professorship in Bethel College. His successor in the presidency of Liberty College was Rev. J. B. Reynolds, whose administration continued during one year. It was about this time, when the institution experienced considerable distress financially, that it found a valuable friend and helper in the late Rev. W. W. Gardner, D. D. The original building had not been completed without accumulating a debt of about $8,000, which was now pressing heavily upon it. It was rescued from this embarrassment by the efforts and energy of Dr. Gardner, who was long connected with the educational work of his church in Kentucky, being for many years professor of theology at Bethel College, and whose labors for and devotion to the cause of education in the State well deserve a special mention. Seeing at this time the work of Liberty College liable to be seriously hindered, he took the field in its behalf and was able to secure money and pledges sufficient to free the institution from debt.

After President Reynolds's retirement from the executive chair of the college Profs. E. W. Elrod and J. P. Fruit were then associated for two years in its presidency. At the end of this time Professor Fruit resigned to accept the chair of English in his alma mater, Bethel College, and his place was supplied by Prof. E. W. White, who remained associated with Professor Elrod in the management of Liberty until 1889, when both resigned to take charge of Lynnland Institute, which they had jointly purchased. The college at Glasgow had had a good patronage during their administration, its alumnæ for the past eight years having numbered 33.

In the summer of 1889 Rev. T. S. McCall was elected to the presidency of the institution, a position held by him two years, when he resigned to become president of Bethel Female College at Hopkinsville, Ky. The average annual attendance during his administration was about 120 and the number of graduates for the time 11.

The next incumbent of the executive chair of Liberty College was Rev. J. M. Bent, D. D., who resigned the presidency of the Baptist

College at Pierce City, Mo., in order to accept the position. An unfortunate accident caused the death of Dr. Bent before the end of his second year, and in 1893 Rev. J. M. Bruce, A. M., then pastor of the Baptist Church at Glasgow, was induced to take charge of the college.

Mr. Bruce, after Mr. Terry and Dr. Gardner, may be considered in a sense a third founder of the institution, for he rescued it a second time from financial difficulties. Some of the pledges secured by Dr. Gardner could not be collected, and the resulting deficiency, together with some other necessary indebtedness, had accumulated to about $4,000. Through the efforts of President Bruce this amount was raised and enough more to make considerable improvements in the college property, so that at his resignation in 1895 the institution was left free from debt and prepared for greater usefulness in the future. A primary department was attached to the institution during this administration and, in 1893–94, the number of students rose to 217, the largest in the history of the college. The faculty at that time numbered 7 members.

In the summer of 1895, H. J. Greenwell, A. M., an alumnus of Georgetown College, Kentucky, who had had many years' successful experience at the head of educational enterprises at Bardstown and other places in Kentucky, became president of the college, which he has since efficiently conducted. Under his administration the institution has steadily increased its matriculation, which was at first considerably reduced by the general financial stringency. The present faculty contains six members, with George J. Burnett, A. B., as vice-president. Arrangements are in progress during the present summer to materially improve the college grounds and buildings and to add several new teachers to the faculty, a large commercial department being among the new features contemplated. The present regular college course in literature and science, together with departments of music and art and a normal course for training teachers, is to be maintained, and improved as the times demand.

A gradual movement toward what may be called popularizing the institution and making its advantages more accessible to the patronizing association as a whole and to the public generally had been perceptible in its history for several years at the time of the accession of President Greenwell. During Dr. Bent's administration business and normal courses had been added to its curriculum, and, under Mr. Bruce, it had opened its doors to young men as day pupils. As the logical result of this movement, at the beginning of the present administration all departments of the college were fully opened to young men, separate boarding departments having been provided for the two sexes, and the institution became fully coeducational, thus joining in the general coeducational movement apparent in the educational history of Kentucky in recent years.

The total number of graduates of Liberty College, according to the best information at hand, which is approximately correct, is 82, of whom 79 are young ladies and 3 young men; a number of these adorn various stations in different walks of life.

BIBLIOGRAPHY.

This sketch is based entirely on correspondence and catalogues.

OGDEN COLLEGE, BOWLING GREEN.

Ogden College owes its existence to the wise beneficence of Maj. Robert W. Ogden, who by his will, dated December 7, 1870, left the sum of $50,000, "or so much thereof as may be necessary," to be used "in the purchase of suitable grounds and the erection thereon of appropriate buildings in or near the town of Bowling Green, Ky., to be dedicated and devoted to the education therein of males or females, young men or young women, as my executor or executors may elect."[1] By further provisions of the will the proposed institution was to be called Ogden College, if a male school should be decided upon, or Ogden Seminary if a female school. It was also made the residuary legatee of his estate, the income on the amount thus realized, which was estimated at the time of his death to be something over $60,000,[2] was "to form a fund out of which to pay, as far as it will go, the tuition fees of any of the young men [or young women] of Warren County or the State of Kentucky who may choose to avail themselves of this fund."[1] Preference was also expressed for a male college, although the decision of that matter was left entirely to his executors, Judge William V. Loving and his son, Hon. H. V. Loving, of Louisville, Ky., who, under the name of regents, were to have full general control over the institution, the more immediate government of which was to be intrusted to a board of five trustees, appointed by the regents.

Major Ogden died on November 10, 1873. Hon. H. V. Loving, the only one of his executors to accept the trust, decided in favor of a male college, according to the preference expressed in the will, and in September, 1874, selected as the first board of trustees for the institution Hon. Robert Rodes, Hon. H. T. Clark, Judge H. K. Thomas, Col. W. E. Holson, and Hon. D. W. Wright. Mr. Rodes became president and Mr. Wright secretary and treasurer. This board for a number of years looked after the interests of the infant institution faithfully and efficiently, and it was through their labors that much of the impetus which has made it what it now is was imparted. Mr. Wright especially, who still retains the same official position, has given much time and attention to the success of the enterprise.

Some time was necessarily occupied in settling up the estate, but,

---

[1] Records of the Warren County court.

[2] Collins's History of Kentucky, Vol. I, p. 246. Somewhat more than this amount was, it appears, realized from the residuary estate.

by resolution of the board of trustees adopted on June 12, 1877, it was decided to open the college for students on the first Monday of the following September, and on July 16, 1877, the first faculty was elected, composed of Rev. J. W. Wightman, D. D., president, and M. H. Crump and John P. Leotsakos, professors. A charter was later secured for the institution, which bears the date of March 8, 1878, and confers all the usual collegiate powers and privileges.

The amount of the residuary funds which could be depended upon at the time of the opening of the college or that have been realized since were not and have not been sufficient to support a large faculty or properly train a large number of students. Hence the policy of the trustees has been to limit the number of students to such as can be properly cared for by the institution, while at the same time giving as much free tuition as its means will justify. The number of students to be received was limited to 100 by a resolution of the board adopted on August 18, 1877. Tuition was practically free from the beginning to students from Kentucky, and especially from Warren County, these being only required to pay a small incidental fee[1] each term, which was often remitted entirely in the case of deserving students of limited means. Students from other States were required to pay in addition the comparatively small tuition fee of $30 a year. Until quite recently as many as 60 students have always been admitted free of tuition. Upon this basis the matriculation of the institution has necessarily remained local to a large extent, as the local attendance has always been quite equal to the capacity of the college under its regular income, and the tuition of nonresident students, few in numbers as they have been, could not be depended upon for an enlargement of the institution, either in the way of furnishing additional teaching force or better general equipment.

The first session of the college was opened on September 3, 1877, the property having been leased for its use which had been lately occupied by Warren College, an institution inaugurated at Bowling Green, in 1872, under the patronage of the Methodist Episcopal Church South and quite prosperous for a time, but which had recently been forced to suspend on account of lack of sufficient financial support. The course of instruction in the new institution, as originally outlined, consisted of a preparatory course of two years and a college course of four years. By reason of many students dropping out and others taking their places 128 matriculates were in attendance the first year, nearly all of them pursuing preparatory work. College classes were more fully organized at the beginning of the next session, when William A. Obenchain, A. M., was added to the previous faculty as professor of mathematics.

[1] This fee in 1877 was $5 a year. In 1878 it was made $6 a year and in 1880 $10 a year, which it has since remained.

1. Academic building. 2. Fourteenth street entrance.
3. View down State street from State street entrance.

OGDEN COLLEGE, BOWLING GREEN.

In 1878 the means of the institution were further increased by its becoming the residuary legatee of the estate of Maj. John E. Robinson, of Bowling Green. This bequest, amounting to about $25,000, was given for the endowment of a professorship. Subsequent litigation over the will, however, only left to the college about half that amount, the income from which has been set apart to the chair of natural science, which, in accordance with the terms of the bequest, is styled the John E. Robinson chair of natural science. In 1880 the desirable grounds and buildings hitherto used by the institution, which are beautifully situated in the suburbs of Bowling Green, well adapted to college purposes, and estimated to be worth about $25,000, were purchased by its trustees. The already handsome campus of about 10 acres was further beautified. The buildings were also considerably improved internally, the accommodations enlarged, and the equipment of the college otherwise much enhanced, among the other additions being a good complement of mathematical, chemical, and physical apparatus.

The average attendance during the first three years of its history remained about the same. In 1880, however, the course of study was more thoroughly systematized, being divided into the eight schools of ancient languages, mathematics, natural science, philosophy, civil engineering, modern languages, English language and literature, and commercial science, and a more rigid test of scholarship having been applied, the number of students in 1880–81 was reduced to 87, which has since remained about the usual average annual matriculation. At the end of this session the first graduating class of three members, upon whom the degree of bachelor of arts was conferred, was sent out by the college.

In August, 1883, Dr. Wightman resigned the presidency of the college, which he had done much to start on its career of usefulness, and was shortly afterwards succeeded by Prof. William A. Obenchain, who has since efficiently discharged the duties of the position. At the same time a bachelor of science course, strong especially in mathematics and modern languages, was added to the previous course of bachelor of arts, thus allowing a partial specialization of studies. This principle was still further extended, in 1885, by the addition of a bachelor of philosophy course, which has as its distinctive basis English, modern languages, and history, the last subject, including political economy, constituting a new school in the curriculum, which then became substantially what it has since remained.

Local conditions have been such that the college has always found it necessary, as is the case with most other institutions of higher education in the State, to have attached to it a preparatory department, in order that its students may be properly trained for its collegiate classes. The course in this department extends through two years and necessarily takes up a great deal of the time and attention of the faculty. The standard of the collegiate department has, however, not only been maintained from the first, but has been from time to time improved, as in 1889, when more rigid requirements for entrance were instituted by reason of the improved condition of the graded school system of Bowling Green, from which a large proportion of its students naturally come.

In 1895 it was found that under the practically free tuition system which had been in use the college had been conducted on a scale too liberal for its own resources. Its future growth and expansion were in danger, as the income from its endowment fund had decreased considerably, owing to the general decline in the rate of interest. Two courses of action then confronted its trustees—either to curtail its work and lower its grade or to limit the number of free scholarships, only awarding these to deserving young men in need of aid, and requiring all others to pay a moderate tuition fee in addition to the regular incidental fee, required of all students, and the special laboratory fees, required in the scientific departments. The board wisely adopted the second of these plans, fixing the number of free scholarships at 40, and the rate of tuition in the collegiate department at $40, and in the preparatory department, $25 a year. The experience of the institution has since abundantly confirmed the wisdom of this choice, as the attendance has not been diminished, at least materially, and with the additional income thus secured another member has been added to the faculty. The college has been able to maintain its former good standard of scholarship and to increase rather than diminish its usefulness, and an avenue for further enlargement in the future has been provided.

The courses of instruction are uniformly well arranged and thorough as far as they go, and its equipments and facilities for instruction in its chosen line of work have been kept up with the demands of modern education. It has a well-selected library of miscellaneous books and works of reference, and has a well-appointed equipment for illustration and practical instruction in the different branches of science. The college has not striven for numbers, either in attendance or in the graduates it has sent forth. Its average annual matriculation during the twenty-one years of its existence has been about 95, and during that time it has had only 41 graduates. Those of its graduates who have pursued advanced courses of study in Eastern universities or in professional schools have as a rule taken a high standing and acquitted themselves with honor, while the success of all, in business life and in the various professions, will compare favorably with that of the alumni of other institutions in the State during the same period. The majority of its present board of trustees are graduates of the institution.

The grounds and buildings of the institution are estimated to be worth about $40,000, while its productive funds now approximate $120,000. Its present faculty is constituted as follows: William A. Obenchain, A. M., president and professor of mathematics and political science; William F. Perry, A. M., professor of English language and literature, elocution, and history; John B. Preston, M. A., professor of ancient languages and French; S. R. McKee, Ph. D., John E. Robinson professor of natural science; Henry K. McGoodwin, B. S., instructor in history.

BIBLIOGRAPHY.

Collins's History of Kentucky.
Records of the Warren County Court.
Minutes of the Board of Trustees.

UNION COLLEGE, BARBOURVILLE.

Union College is the adopted college of Kentucky Conference of the Methodist Episcopal Church, standing in the same relation to that body that Kentucky Wesleyan College does to Kentucky Conference of the Methodist Episcopal Church South. The former, therefore, although one of the most recently organized institutions of higher education in Kentucky, is, as well as the latter, as old in conception and spirit as Bethel Academy and has an equal right to trace its lineage from that source down through Augusta College and the period of Methodist control of Transylvania University.

The establishment of Union College is largely due to the foresight and energy of Rev. Daniel Stevenson, D. D., who was in many ways prominent in educational matters in Kentucky, being influential in the establishment of Kentucky Wesleyan College in 1859, and State superintendent of public instruction from 1863 to 1867. Dr. Stevenson had, with a considerable number of others, withdrawn from the Methodist Episcopal Church South at the close of the civil war and united with the comparatively small number of members left in Kentucky at that time of the older branch of the Methodist Episcopal Church in the United States, commonly called in contradistinction the Northern Methodist Church, from which organization the separation of the Southern church had taken place in 1844–45.

In the change of church relations the larger part of the church property and at least all of the important educational institutions had been left in the hands of the Southern Church, and so the Methodist Episcopal Church found itself without any representative college. Dr. Stevenson, considering, as expressed substantially in his own words,[1] the promotion of the cause of education as a duty and privilege of the church next to preaching the gospel, and as a necessity to the permanent progress of any religious movement, saw the imperative need of establishing schools for his denomination as well as build-

[1] In a personal letter of January 30, 1896.

ing churches and parsonages. Accordingly steps were taken by him and others looking toward the accomplishment of this purpose, and in 1866 a charter was obtained from the State legislature for a board of education of Kentucky Conference of the Methodist Episcopal Church. This board, according to its charter, is composed of 10 members, 2 of whom are elected each year by the conference, and has control of a number of educational institutions belonging to its church in Kentucky, of which Union College is the only one of collegiate grade. It also possesses all the usual powers and privileges of a college board of trustees.

Nothing was done by this board of education for several years after its organization, owing to the lack of funds, the means of the church, during this period, being absorbed in more direct and pressing church undertakings; but in 1879, under their supervision, Dr. Stevenson leased the old Augusta College building, thus returning to an old educational center of his church, and opened, in the autumn of that year, the Augusta Collegiate Institute. This step, however, since the Augusta property, by reason of its legal status, could never be permanently acquired, was only considered preparatory to an enlarged educational enterprise elsewhere when a propitious opening should occur. The collegiate institute was conducted at Augusta for eight years, where it did an excellent educational work under Dr. Stevenson's efficient management.

Meanwhile the desired opportunity to secure a suitable equipment and a good location was found when the property of Union College was sold in 1886. This institution had been incorporated in 1879 and a building erected for it at Barbourville in 1880 by a joint stock company. Mainly through the influence of Mr. A. H. Harritt, $7,470 had been spent for grounds and a partially completed building, in which a school had been opened in the autumn of 1880. The property, however, had soon become involved in litigation, and the school had been closed for some time when its property was sold, by order of court, on October 25, 1886. It was at that time purchased and held for the conference by Dr. Stevenson, with the financial assistance of Mr. Green Elliot and Mrs. M. P. Dowis, of Barbourville, Dr. Stevenson having secured authority for this action from the conference at its meeting in Lexington in the preceding September.

The year 1886, in which this purchase took place, is considered the foundation date of Union College under its present organization. In December, 1886, a school was opened in its building, under the care of the conference, with George H. Dains, A. M., as principal. Professor Dains had been associated with Dr. Stevenson in the faculty of Augusta Collegiate Institute. He had full charge of Union College until June, 1887, and also for part of the scholastic year 1887–88, Rev. J. D. H. Corwine being principal for the other part of that year. The other teachers during this time were Mr. Francis Goetz and Miss

Emma B. Wykes, while some assistance was rendered by Professor Dains's mother.

In September, 1887, Dr. Stevenson was appointed president and financial agent of the college by the board of education, who then took direct charge of the institution. Dr. Stevenson accepted the position, resigning the presidency of Augusta Collegiate Institute in order to do so, but devoted himself for the first year to raising the money to pay for the property and make needed improvements. He proceeded with his characteristic energy, always going ahead, whether the circumstances appeared favorable or unfavorable, and was able, by the next session of the conference in Louisville, to present to the board of education a deed for the property, having secured funds not only sufficient to pay for it, but also to complete the building, make some necessary repairs and improvements, and supply needed furniture. The one who was the chief contributor toward purchasing the property, and who has since been largely instrumental in supplying the pressing needs of the college by meeting deficiencies in its current expenses, and has besides laid the foundation of its endowment, is Mrs. Fanny Speed, of Louisville. The completed college building contains a chapel capable of seating from 300 to 350 persons; also four large recitation rooms, a room for a library, and one for the literary societies, besides several other smaller rooms. It is situated in the center of a campus of 3 acres, beautifully adorned by shade trees.

In the autumn of 1888 Dr. Stevenson assumed the active duties of the presidency of the college, which he continued to discharge with great acceptability until his death in 1897. The institution had found it necessary, in order to meet local needs, to establish, besides its collegiate department, not only a preparatory department, but also primary and intermediate departments, and has not yet been able to discontinue these. It has also continued upon its former coeducational basis. It had been a college in name, but an academy in fact, prior to the presidency of Dr. Stevenson, but under his management, although the lower departments were still retained, its collegiate department was soon developed into what its name implied. Its course, which had been previously very much strengthened, had a whole year's requirements, chiefly in Latin, Greek, and mathematics, added in 1894–95 and was in that year brought up to the requirements of the university senate of the Methodist Episcopal Church.

This body, which is somewhat unique in character and already an important educational factor, while likely to be more so in the future, is worthy of some description in this connection. It was provided for by the general conference of 1892, and has for its object the unification of the colleges of Methodism by placing them in federal relations to each other and bringing them all under the direct supervision of the church in respect to their scholastic requirements. It is composed of practical educators, whose duty it is to determine the minimum amount of actual academic work necessary for the baccalaureate degree in the educational institutions of the church. Reports are made by it quadrennially to the board of education of the church at large. This body is authorized to determine the institutions which meet these requirements and are therefore entitled to be designated "as colleges in the official list of the educational institutions of the church." The senate held its first meeting and made its first report in November, 1893. The standard then formulated has since resulted, under its diligent application by the board of education, in the raising of the courses of more than forty colleges of the church.

The faculty of Union College during Dr. Stevenson's administration contained from 4 to 6 teachers, and besides those who are still members the following were at different times connected with it during this period: Professor Dains, Miss Wykes, Miss Nettie Gray, W. E. Shaw, A. B., Miss Mesleyana Gardiner, Miss May E. Bowmer, Miss Maude England, Fred. C. Reeter, A. B., and A. H. Harrop, A. B.

In 1893 the institution sent out its first graduating class of two members, one of whom was Professor Faulkner, its present president. The college only maintains one regular course—the classical one, which, since it has been brought up to the requirements of the university senate, is not behind similar courses in other colleges of the State, particularly in the amount of Latin and Greek it requires for the degree of A. B. It also confers the degree of A. M. upon the satisfactory completion of a course equivalent to a year's residence at the institution subsequent to taking the bachelor's degree and the presentation of an acceptable thesis. One of the objects of its establishment was the proper training of candidates for the ministry. A number of these have been members of its regular classes from the first. Some professional training has been furnished to these each year since 1895 by a special course of lectures on theological topics, and during the present summer a regular professor of theology has been added to the college faculty. The institution also maintains the ornamental branches of instruction usually pursued in female colleges.

Dr. Stevenson died on January 2, 1897, and the executive duties of the institution devolved temporarily upon Rev. J. P. Faulkner, A. M., a member, as already noted, of its first graduating class, and later one of its professors. On March 22 following he was regularly elected as its president by the board of education. Professor Faulkner had been associated with Dr. Stevenson, either as student or teacher, almost from the establishment of the college, and it was the latter's desire that he should succeed to the presidential office and carry forward the work of the institution along the lines already planned—an undertaking in which it seems likely from the beginning[1] which he has made he

[1] During his administration, besides the addition of the new department of theology, the former matriculation of the college has been almost doubled, a new member has been added to the faculty, and a new boarding department for young ladies opened.

will achieve success. After Dr. Stevenson's death his library was donated to the college, and makes, with previous donations, mainly given by Mrs. Speed, something over 1,000 volumes as the foundation of a future collection. The college has also made a beginning in securing an endowment, its funds for that purpose now being about $8,000, all but about $2,200 of which has been contributed by Mrs. Speed.

The institution has a wide field of usefulness before it, occupying as it does a region in the southeastern part of the State in which institutions of higher education are very few in number. Its character for intellectual and moral influence has been constantly rising, as it has been better in tone and grade than in the size of its matriculation. Its average annual attendance since its foundation has been about 118 students in all departments. Its graduates up to 1898, inclusive, number 17, among whom are all the members of its present collegiate faculty, while others have entered the professions of law, medicine, and theology.

The faculty of the college, in addition to two teachers connected with the primary and intermediate departments, has the following regular professors: Rev. James P. Faulkner, A. M., president and professor of mental and moral science and mathematics; George Harmon Wilson, A. B., vice-president, professor of Greek, political economy, and civics; Sarah Elizabeth Lock, A. B., professor of literature and history; George Ewin Hancock, A. B., professor of Latin and sciences; Rev. J. E. Thomas, A. B., B. D., professor of theology.

BIBLIOGRAPHY.

Much of the material used in this sketch was obtained through correspondence with Dr. Stevenson. Much has also been obtained from the usual sources of information, and something from the minutes of Kentucky Conference for 1895.

Chapter VI.

FEMALE COLLEGES.

LORETTO LITERARY AND BENEVOLENT INSTITUTION, MARION COUNTY.

This is the official title of what is ordinarily called Loretto Academy, a school which enjoys the honor of being the first institution for the higher education of women established in the Mississippi Valley, with a continuous history to the present time. This honor it shares to some extent with Nazareth Academy, founded soon after. The long and useful career of both these schools entitles them to treatment in this monograph, although, if judged strictly according to the greater part of their present curricula, they would be classed among secondary institutions.

The humble beginning of the present Loretto is to be found in a little school opened on Hardins Creek, Marion County, by Miss Anne Rhodes, early in 1812. Within a few months she was joined by Misses Christine Stuart and Anna Havern. Misses Mary Rhodes and Nellie Morgan were soon added to their number, these five becoming the nucleus of a Catholic sisterhood,[1] a religious order for the education of young ladies. The school was meant to provide for the education of the rising generation in what was then the wilderness of Kentucky, and its foundation was encouraged by Bishop Flaget, the first bishop of the West, including Kentucky. He was ably assisted by Rev. Charles Nerinckx,[2] a Belgian priest lately attached to the diocese and greatly interested in the education of the people. Both were seeking for some permanent establishment by which the work of education might be inaugurated and perpetuated, and were greatly pleased with the proposition of the young ladies mentioned above to found a sisterhood one of whose special objects should be the moral and intellectual training of the young. The original members of the organization applied to Father Nerinckx for a few rules to be a guide to their daily lives. These he gave them, and he is thus considered the founder of the order.

---

[1] The name of the sisterhood is Sisters of Loretto, or The Friends of Mary at the Foot of the Cross.

[2] Father Nerinckx came to Kentucky in 1805, and died in 1824. For his biography see bibliography at the end of the sketch of St. Mary's College.

The three oldest members were clothed with the religious habit and veil of their sisterhood on April 25, 1812, in St. Charles Church, Marion County. The first home of the order, located about 6 miles from the present mother house, was a rude log cabin, a deal table and wooden benches constituting the furniture, hard work and poverty the endowment. The original teachers supported themselves from such small fees as could be paid by the more well-to-do farmers of the neighborhood, and the establishment has since been supported entirely by tuition fees, which have always been very moderate. The sisterhood is governed by mother superiors, who are elected by the members, according to rule, every three and every six years. Sister Anne Rhodes became the first mother superior, but as no one is publicly distinguished above another in the order no other names have been handed down to us as especially prominent in the administration of its affairs.

By 1816 the sisterhood had grown to 26 members, and branch houses began to be established, first in Kentucky and then in other States, especially in the West. The sisterhood has since become one of the most successful organizations engaged in female education in the country, having now 45 branches in Kentucky, Missouri, Illinois, Colorado, New Mexico, Texas, and other Southern and Western States. Teachers are provided for all these by a normal school at Loretto, which all young members are required to attend in order to cultivate under experienced teachers any special talent they may have. The superior of the order appoints the faculties for the various schools wherever they may be located. In 1896 there were 65 young ladies in the novitiate department, who must all spend five years in preparation in the normal school before entering upon the work of teaching, the residence and occupation of each being assigned by the superior.

In the original school the curriculum was gradually extended and equipments added, according to the progress of the times and the means of the order. On December 29, 1829,[1] a charter was secured from the legislature granting the usual corporate and literary powers. The institution is managed by the sisterhood, all its teachers being members of the order, but is by its charter under the general supervision of a board of trustees, composed of a moderator and six members, who are a self-perpetuating body.

In 1888, having outgrown its quarters, a fine building was erected, which presented quite a contrast to the old log house of early days. Besides this spacious and handsome academy, there is now at the mother house a substantial array of brick buildings, constituting quite a village, and located in the midst of a large farm, partly planted in orchards and gardens and partly used for raising grain and other food products.

The academy building has all the modern improvements, and the school has a library, museum, and other equipments needed for suc-

[1] Acts of 1829-30, pp. 27-30.

cessful teaching. Music, art, and the different languages and literatures have been prominent departments of its course, which extends from a primary department to work of collegiate grade. It has always maintained a large and experienced corps of teachers, and has had a good patronage, especially from the South and West, ranking, as it does, as one of the leading educational institutions of its church in the Southwest. Its pupils have come mainly from Kentucky, Missouri, Illinois, Alabama, Tennessee, Colorado, Kansas, and Montana, and among its graduates have been a number who have held reputable positions in art, literature, journalism, and as teachers.

BIBLIOGRAPHY.

Maes's Life of Nerinckx.
Acts of the State legislature.
Correspondence and catalogues.

NAZARETH LITERARY AND BENEVOLENT INSTITUTION, NELSON COUNTY.

This school, like Loretto, is ordinarily known simply as Nazareth Academy. It was almost contemporary with Loretto in its foundation, and has enjoyed to some extent a greater and wider celebrity. It was for many years one of the most famous schools in its section, and has since held an honorable position among educational institutions for women in Kentucky, although, as has been already noted, much of its work would now be classed as secondary.

The establishment of Nazareth was due to the efforts of three ladies, whose number was soon increased to five, to assist Bishop Flaget, lately appointed (in 1808) the pioneer bishop of the West, in educating the children of the sturdy farmers who lived around the first episcopal residence, then a log cabin, located at St. Thomas, amidst the picturesque knobs of Nelson County, about 9 miles from Bardstown. These ladies, eager to devote themselves to this good work, came to make their residence at St. Thomas on December 1, 1812. Soon additions were made to their ranks, and having been organized into a community of Sisters of Charity,[1] they founded the school of Nazareth in August, 1814. Although Bishop Flaget originated the plan of its organization, yet upon Bishop David, his coadjutor, fell the greater part of the care of watching over the foundation and looking after the interests of the little community, and the latter is therefore looked upon as its real founder.

The original home of the sisterhood was a log cabin, built by the seminary students of St. Thomas, under the direction of Bishop David, and the new religious organization was composed at first of only five earnest souls. The principal object of the order, as in the case of that of the Sisterhood of Loretto, is the instruction of young girls, but the Sisters of Charity also have charge of orphan asylums, hospitals, and similar institutions.

[1] The name of the organization is The Sisters of Charity of Nazareth.

The most prominent of the early members of the order were Mother Catherine Spalding, Sister Ellen O'Connell, and Sister Harriet Gardiner. Mother Catherine Spalding was a cousin of Archbishop Spalding, the seventh archbishop of Baltimore, and was chosen the first mother superior of the order, a position which she held for twenty-four years. She was the pivot upon which the affairs of the growing sisterhood turned for many years, and was noted for her clear convictions of duty and her faithful performance of its demands. Sister Ellen O'Connell was the first directress of studies, a position which she held for thirty-five years, dating from the first opening of the school at St. Thomas. She imparted to the course from the beginning that thoroughness and strength which soon made Nazareth prominent and attracted pupils from a distance. Sister Scholastica O'Connor was the first music teacher in the school.

The original school at St. Thomas was both a day school and boarding school, but in 1822 the academy was moved to its present location, 7 miles distant from its original one, the new site being called Nazareth and the day school at that time being discontinued. On December 29, 1829,[1] the school was chartered under its official title, as given above, and was granted the usual scholastic powers and privileges. Under this charter the institution is managed by the members of the community, under the general supervision, in certain respects, of a board of seven trustees, of whom the Bishop of Louisville is moderator.

The funds at the time of the removal to Nazareth were barely sufficient to purchase the farm on which the buildings now stand. The school has since had no further endowment, but has devoted the income derived from tuition, as this increased, to improvement and expansion, improved buildings and other means of instruction having been gradually added as means have come in. Within six years after the change of location $20,000 was spent in improving the place, and in 1844 there were 120 boarders, whereas there had been only 30 the last year at St. Thomas. The succeeding years have found spacious, handsome, and well-arranged buildings added, until Nazareth has become one of the most extensive and best-equipped boarding schools in the country. A large farm is attached to the school to furnish recreation grounds and to aid in supplying the table. A view of the school as it was in 1822 and as it now is, would well display not only the growth of this institution, but also, in a general way, the expansion of higher education in Kentucky during this time.

Not only has the parent school been maintained at Nazareth, but as many as sixty-seven branch schools have been established in Kentucky and other States of the South and West. Teachers are furnished for all these schools by a normal school conducted at Nazareth, where these teachers are carefully trained for their work.

Besides those already named, among others eminently instrumental

[1] Acts of 1829-30, pp. 24-27.

in building up Nazareth, may be mentioned Mother Frances Gardiner, who came with her sister to St. Thomas in 1819, and was, after the retirement of Mother Catherine Spalding, for thirty-five years the mother superior of the community. She had a great talent for administration, and for this long period successfully managed the affairs of the institution. Even more noted is Mother Columba Carroll, who was Sister Ellen O'Connell's successor as directress of studies, holding that position for thirty-five years, and was, after Mother Frances Gardiner's retirement, for more than ten years mother superior. Mother Columba possessed extraordinary zeal and tact in ruling the sisterhood. Among those who have presided over the community in recent years are Mother Cleophas Mills, the present mother superior of the order, who was also at the head of its affairs from 1885 to 1891, and Mother Helena Tormey, who was mother superior from 1891 to 1897. Sisters Columba Tarleton and Emily Elder are noted as having been very highly accomplished teachers.

The course of instruction at Nazareth extends through seven years, ranging from primary work to that of collegiate grade and having such modern features as normal and business departments. A large and well-trained faculty has always been maintained, and a library, museum, and laboratories furnish good facilities for teaching. The patronage of the school has been quite large, the attendance having been frequently over two hundred in a year, and has come from Kentucky and the Southern States generally, Louisiana, Mississippi, Tennessee, Texas, and Alabama having been and still being well represented. The average number of graduates in recent years has been about twelve, and the total number of alumnæ is something over six hundred. The latter are quite widely distributed throughout the Union, and many of them occupy prominent positions in teaching and other professions, especially in the West.

BIBLIOGRAPHY.

Spalding's Early Catholic Missions.
Acts of the State legislature.
Reprint of an article in the Catholic World (New York) for January, 1893.
Catalogues and correspondence.

SCIENCE HILL SCHOOL, SHELBYVILLE.

This school, although its work is now avowedly largely secondary, is worthy of consideration on account of the especially prominent position it has occupied for a long time in the educational annals, not only of Kentucky, but of the South and West generally, and the distinguished services rendered to the cause of education by Mrs. Julia Tevis, its founder and so long its principal. It also still holds an honored rank among the State's educational institutions and does much teaching of a grade even superior to that done by many schools bearing more pretentious titles.

Science Hill had its beginning in a private school, opened in Shelbyville, March 25, 1825, by Mrs. Julia A. Tevis and her husband, Rev. John Tevis, of Kentucky Conference of the Methodist Episcopal Church. It is quite proper that Mrs. Tevis's name should be mentioned first in this connection, for although her husband was associated with her for some time in conducting the school and rendered efficient services in its behalf, yet the main burden of the enterprise, even from its inception, was borne by Mrs. Tevis, and to her is to be attributed the largest share of its success. She also conducted it alone for many years after Mr. Tevis's death. It has been well said that "few institutions were so entirely the work of one mind and hand."[1] At the time of its establishment it was only antedated in Kentucky as a female school by Loretto and Nazareth, and was, with one exception,[2] the first Protestant institution for girls which has had a continuous history founded in the Mississippi Valley. The school has always been and still is purely an individual enterprise, for, although nominally placed under care of Kentucky Conference as early as 1829, the conference has never had any part in its management, nor has it ever contributed anything to its support. Naturally the enterprise was welcomed and encouraged by the citizens of Shelbyville, but they have never given anything for either its equipment or endowment.

The number of students enrolled in the school was at first quite small, there being only 20 the first term, of whom 4 were boarders, and only 43 were in attendance in the first part of 1827. In its early days it encountered a prejudice against the higher education of women, then quite prevalent in Kentucky, which it gradually overcame. Soon, however, its reputation was established and its rooms were crowded with students, the South generally, as well as Kentucky, becoming its special patron and friend. It was not long before its matriculation was only limited by the accommodations it could furnish. Its enrollment, whose names represented each year almost every State in the South and West, soon reached 200, and, between 1850 and 1860, frequently was as much as 300. From 1840 to 1866 the reputation of Science Hill may be said to have been second to that of no female college in the South. Mr. Tevis died in 1861, but his wife continued to conduct the institution successfully for many years afterwards. Not only were its operations not suspended by the civil war, but even its attendance seems not to have been materially reduced, there being in 1864-65, over 200 students in its halls, although business, generally, in the South was quite fully interrupted.

[1] Anniversary sermon, p. 21.

[2] This exception is given in Sixty Years in the School Room, p. 356, as the school established a few years before Science Hill by Rev. Mr. Fall at Nashville, Tenn. The reference is probably to Nashville Female Academy, founded in 1817 (see Merriam's Higher Education in Tennesse, p. 245).

The school's original material equipment was a private dwelling of rather limited capacity, and as more suitable buildings, furniture, and apparatus had to be supplied from the profits of the enterprise, they were only gradually acquired. The income was, however, soon sufficient to supply enlarged accommodations and better facilities for instruction. After a time the buildings had to be improved and extended during every vacation to provide for the increased number of students, until the equipment became ample in comparison with other similar institutions. The last important building erected under the old management was a large chapel which was opened in 1860. The course offered during this early period of the school's history was the common one in vogue in female colleges in the South, the English branches constituting its basis, and making with music and art what was then considered sufficient for a girl's equipment for life. Science Hill added to these more of natural science than was usual among schools for women.

Mrs. Tevis remained in the school and, for the most part, guided its fortunes until just prior to her death in 1880. Dr. B. P. Tevis had for some time previous been associated with her in its management, when, on March 25, 1879, the fifty-fourth anniversary of its foundation, the proprietorship of the enterprise was transferred to W. T. Poynter, D. D., a member of the Kentucky Conference. Mrs. Tevis died April 21, 1880, full of years, labors, and honors, having influenced for good by her work almost every section of the South and West, where, in almost every city, village, and hamlet, the graduates of Science Hill are to be found. She was noted for her liberality, having given free education, amounting to thousands of dollars, to many poor deserving students, and otherwise so conducted her school that it may truly be said to have been "a blessing to thousands of pupils, to the church, and to the country."[1] She was also a great and original teacher and has been rarely equaled for dignified and finished style of instruction. No record has been kept of the number of alumnæ during her administration, but this[2] may safely be said to have been larger than that of most private schools in the country, or of most other Southern schools for girls.

When Dr. Poynter took charge of the school he changed the character of its work in such a way as to make it distinctively a secondary school in the fullest sense of that term, its requirements being made to conform with those lately laid down by the Committee of Ten. He also secured for it during the first year of his administration a charter, something it had never possessed before, conferring upon it the usual scholastic powers and privileges. It is now called an English and classical school for girls and has become known especially as a pre-

[1] Anniversary sermon, p. 27.

[2] It is known that more than 2,000 pupils had been educated in the school in Mr. Tevis's lifetime and more than 3,000 up to 1875.

paratory school to Wellesley College, where its graduates have maintained an excellent standing. Much of its work is still, however, of a high grade in comparison to that of other female schools in Kentucky, and the diplomas it grants represent better work than that done in many so-called colleges. The attendance of late years has not been so large as formerly, but continues good considering the multiplicity of schools and the financial distress of recent years. It includes, in many instances, the daughters and even granddaughters of former graduates of the institution. The library, scientific apparatus, and other means of instruction have been enlarged and otherwise kept up to the requirements of modern education, and, as a rule, only graduates of the best Eastern colleges have been employed as teachers. Dr. Poynter died July 30, 1896, in the midst of a career of usefulness. He had kept up the reputation of Science Hill for doing thoroughly the work it undertakes to do. Since his death Mrs. Clara M. Poynter, his wife, who had been previously associated with him in the faculty as lady principal, has efficiently conducted the institution, which bids fair to maintain its former position of usefulness as an educational factor in the State.

BIBLIOGRAPHY.

Sixty Years in the School Room, by Mrs. Julia A. Tevis, Cincinnati, 1878.

Sermon on the Fortieth Anniversary of Science Hill, by Rev. G. E. Cunningham, Louisville, 1865.

The Gospel Herald, for November, 1829.

The Southern School, for January, 1896.

A History of Methodism in Kentucky, by A. H. Redford, D. D., 3 vols., Nashville, 1871.

Collins's and Smith's History of Kentucky.

Some additional information was also given by the late president, Dr. Poynter.

LOGAN FEMALE COLLEGE—RUSSELLVILLE.

As early as 1846 Prof. William Wines founded a school in Russellville for boys and girls, as an individual enterprise, to meet the demands of the local need of higher education. Out of this school, known as "The Academy," by small increments has grown Logan Female College, with her fifty-two years of history, which is practically continuous, although her life, on more than one occasion, has been temporarily suspended, and has at times seemed in danger of being extinguished. Professor Wines was an excellent teacher, and succeeded in building up quite a good school, in which many of the leading citizens of Russellville and vicinity either were fitted for college or received the greater part of their education. Among these may be mentioned particularly the late Ecstein Norton, so long prominent in business circles in Kentucky and New York and a liberal patron of education, and the late Rev. David Morton, D. D., afterwards so intimately connected with the history and prosperity of Logan Female College and noted in the enterprises of the Methodist Episcopal Church South.

Equal advantages were offered in the school to girls and boys, and a large proportion of the attendance during this early period was composed of girls. The desire to perpetuate such an institution in their midst led a number of the citizens of Russellville and the surrounding community to organize a company in 1856 and purchase the property hitherto occupied by the school from Professor Wines, who at that time severed his connection with the enterprise. The amount paid for the property was $3,500, raised by the company in shares of $100 each.

Under the new régime, Rev. J. E. Carnes, of Louisville Conference of the Methodist Episcopal Church South, became principal of the school and remained at its head for two years, during which time he seems to have given it a fair impetus for its future career.

In 1858 he was succeeded by Rev. Edward Stevenson, D. D., of the same church, who, through his ability and energy, did much to build up the character of the institution as an important educational center. He inaugurated a plan for the purchase of the property by his church and succeeded in raising the money for this purpose from the members of his denomination. He also secured several thousand dollars besides, which was used in improving the property generally and making important additions to the buildings. He obtained for the institution in 1860 a charter changing its name to the Russellville Collegiate Institute and granting it the power of conferring diplomas. At the same time it was received regularly under the care of the Louisville Conference, under whose patronage it has since remained. The success of the institute was very great under the vigorous administration of Dr. Stevenson, even during the civil war, but it was much disorganized by his long illness, resulting in his death in 1864.

Rev. David Morton then became principal. He conducted the school with such success, took such a prominent part in its history, and wrought such changes in its character that he may be denominated the principal founder of the institution as it exists to-day. Although the work of the college was seriously hindered during the first part of his administration because its grounds and part of its buildings were occupied by Federal troops during the greater part of two years, yet he not only managed to keep it in operation, but even raised some funds for its improvement. He also began at this juncture to contemplate the enlarging of the enterprise in both a material and educational way.

In 1866 a stock company, known as the Logan Female College Company, was organized and the plan formed of erecting a large new building on a lot opposite the original one, the principal part of the money for which was raised by Dr. Morton in the fall and winter of 1867. The previous establishment in Russellville of Bethel College, an institution for young men, by the Baptists of southern Kentucky having rendered the department for boys and young men in the institute unnecessary, it was discontinued and the school limited to the education of girls only. Its curriculum was extended, and in 1867 a new charter was obtained from the legislature converting it into a regular female college under its present title. Under this charter the institution is controlled by a board of eight trustees, elected partly by the stockholders and partly by the conference. Conference appoints for it annually a visiting committee of three members. Dr. Morton retired from the active management of the school at the close of the next school year, but remained for some time its financial agent and was until 1892 one of its trustees. During this time he raised a considerable amount of funds for its use and otherwise contributed to its prosperity.

In 1868, when the new charter went into operation, Rev. R. H. Rivers, D. D., became by the appointment of conference the first president of Logan Female College. Dr. Rivers was a teacher of thirty years' successful experience and would doubtless have done much toward building up the institution, but at the end of a year, before his administration had fairly gotten started, he was transferred by his church to other fields of usefulness.

Rev. N. H. Lee, D. D., was appointed president upon the retirement of Dr. Rivers. Dr. Lee was a man of high attainments and enlarged views and was able to successfully uphold the work of the college for four years. But the financial panic of 1873 had greatly delayed the collection of funds for the new building, and as the old one had been sold and the new one was not yet sufficiently completed to be occupied, the institution was suspended for a year after Dr. Lee resigned its presidency in 1873.

In 1874, although the building was yet incomplete, the college was reopened under A. B. Stark, LL. D., as president. He was a man of broad culture and scholarly attainments, and under his management the curriculum of the institution was further extended and regularly arranged into different schools of instruction in the various departments, substantially as it has since remained. The reputation of the college was during this adminstration considerably increased, especially by its work in English and Anglo-Saxon, which was of such a character as to call forth encomiums from Dr. Furnival, of the New Shakespeare Society of London. The attendance during this period averaged about one hundred pupils annually, and considerable additions were made to the scientific apparatus, the library, and other means of instruction. A number of additional rooms were also completed in the building, but the college was by this put somewhat in debt. Failing health compelled Dr. Stark to resign in 1883, when he was succeeded by H. K. Taylor, A. M., as president.

Professor Taylor's administration was energetic and prosperous. Under his management the department of natural science was much emphasized and the work of the college in that direction much strengthened. In 1889 Professor Taylor retired from the presidency of the institution and A. G. Murphey, A. M., who had for the last three years been connected with the faculty, was elected in his stead.

Professor Murphey, who had had a ripe experience in various other colleges of his church in Kentucky, has since remained in charge of the institution, and has been eminently successful in upholding its standard of scholarship and otherwise maintaining its reputation. The course of instruction, especially in the departments of English history and music, has been improved, the foundations laid for a larger and better library, and the facilities for teaching otherwise enlarged.

The debt, which had been hanging over the institution for some time, has also been paid, and the college building finally completed, at a total cost of about $30,000. This building, in its arrangement, size, and general accommodations, is probably the equal of any similar structure in the State. It is situated in a tasteful campus containing 6 acres. The average attendance during the first five years of President Murphey's administration was about a hundred and fifty students each year, an average somewhat larger than that of former times and wider in its geographical distribution, as many as nine or ten of the Southern and Western States being represented. The attendance has of late been somewhat reduced by the general financial depression, but still remains good.

The institute had sent out its first graduating class of 2 in 1861, and the college its first class of 7 in 1869. There have been up to 1898, inclusive, 185 regular graduates in the different courses, besides a number upon whom special certificates have been conferred in various departments. The present graduating class of 12 members is the largest in the history of the institution. The present faculty is composed of 12 well-trained teachers. The college curriculum embraces the departments of Latin, English, mathematics, natural science, history, Bible studies, philosophy, political science, elocution, Anglo-Saxon, Greek, French, and German, different combinations of which lead to the three degrees of bachelor of arts, bachelor of science, and bachelor of laws. There are, in addition, primary and preparatory departments and departments of music and art.

BIBLIOGRAPHY.

This sketch has been compiled almost entirely from catalogues and correspondence, with some reference to Redford's Methodism in Kentucky and Henderson's Centennial Exhibit. A few facts have been taken from A History of Education in the Louisville Conference, by Gross Alexander, S. T. D., Nashville, 1897, which was published after this sketch had practically been completed.

MILLERSBURG FEMALE COLLEGE, MILLERSBURG.

The lineal predecessor of this institution may be found in a school for girls opened in Millersburg in 1849 or 1850 by Col. Thornton F. Johnson. Colonel Johnson had for a number of years previously taught at Georgetown, Ky., and later had established, first at Georgetown and then at Blue Lick Springs, a private military academy. This was a novel enterprise in this country, in conducting which he had been assisted by James G. Blaine, then quite a young man, but destined to become subsequently so famous in American political history. The school at Millersburg was founded to supply the need of better facilities for the higher education of girls in the immediate community and the adjoining section of Kentucky, and was first conducted in the building of the Christian Church. In this school Colonel Johnson was assisted by three sisters, the Misses Stanwood, one of whom afterwards became the wife of Mr. Blaine. The school was soon transferred from the church to the Batterson residence, which had been purchased for it and which was located on the site of the present college buildings.

In 1852 Rev. John Miller, M. D., then pastor of the Methodist Episcopal Church South, in Millersburg, bought the property and changed its character by making the school coeducational. Dr. Miller conducted it for two years as principal, when he retired on account of poor health, and the institution passed, in 1854, into the hands of Rev. George S. Savage, M. D., a well-known and able teacher of several years' experience.

Dr. Savage, assisted by his wife, also an excellent teacher, conducted the school successfully for several years as a mixed, common, and high school, under the name of Millersburg Male and Female Collegiate Institute. When, in 1857, under the leadership, principally, of Rev. T. P. Shellman, the plan of establishing a college for the Kentucky conference was originated, the aim at first seems to have been to convert Dr. Savage's school into the proposed institution. But when it was decided to make the new college exclusively male, and it was opened in the fall of 1859, as the precursor of what is now Kentucky Wesleyan College, the original school was made exclusively female and its name changed to Millersburg Female College by a charter obtained for it on February 20, 1860, which granted to it the power of conferring the usual degrees. The buildings, which were not showy, but ample, were at that time thoroughly refitted and its previous course considerably extended. The institution was originally and still remains entirely a private enterprise, but is, in a general way, under the patronage of Kentucky conference, which annually appoints a visiting committee to inspect its work.

Dr. Savage remained at the head of the institution until 1866, when he retired from its presidency on account of ill health, and was succeeded by Prof. J. W Hamilton. Dr. Savage has since, for many years, been the efficient general agent of the Americal Bible Society for Kentucky and Tennessee. The general prosperity of the college during his administration is attested by the fact that its attendance averaged from 150 to 200 students yearly during this period, and although its patronage was somewhat reduced, its operations were not interrupted nor its success materially impaired by the civil war. During the war, on account of the suspension of Kentucky Wesleyan College, a number of boys were received as students, its old plan of coeducation thus being temporarily restored. The school had originally a very good course for the time, and its extension under Dr. Savage made it the equal of that usually offered at female colleges in the South, a standard which has since been maintained. The instruction given has also been modernized as the times have demanded. A normal department was established as early as 1862.

Profes or Hamilton held the presidency of the college only three years, after which for several years there were a number of changes in its proprietorship, Professor Hamilton being succeeded by Prof. J. A. Brown, and Judge William H. Savage taking Professor Brown's place in 1870. In 1872 Rev. George T. Gould, A. M., was associated with Judge Savage in the control of the institution, and in 1874 Rev. H. W. Abbett, A. M., was added to the management. In 1875 Judge Savage severed his connection with the institution, which was conducted by professors Gould and Abbett jointly until 1877, when Professor Gould became sole proprietor, remaining so until 1884. During this period of the institution's history, especially under Professor Gould's administration, its scope was considerably enlarged and its teaching force materially increased, the aim being, as stated in its catalogues, to make of it a polytechnic institute, with a course ranging from a primary department to a college course of good compass, and including the usual ornamental branches, and normal and commercial departments. Its patronage was also considerably increased during this time, rising to 229 students in 1881-82, as many as 13 States being at times represented in its matriculation.

On December 29, 1878, the school met with the misfortune of having its principal building, including all of its furniture and educational appliances generally, destroyed by fire. Professor Gould's energy is illustrated by the fact that not a single day's exercises were interrupted by this calamity. New quarters, with the necessary equipments, were rented and the school's affairs proceeded as if nothing very unusual had happened. With the aid of the insurance on the old building and a moderate subscription, secured from the citizens of Millersburg and vicinity, a new and more commodious building was at once begun, and was completed and occupied in June, 1879. The new structure is a large three-story brick building with all the modern improvements, and furnishes accommodations for 150 boarders. President Gould was, however, unable to overcome the financial loss due to the fire, and so was forced to relinquish the proprietorship of the college in 1884, when he was succeeded in its presidency by Rev. Morris Evans, D. D., who, however, remained only one year.

In September, 1885, Rev. Cadesman Pope, who had previously purchased the property, took charge of the college. He associated with himself in its faculty two veteran teachers—Mrs. S. C. Truehart, for the past thirteen years principal of Stanford Female College, and Prof. A. G. Murphey, who had had many years' experience in Kentucky Wesleyan College and other institutions. The general scope of the institution was also considerably broadened and its work otherwise strengthened, so that it may be fairly said to rank among the best female colleges of the State. The course has been subsequently arranged on a more distinctively collegiate basis, the branches of instruction being classed under different schools, and the faculty has been considerably enlarged. The patronage of the institution during the greater part of Rev. Mr. Pope's administration was quite as good as at any former period in the history of the college, and was wider than ever before, extending as it did from Virginia to Texas and from Florida to Illinois.

In July, 1897, Mr. Pope retired from the management of the institution, and Rev. C. C. Fisher, A. M., who had previously become its proprietor by purchase, assumed its presidency. Professor Fisher is a graduate of Emory and Henry College, and has had a number of years' experience as a teacher in high schools and colleges. His aim has been to maintain the school's former high ideal of female education. Upon his accession the buildings were largely refitted and the equipment of the school otherwise materially improved. The present faculty of the college is composed of 13 teachers, who by their experience and ability should be well calculated to perpetuate its former usefulness.

Millersburg Female College has almost every year since 1857 sent forth from 1 to 17 graduates, so that her alumnæ in 1898 numbered 339, many of whom have distinguished themselves, especially as musicians and teachers.

BIBLIOGRAPHY.

Perrin's History of Bourbon, Scott, Harrison, and Nicholas Counties. Henderson's Centennial Exhibit. The information obtained from these has been materially enlarged by that obtained from catalogues, and that furnished by President Pope and Miss Ella Fleming, of Millersburg.

BETHEL FEMALE COLLEGE, HOPKINSVILLE.

The Baptists of Hopkinsville appear as early as 1851 to have planned for a female school to be conducted under their auspices, as is shown by the charter secured that year for the Baptist Female Institute. The scope of the enterprise seems, however, to have been widened, and the present Bethel Female College is the culmination of the desire, not only of the Baptists of Hopkinsville, but of Bethel Association, to foster female education. This association, from which the college takes its name, embraces in its territory a considerable part of southwestern Kentucky and a portion of Tennessee. The movement for the proposed school began to take shape in 1854, when John P. Campbell, A. D. Sears, Shandy Holland, L. L. Leavell, A. Palmer, S. D. Buckner, H. A. Phelps, E. B. Richardson, and E. Y. Vaughan were appointed its trustees. This board of trustees includes the names of those who were probably mainly instrumental in promoting the enterprise, and who largely looked after it in its incipiency.

Steps were soon taken to raise funds for its inauguration, and a charter was secured for it on March 9, 1854, under the name of Bethel High School. It was decided to locate the school in Hopkinsville, and a plan for a building for it was proposed by the trustees as early as April 21, 1854, but the money for the building, which came mainly from local and associational sources, seems to have been collected rather slowly, so that its erection was not ordered by the trustees until September 18, 1854. The corner stone of this building was laid with Masonic ceremonies on April 7, 1855, but it was not entirely finished until the early part of 1857, although it was occupied by the school for some time before that date. It is constructed of brick; has three stories and a basement, with a frontage of 80 feet and a depth of 50 feet, and cost, when completed, about $30,000. It is situated in the midst of handsome and spacious grounds.

The trustees, in the summer of 1854, had outlined a course of instruction which they declared should be "that of the best female seminaries of the South and West," and on July 17 of that year appointed W. W. Rossington as professor of music in the school. It does not appear whether or not Professor Rossington ever taught in the present building, but he is the first teacher ever regularly appointed to a position in the school. While its building was being prepared for occupancy its principalship was offered successively to Joseph Warder and R. L. Thurman, each of whom, for some reason, declined it. The board had, by resolution, determined to look for a presiding officer "of preeminent classical training" and to make Bethel Female High School "equal to any female college in the Southwest." Finally, on July 9, 1856, W. F. Hill was elected principal for a term of years, and the school was opened in the fall of that year under his management, although its building was yet incomplete.

Professor Hill remained in charge of the institution only one year, being succeeded on June 16, 1857, by Prof. J. W. Rust, who remained at its head until it was suspended by the civil war, and who may be said, more than any other man, to have established its reputation for good scholarship and excellent discipline. During all the early years its successful operation was much hindered by a lack of funds, to secure which a number of agents were at different times appointed by Bethel Association. The one who appears mainly to have at last put the institution on its feet financially is Rev. J. M. Burnett.

In 1858, at the instance of Bethel Association, the school was placed under the control of Green River Educational Convention, and it was rechartered under the name of Bethel Female College. The new plan of management was, however, found to be unsatisfactory, and after a time the new charter was repealed, and the school has since been operated, until recent years, under its original charter, although still retaining in popular usage the name of college. Professor Rust was able to conduct the school with such success that considerable improvements were made from its accumulated income in 1860. The war, however, cut off a large part of its patronage and otherwise so interfered with its operation that Professor Rust found it necessary to resign on August 17, 1863, after which for several months its work was suspended. During this suspension its building seems, at least temporarily, to have been occupied by the Federal military authorities, as is shown by a protest recorded in the minutes of the board of trustees against their use of it for a dance.

In March, 1864, the school was reopened by Rev. T. G. Keene, who at first bore the title simply of professor, but became principal the next year and remained so until June, 1866. The prosperity of the institution revived during his administration, in the latter part of which his efforts were ably seconded by those of Rev. M. G. Alexander, who became his successor. Professor Alexander retained the principalship until July, 1868, when he entered other fields of usefulness, and Rev. J. F. Dagg was elected as his successor. Professor Dagg successfully conducted the enterprise until his resignation, in 1874, when the position of principal was again tendered to Prof. J. W. Rust, who had been at its head from 1857 to 1863 and had been president of Bethel College, at Russellville, from 1864 to 1868.

Professor Rust, who had been recuperating his health for the past six years, accepted the position upon the condition that about $6,000 be spent in repairing and improving the school property. He entered upon his new administration with vigor and soon had the prosperity of the school well established. Professor Rust remained in charge of the institution until his death, in 1890, and, in the language of its board of trustees, is said to deserve the thanks of the board and of the association for the energetic and skillful manner in which he managed it and kept it alive. He was "an efficient and successful educator, possessing energy, enthusiasm, tact, and fidelity." Under his management the college had a faculty of from six to ten teachers and an average attendance of something over one hundred students each year. Its course of study had been outlined by a committee of Bethel Association, consisting of Rev. George Hunt and W. B. Walker, in 1866, and had been divided into the five departments of languages, mathematics, mental and moral science, and belles-lettres, natural science, and fine arts. This course was carried out by Professor Rust in such a way as to attain an excellent standard of scholarship.

For about a year after the death of Professor Rust no one was elected to the vacant presidency. In January, 1891, the position was tendered to Rev. T. S. McCall, M. A., for the past two years the successful president of Liberty Female College, at Glasgow, Ky. Professor McCall accepted soon afterwards, and took charge of the institution in the following summer, the college building having meanwhile been enlarged, improved, and refurnished, at a cost of about $9,000. In the spring of 1890 a new charter had been secured for the school, changing its name to Bethel Female College, a name it had really borne before the public since 1858, and granting to it the power to confer the usual collegiate degrees. As this charter was granted shortly before Professor Rust's death, he thus became the first regular president of the college, but Professor McCall was the first one to enter upon his duties under that title. President McCall maintained the former standard of the school during his administration of five years, ending in June, 1896.

Soon after the resignation of Professor McCall had been tendered and accepted, in the spring of 1896, Rev. Edmund Harrison, A. M., was elected president, and the office of vice-president created, to which his son, W. H. Harrison, M. A., was elected. President Harrison had been for a number of years a professor in Richmond College, Virginia, while his son had had considerable experience as an educator. The new administration took charge in the summer of 1896. Its first two years argue well for the future growth and improvement of the institution. The course of instruction has been modeled upon that of the University of Virginia, and the aim is to make it equal to that of any of the male colleges in the State, parallel degrees to those granted by them being offered.

Bethel Female High School sent out its first graduating class, of seven members, in 1858, but did not graduate a much larger one for many years afterwards, excellence of scholarship rather than numbers, it seems, being aimed at by her in granting diplomas. Her alumnæ altogether number 167. Bethel Association has mainly furnished the means to build the institution and equip it fairly well for its work, but has never granted it the endowment so much needed for greater efficiency. Various appeals for an endowment have at different times been made by Professor Rust and others interested in the welfare of the college, but have so far met with only an indifferent response on the part of the association. It is to be hoped that the movement, which is still being agitated by the friends of the institution, will be more successful in the future.

BIBLIOGRAPHY.

The minutes of the board of trustees. (These are quite complete and have been carefully examined.)

Perrin's History of Christian County.

Spenser's History of the Baptists of Kentucky.

Cathcart's Baptist Encyclopedia.

The Russellville Herald of June 10, 1891.

BEAUMONT COLLEGE, HARRODSBURG.

Beaumont College is the successor, in location and at least in the major part of its equipment, of Daughters' College, one of the oldest and for a long time one of the most prominent female colleges of Kentucky and the Southwest, and therefore worthy of having some account given of its history.

DAUGHTERS' COLLEGE.

This institution was almost entirely the work of one man, as it was established and successfully conducted for nearly forty years by John Augustus Williams, A. M., LL. D., its president during practically its entire history. President Williams, who is still living and who has been for many years a prominent minister of the Christian Church, had graduated from Bacon College in 1843, when only 19 years old, and subsequently devoted himself mainly to teaching, for which he had a special talent. After several years' successful experience in his profession, he in 1851 established Christian College, at Columbia, Mo., which was very prosperous under his management for five years. However, in 1856 he resolved to return to his native State, and accordingly purchased Greenville Springs, a beautiful estate of some 30 acres, formerly noted as a watering place, located near Harrodsburg, Ky., where in September of that year he opened Daughters' College for the education of young women, as its name implies. The buildings of the Springs were commodious and well adapted to educational purposes, and the location was excellent and otherwise well suited for the establishment of such an institution. A charter was secured for the enterprise in the summer of 1856, conferring upon the proposed college all the usual powers and privileges. Professor Williams's father, Dr. C. E. Williams, was a joint proprietor of the school, and remained a business partner for many years, but its educational work was from the first under the exclusive management of Professor Williams, who was the president of its faculty. This faculty was an able and experienced one from the beginning, and the course of instruction offered was excellent, especially in comparison with that usually given in female colleges. It included the following departments: Philosophy, English language and literature, mathematics, natural science, history, ancient and modern languages, the school of the Bible, and the school of fine arts.

At the opening of the college all the rooms of its building then available were filled within a week, and its prosperity was uninterrupted for a long period, excepting two years during the civil war, and even then its patronage was not greatly reduced. Professor Williams's popularity as a teacher is well attested by the fact that fifty or more of his former pupils had followed him from Missouri to Kentucky at the establishment of the college. In 1865 he was induced to accept the chair of moral and mental philosophy in Kentucky University at Lexington, where, in 1866, as its first presiding officer, he did much toward organizing the work of the Agricultural and Mechanical College, but in 1868 he resumed the presidency of Daughters' College, which he then retained continuously throughout its remaining history.

In 1892, on account of ill health, he retired from the profession of teaching, and Daughters' College, as it had been formerly constituted, was suspended, the name and good will of the institution being retained by Professor Williams with a view to reopening in the future should his strength permit. Professor Williams has been instrumental in molding the education of many young women throughout the South, as the patronage of his school was comparatively large, and in many years represented most of the Southern States. Its graduates numbered from 2 to 17 each year after 1857, and altogether amounted to about 350, coming from as many as 26 of the Southern and Western States. The college early developed a pedagogical tendency, having soon a regular normal department added to its course of instruction, and became noted for the large number of successful teachers it produced, more than one-third of all its graduates having devoted themselves, more or less, to this profession.

BEAUMONT COLLEGE.

After two unsuccessful attempts had been made to establish a new institution upon the foundation of Daughters' College the property formerly occupied by it was purchased in July, 1894, by Th. Smith, A. M., who opened in its buildings, in the autumn of that year, a new educational enterprise under the name of Beaumont College. The new school was incorporated under the general laws of the State in April, 1895, with full power to confer degrees. Professor Smith is an alumnus of the University of Virginia and a teacher of many years' successful experience in Georgetown College, Kentucky, and elsewhere. His aim has been to have Beaumont College do more distinctively university work than is usually attempted in at least most of the female colleges of the South. To this end, the former Daughters' College curriculum has been considerably widened, especially in the departments of ancient and modern languages and higher mathematics, and a strong faculty has been employed, several of whom are prominent specialists. Special stress has also been put upon the school of music, which employs only graduates of the best conservatories, while the former normal and business courses have been retained. The new college has ample apparatus and a well-selected reference library. It is, however, like Daughters' College, still purely an individual enterprise and lacks that endowment which would enable it to enlarge its operations and extend its field of usefulness. It has, nevertheless, acquired considerable prestige in the past four years and is widening its patronage, drawing its students from a number of States outside of Kentucky.

BIBLIOGRAPHY.

On Daughters' College: The Biographical Encyclopedia of Kentucky; Mrs. Daviess's History of Mercer and Boyle Counties; Henderson's Centennial Exhibit: The Disciple of Christ (Cincinnati) for July 1, 1884; The Kentucky Craftsman (Lexington) for August, 1895.

The account of Beaumont College is based entirely on catalogues and correspondence.

SAYRE FEMALE INSTITUTE, LEXINGTON.

This school has long held an excellent rank among the institutions for the higher education of women in Kentucky. It owes its existence to the munificence of David A. Sayre, of Lexington, after whom it is named. Mr. Sayre had come to Lexington from New Jersey in 1811, when quite a young man. From absolute poverty he had, by thrift and economy, become a banker as early as 1829, and subsequently amassed large wealth, a considerable part of which was devoted to the use of public institutions connected with the Presbyterian Church, of which he was a member. He became interested in educational matters largely through the influence of his wife, who had been a teacher, and who still retained an enthusiastic interest for the profession, and determined to establish in Lexington a first-class school for girls, whose benefits should be as widely distributed as possible.

The institute which bears his name was accordingly organized November 1, 1854, under Rev. H. V. D. Nevins as principal. It was first located on the corner of Mill and Church streets, and was then called Transylvania Female Seminary. On October 1, 1855, it was moved to its present location on Limestone street, near the center of the city, which had been purchased and specially prepared for it by Mr. Sayre, after whom it was then named. On March 10, 1856, it was chartered under its present title, with general power to confer collegiate degrees. According to this new charter the institution is managed by a board of 13 self-perpetuating trustees, of whom the mayor and city judge of Lexington are ex officio members. Its property can never be used for anything else except the education of girls, and all its income must be used either to increase its facilities for instruction or to add to the number of its beneficiary pupils. A moderate rate of tuition is charged by the school for its benefits in the case of most of its pupils, but it offers a free scholarship to one pupil from each of the public schools of Lexington each year, and besides this, grants gratuitous instruction to many deserving students. Its course includes all grades from a primary department to collegiate work of good compass. It is conducted under Presbyterian auspices, although nonsectarian in management.

Mr. Nevins remained at the head of the school until 1859, when Prof. S. R. Williams became his successor. Professor Williams conducted the enterprise with success until his death in June, 1869, although part of the time was the disturbed period of the civil war.

Prof. James Dinwiddie took charge in 1869, but remained only one year, being succeeded in June, 1870, by the present efficient principal, Maj. H. B. McClellan.[1] In September of that year occurred the death of Mr. Sayre, who had carefully watched over the interests of the institution since its inception. He left to it in perpetuity its excellent building and fine grounds, the latter including about 5 acres. He had added other gifts during his life, making his total donations about $100,000, and furnishing the school an equipment which was one of the best of its kind in the South. He had been its sole founder and its only benefactor up to the time of his death. In the latter part of 1870 his nephew, Mr. E. D. Sayre, expended about $3,000 in improving the property, and his sister, Mrs. Priscilla Cromey, who died in 1877, bequeathed to it $10,000, of which, however, it received only $5,000, owing to a contest over her will.

Major McClellan, during an administration which has lasted twenty-eight years, has had a large measure of success in the management of the institute, and has made it eminently useful as an educational factor in Kentucky and the South especially. The attendance, which had been 60 in 1868–69, was 80 in 1870–71, and 119 in 1872–73. By this time the school had outgrown its original quarters, and an enlargement and improvement of its buildings were necessary. This was done between 1872 and 1875, at a cost of $13,000, the chapel being enlarged and additional rooms for boarding pupils provided.

In 1886–87 about $10,000 more was expended in adding a new recitation room and furnishing improved heating apparatus and other modern appliances. Of these amounts $15,000 came from the income of the institution, the rest being derived from the gift of Mr. E. D. Sayre and the bequest of Mrs. Cromey. A valuable reference library and a good collection of scientific apparatus constitute part of the general equipment of the institution, which has been kept up well with the times, as is illustrated by the fact that Principal McClellan was prepared, in 1896, to verify Professor Rœntgen's X-ray experiments within five days after the discovery had been announced.

The enlarged accommodations made possible a larger patronage, which speedily came, there being 197 pupils in 1875–76, and an average of about 230 yearly between 1873 and 1893, the highest number being 305 in 1890–91. The faculty during this period numbered from 8 to 14 teachers. The present faculty contains 10 teachers. Since the panic of 1893 the average attendance has been about 130. The students come mainly from Kentucky and other Southern States. The graduating class of 1856, which was the first one to go out, numbered 11 members, and since then it has sent out almost every year a class of from 1 to 20. The alumnæ now number altogether 415, and are scattered over 20 of the Southern and Western States.

[1] Major McClellan, besides being a prominent educator, is the author of the Life and Campaigns of Maj. Gen. J. E. B. Stuart.

The school has power to confer all the regular college degrees, but has chosen only to grant diplomas in two courses called regular and English. The latter of these embraces the elements of a well-rounded English education, while the former includes, in addition, a comprehensive course in Latin or one of the modern languages. The institute has furnished a large proportion of the successful teachers of Lexington and Fayette County, and has given much free tuition to those and others, the amount so bestowed between 1870 and 1889 having been estimated[1] to be as much as $10,000. It has, under Major McClellan's management, been brought up to a high standard of usefulness and exerted a wholesome influence in behalf of an excellent standard of scholarship. The financial foundation granted to it by Mr. Sayre places before it the prospect of widening and extending its influence for good in the future.

BIBLIOGRAPHY.

Collins's History of Kentucky.
Peter's History of Fayette County.
Henderson's Centennial Exhibit.
Lexington Press Transcript of February 18, 1895.
Newspaper clipping of 1889.

CALDWELL COLLEGE, DANVILLE.

Schools for girls were early established in Danville, the first one of any note being one founded by Rev. J. K. Burch, for a time a professor in a theological department attached to Center College. None of these schools, however, had a first-class equipment, and their duration was, as a rule, short. The community had long been an educational center for young men, especially among the Presbyterians, who had also endeavored to have their daughters given equal advantages with their sons. A united and determined effort looking toward the accomplishment of this end was finally made in 1856.

In this enterprise the more intelligent part of the citizens of Danville and Boyle County generally were interested, but the Presbyterians were prime movers. Several prominent citizens were at first appointed to canvass for funds for the undertaking, and secured subscriptions amounting to about $5,000, the largest single subscription being $500. At a public meeting called in the Second Presbyterian Church in Danville to hear the report of this committee, the late Rev. E. P. Humphrey, D. D., at that time a professor in Danville Theological Seminary, made a stirring address in favor of the higher education of women, and perhaps did more than anyone else to arouse enthusiasm in favor of the proposed institution. After several other addresses had been made and various plans suggested, Dr J. M. Meyer, who is still living in Danville, arose and having stated that, if the

[1]Newspaper clipping of 1889.

enterprise was to be a success larger subscriptions must be made, proposed to be one of ten to give $1,000 each for the school. To this proposition G. W. Welsh, Charles Henderson, George F. Lee, Charles Caldwell, and perhaps one or two others responded. These subscriptions, together with other smaller amounts subscribed at the time, made about $8,000 raised at this meeting. A further canvass of the community was made in which about $3,000 additional was secured. A building committee was appointed, and with the money in hand an eligible lot on Lexington street in Danville was purchased, and the front of the original building erected in the latter part of 1859.

In this year Prof. E. A. Sloan, of Alabama, was elected the first principal of the institution, who, upon his arrival in Danville, considered its accommodations insufficient, and so, upon his request, an extra subscription of $10,000 was raised, with which, in 1860, an ell 100 feet long and two stories high, with galleries on either side, was added to the front previously erected. The school had originally been called Henderson Institute, but in order to secure the addition to the building Mr. Charles Caldwell had raised his subscription to $3,000, in gratitude for which its name was changed to Caldwell Institute. Mr. Caldwell was an elder in the First Presbyterian Church in Danville, and a warm friend of the institution as long as he lived. Under its new name a charter was secured for the enterprise, placing it under the control of the elders of the two Presbyterian churches of Danville.

The institute was first opened by Professor Sloan in the fall of 1860. Its completed building was equipped in such a manner as to be one of the finest of its kind in the State, the total cost of buildings, ground, and equipment being about $80,000. The faculty was composed of an efficient corps of teachers and the opening attendance was large. So the school at the time had every prospect of success; but the civil war soon cut off its patronage from the South, upon which the management had largely depended, and consequently its operations had to be suspended in 1862.

It remained closed for about two years, when a Mr. Hart seems to have had charge of it for about the same length of time. In 1866 Rev. L. G. Barbour, D. D., was elected principal and conducted a good school for eight years, when he resigned, 1874, to accept a chair in the newly established Central University.

The usefulness of the institution had for some time been greatly impaired by the lack of cooperation between the two controlling Presbyterian churches, who had become divided by the issues of the war and who did not care to occupy the property jointly. This was one reason for its suspension. At length an arrangement was made whereby the Second Presbyterian Church was to assume a debt remaining from Professor Sloan's administration, amounting to about $20,000, and was to have control of the school. It has until recently remained under the management of that church, whose elders have acted as its board of trustees.

Upon Dr. Barbour's resignation as principal, Prof. W. P. Hussey, of Boston, Mass., became his successor. The latter entered upon his work with great enthusiasm, inducing the board of trustees to apply to the legislature for a new charter, which changed the name of the institution to Caldwell College and otherwise enlarged the scope of the enterprise. Professor Hussey's plans were, however, cut short and the work of the college again suspended by the misfortune of having its building entirely destroyed by fire in April, 1876.

Nothing remained to it from this calamity except its grounds, which, not long afterwards, were divided into building lots and sold. With the funds thus obtained the present main building, well suited to its purposes and almost directly opposite the original location, was purchased. In the autumn of 1880 the college was reopened in its new quarters with Rev. John Montgomery as president. President Montgomery remained at its head for six years, during which time it seems to have been fairly prosperous. In his administration a brick chapel was added to the material equipment of this institution.

In the fall of 1886, Miss C. A. Campbell, of Danville, succeeded Rev. Mr. Montgomery in its presidency and remained its successful manager for eleven years. Soon after her accession an addition, containing four large recitation rooms and a gymnasium, was made to the buildings. Not long after this, a charter was secured granting full power to confer the usual degrees, a right which the college does not seem to have had, at least in full, under its previous charter. The course of instruction was also very materially strengthened, the aim being to make it the equal of that pursued in the male colleges of the State. It also includes a normal course, intended especially for students who wish to become teachers. Miss Campbell associated with herself a well trained faculty of 11 teachers and was able to build up the patronage of the institution considerably during her administration.

She retired from the presidency in the summer of 1897, and was succeeded by Rev. J. C. Ely, D. D., who has upheld the former prosperity of the school during the past year. Caldwell College has sent forth many well trained graduates since its first opening in 1860. The number of these can not be accurately ascertained from the somewhat imperfect records at hand, but enough is known to say that at present there are over 200 alumnæ.

BIBLIOGRAPHY.

The facts used in this sketch have been chiefly obtained from Dr. J. M. Meyer, of Danville. They have been considerably elaborated by reference to catalogues, Henderson's Centennial Exhibit, and other general sources of information.

HAMILTON FEMALE COLLEGE, LEXINGTON.

This institution was originally called Hocker Female College, after its founder, and was opened in Lexington in the autumn of 1869 by Mr. James M. Hocker, who, as announced in the first catalogue of the college, had had for years the cherished purpose of consecrating a large portion of his time and means to the "upbuilding of an institution for young women, founded on Christian and scientific principles." The school was intended to meet a public want by supplying an education for girls equal to that usually afforded boys. It was from the first conducted in the interest of the Christian Church, of which Mr. Hocker was a member. He was the founder and sole proprietor, but some of the prominent members of his church in Lexington and vicinity were associated with him in its management. A number of these constituted its trustees under its first act of incorporation, which was secured early in its history and gave to it the right of granting diplomas.

Prior to the opening of the college a substantial and artistic building was erected for it, which has a frontage of 160 feet and a depth of 88 feet, and is four stories in height. It has accommodations for 150 boarding pupils, and is situated in the midst of a handsome campus on North Broadway street. In 1870 an addition was made to it, containing a gymnasium, music hall, and art gallery, which, including the excellent equipment, brought the total cost of the entire educational plant above $100,000.

The first president of the new college was Robert Graham, A. M., who has been so long prominently connected with the educational enterprises of his church, especially with Kentucky University and the College of the Bible. The first faculty included 12 experienced teachers, and the course offered embraced the following departments: Mental and moral philosophy, physical science, mathematics, English language and literature, sacred and civil history, modern languages, ancient languages, and the fine arts. There was also a preparatory department. President Graham remained in charge of the institution for six years, during which the average annual attendance was something over 120, and represented most of the Southern States. The first graduating class, that of 1870, contained 3 members, and there were 48 other graduates during this administration.

Upon President Graham's retirement in 1875 to become the presiding officer of the College of the Bible, Henry Turner, A. M., became his successor and held the position for two years. Mr. Hocker's financial management of the college had not been a success, and so, in the summer of 1877, its proprietorship was transferred to a joint stock company, composed of its first board of trustees and other enlightened and public-spirited citizens of central Kentucky, all of whom were members of the Christian Church. This company was incorporated on July 1, 1877, and a new charter was secured for the institution placing it under the control of a board of 15 trustees elected by the stockholders, its management in the interest of the Christian Church being still secured by the charter requiring its trustees to be members in good standing of some Christian congregation. Those chiefly instrumental in bringing about the reorganization in this way were Elders M. E. Lard, J. W. McGarvey, and Robert Graham, although others assisted prominently in the enterprise. The money for the purchase of the property by the joint stock company was raised by donations and loans from liberal citizens and amounted to about $50,000, of which $10,000 was given by Mr. William Hamilton, of Woodford County, in honor of whom, as the chief contributor, the school was named Hamilton College by its new charter. It has since been operated under this charter with some slight amendments.

Under the reorganization Prof. J. T. Patterson, who was one of the chief stockholders and had had twenty-two years' successful experience in conducting similar institutions, became president. The college prospered under its new auspices and Professor Patterson remained at its head fourteen years, steadily increasing its reputation and attendance. Its students during this time averaged each year about 165, their number in 1890–91 rising to as many as 226. They frequently represented 13 of the Southern States. The faculty also increased from 10 at the opening of the administration to 17 at its close.

In 1889 Professor Patterson, on account of impaired health, retired from the active management of the institution, having associated with himself Prof. J. B. Skinner as principal and financial agent. The former, however, still retained his connection with the faculty and conducted his classes as usual until 1891, when he finally severed his connection with the institution. Under his management from 4 to 22 graduates had gone forth each year, and the total roll of alumnæ for the time is 173.

Upon President Patterson's retirement in 1891, Professor Skinner assumed entire charge of the school as its president. A primary department was then added to the course of instruction, and for it a new building was erected in 1892. In 1895 an extra calisthenic room, laboratory, and library were added and in the summer of 1896 the college grounds considerably enlarged and improved, about $5,000 being expended for these purposes. President Skinner had a large measure of success in sustaining the previous standard of scholarship of the institution and in upholding its attendance, notwithstanding the financial distress of recent years. The original large faculty was still retained, and about 200 students were usually to be found in the rooms of the college during his administration, which lasted about seven years. There were 114 graduates during this time, 24, the largest number in the history of the college, having been sent out in 1896, thus making the total alumnæ of the institution, up to 1898, inclusive, 351, who have come from 15 States of the Union.

President Skinner died in office February 28, 1898, thus being cut off in the midst of a career of educational usefulness, which, besides his nine years' connection with Hamilton College, had included a professorship in Christian College, Columbia, Mo., for five years and the presidency of Garrard College, Lancaster, Ky., for one year.

B. C. Hagerman, A. M., for a number of years the successful president of Madison Female Institute, at Richmond, Ky., and since then of Bethany College, Va., has recently been chosen as President Skinner's successor. His past record is such that Hamilton College may be expected to continue its present prosperity under his management.

BIBLIOGRAPHY.

This sketch has been founded largely upon facts obtained from a file of catalogues, which have been supplemented considerably by reference to Peter's History of Fayette County and by some information furnished by Professors Grahamr and Skinner.

JESSAMINE FEMALE INSTITUTE, NICHOLASVILLE.

Although bearing the name of institute simply, this school has for some time held an honorable position among the female colleges of the State. The purpose for which it was founded may be well expressed in the language of a recent catalogue, which declares it to be "the outgrowth of the intelligent demand of a cultured and earnest community, which realizes its best interests are met in an educated womanhood."

The preliminary steps looking toward the establishment of the institution were taken at a public meeting held at Nicholasville on May 20, 1854, when a series of resolutions were adopted, with a preamble reading as follows, viz:

We whose names are hereto subscribed, being desirous of establishing in the town of Nicholasville, Ky., a female school of such a character as will attract patronage from abroad as well as give the highest facilities for education in our own midst, have united ourselves into an association for this purpose, pursuant to an act of the legislature of Kentucky, passed at its last session, providing for and regulating voluntary associations. And that we may secure to ourselves the privileges and benefits therein set forth of a body corporate and politic, under the name and style of the Jessamine Female Institute, do hereby adopt the following articles of agreement.

According to the articles of agreement, which follow, the educational affairs of the association were to be managed by its principal officers in conjunction with a board of trustees appointed by the members from among their own number. The agreement was signed by twenty prominent citizens of Nicholasville and vicinity, who thus became chiefly instrumental in promoting the enterprise. They were mainly members of the Presbyterian Church. Only $2,500 was at first subscribed toward the equipment of the school, and the first building erected for it was a brick chapel for recitation purposes, with a seating capacity of fifty pupils.

As the Presbyterians took the leading part in organizing the institute it was opened under their auspices, with Rev. Branch Price, a Presbyterian minister, as its first principal. He took charge in the autumn of 1855, and was assisted by a full faculty. The curriculum offered consisted of courses in English, Latin, Greek, mathematics, modern language, music, and art, and was aimed to be the equal of that of any of the female colleges in the Southwest. The policy of the trustees has been to leave the property to the principal, who takes direct charge of the school affairs, appointing and governing its faculty and selecting its course of study.

In February, 1866, the legislature of the State, upon application, granted a very liberal new charter to the institution, giving to it the power to confer the usual degrees and putting it more distinctively on a nonsectarian basis. It was to be managed by a board of six trustees, elected every three years by the members of the corporation. The first trustees elected under this charter purchased a residence for the principal, adjacent to the chapel, and in 1867 Prof. M. C. McCrohan, who had succeeded Rev. William Price, opened a boarding department, which added considerably to the patronage of the school already very good.

In 1870 Prof. G. G. Butler became Professor McCrohan's successor in the principalship. Under his direction the school prospered for three years, but during the next two years the attendance declined considerably. In 1875 Prof. J. B. Tharp took charge of the institution, and had a good school for three years; but from 1878 to 1881 the affairs of the institute were badly managed and its patronage became so poor that it was closed for a short while in the spring of 1881.

In the autumn of that year Miss M. F. Hewitt, who for the past six years had been principal of Warrendale Female Seminary, at Georgetown, Ky., was induced to attempt the reorganization of the school. It had become so much disorganized and its prospects were so poor that the trustees had to guarantee Miss Hewitt her support for a year in order to induce her to undertake the work. She, however, succeeded in the task from the beginning, and conducted the institution very successfully for twelve years. The attendance increased from year to year so that the original building had soon to be much improved and enlarged. By 1888 the institute had outgrown entirely its original quarters, and in September of that year an elegant and imposing new building was completed by the trustees, at a cost of $20,000, most of the money for the purpose having been subscribed by the citizens of Nicholasville and Jessamine County. The new building is quite complete in all its appointments and is one of the handsomest structures of its kind in the State. It stands in the midst of a well-kept campus of 3 acres beautifully situated on a commanding elevation west of the town. The patronage of the institute during Miss Hewitt's administration was more than double what it had usually been previously, and at times included representatives from as many as eleven of the Southern and Western States.

In 1893 declining health caused Miss Hewitt to resign, and the present principal, Mrs. B. W. Vineyard, was then elected. Under the latter's management the previous reputation of the school has been sustained and considerable improvements have been made, particularly in the way of additions to its library, scientific apparatus, and other facilities for instruction. The present faculty is a large and well qualified one, and the institution is prepared to do excellent work in the future, aiming as it does to stand abreast of any college in the South. Like all the other female colleges of Kentucky, however, it has no endowment upon which the security of its future growth and expansion may depend. No record of its alumnæ was kept prior to 1882, but from that time to 1898, inclusive, there have been 181 graduates, many of whom have become teachers of considerable reputation.

BIBLIOGRAPHY.

This sketch is based primarily upon information furnished by Dr. Charles Mann, secretary of the board of trustees, which has been confirmed and enlarged by reference to the usual sources of general information.

STANFORD FEMALE COLLEGE, STANFORD.

This institution was organized in 1871, at the instance of some of the prominent citizens of Stanford and vicinity, for the purpose of giving their daughters a collegiate education and also attracting patronage from a distance. It was chartered the year of its establishment with the usual collegiate powers and privileges. John B. Owsley, S. H. Shanks, J. W. Alcorn, M. C. Saufley, John Reid, and H. S. Withers were prominently connected with the enterprise from its inception, and may be mentioned as its chief founders and promoters. These and others organized themselves into a joint stock company to raise the necessary funds and to provide for a plan of management. The money for the building was subscribed by the incorporators and other citizens of the community and was supplemented by a donation from the town of Stanford.

The original building is a substantial brick structure costing about $15,000. It is admirably adapted to its purpose and is located in the midst of tastefully ornamented grounds. It was completed shortly before the opening of the college. Considerable additions and improvements have since been made to it by the company securing authority to issue bonds upon the property. This plan has caused the accumulation of an indebtedness by the institution which has not yet been entirely liquidated.

The school was opened in the fall of 1872 with Mrs. Sallie C. Truehart, A. M., as the first president. Mrs. Truehart held the position with success for thirteen years. Under her direction the original course of instruction, consisting of the departments of ancient languages, modern languages, mathematics, mental and moral philosophy, English literature, natural science, history, and the usual ornamental branches, was laid out and a good complement of educational apparatus, including the foundation of a well-selected library, accumulated. During this administration the faculty included from 6 to 11 teachers and there were usually about 100 students in attendance upon the various courses, which included primary and preparatory as well as collegiate instruction. The total number of graduates for the period is 41, there being from 1 to 10 in each class after 1875.

In 1885 Mrs. Truehart resigned her position and was succeeded in the presidency by A. S. Paxton, A. B., who remained in charge of the institution for three years. Professor Paxton remodeled the course after the plan of that of his alma mater, Washington and Lee University, an arrangement which has since been substantially retained.

J. M. Hubbard, A. M., next became president, assuming the position in 1888 and retaining it for seven years. During this time the condition of the institution was that of general prosperity. Its matriculation was considerably increased, its curriculum somewhat enlarged, and its buildings extensively improved. Professor Hubbard employed only well qualified teachers and used modern methods of instruction. He resigned in 1895 to accept the presidency of Howard Female College, Gallatin, Tenn.

His successor at Stanford was Rev. William Shelton, LL. D., who is the present head of the institution. Dr. Shelton has for a number of years been a prominent educator, having been the president of several colleges in Tennessee. His administration of Stanford College has so far been successful and the future prospects of the institution are good. His daughter, Mrs. Nannie S. Saufley, is the efficient lady principal of its faculty. A number of improvements have recently been made in the buildings and the scientific apparatus considerably enlarged. Mr. George H. McKinney, of Stanford, presented to the college in 1897 a valuable cabinet of minerals and other geological specimens.

Stanford Female College, while Christian in spirit, is one of the few educational institutions in Kentucky which is not under the patronage, if not direct control, of some religious denomination. According to its charter it is managed by a board of eight trustees, who are authorized to fill their own vacancies. The course of instruction offered by the institution has been from time to time improved so as to compare very favorably with that of other Southern female colleges. If four of its "schools" are completed the student is entitled to a diploma without degree. The completion of the English course leads to the degree of M. E. L. The addition of Latin to the latter course entitles one to the degree of A. B. The standard of scholarship in the degree courses seems to have been very well upheld, as the institution has had only 83 graduates throughout its history.

BIBLIOGRAPHY.

This sketch has as its chief foundation a number of data furnished by President Hubbard, now president of Howard Female College, Gallatin, Tenn. Other facts have come from catalogues and similar sources.

VILLA RIDGE COLLEGE, PEWEE VALLEY.

This institution was known until 1896 as Kentucky College for Young Ladies, and its object and purpose, as expressed in a clipping from the Oldham News of December 20, 1894, is "to promote the education of young women in literature, science, and art." The college was founded originally by a stock company, of which a number of prominent citizens of Pewee Valley and vicinity were members, 22 of whom, its chief promoters, constituting its first board of trustees. Those mainly instrumental in establishing the school seem to have been Presbyterians, but it was placed from the beginning on an undenominational basis. A well-located tract of 20 acres of land, one-half of which constitutes the present campus of the college, was purchased by the company and from funds subscribed by its members a large and comfortable building was erected, which was dedicated on December 23, 1873.

The school had been opened in the previous autumn and had E. A. Sloan, A. M., as its first president. Professor Sloan had previously been at the head of female colleges in Alabama and Kentucky, and successfully conducted the institution for six years. The original faculty consisted of 8 teachers, and the course of instruction as first outlined contained the usual ornamental departments, besides a two years' preparatory course and a four years' collegiate course of very good compass in comparison with that of similar institutions. There were 63 students in attendance the first year the school opened. In 1874 it was incorporated by the legislature under the name of Kentucky College for Young Ladies and was given all the powers and privileges of "any university, college, or seminary of learning in the State." In its second year the foundations of an excellent library for the institution were laid through the liberality of Mrs. B. J. Clay, of Richmond, Ky. In that year there were 68 students in attendance, most of whom were in the collegiate department, and the first class, consisting of 9 members, was graduated. There were 33 graduates during President Sloan's administration, which was terminated by resignation in 1879.

Soon after Professor Sloan's retirement an arrangement was made between the trustees and Rev. Erastus Rowley, D D., whereby the latter leased its property and took entire charge of the college as its president. Dr. Rowley was a prominent minister in the Methodist Episcopal Church South. He was an alumnus of Union College, New York, and a teacher of twenty-six years' experience. Not long after his accession to its presidency he became sole proprietor of the institution by the purchase of its property from the trustees. It has since remained a purely private enterprise.

Early in Dr. Rowley's administration a primary department was added to the course of instruction and a scientific course was arranged for in the collegiate department. In 1891 normal and business departments were also added and in the same year the building of the primary and preparatory departments was considerably enlarged. The library was also increased during this administration, in which the average attendance was somewhat larger than it had been formerly. From two to six students completed the course each year during the time, making the total number of graduates 43 up to the time of Dr. Rowley's retirement from the presidency of the institution in 1894.

In the summer of this year G. B. Perry, A. M., became president of the faculty, Dr. Rowley still remaining in connection with the institution as its professor of moral philosophy and the manager in certain respects of its business affairs. He retained this relation with the institution until his death, on February 28, 1896. President Perry had had several years' experience before coming to Pewee Valley, and has been able by his executive ability to uphold the former reputation of the institution and somewhat enlarge its patronage which now comes from a number of the Southern States outside of Kentucky. All the earlier departments of study have been retained, the former primary and preparatory departments having been combined into a preparatory course of four years, and a one-year postgraduate course having been added to the collegiate department, which embraces the schools of history, mathematics, science, Latin, mental and moral philosophy, and English, besides the usual ornamental branches. The present faculty has 10 members.

BIBLIOGRAPHY.

Clipping from the Oldham News of December 20, 1894, with additional information mainly obtained from catalogues.

POTTER COLLEGE, BOWLING GREEN.

The following sentence, taken substantially from one of its recent catalogues, describes in a general way the origin of this institution: Potter College is an expression of the generosity and liberal spirit of the citizens of Bowling Green, who, irrespective of church connections, heartily united in establishing in their midst an institution for the higher education of young women. The chief promoter of the enterprise was Rev. B. F. Cabell, who had been for twelve years the president of Cedar Bluff Female College, located in Warren County, and who in January, 1889, first conceived the idea of establishing a similar institution in Bowling Green, which in many ways offered excellent advantages as a location for such a school. This plan having been submitted to a few of the prominent citizens of the community received a hearty response from them, and steps were at once taken to raise by subscription the money needed to erect and equip for the proposed institution a building which should be first class in all its appointments. A stock company was soon organized, the soliciting committee of which secured subscriptions amounting to about $17,000. This was, however, not deemed a sufficiently large amount with which to inaugurate the enterprise, and Mr. P. J. Potter, unwilling that the project should fail, raised his subscription to $5,000, in consideration of which liberal gift the college was named by its trustees in his honor.

About a year was consumed in raising the needed funds and erecting the front building, which was not fully completed until December, 1889. Meanwhile a charter was obtained for the college, conferring upon it all the usual powers and privileges, and the institution was opened on September 9, 1889, with Rev. B. F. Cabell as its president, its property having been leased to him for a number of years. The college building, to which a new wing was added in 1891, was finely equipped throughout, making its total cost about $50,000, its appointments, including an excellent gymnasium, being modern in all respects. It is a three-story brick building of improved architecture, one of the largest of its kind in the State, and is splendidly located, in a compass of about 7 acres, on a commanding eminence west of the town. A part of the equipment of the college at its opening was a very good complement of physical and chemical apparatus and an excellent geological collection.

The institution is Christian in spirit, but is insured against sectarian control by the provision of its charter that not more than two of its ten trustees, who are elected by the stockholders, shall be members of the same religious denomination. The course of instruction at first embraced primary, preparatory, academic (secondary), and collegiate departments, but only the last two, extending through two and four years, respectively, are at present retained. There are in addition the usual departments of music and art. The regular curriculum includes the departments of English, history, natural sciences, Latin, mathematics, philosophy, elocution, Greek, French, and German, in the last three of which elective courses are offered, as well as in English. Certificates of proficiency are granted in various departments, but only one degree, that of A. B., is conferred. The original faculty contained 11 members, and the students in attendance the first year, who numbered about 200, represented 13 States, principally in the South and West. A number of them were advanced students from other institutions, and at the end of the year there were 9 graduates in the various departments of the college.

The average annual enrollment since the opening of the institution has been about 200, and 26 different States have been represented by its students up to the present time. Its faculty has been usually composed of about 15 teachers in the various departments, and it has had altogether, up to 1898 inclusive, 77 regular graduates, several of whom are holding lucrative positions as teachers in different sections of the country.

During the nine years of its history the equipment of the college has been considerably improved, especially in the way of libraries and scientific apparatus. In 1896 an annex building was erected near the main building. Since the institution was opened President Cabell has been its active manager and the promoter of its success. He has lately secured a sufficiently large amount of its stock to give him a controlling interest in its affairs, which makes the institution now really a private enterprise. The scholastic year 1897–98 was one of the most successful in its history—a history which has been marked by almost unexampled prosperity, for, although one of the youngest of the female colleges of the South, its career has been very successful from the start.

BIBLIOGRAPHY.

The Chicago Commercial Journal of April 7, 1892, supplemented by the usual sources of general information.

OWENSBORO FEMALE COLLEGE, OWENSBORO.

This institution opened its doors in the autumn of 1890, and is therefore the youngest candidate for public favor among the female colleges of Kentucky. The college is said in its first announcement to be "the outgrowth of a desire on the part of the citizens of Owensboro to have brought to their door the largest advantages for their daughters in the higher branches of education." A few earnest men took hold of the matter in a determined way, and having organized themselves into a stock company in a short time raised $30,000 with which they purchased an admirable site and erected thereon an excellent building, the cost of the latter being about $24,000. R. P. McJohnston, Thomas Pettit, J. D. Powers, Robert Brodie, J. G. Delker, A. C. Thompkins, J. H. Parrish, E. G. Buckner, and T. S. McAtee were, among others, especially active in promoting the enterprise.

The institution is incorporated under the general laws of the State. Its articles of incorporation were filed on March 26, 1893, and give to it the right to confer the usual literary degrees. It is placed under the management of a board of 10 directors chosen by the members of the stock company from their own number. R. P. McJohnston was the president of its first board of directors, while Thomas Pettit was the secretary and J. H. Parrish treasurer. The committee under which the building was completed was composed of A. C. Thompkins, Alexander Hill, and E. G. Buckner. The building is of brick, is 3 stories in height, and is quite modern in its equipment. It contains, besides the class-rooms, a gymnasium and laboratories, and has, in addition, accommodation for 30 boarding pupils. The college has acquired since its foundation a good geological collection and an excellent herbarium.

Prof. W. H. Stuart, who had been for several years at the head of Stuart College at Shelbyville, Ky., was elected its first president, and opened the institution on November 1, 1890, at the time its building was completed. Professor Stuart was assisted by a faculty of 8 members. The course offered at the opening was similar to that usually given in female colleges in the South, having besides the usual ornamental branches and primary and preparatory departments, two college courses of four years each, leading respectively to the degree mistress of arts, and mistress of belles-lettres. These courses embrace the departments of ancient languages, modern languages, mathematics, natural science, and English. There were 70 regular and 12 special students in attendance the first year. In the second year there were 83 regular and 12 special students.

President Stuart was not able to make a financial success of the school and so, in 1895, retired from its management, its property being at that time leased for a term of years to A. C. Goodwin, Ph. D. Professor Goodwin had been for the previous nine years superintendent of the Owensboro city schools, after having previously been connected with the faculty of South Kentucky College. He has since conducted Owensboro Female College with success, having been able to considerably widen its reputation and extend its patronage.

Under his contract with the directors boys were to be allowed to enter this institution as day pupils, thus making the school partly coeducational and so far changing its original design. The enterprise has also of late become largely individual through President Goodwin's having acquired the greater part of its stock. In its course of instruction natural science and literature have recently been given special emphasis, while a commercial course and a normal department have been added to the branches previously taught. The college has had a number of graduates, several of whom have sustained themselves well in advanced work in Eastern institutions.

BIBLIOGRAPHY.

This sketch is based entirely upon catalogues and correspondence.

Chapter VII.

SPECIAL PROFESSIONAL SCHOOLS.

THE UNIVERSITY OF LOUISVILLE.

The charter of the University of Louisville, granted by the legislature of Kentucky on February 7, 1846, contemplated the founding of "all the departments of a university for the promotion of every branch of science, literature, and the liberal arts." Its basis was to be the Louisville Medical Institute, then a flourishing institution; a law department was to be at once established, and power was given to convert Louisville College, the successor of old Jefferson Seminary, founded in 1816, into the collegiate department. The proposed institution was, according to the plan of management adopted for the Louisville Medical Institute in 1837, to be governed by a board of eleven trustees, who were to be appointed by the mayor and city council of Louisville and were given the right to confer all degrees usually conferred in colleges or universities. This board has since exercised supervision over the original medical department and over the law department, which was soon added, but the contemplated conversion of Louisville College into its academic department was never regularly completed, and so the University of Louisville, as at present constituted, embraces only medical and law schools, located in the city of Louisville. Jefferson Seminary, or Louisville College as it came to be called after 1830, is, however, worthy of some notice in this connection on account of the important educational position it held for some time in the early history of the city.

JEFFERSON SEMINARY.

This was one of the State academies created by the act of February 10, 1798, which gave to it an endowment of 6,000 acres of public land. An additional act of December 17, 1798, gave to it the privilege of raising $5,000 by lottery for building purposes. The control of the proposed institution was vested originally in a board of eight trustees, whose number was for some reason increased to sixteen in 1800. The land granted was later surveyed and located in Union County, but no use seems ever to have been made of the lottery privilege.

Nothing was done toward opening the school for several years, owing largely, it seems, to the little interest taken in it on the part of its unwieldy board of trustees, whose rights had several times to be confirmed by subsequent legislative action, but owing partly, perhaps, to the lack of funds for inaugurating the enterprise. At last, on July 2, 1813, the trustees, now reduced in number to ten, purchased for $800 a lot of 2¾ acres on Eighth street, between what is now Walnut and Green streets, upon which, soon after, a brick house, one and a half stories high, with two large ground rooms opening toward Grayson street, was erected.

In this building the school was opened in 1816, with the historian, Mann Butler, as its first principal. Mr. Butler was assisted by Reuben Murray and William Thompkins, the principal's salary being $600 a year and that of the other teachers $500 each. The school term was six months in length, and the rate of tuition was $20 per term. Between 40 and 50 students were in attendance upon the seminary during its first term. It was from the beginning of comparatively high grade, and was the finishing school for the more elementary old-field schools then located throughout the city. In 1817 an unsuccessful attempt was made to improve the institution's financial condition by starting a town on its Union County lands, and in 1820 authority was obtained from the legislature to dispose of these lands at auction. It does not appear how much was realized from this transaction. In 1829 the plan of governing the school was much improved by having the number of its trustees reduced to seven, who were appointed by the county court of Jefferson County

On September 30, 1830,[1] inspired by the success of the new city school which had taken away its principal, Mann Butler, its trustees secured legislative authority for transferring one-half of its property to the city of Louisville for a high school. The city accordingly took possession soon afterwards of the city property of the seminary, which it converted into what was known as Louisville College, the city agreeing to augment, as far as necessary, its tuition fees by an annual appropriation. Its first regular college faculty, organized in 1830, was composed as follows: Rev. B. F Farnsworth, president and professor of intellectual and moral philosophy and political economy; John H. Harney, professor of mathematics, natural science, and civil engineering; James Brown, professor of the Latin and Greek languages and literatures; Leonard Bliss, professor of belles-lettres and history; H. F. Farnsworth, tutor in the preparatory department. Rather a modern tone is given to the school by the fact that chairs of modern languages, of commercial science, and of agricultural and mechanical arts were contemplated as future departments. These were, however, probably never established.

Although popularly having the name of college and really doing considerable work of collegiate grade, the legal title of the institution was still Jefferson Seminary until January 17, 1840,[2] when it was, by

[1] The conveyance was not formally made until April 7, 1844.

[2] Collins's History of Kentucky, Vol. I, p. 45.

legislative action, regularly incorporated as Louisville College, and became the official head of the city public-school system, then consisting of primary and grammar schools and a college. The city was then to pay $2,000 a year into the funds of the college and to receive in return 30 free scholarships for its most deserving grammar school students. The college, however, seems later to have received regular tuition fees for these pupils in addition to the regular appropriation. Its faculty at this period in its history was an able one, including among its members for some time Prof. Noble Butler, noted throughout the State as an eminent educator and the author of popular text-books.

Under the legislative act of February 7, 1846, it was proposed to make the institution the academical department of the contemplated University of Louisville provided for by the act, but this union was never regularly consummated, and by the terms of the second charter of Louisville, adopted March 4, 1851, all tuition fees in Louisville College were abolished, and it lost its identity in the city public-school system, of which it has since remained a part, as the male high school. Some mention will again be made of it in describing the public-school system of Louisville.

The old seminary property was sold in different parcels in 1845 and soon after, and the proceeds subsequently used to erect on the university grounds, on Chestnut street near Ninth street, the building of the law department of the university, which has, however, since its construction been used almost exclusively as the home of the male high school, that school thus remaining, in location at least, if not otherwise, a department of the university. As old Jefferson Seminary and Louisville College it had, from the beginning, taken a high standing, partly on account of Mann Butler, its first principal, and was for a long time the only seat of higher learning in the city. In this capacity it furnished to many of the early citizens of Louisville the elements of a liberal education, of the benefits of which they would otherwise have been deprived.

THE MEDICAL DEPARTMENT.

The medical department of the University of Louisville is the oldest medical school now existing in Kentucky with a continuous history to date. Its origin may be traced, in name at least, to the Louisville Medical Institute, which was established in Louisville on February 7, 1833, and was, it seems, operated for a short time under the charter of Centre College, at Danville. It appears, however, never to have had any vigor, and was succeeded in 1837 by a new institution, under the same name, out of which has grown organically the present medical department of the University of Louisville, which has thus had a continuous corporate history since 1837.

The leading spirit in the establishment of the school was Dr. Charles Caldwell, who had been connected for a number of years with the medical faculty of Transylvania University, but had begun to recognize in Louisville, which in 1837 had much outgrown Lexington in size, a more eligible location for a medical college, largely by reason of the superior clinical advantages it offered. Accordingly, after an unsuccessful attempt, in which he was joined by Professors Cooke, Yandell, and Short, of the Transylvania medical department, to have that school moved bodily to Louisville, he and those gentlemen resigned their positions at Lexington and resolved to open the new institution on their own responsibility.

Largely through Dr. Caldwell's influence the city council[1] of Louisville was induced to give 4 acres of ground, centrally located with reference to the city, and $50,000 in money toward the new enterprise, $30,000 being given to provide a suitable building on the lot donated and $20,000 to furnish a library and apparatus. Dr. Joshua B. Flint, a member of its first faculty, was sent to Europe by order of the city council to purchase a suitable equipment of apparatus for the new school, and succeeded in securing a very fine one for the time. The corner stone of a splendid new building was laid with appropriate ceremonies on February 22, 1838. The institution had already been opened, however, in the fall of 1837, and until its building could be completed occupied temporary quarters in the upper rooms of the city workhouse, which stood on the site of the present university building.

The first faculty of the school was constituted as follows: Charles Caldwell, M. D., institutes of medicine; John Esten Cooke, M. D., theory and practice of medicine; Lunsford P. Yandell, M. D., chemistry; Henry Miller, M. D., obstetric medicine; Jedediah Cobb, M. D., anatomy; Joshua B. Flint, M. D., surgery. Drs. Caldwell, Cooke, and Yandell held the same chairs as those held by them in Lexington, where they had been long and favorably known, and the faculty was altogether a strong one. Dr. Cobb was a well-known medical professor from Cincinnati, and was for many years the efficient dean of the institute faculty. There were only 25 students present at the opening of the new institution, but 80—a number of them from other institutions—were in attendance during its first session, and at its close the degree of M. D. was conferred on 24 candidates.

The fine new building was finished in time for the opening of the second session of the school, and, with its library and apparatus purchased by Professor Flint, its equipment was then unexcelled in the country. Its faculty was completed the second year by the addition of Dr. Charles W. Short, who came to Louisville at that time to occupy in the institute his old Lexington chair of meteria medica, the

[1] Fred. A. Kaye was mayor of Louisville at the time and was one of the foremost and warmest advocates of the school.

duties of which had been discharged the previous year by Professor Yandell. During the second session 120 matriculates were in attendance, and at its close 27 M. D.'s were conferred.

In 1839, a new chair of clinical medicine and pathological anatomy was created, to which was called the celebrated Dr. Daniel Drake, formerly connected with Transylvania University and the Cincinnati Medical College, and noted for his strength, versatility, and eloquence as a teacher of medicine. The students that year rose in number to 205, and there were 38 graduates. In 1840, a clinical amphitheater was erected by the faculty at their own expense, adjoining the Marine Hospital, in order that better results might be obtained in witnessing operations.

The number of students regularly increased until 347 were in attendance, in 1845–46, and 73 were graduated. This made the school second in number only to the two medical schools of Philadelphia. It had had, up to the end of that year, 1,955 matriculates and 418 graduates. No other medical school had, probably up to that time, attracted a larger number of pupils in so short a time.

A larger institution was now proposed and, as has been said, was organized, by a charter secured from the legislature, on February 7, 1846, according to the terms of which Louisville Medical Institute became the medical department of the University of Louisville, the buildings and grounds of the former institution being transferred to the latter by request of the city council. This reorganization took place on May 18, 1846, through by-laws adopted by the board of trustees, who took the place of the old board of managers. This change of name and charter had really no other effect on the institution, which has been conducted on the same plan as formerly, and has not been materially affected in any way in its history by the founding of a law department under the same board of trustees.

The history of the medical department of the university has since been one of uniform success, its aim having been to keep abreast of the demands of medical science and to furnish proper facilities for the changed conditions of practice and teaching as these have arisen. Some notice will be taken of the important advances in its work from time to time, together with other incidents in its history of more than usual interest.

The progress of the school was steady until interrupted somewhat by the advent of the civil war, which suspended its lectures entirely during the year 1862–63. Meanwhile, on December 31, 1856, it had lost its original building by fire; but the lectures of that session were completed in the amphitheater of the marine hospital by the courtesy of its trustees, and a new building, in many respects more commodious than the old one, was erected in the spring and summer of 1857. The loss on the former building and apparatus, while approximating $100,000, had been mainly covered by insurance, so that the facilities of the school were not decreased by the fire, but rather increased, as its building was improved and new apparatus speedily supplied.

In 1859 a valuable addition was made to its equipment by the erection of a small dispensary building, where the treatment of disease could be brought more directly under the inspection of its students. Up to its temporary suspension in 1862, the school had had 1,067 graduates, the largest single class during this period being that of 1850, which graduated 113 members. The classes of 1864 and 1865 were comparatively small, but that of 1866 again reached the respectable proportions of 87 graduates.

In September of this last year the Kentucky School of Medicine was temporarily united with the university, a combined faculty of ten members taking the place of the former separate faculties. This faculty was constituted as follows: Llewellyn Powell, M. D., professor of obstetric medicine; H. M. Bullitt, M. D., professor of the principles and practice of medicine; G. W. Bayless, M. D., professor of the principles and practice of surgery; C. W. Wright, M. D., professor of chemistry; J. M. Holloway, M. D., professor of physiology; L. J. Frazee, M. D., professor of materia medica and therapeutics; J. M. Bodine, M. D., professor of anatomy; A. B. Cook, M. D., professor of surgical diseases of the genito-urinary organs and rectum; J. A. Ireland, M. D., professor of clinical medicine; J. W. Benson, M. D., professor of clinical surgery. Drs. T. S. Bell and Lewis Rogers were also emeritus professors, respectively, of the science and practice of medicine and public hygiene, and materia medica and clinical medicine. Dr. Benson was dean of the faculty.

This union of the two schools only lasted about a year, as the university faculty was reorganized in May, 1867. It was then composed of Drs. Powell, Rogers, Bayless, Bullitt, Wright, and Bodine, mentioned above, with the addition of Drs. Henry Miller and D. W. Yandell, who had formerly been connected with it. Drs. Powell, Bayless, Wright, and Bodine held their former chairs, while Dr. Rogers, now an active professor, held that of materia medica and therapeutics; Dr. Bullitt, that of physiology and pathology; Dr. Miller, that of medical and surgical diseases of women, and Dr. Yandell, that of the science and practice of medicine. Dr. Bodine had become dean of the united faculty in January, 1867, upon the resignation of the position by Dr. Benson, a relation which was continued under the reorganized university faculty, and one which has since been maintained, much to the advantage of the institution.

The university has always been in hearty sympathy with every proposition to advance the standard of medical education, but, looking as it necessarily does to the South and West for patronage, has not always been able to take the stand in favor of these that it would have otherwise done, owing to the competition of other colleges in the same territory. Its course was originally one year of lectures, with a preliminary requirement of three years' office study, and remained so for many years. In 1876, upon the formation of the American Medical College Association, of which it became a member, its requirements for graduation were made two years' lecture courses with one year's preliminary study. In 1892 it took part in the organization of the Southern Medical College Association, and in 1893, according to the laws of that body, required a preliminary admission requirement at least equal to a second-grade teacher's certificate, and the student was required to take instruction in the laboratories of practical chemistry, microscopical technology, normal and pathological histology, bacteriology, ophthalmoscopy, laryngoscopy, otoscopy, operative surgery and surgical dressings, besides attending upon three courses of lectures of not less than six months each in three separate years, during which the student must take two courses in dissection and two courses of clinical or hospital instruction as a prerequisite to graduation. In 1895 the institution became a member of the association of American medical colleges and advanced its matriculation requirements and its standard of graduation up to the rules of that association, which require attendance upon four years' lectures for students graduating after 1899.

Meanwhile the equipment of the school has been kept abreast of these increasing requirements for its doctorate. In 1888 a commodious dispensary was constructed, the plans and arrangements of which were well suited for conducting a large polyclinic. Besides its original chemical equipment, it has from time to time established special laboratories for practical demonstration and for teaching students the use of instruments, especially those of precision required in diagnosis. In 1879 special laboratories in medical chemistry, ophthalmoscopy, laryngoscopy, otoscopy, histology, and microscopy were opened, and in 1880 one for surgical dressings was added. These various laboratories have been steadily enlarged and increasingly provided with all the instruments and appliances which experience has shown to be needed in a well-conducted institution. The regular chemical laboratory is one of the largest in America. The library and anatomical apparatus of the school are also modern. In 1896 its clinical instruction was enlarged by the addition of three new chairs to its faculty, those of clinical professor of diseases of the eye, ear, nose, and throat, clinical professor of diseases of children, and clinical professor of genito-urinary diseases. Medical jurisprudence has been taught for many years by a competent lecturer, and instruction in all the departments of a modern medical course is now offered annually by the members of the faculty of the institution.

The number of students in attendence upon the medical department of the university since 1869 has rarely fallen below 200 annually, and has frequently gone over 300. The largest attendance in any single year was 426 in 1892–93. The average attendance for the last ten years has been 313.[1] The number of graduates each year has usually been about 100, the largest number in any one year being 209 in 1893–94. The average for the past ten years has been 125. The total number of graduates, from the foundation of the school up to 1898, inclusive, is 4,831.

The advancement of the requirements for matriculation and graduation in recent years has somewhat reduced the number of matriculates and graduates, but the reduction has not been greater than has been usual in other similar institutions. The graduates of the school have won much distinction in their profession and as teachers, those who have gone into teaching having filled chairs in New York, Philadelphia, New Orleans and other centers of medical education. It has furnished seven presidents to the American Medical Association.

The following, a practically complete list of its professors from its foundation to the present time, will doubtless be of some interest: Charles Caldwell, 1837–1849; John Esten Cooke, 1837–1844; Lunsford P. Yandell, sr., 1837–1859; Henry Miller, 1837–1858 and 1867–1869; Jedediah Cobb, 1837–1852; Joshua B. Flint, 1837–1840 and 1856–1858; Charles W. Short, 1838–1849; Daniel Drake, 1839–1849 and 1850–1852; Samuel D. Gross, 1840–1850 and 1851–1855;[2] Elisha Bartlett, 1849–1850; Lewis Rogers, 1849–1856[2] and 1863–1868; Benjamin Silliman, jr., 1849–1854; Paul F. Eve, 1849–1850; Austin Flint, 1852–1855;[2] Benjamin R. Palmer, 1852–1865; J. Lawrence Smith, 1854–1866; Robert J. Breckinridge, 1855–1861;[2] T. S. Bell, 1856–1867[2] and 1868–1885; Llewellyn Powell, 1858–1868; J. W. Benson, 1858–1864 and 1866–67; David W. Yandell, 1859–1861 and 1867–1897; S. M. Bemiss, 1861–62 and 1865–66; G. W Bayless, 1863–1873; J. M. Holloway, 1865–1867; H. M. Bullitt, 1866–1868; C. W. Wright, 1866–1868; J. M. Bodine, 1866 to date; Edward Palmer, 1868–1895; L. P. Yandell, jr., 1868–1884; John E. Crowe, 1868–1881; James W. Holland, 1869–1885; Theophilus Parvin, 1869–1872 and 1882–83; Richard O. Cowling, 1873–1881; W. O. Roberts, 1881 to date; J. A. Ouchterlony, 1882 to date; Turner Anderson, 1884 to date; H. A. Cottell, 1884 to date; William Bailey, 1885 to date; H. M. Goodman, 1895 to date; J. M. Ray, 1896 to date; R. B. Gilbert, 1896 to date; I. N. Bloom, 1896 to date.

This list includes the combined faculty of the University and the Kentucky School of Medicine in 1866–67. No attempt has been made to give the chairs of the different professors, as these have been changed so often as to make the task quite impossible.

The following have been the deans, or chief executive officers, of the faculty, to whom a large part of the success of the school is to be attributed: Jedediah Cobb, from 1837 to 1852; Lunsford P. Yandell, sr.,

[1] The students come mainly from the Southern and Western States, but have at times represented as many as 33 of the States and Territories, and 3 foreign countries.

[2] These dates are a little uncertain, but are approximately correct.

from 1852 to 1859; J. W. Benson, from 1859 to 1863, and again from 1866 to 1867 (January); G. W. Bayless, from 1863 to 1866, and J. M. Bodine, from 1867 (January) to the present time.

The following are the present regular professors of the institution, with the chair of each: J. M. Bodine, M. D., professor of anatomy and dean of the faculty; W. O. Roberts, M. D., professor of principles and practice of surgery and clinical surgery; J. A. Ouchterlony, A. M., M. D., LL. D., professor of principles and practice of medicine and clinical medicine; H. A. Cottell, M. D., professor of physiology, histology, and clinical diseases of the nervous system; Turner Anderson, M. D., professor of obstetrics and gynecology; William Bailey, A. M., M. D., professor of materia medica, therapeutics, and public hygiene; H. M. Goodman, A. B., M. D., professor of medical chemistry; J. M. Ray, M. D., clinical professor of diseases of the eye, ear, nose, and throat; R. B. Gilbert, M. D., clinical professor of diseases of children and demonstrator of anatomy; I. N. Bloom, A. B., M. D., clinical professor of genito-urinary diseases. The faculty includes, besides these, sixteen lecturers, demonstrators, and assistants of various kinds.

THE LAW DEPARTMENT.

This department of the university is ordinarily called the Louisville Law School, and was organized, according to the terms of the university charter of February 7, 1846, at the same time that Louisville Medical Institute became the medical department of the university under by-laws adopted by the board of trustees on May 18, 1846. Those who may be mentioned as taking perhaps the leading part in its establishment are Hon. James Guthrie and Judge Henry Pirtle, the latter for a long time being one of its most prominent professors. Mr. Guthrie, who was prominent in local, State, and national politics before and after this time, had been previously connected with the board of managers of Louisville Medical Institute and had taken a great interest in its welfare. He did much to promote the foundation of the larger institution, with all the departments of a university, contemplated by the charter of 1846, which movement, as already noticed, only resulted in the addition of a law school to the former medical school, the two forming the professional departments of a university which as yet has had no others.

The law department of the university was opened in the fall of 1846, and had as its first faculty Henry Pirtle, professor of constitutional law, equity and equity pleadings, and commercial law; Garnett Duncan, professor of the science of law and the law of nations; Preston S. Loughborough, professor of the practice of law, including actions, pleadings, evidence, and criminal law. This faculty, as has been the case with subsequent ones, was composed of able lawyers and jurists, but of these Judge Pirtle, as he was ordinarily called, was perhaps the most distinguished and the one destined to be most closely connected with the school. He had studied under the noted John Rowan, greatly distinguished as an advocate, a judge, and a United States Senator; had become a circuit judge at the early age of 28, and had subsequently held some of the highest judicial positions in the State.

He was for twenty-seven years a professor of the law school, and was more potent than any other one man in shaping its destinies. He was a profound lawyer, particularly in the equity branches, and was to the end of his life an enthusiastic and laborious student in many fields of learning.[1]

Professor Duncan was one of the leaders of the bar of Kentucky, and was possessed of a deep knowledge of legal science. He only remained connected with the school for one year, being succeeded in 1847 by Ephraim M. Ewing, who also held an honorable position in the judicial annals of the State.

Of Professor Loughborough it has been said:

As a professor he moved with familiar steps over the department of jurisprudence confided to his teaching, and as a practitioner he may be said to have illustrated the law by his learning and sagacity.[2]

He remained identified with the school until just prior to his death in 1852, when he was succeeded by James Pryor.

The original requirements of the law department of the university were one year's office practice and one year's lectures, or two years' lectures. The latter has been the uniform requirement in recent years. There were 30 students in attendance during its first term, of whom 12 received diplomas at the end of the year. The attendance of the second year was considerably larger, and at its end 23 degrees were conferred. The school was uniformly successful up to the period of the civil war, its graduating class numbering 36 in 1860, and almost as many in 1861. It continued its sessions during the war, but of course its matriculation was very much reduced, the operations of the war covering for some time a considerable part of the territory from which it drew its students. By 1866 its classes had again risen to somewhat of their former size, and its patronage has since continued generally good, the graduating class it now usually sends out annually approximating very closely the largest one of antebellum days.

The present course of study is designed for two sessions of seven months each. The junior class pursues courses in elementary and constitutional law, mercantile law, law of corporations, law of contracts, law of pleading, criminal law, and law of torts; while the senior class investigates equity jurisprudence, law of corporations, law of evidence, law of code pleading, and law of real property. The method of instruction is one in which the use of lectures, of textbooks, and the discussion and dissection of test cases are combined. The whole is illustrated and enforced by a moot court, which meets

[1] Announcement of 1896-97, p. 6.
[2] Announcement of 1897-98, p. 7.

regularly and conforms to all the rules and practices of judicial procedure. The students have free access to the Louisville Law Library, which contains about 10,000 volumes. They can also attend without extra expense the lectures on medical jurisprudence in the medical department of the university. By an act of the State legislature of December 20, 1873, the diploma of the law school is equivalent to a license to practice law in Kentucky.

The matriculates of the school have come mainly from Kentucky and the adjoining States, but its alumni, who up to 1898, inclusive, number 1,034, are to be found in almost every State of the Union. Many of these have reached distinction at the bar and in politics. They include in their number many judges and Congressmen, a nominee for the Vice-Presidency, and at least one governor of a State.

The following is a complete list of the professors of the institution from its foundation: Henry Pirtle, 1846–1873; Garnett Duncan, 1846–47; Preston S. Loughborough, 1846–1852; Ephraim M. Ewing, 1847–1849; William F. Bullock, 1849–1871; James Pryor, 1852–1856; James Speed, 1856–1858 and 1873–1876; John Preston, 1858–59; Horatio F. Simrall, 1859–1862; Peter B. Muir, 1862–1868; Henry J. Stites, 1868–1872; Bland Ballard, 1871–1873; Thomas E. Bramlette, 1872–73; James S. Pirtle, 1873–1881; Horatio W. Bruce, 1873–1880; William Chenault, 1879–1886; Henry C. Pinnell, 1880–81; Rozel Weissinger, 1884–1890; Emmet Field, 1884 to date; W. O. Harris, 1886 to date; Charles B. Seymour, 1890 to date.

For many years prior to 1897, for the greater convenience of its professors, its sessions were conducted in the building known as the Bull Block, on the northeast corner of Fifth and Market streets, but having in that year outgrown those quarters, the session of 1897–98 was held in the home originally designed for it—the law building of the university, on Chestnut street near Ninth street, occupied since 1856 by the city male high school.

The present faculty consists of: Hon. W. O. Harris, LL. B., professor of the law of real property, of criminal law, and law of torts; Hon. Emmet Field, LL. B., professor of pleading, evidence, and law of contracts; Charles B. Seymour, A. M., B. S., professor of equity jurisprudence, of mercantile law, and law of corporations.

As has been said, Judge Henry Pirtle was for a long time a leading spirit in the school. Since 1890 Hon. W. O. Harris has been its efficient dean, or chief executive officer.

BIBLIOGRAPHY.

Collins's Sketches; Collins's History; McMurtrie's Sketches of Louisville; Colonel Durrett's articles in Courier-Journal of January 2, 9, 16, 23, and 30, 1881.

Sketch of the Medical Department, in Courier-Journal of August 9, 1869; Williams's Ohio Falls Cities and their Counties.

Louisville, her Commercial, Manufacturing, and Social Advantages, by Richard Deering, Louisville, 1859.

A History of Louisville, by Ben Casseday, Louisville, 1852.

Louisville, Past and Present, by M. Joblin & Co., Louisville, 1875.

Address by Dr. D. W. Yandell on the Semicentennial of the Medical Department, Fifty-first Announcement, pp. 24-32.

Articles by T. M. Goodknight in the Southern School.

A sketch of the law department and its first faculty is to be found in the announcements of that department for 1894-95, 1897-98, and 1898-99.

DANVILLE THEOLOGICAL SEMINARY, DANVILLE.

The official title of this institution, according to the plan adopted for its regulation in 1854, is The Danville Theological Seminary, under the care of the General Assembly of the Presbyterian Church in the United States of America. It was established by that church in 1853 to supply proper theological training for its ministry, primarily in the Southwest and West. The Presbyterians of Kentucky early contemplated the establishment of a theological seminary in their midst. The amendment to the charter of Centre College, secured on January 27, 1824, and placing the institution under their control, made provision for a theological department, with one or more professors, and we have seen in connection with the history of that institution that such a department, with one professor, Rev. James K. Burch, was attached to it in 1828, but was not long maintained, owing to a lack of sufficient endowment. However, the $2,000 raised toward an endowment at that time was carefully husbanded and afterwards formed a part of the funds offered by the synod of Kentucky for the establishment of Danville Theological Seminary, amounting then to about $5,500. Subsequent to the abandonment of the theological department of Centre, another fund was raised by this synod for theological education. It amounted to about $22,000, and was later united with the Centre College fund into what was known as the Seminary fund. This was, by a legislative act of March 1, 1850, put under the control of trustees, and its income was for a time used to support a professor in the Presbyterian Theological Seminary at New Albany, Ind., an institution supported and controlled by seven of the western synods of the church.

There was a desire, however, on the part of these synods, especially that of Kentucky, to have located in the West, as the central Mississippi Valley was then called, a seminary of the first class under the control of the General Assembly of the church. This desire was voiced by a meeting of representatives of these synods, joined by four other western ones, held in conjunction with the session of the General Assemby of the church in Philadelphia, Pa., in May, 1853. The participating synods were those of Nashville, Kentucky, Cincinnati, Indiana, North Indiana, Missouri, Mississippi, Memphis, Illinois, Ohio, and Arkansas, and their representatives passed unanimously the following resolution, together with some others in regard to the location and other specific matters concerning the proposed institution:

> That we are of the opinion that the General Assembly ought at this time to establish in the West, under its own care, a theological seminary of the first class, and that we will earnestly labor to have it done.

The matter was duly brought before the assembly,[1] its presentation being accompanied by an overture from the twelve commissioners from Kentucky, proposing, if the assembly should establish such a seminary, to give toward its endowment, wherever it should be located, $20,000, and if it should be located at Danville, Ky., to make their contribution $60,000 and 10 acres of land.

Rev. Robert J. Breckinridge, who had taken a prominent part in the meeting of the representatives of the synods, and also in drawing up the overture from the Kentucky commissioners, presented the latter, with other papers, before the assembly, as chairman of the committee on theological seminaries, in a very forcible way, and was largely instrumental in bringing about the subsequent action. He may thus, more than anyone else perhaps, be called the founder of Danville Theological Seminary, of whose faculty he was also for many years a very prominent member.

The assembly on May 26 voted to establish the desired seminary, on May 27 accepted the proposition of the Kentucky commissioners and located it at Danville, and on May 30 placed it under the immediate control of a board of 54 directors, one-third of whom were to be elected each year. On the same day it declared the institution should be conducted provisionally on the plan of Princeton Seminary, New Jersey, and should be opened on October 13, 1853. On the next day it elected the first faculty of the school, composed as follows: Rev. Robert J. Breckinridge, D. D., LL. D., professor of exegetical, didactic, and polemic theology; Rev. E. P. Humphrey, D. D., professor of Biblical and ecclesiastical history; Rev. B. M. Palmer, D. D., professor of oriental and Biblical literature; Rev. Phineas B. Gurley, D. D., professor of pastoral theology, church government, and construction and delivery of sermons.

A charter was afterwards secured for the institution by a legislative act of January 28, 1854, which placed the management of its finances in the hands of a board of not more than 18 trustees, 9 of whom must be from Kentucky, and whose appointment was vested in the assembly. Its affairs, outside of its finances, still remained under the control of its directors.

Drs. Gurley and Palmer having declined the chairs to which they had been elected, the seminary was opened at the appointed date, with Drs. Breckinridge and Humphrey as professors, assisted by Joseph G. Reasor as instructor in oriental and Biblical literature. An arrange-

[1] Catalogue of 1853-54, p. 14.

ment had been made on June 30, 1853, between a committee of the assembly and the trustees of Centre College by which, until the seminary could provide itself with suitable quarters, it was to have the use of the college buildings as far as such use would not interfere with the latter's interests. This is the beginning of a close alliance in spirit and management between the two institutions, although there has never been any organic connection between them. The students of the seminary have always had free access to the college classes, and the library of each institution has always been freely accessible to the professors and students of the other.

The seminary was conducted the first year under the Princeton plan, but the assembly of 1854 adopted for it a plan drawn up by a committee appointed for the purpose the previous year, the essential principle of which was that the students should not be arranged in regular classes except in Hebrew, in which there were to be two divisions according to the stage of advancement, but were to be taught together, as in other professional schools, every student attending every public exercise of every professor as long as he was connected with the institution. The completion of a certain number of exercises in a creditable manner, which usually required three years, qualified for graduation. This plan was used continuously in the seminary until 1876.

There were 23 regular students, from five of the Southern and Western States, in attendance on the seminary during its first year. By 1854 the church in Kentucky had done more than had been pledged, as she had subscribed $65,000 toward the funds of the institution, and in the summer of this year a substantial and commodious building was purchased for its accommodation. The means to purchase this, as well as to pay the running expenses of the school for three years, were entirely contributed by the synod of Kentucky, as has also been the case with its endowment mainly, which has been given almost entirely by Kentucky and the eastern half of Tennessee. Its funds had in 1859 accumulated to $131,749, of which amount all but about $20,000 came from Kentucky. In 1854–55 there were 37 students in attendance, and in 1855–56, 45. In the latter year Rev. Stuart Robinson, D. D., became professor of pastoral theology and church government in the institution. He only remained connected with the faculty for about two years, but before his resignation Rev. Stephen Yerkes, in June, 1857, took Instructor Reasor's place as professor of oriental and Biblical literature, thus for the first time completing the faculty as originally contemplated. During the next session there were 40 students in attendance, who represented fourteen States of the Union and one foreign country.

Dr. Yerkes remained closely identified with the history of the seminary until his death and had a very potent influence on its later development, perhaps more so than any other one man outside of

Dr. Breckinridge. Rev. Joseph T. Smith was professor of church government and pastoral theology for a part of the year 1860–61, but that chair was not occupied again regularly until 1867. The highest number of students during any year prior to the civil war, in fact any year in the history of the institution, was in 1859–60, when 53 were in attendance. Up to 1859, inclusive, there had been altogether 115 separate students and 43 graduates.

The seminary was in operation all during the war, but its attendance was very much reduced, not only by the disturbed state of affairs generally, but by the disruption which began in the church. The total enrollment of the institution up to September, 1865, had been 372 students, of whom 81 had completed the course. The Synod of Kentucky divided in 1866 between the original church organization and that of the new Southern Presbyterian Church, but the seminary, as well as Centre College, remained under the control of the original assembly, ordinarily called that of the Northern Presbyterian Church. The results of the war practically in large measure isolated the institution, as a large part of the church in its original field went over into the Southern Presbytery, and, moreover, in 1869, by the union of the old school and new school branches of its own church organization, it was brought into competition in the same field with Lane Seminary, at Cincinnati, Ohio. These facts account for its slow process of recuperation and growth since the war.

At the end of that struggle the institution was left in a very crippled condition, with two of its professorships vacant. So, in 1868, as also in 1869, it held only a short summer session, 8 students being in attendance the first of these years and 10 the second.

On December 1, 1869, Dr. Breckinridge, after having taught with great distinction and success in the seminary for about sixteen years, resigned his professorship on account of failing health. He died on December 27, 1871. A member of a celebrated Kentucky family, he had graduated at Union College, New York, in 1819, when 19 years of age. At first he turned his attention to the law, but in 1832 he entered the ministry and was for about thirteen years the brilliant and successful pastor of the Second Presbyterian Church of Baltimore, Md. He was then the president, for two years, of Jefferson College, Washington, Pa., after which he removed to his native State to engage for a short while in pastoral work in Lexington, but mainly to devote his great energy and ability to the cause of education in the service of the State and his church. We have already noticed that he was mainly instrumental in establishing the seminary, and shall see in another connection what a great work he did for the cause of common-school education in Kentucky. His influence was great not only in Kentucky but throughout the country, especially in church and educational circles. He was noted as a preacher, debater, and journalist, as well as a teacher.

After Dr. Breckinridge's resignation in 1869, Dr. Yerkes's chair was made that of Biblical literature and exegetical theology, and as senior professor he became chairman of the faculty, a position he retained for about twenty-seven years, during which time his was the guiding hand in seminary affairs. In 1870, a full faculty was secured for the institution and a regular session held, which had, however, only 6 students in attendance. From 1871 to 1874 its sessions were practically suspended. One of its professors, however, remained in charge during this time to give such instruction as might be requested. During this period, in 1873, the plan of management was changed in such a way as to bring it into harmony with that adopted in 1869 for the control of all the seminaries of the church. Under this arrangement the institution has since been controlled by a body of 30 self-perpetuating directors, one-third of whom are replaced each year, and who have in the first instance the management of all the affairs of the seminary, the general assembly reserving to itself only a final residuary control by being able to veto absolutely the election of any director or professor of the school.

In 1876, the plan of instruction previously used in the institution was changed so as to become similar to that of the other seminaries, and its students were for the first time divided into three regular classes. Soon after this several resignations occurred in its faculty and as the number of students had declined to 7 in 1882–83, it was thought best to suspend its sessions for a time. This was done with the sanction of the General Assembly, and no regular session was again held for three years, Dr. Yerkes meanwhile remaining in charge and giving such instruction as was desired by a few students.

In 1886, an arrangement was made, by an agreement between its board of directors and the trustees of Centre College, to open the seminary again on a broader basis, its management, especially in regard to the personnel of its faculty, being more closely associated with that of the college than formerly, a plan which has since been continued to a considerable extent. The reorganized faculty which opened the institution in September, 1886, was constituted as follows: Rev. Stephen Yerkes, D. D., Biblical literature and exegetical theology; Ormond Beatty, LL. D., historical theology; Rev. C. H. B. Martin, D. D., systematic[1] theology; Rev. John L. McKee, homiletics and pastoral theology. Dr. Beatty was, at that time, the president of Centre College and Dr. DeKee its vice-president, while Dr. Martin was then pastor of the Second Presbyterian Church in Danville. A full and regular course was given the first year of the reopening of the seminary and 10 regular students were that session in attendance upon its exercises. Its classes have not been large since, but have gradually increased until there were altogether 42 students in 1896–97, the largest number in recent years. However comparatively small

[1] This was the name of the old chair of didactic and polemic theology.

DANVILLE THEOLOGICAL SEMINARY—BRECKINRIDGE HALL.

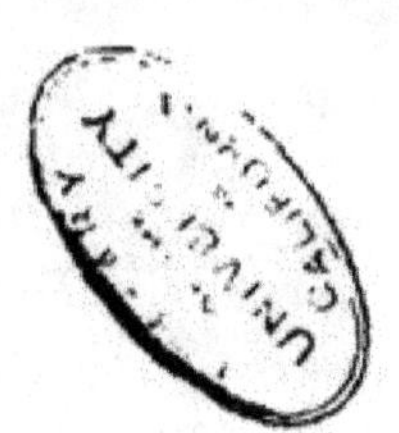

the attendance has been at any time since the reopening, the amount and quality of the instruction given has not been diminished, a full faculty having been constantly maintained and a regular course offered.

The facilities for instruction have also been kept first-class and the accommodations offered excellent. The library, which was already called extensive and valuable in 1856, has been added to from year to year, by donations and purchases, so as to meet the demands of modern education. It has recently received the addition of the extensive private library of the late Dr. Yerkes, and of a special library of about 1,000 volumes of the best modern works, given by Mr. Anthony Dey, of New York City, and named the David C. Humphrey library. In 1890 the erection of a fine, new building, containing commodious lecture and library rooms, besides a dormitory for students, was begun on a site leased from Centre College, and more eligible than the old one. It was completed in 1893, at a cost of $25,000, and was named Breckinridge Hall, in honor of Dr. Breckinridge, the revered member of the first seminary faculty.

The endowment of the institution, as at first contemplated, has never been completed, no important benefactions having been asked for or received by it in recent years, but its funds contributed originally, as has been seen, largely by Kentucky, have been carefully managed and have accumulated by savings until, in 1896, its entire property, including its library, was valued at about $245,000.

A number of changes have in recent years taken place in the seminary faculty. In 1887 John W. Redd, A. M., of the Centre College faculty, was added to it as professor of Biblical Greek and New Tesment history, and Clarence K. Crawford, A. M., as instructor in Hebrew, thus making provision for a more extended course of study. In 1888 Rev. W. C. Young, D. D., who had that year assumed the presidency of Centre College, became its professor of pastoral theology, a chair to which homiletics was attached in 1891. In 1890 Professor Redd and Dr. Beatty[1] retired from its faculty, and Rev. John M. Worrall, D. D., was elected professor of ecclesiastical history, church government, and English Bible. Upon the resignation of the regular duties of his chair by Dr. McKee in 1891, most of these were assigned to Dr. Young, while at the same time Mr. Crawford was made professor of Hebrew and Biblical antiquities.

On March 28, 1896, the seminary lost by death its senior professor, Dr. Yerkes, so long the honored and capable chairman of its faculty. Dr. Yerkes had graduated at Yale in 1837, when 20 years of age, in the class with Chief Justice Waite, Professor Silliman, Hon. Edwards Pierrepont, Hon. William M. Evarts, and other prominent public men. He had then taught in a Presbyterian high school near Baltimore, Md., until 1852, meanwhile studying theology under Dr. Breck-

[1] Dr. Beatty has since died.

inridge, and engaging somewhat in the work of the ministry. In 1852 he was elected professor of ancient languages in Transylvania University at Lexington, Ky., from which position he was called in 1857 to a professorship in the seminary, where he remained for nearly thirty-nine years, accomplishing there the great work of his life. He was scholarly, able, and faithful, and withal, warmly devoted to his work. He has been characterized as a strong man, an able divine, a wise counselor, a ripe scholar, and a grand teacher,[1] and was one who left a strong impression for good upon all who came under his instruction. On September 16 of the year of Dr. Yerkes's death, Dr. Young, the distinguished and efficient president of Centre College, who had been connected with the seminary faculty since 1888, also died. Consequently, in September, 1897, two new members were added to the faculty, William H. Johnson, M. A., and J. C. Ely, D. D., making the present teaching body, with their chairs, to consist as follows: John M. Worrall, D. D., Biblical and ecclesiastical history and church government; Claude B. H. Martin, D. D., systematic theology and study of the English Bible; Clarence K. Crawford, A. M., Old Testament languages and exegesis and Biblical antiquities; William H. Johnson, M. A., New Testament literature and exegesis; John C. Ely, D. D., homiletics. Dr. Worrall, by virtue of his rank as the oldest regular professor, is chairman of the faculty.

The following is a list of all the professors of the seminary from its foundation, with their chairs and terms of service: Robert J. Breckinridge, exegetical, didactic, and polemic theology, May, 1853, to December, 1869; Edward P. Humphrey, Biblical and ecclesiastical history, May, 1853, to May, 1866; Joseph G. Reasor, instructor, Biblical and oriental literature, September, 1853, to May, 1857; Stuart Robinson, church government and pastoral theology, September, 1856, to April, 1858; Stephen Yerkes, Biblical and oriental literature, June, 1857, to November, 1869, biblical literature and exegetical theology, November, 1869, to March, 1896; Joseph T. Smith, church government and pastoral theology, May, 1860, to December, 1860; Robert W. Landis, church government and pastoral theology, May, 1867, to November, 1869; Nathaniel West, Biblical and ecclesiastical history, June, 1868, to June, 1870, didactic and polemic theology, June, 1870, to June, 1873; George D. Archibald, church government and pastoral theology, June, 1870, to September, 1872, church government and pastoral theology, June, 1874, to May, 1883; Samuel J. McMullin, Biblical and ecclesiastical history, June, 1870, to September, 1872; Nathan L. Rice, didactic and polemic theology, June, 1874, to April, 1877; John S. Hays, Biblical and ecclesiastical history, June, 1874, to April, 1883; Jonathan Edwards, systematic theology,[2] Sep-

[1] Minutes of the Synod of Kentucky for 1896, p. 44.

[2] The name was adopted at this time instead of the former title of didactic and polemic theology.

tember, 1877, to May, 1880; Ormond Beatty, church history, September, 1886, to May, 1890; Claude B. H. Martin, systematic theology, September, 1886 to date; John L. McKee, homiletics and pastoral theology, September, 1886, to May, 1891; John W. Redd, Biblical Greek and New Testament history, September, 1887, to May, 1890; Clarence K. Crawford, tutor in Hebrew, September, 1887, to May, 1891, professor of Old Testament languages and Biblical antiquities, May, 1891 to date; William C. Young, pastoral theology, September, 1888, to May, 1891, homiletics and pastoral theology, May, 1891, to September, 1896; John M. Worrall, Biblical and ecclesiastical history and church government, September, 1890 to date; William H. Johnson, New Testament literature and exegesis, September, 1897 to date; John C. Ely, homiletics, September, 1897 to date.

The course of instruction in the seminary embraces all the departments of a modern theological education, and is strictly professional in character, being directed to the one end of properly preparing students for the ministry. The methods of instruction, besides regular class-room exercises, embrace various practical exercises and conferences in different departments. Only those are admitted to the courses that have received a regular college education, or at least so much thereof as will enable them to pursue with profit the courses taken. The work of the institution is so coordinated with that of Centre College as to offer excellent advantages to those who wish to take special courses in the latter, to all of which the admission is gratuitous.

BIBLIOGRAPHY.

Collins's History of Kentucky

The Presbyterian Almanac for 1860, edited by J. M. Wilson, Philadelphia, Pa.

Plan of the Danville Theological Seminary, Louisville, 1854.

Plan of the Danville Theological Seminary, Louisville, 1873.

An address to the Alumni Association of Centre College, by James Barbour, Cincinnati, 1874.

The Presbyterian Encyclopedia, edited by Alfred Nevin, D. D., LL. D., and other eminent ministers of the church, Philadelphia. 1884.

Minutes of the Ninety-Fifth Annual Session of the Synod of Kentucky, Mount Sterling, 1896.

Considerable information was also obtained from catalogues, especially those of 1853-54, 1874-75, and 1886-87.

SOUTHERN BAPTIST THEOLOGICAL SEMINARY, LOUISVILLE.

From the very organization of the Southern Baptist Convention in 1845, persistent efforts were put forth by some of the prominent members of the denomination to establish a general theological seminary which should furnish a professional education to the ministry of the church of wider scope and better adapted to the special needs of individuals than could be offered in the theological departments of the various church colleges, whose endowments were meager and whose instruction was necessarily limited in character. Even at the first meeting of the convention, held at Atlanta, Ga., in May, 1845, a special conference looking toward this object was held by those particularly interested, and similar discussions were held from time to time at various other denominational gatherings. Among those particularly active in urging on the enterprise at the different church meetings in which they took part may be mentioned: R. C. B. Howell; John L. Waller; Basil Manly, sr.; William B. Johnson; J. L. Burrows; J. B. Jeter; J. B. Taylor; A. M. Poindexter; G. W. Samson; J. W. M. Williams; J. O. B. Dargan; R. Furman; Basil Manly, jr.; J. H. De Votie; J. M. Pendleton; and S. L. Helm.

At the meeting of the general convention in Charleston, S. C., in 1849, a large committee, with A. M. Poindexter as chairman, was, after deliberation, appointed with the object of getting the church colleges to favor and assist the general seminary idea, but these were found not to be prepared to unite in the enterprise at that time and so its friends were for a time discouraged, and by mutual consent agitation in its behalf was temporarily discontinued. At length, in June, 1854, the General Association of Virginia, meeting in Richmond, proposed a convention of the friends of theological education, to be held at Montgomery, Ala., on May 11, 1853, in conjunction with the general convention of the church. The proposition was favorably received and the Montgomery convention was a decided success, being especially noteworthy from the fact that James P. Boyce and John A. Broadus, men afterwards so potent in shaping the destinies of the proposed seminary, here became prominently identified with the movement for its establishment.

At Montgomery it was decided to call another educational convention to meet at Augusta, Ga., in May, 1856, to discuss the question in all its bearings. Numerous delegates were present at Augusta, but the difficulties in the way of accomplishing the proposed object seemed so great that nothing further was done than to solicit bids for the location of the seminary, should it be established, after which the whole matter was referred to another convention, to assemble in Louisville, Ky., in May, 1857. At this time the Baptists of South Carolina, who, under Dr. Boyce's leadership, had then become thoroughly committed to the plan of having a general seminary rather than scattered colleges and theological schools, proposed to give $100,000 for its establishment at Greenville, in their State, provided a like amount should be raised by the church in the other Southern States. This proposition was, after a full discussion, accepted by the Louisville convention and steps taken to raise the needed funds and open the institution in the autumn of the following year. A committee was appointed to draw up a plan for its organization, which was to be effected by a fourth educational convention to meet in Greenville in May, 1858. Dr. Boyce reported to the Greenville convention that he

SOUTHERN BAPTIST THEOLOGICAL SEMINARY—NEW YORK HALL.

had raised in cash and good pledges the whole of the amount promised by South Carolina, and that body, after adopting a plan for the seminary, elected its first corps of professors and arranged to inaugurate the institution on October 1, following.

The plan to be used for the seminary had already been outlined in an inaugural address delivered by Dr. Boyce in June, 1856, while a professor in the theological department of Furman University. The instruction given was to be based on a certain declaration of fundamental doctrine to which all professors were to be required to subscribe and conform their teaching, but which was not to be imposed by the seminary in any authoritative way upon its students. While instruction was to be offered of the widest scope and highest grade, such as should suit those prepared for advanced work in the original languages of the Scriptures, others of less scholarly acquirements were to be welcomed for shorter or longer times to courses designed to better prepare them for the successful performance of the active work of the ministry. To this end the usual range of studies was divided into a number of "schools," which might be taken by students according to their ability and desires, and different combinations of which, when properly completed, would lead to various degrees in the different departments. This original plan has since been substantially maintained, its development leading naturally to the present English, eclectic, and full graduate courses. The control of the seminary was placed by the Greenville convention in the hands of the Church Board of Education Society, where it remained until 1866, when it was by general consent placed under the management of the general convention of the church.[1]

The first faculty selected for the institution was composed of Rev. James P. Boyce, D. D.; Rev. John A. Broadus, D. D.; Rev. Basil Manly, jr., D. D.; and Rev. E. T. Winkler, D. D.; but two of these, Drs. Broadus and Winkler, declined their appointments at first, and so the seminary was not opened as expected in 1858. Dr. Broadus, however, was led later to reconsider his declination, and Dr. William Williams having been elected in the place of Dr. Winkler, the seminary was opened on the first Monday in October, 1859, with a faculty of four professors, of which Dr. Boyce was chairman.

The aim of the institution has always been to retain an able faculty rather than have expensive buildings, when it could not afford both, so its original equipment in the way of buildings, and indeed all it had in the way of general accommodations while in Greenville was

[1] This body elects the board of trustees, which is composed of one member from each State contributing as much as $5,000 to the seminary funds, and one member for each additional $5,000 contributed up to eleven members. There are at present 5 trustees from Maryland, 5 from Virginia, 11 from Georgia, 4 from North Carolina, 3 from Alabama, 2 from Texas, 11 from Kentucky, 11 from South Carolina, 3 from Missouri, 2 from Mississippi, and 2 from Tennessee.

a leased church, previously unoccupied, in which by inexpensive partitions two lecture rooms and a library room were provided. Its students at first boarded in private families. Its library was from the beginning an excellent one, as the large and well-selected collection of the theological department of Furman University had been transferred to the seminary.

There were 26 students, representing six States, in attendance upon its first session, and 36 from a wider territory the second session. This is claimed[1] to be a larger beginning than any other theological seminary in America had hitherto had in the same time. By the end of the second year the second $100,000 of the endowment, pledged by the States outside of South Carolina, had been secured in money and good subscriptions, and the outlook for the institution was exceedingly bright. When the civil war came on the attendance was reduced to 20 the third year, several of the students having joined the army before the end of that session, so the seminary was suspended from June, 1862, to the autumn of 1865, the professors meanwhile maintaining their nominal connection with the institution while engaged in various other church enterprises.

The prospects of the seminary in 1865 were indeed gloomy, as practically all its paid-in endowment had been lost by the war and such pledges to its funds as remained unpaid were now practically worthless on account of the poverty of those who had given them. The prospects for future contributions, even for current support, were also very poor amid the general desolation wrought by the war and the social changes produced by it. But under the leadership of Dr. Boyce, who himself contributed $1,000 toward the expenses of its first session, the faculty and friends of the institution persevered, and it was reopened on October 2, 1865, with a full faculty, and, although only 7 students were in attendance during the year, a regular course in all departments was maintained as far as desired by any of the students. Dr. Boyce was able from year to year, by diligent and persistent efforts through correspondence and personal application, to meet the needs of the institution, always drawing freely upon his own private means in order to do so, and thus it managed to live, and the number of its students gradually increased, numbering as many as 46 in 1868–69 and 61 in 1869–70, its faculty having been strengthened at the beginning of this last year by the addition of Rev. C. H. Toy, D. D., LL. D., as professsor of Old Testament interpretation. No permanent endowment was, however, being secured, and so even the permanency of the seminary was endangered, precariously maintained as it was by annual contributions, and future growth and expansion to any extent seemed, under the conditions, entirely impossible.

---

[1] First Thirty Years, p. 11.

SOUTHERN BAPTIST THEOLOGICAL SEMINARY—NORTON HALL.

As a sufficient endowment, which experience had shown must be largely local, could not be hoped for from the denomination in South Carolina on account of the great losses they had suffered by the war and the pressing need of other church enterprises located in their midst, the question of the location of the institution was reopened at the general convention in St. Louis, Mo., in 1871, when the Baptists of Kentucky proposed that, if it should be removed to Louisville, they would pledge $300,000 toward its endowment, provided the other Southern States would contribute $200,000 more. This proposition was accepted by the denomination in August, 1872, and was formally ratified by the general convention at Mobile, Ala., on May 10, 1873.

The removal was not carried out until 1877, the interval being spent in raising the proposed endowment, to which work Dr. Boyce devoted himself, having removed to Louisville in 1872 for that purpose. Nearly the whole of this endowment had been secured in real estate, stocks, and individual pledges when the financial panic of 1873 made much of this unavailable, and it seemed in 1874 that the proposed plan would after all fail, but it was saved by the prompt subscription by some of its friends of $90,000, to be paid in five annual installments. Meanwhile the sessions of the seminary had continued at Greenville and had had an average attendance of something over 60 students, there being 68 present in 1876-77. Dr. Broadus had become acting chairman of its faculty upon Dr. Boyce's removal to Louisville, at which time Rev. W. H. Whitsitt, D. D., its present president, became its professor of ecclesiastical history and Biblical introduction, Dr. Williams being transferred to Dr. Boyce's chair of systematic theology. Dr. Manly had resigned his chair in 1871 to accept the presidency of Georgetown College, Ky., and from 1875 to 1877 Rev. A. J. A. Jaeger was an assistant professor in the seminary. On March 20, 1877, the institution was deprived by death of the services of Dr. Williams, who is described as "a warm friend, a fervid and vigorous preacher, a teacher of singular clearness and attractiveness, a Christian of deep and simple piety."[1]

The seminary was first opened in Louisville on September 1, 1877, when its faculty was constituted as follows: Rev. James P. Boyce, D. D., LL. D., professor of ecclesiastical history, church government, and pastoral duties; Rev. John A. Broadus, D. D., LL. D., professor of New Testament interpretation and the preparation and delivery of sermons; Rev. Crawford H. Toy, D. D., LL. D., professor of Old Testament interpretation; Rev. William H. Whitsitt, D. D., professor of Biblical introduction and polemic theology.

In 1879 Professor Toy resigned to accept the chair of Semitic languages in Harvard University and Dr. Manly returned to his old chair in the seminary, which he retained until his death. Eighty-nine students were in attendance upon the first session of the institution at

[1] First Thirty Years, p. 36.

its new location, and an average of more than 90 were present during the next three years. Its numbers soon increased so as to make it the largest Baptist theological seminary in existence, and it became necessary to enlarge its faculty, as was done in 1881, by the addition of George W. Riggan, D. D., who at that time was made an instructor of Hebrew, Greek, and homiletics. He became an assistant professor in 1883. Meanwhile the institution had again experienced financial difficulties, from which it was again happily relieved. In the latter part of 1879, little of the prospective endowment having been paid in, the seminary was about to become embarrassed financially, when, on February 11, 1880, it received from Governor Joseph E. Brown, of Georgia, the unexpected gift of $50,000[1] to endow a professorship. This movement to increase the endowment was joined in by various friends of the institution in Louisville, New York City, and elsewhere to such an extent that its permanency was soon assured.

The same policy in regard to buildings was pursued by the seminary in Louisville as in Greenville. Until its building funds were supplied it occupied temporary quarters for a time in the public library building on Fourth near Walnut street, which it used for lecture rooms and library purposes, while the Waverly Hotel, on Walnut street near Sixth, was rented as a dormitory for students. In 1885 eligible and spacious grounds on Broadway between Fourth and Fifth streets were purchased by Louisville friends as a proposed site for the early construction of suitable buildings, and in the following year very liberal contributions were made by Mr. John D. Rockefeller and other generous friends in New York City and vicinity for the erection of the first seminary building. This was completed in 1887, at a cost of $80,000, an amount about equal to the cost of the seminary grounds, and was called, in honor of the home of its donors, New York Hall. It is a fine large 4-story building, located on Fifth street near Broadway, and was intended primarily as a dormitory for students. It was also for a time furnished with lecture-room and library accommodations. In 1890 a separate and beautiful library building was erected at a cost of $50,000. It was given by Mrs. J. Lawrence Smith, of Louisville, as a memorial of four of her deceased nephews and nieces. In 1893 Norton Hall, the imposing structure at present used by the seminary for administrative and lecture-room purposes, was built by the Norton family, of Louisville, at a cost of $60,000. In 1897 the seminary was supplied with a handsome new gymnasium through the liberality of Hon. Joshua Levering, of Baltimore, Md., by whom it was built and equipped with modern apparatus at a cost of $10,000, thus completing a material equipment for the institution surpassed by few, if any, of its kind in the country.

[1] This was set apart to the chair of systematic theology, which has since been called the Joseph Emerson Brown chair.

Considerable additions to its supporting endowment have also been made in recent years, among these[1] being the gift in 1893 of $70,000 by Mrs. Minnie Caldwell (née Norton). The value of the entire seminary property and funds was estimated in 1896 at about $870,000, and is probably now approximately $900,000. The direct means of instruction have in like manner been kept up to modern demands. The library, which already had a good foundation, has been added to from time to time by the purchase of standard works, and has received valuable donations and bequests from the library of Columbian University, Washington, D. C.; from Prof. W. E. Bailey, of South Carolina; Rev. Dr. B. Manly, sr.; Rev. Franklin Wilson; Rev. T. W. Tobey, and others, besides a large donation from Dr. Boyce and one from the library of Dr. Basil Manly, jr.; so that it now numbers over 20,000 volumes.

The number of students attending the seminary in recent years has, however, kept pace somewhat with its enlarged accommodations and improved facilities. In 1882–83 its matriculation was 120, and since then there has been an almost uniform increase until the high-water mark was reached in 1895–96, when 318 students were enrolled. It is believed that it then became the largest theological seminary of any denomination in the whole country. In 1897–98, 301 students were present, who represented 31 States and 1 Territory of this country and three other countries; 676 students were enrolled altogether in Greenville, and 3,621 have been enrolled since the removal to Louisville, making a total registration up to 1898, inclusive, of 4,297, of which about 1,800 names are counted twice. Of the Louisville registration 2,433 names have been enrolled since 1888—a fact which shows the rapid growth of the institution in recent years. A considerable portion of the students who have attended the seminary have graduated in one of its courses. Its present faculty is composed largely of its own graduates.

Its increase in matriculation in recent years has been so nearly commensurate with the enlargement of its funds that, although the latter has been quite large, the income derived from it has only been lately somewhat equal to the additional demands made upon it, thus making the income of the institution meet its expenses. Indeed, for one purpose—to secure the funds needed to assist deserving students who are unable to fully meet their own expenses—it has been found necessary that annual contributions should still be solicited; at least the principal part of the means the seminary now has for this special object consists of the income derived from $15,000 bequeathed by D. A. Chenault in July, 1885, and $10,000 bequeathed by W. F Norton in October, 1886.

A number of changes have taken place in the seminary faculty in recent years. Assistant Professor Riggan died on April 18, 1885, and

[1] A lectureship foundation of $5,000 was also given in 1894 by Rev. William D. Gay, of Montgomery, Ala.

was succeeded in the latter part of that year by J. R. Sampey, D. D., at first as instructor, but after two years as assistant professor. Rev. F. H. Kerfoot, D. D., was elected co-professor of systematic theology in 1887, and full professor of systematic theology, pastoral duties, and church government in 1889. A. T. Robertson, A. M., was made an instructor of Greek and homiletics in 1888 and an assistant professor in 1890.

The office of president of the seminary was created in May, 1887. It was very appropriate that Dr. Boyce, who had so long been the chairman of its faculty, should be the first incumbent of the new office, the duties of which he was, however, not long to discharge, as he was removed by death on December 28, 1888. He had been connected with the institution for more than thirty years, counting from the incipiency of the movement for its establishment, and had devoted to its interests untiring exertions and made great sacrifices in its behalf. He had graduated at Brown University in 1847, when just over 20 years of age. After having engaged in religious journalism for something over a year, he studied theology at Princeton, N. J., for two years, and then entered the work of the pastorate until 1855, when he accepted a call to the chair of theology in Furman University, at Greenville, S. C. While holding this professorship he became prominently identified with those laboring to found a general seminary for the church, his efforts in behalf of which, both before and after its establishment, we have already in a general way largely recounted. He has been called "a sturdy, honest, Godly man, an elevated and genial character, a safe and wise counselor,"[1] and his work in behalf of the seminary has been characterized as follows: Dr. Boyce was chairman of the faculty, treasurer of the board, general financial agent, and has been the life power of the institution from its inception until the present time.[2]

Upon Dr. Boyce's death Dr. Broadus became chairman of the faculty, a position he had already successfully held for five years at Greenville. In May, 1889, he was regularly elected president of the seminary, a position he continued to occupy with honor to himself and the institution until his death on March 16, 1895. He had taken his A. M. at the University of Virginia in 1851; had been an assistant professor in that institution from 1851 to 1853, and had been engaged in pastoral work until he became connected with the seminary faculty in 1859. His labors for that institution could only be placed second to those of Dr. Boyce, if to those of anyone.

Dr. Manly, the only remaining member of the original faculty, who, as we have seen, after eight years' efficient service as the president of

[1] First Thirty Years, p. 31.

[2] Cathcart's Encyclopedia, p. 1087. Dr. Boyce is the author of a text-book on theology and also of a number of addresses. He also wrote extensively for religious newspapers and reviews.

SOUTHERN BAPTIST THEOLOGICAL SEMINARY—LIBRARY BUILDING.

Southwest corner Fifth and Broadway.

Georgetown College, had returned to the seminary in 1879, had died in office about three years before Dr. Broadus, on January 31, 1892. He was a tireless worker and fine teacher. It is through his efforts, combined with those of Dr. Broadus, that the funds of the seminary to aid needy students were for many years raised.

The course of instruction, while, as has been said, in the main following the original plan, has lately been considerably enlarged. A chair of ecclesiology was added to the regular course in 1896, as has also been a lecture course on the history of missions. The school of Latin theology has been replaced by a school of special theology taught in English, and many special courses for graduate students have also been established. The regular course of instruction is divided into the nine schools of biblical introduction, Old Testament interpretation, New Testament interpretation, systematic theology, polemic theology, homiletics and elocution, church history, ecclesiology, and pastoral duties. Each of these schools is entirely independent of the others, and is, with the exception of Hebrew and Greek, completed in one year. Combinations of the different schools lead to the degrees of English graduate, eclectic graduate, and full graduate. It requires three years for a student with a degree from a good college to complete the full course. A graduate course leading to the degree of doctor in theology is open to full graduates.

We have already mentioned the addition to the seminary faculty of Dr. Kerfoot and Professor Robertson, whose elections were due partly to the illness and subsequent death of Dr. Boyce and partly to furnish additional teaching facilities to the institution. Other changes have since been made, owing to Dr. Broadus's death and the enlarged matriculation. In May, 1893, E. C. Dargan, D. D., became co-professor of homiletics, church government, and Latin theology; in May, 1894, W. J. McGlothlin, A. M., instructor of Old Testament interpretation; in October, 1895, H. H. Harris, D. D., LL. D., professor of Biblical introduction and polemical theology; and in May, 1896, W. O. Carver, instructor in New Testament interpretation and homiletics. Professor Harris died in office on February 4, 1897.

In May, 1895, soon after Dr. Broadus's death, Dr. Whitsitt was elected as his successor in the presidency of the seminary. Dr. Whitsitt graduated at Union University, Tennessee, in 1861, and later studied one year in the University of Virginia. He then spent two years in the seminary at Greenville, after which he studied in Germany for two years, and then, after a short pastorate, became, as we have seen, a professor in the seminary in 1872. Under his administration the former prosperity of the institution has continued, and he has had the satisfaction of seeing it become the largest seminary in his church.[1] On July 14, 1898, he offered his resignation as president

[1] Dr. Whitsitt also has quite a reputation as a writer as well as teacher and administrative officer.

to the board of trustees. No definite arrangements have yet been made in regard to his successor.

The present faculty of the institution, with the changes in their chairs which have recently taken place, are as follows: William H. Whitsitt, D. D., LL. D., president and professor of ecclesiastical history and polemic theology; Franklin H. Kerfoot, D. D., LL. D., professor of pastoral duties and Joseph Emerson Brown professor of systematic theology; John R. Sampey, D. D., professor of interpretation of the Old Testament; Archibald T Robertson, D. D., professor of interpretation of the New Testament; Edwin C. Dargan, D. D., professor of homiletics and ecclesiology; William J. McGlothlin, A. M., D. D., professor of Biblical introduction and assistant professor of Old Testament interpretation; William O. Carver, Th. D., assistant instructor in New Testament interpretation and homiletics.

BIBLIOGRAPHY.

Collins's and Smith's History; Cathcart's Baptist Encyclopedia; Williams's Ohio Falls Cities and their Counties.

The First Thirty Years of the Southern Baptist Theological Seminary, Baltimore, 1890 (contains historical sketch by J. R. Sampey, D. D.).

LOUISVILLE MEDICAL COLLEGE, LOUISVILLE.

The foundation of Louisville Medical College is due to the conviction on the part of its promoters that the great popularity of Louisville as a medical center justified the establishment of a new, modern, and independent college. A previous attempt in the same line had resulted in the incorporation of the Clay School of Medicine, the place of which was taken by Louisville Medical College, its charter being repealed at the same time that of the latter was granted.

Those mainly instrumental in the founding of the new school were the men who composed the major portion of its initial faculty, viz: Drs. Henry M. Bullitt, Henry Miller, John Goodman, J. M. Holloway, J. A. Ireland, John A. Ouchterlony, and E. S. Gaillard, whose aim was to establish an institution which should be first-class in all its appointments and should have a first-class teaching force.

An organization of the faculty had taken place shortly before the application for a charter, which was obtained from the State legislature by an act approved January 26, 1869. This charter places the residuary control of the school in the hands of 8 self-perpetuating trustees, who have a general supervision over its property and faculty Its faculty has a large share in its management, as they elect to professorships which only have to be confirmed by the trustees, and are perpetual unless severed by resignation, ejection, or death. The trustees are authorized to hold property for the benefit of the school to the amount of $100,000, and can also, by an amendment to the charter secured March 22, 1873, which has, however, never been taken advantage of, bond its property, if necessary, to the amount of $25,000. The institution is empowered to confer the usual degrees in medicine, dentistry, and collateral sciences.

The original faculty was composed of the founders mentioned above, supplemented by two other physicians,[1] most of whom have either previously or subsequently been connected with the faculties of some of the other medical colleges of Louisville. Dr. Bullitt was made dean of the new school, which was first opened in September, 1869, in the old law building, on the southwest corner of Fifth and Green streets. The success of the institution was pronounced from the start and its classes soon grew to be quite large. It had 225 students and 51 graduates in 1872-73, and up to that year, inclusive, had had 350 graduates. By 1875-76 its classes were the largest south or west of Philadelphia. Its students came mainly from the South and Southwest, but quite a number of them came from north of the Ohio River.

By 1877 its classes had outgrown their first quarters, and space was secured for it in the autumn of that year in Odd Fellows' Hall, on First and Jefferson streets. Enlarged accommodations were soon again demanded, and in the summer of 1883 a large building on Third street was leased and fitted up for the institution. As the years went by this building was also found to be inadequate, and the faculty determined to erect one which would properly accommodate their ever-increasing classes, a resolution which resulted in the construction of the present fine building, on the corner of First and Chestnut streets, which is one of the handsomest and most commodious of its kind in the country and one of which the institution has a right to be proud It is pleasing in its architecture and splendid in its equipment, containing "every element necessary to give the student of medicine all the facilities which the ideas of the present day deem essential to thorough teaching."[2]

The following description, taken in substance from a recent announcement of the school, will give some idea of its accommodations: It is 184 feet long and 87 feet wide and four stories in height, with a basement under the entire structure. The first floor contains the faculty rooms, reception room, chemical laboratory, library, and janitor's rooms. On the second floor will be found the museum, main amphitheater, chemical room, clinical room, and professors' room. The amphitheater is 55 by 75 feet and extends up through two stories. It will comfortably seat 600 students and is perfect in its acoustic properties. On the third floor are rooms for demonstrating histology, microscopy, and bacteriology. The fourth floor contains the dissecting room, 55 by 75 feet, floored with tiling and furnished with hardwood tables and marble lavatories. It is perfectly ventilated and

[1] These physicians were Drs. Birch and Logan, whose first names the writer has been unable to ascertain.

[2] Announcement of 1892-93, p. 5.

nightly flushed with water, so as to be well-nigh odorless. The dispensary building is located at the north end of the main building and is connected with it by a corridor. It is two stories high and contains a spacious clinical amphitheater, waiting rooms, etherizing room, drug room, special operating room, recovery room, and reading room for students. The new building was occupied by the college in September, 1893, the session of 1892–93 having been spent in the building of the Kentucky School of Medicine on Sixth street.

The institution had previously been progressive in its methods of instruction and in its equipment. While located on Third street, just prior to 1889, it had erected a dispensary and had added a gymnasium to its outfit. It was also one of the first, if not the first, of the medical colleges in the South to use the method of having each dissection practically demonstrated before the class prior to its being undertaken by the students, as it was also to add an infirmary annex, making it possible to perform major operations under perfect asepsis in the presence of the entire class. The equipment of the institution includes, besides a large, regular chemical laboratory, special laboratories in histology, in pathology, and bacteriology, and in operative surgery.

Its original course required for graduation had been the one usually in vogue at the time of its establishment—two years of lectures, with one year's previous office study. This was maintained up to the session of 1892–93, when the college entered the Southern Association of Medical Colleges, and with the opening of the next session in 1893 adopted, in accordance with the requirements of that organization, a three years' course of study for all students then entering for a new course. In 1895 it joined the Association of American Medical Colleges, and in its next session required all students beginning their first course of medicine to take a four years' course before graduation. The association's preliminary matriculation requirements are also enforced. The institution has thus brought its graduation requirements up to those of the best and foremost medical colleges of the country.

The method of instruction is one in which lectures, clinics, recitations, quizzes, and practical demonstrations are all combined. The following are the departments of the course as at present offered: Principles and practice of medicine, anatomy, practical anatomy, physiology, materia medica and therapeutics, obstetrics, gynæcology and abdominal surgery, surgery, clinical surgery, chemistry, diseases of the eye, ear, nose, and throat, diseases of the nervous system, genito-urinary diseases, diseases of children, diseases of the rectum, physical diagnosis, hygiene, and medical jurisprudence.

As in all the other medical colleges of the country, the matriculation of Louisville Medical College has been somewhat reduced of late, owing to the advanced standard of entrance and the length and time necessary for graduation, but its attendance has been comparatively

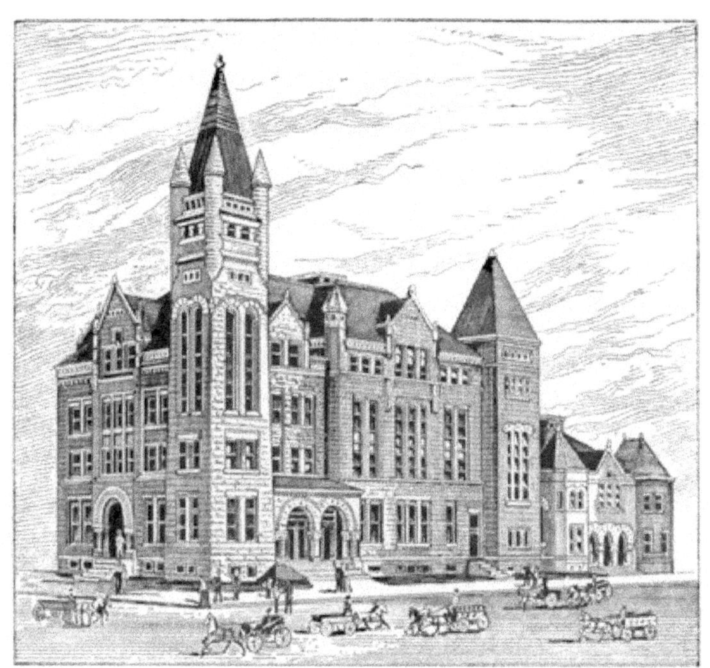

LOUISVILLE MEDICAL COLLEGE.

well sustained. Its combined classes in recent years have at times numbered more than 300 students, who have frequently represented as many as 25 States and Territories of the Union, besides several foreign countries. It is estimated that about 7,000 students altogether have attended the school since its foundation, which would make a yearly average of about 240. The graduating class has numbered as many as 191 (in 1893–94), and the total number of graduates, up to 1898 inclusive, is 1,974, a yearly average of about 68. The graduates are distributed in every State of the United States, especially in the South and West, and particularly in Texas, Indiana, Kentucky, Illinois, and Ohio. Recently a larger number have been residents of the North, Northwest, and East.

Much of the prosperity of the college has been due to its efficient deans who, with their terms of office, have been as follows: Dr. Henry Bullitt, 1869–70; Dr. E. S. Gaillard, 1870–79; Dr. J. A. Ireland, 1879–1895; Dr. C. W. Kelly, since 1895. Dr. Ireland was an emeritus professor in the institution until the present year, and was the last of its original faculty to be connected with it. Its present faculty is composed mainly of comparatively young men who are, however, well to the front in their profession.

The professors and their chairs are as follows: C. W. Kelly, M. D., C. M., professor of descriptive and surgical anatomy and clinical medicine, dean; Geo. M. Warner, M. D., professor of materia medica, therapeutics, and diseases of children; A. Morgan Cartledge, M. D., professor of gynecology and abdominal surgery; H. B. Ritter, M. D., professor of obstetrics and hygiene; Wm. Cheatham, M. D., professor of ophthalmology, otology, and laryngology; John G. Cecil, B. S., M. D., professor of principles and practice of medicine, clinical medicine, and neurology; Wm. C. Dugan, M. D., professor of surgery and clinical surgery; Fouchee Warren Samuel, A. M., M. D., professor of principles and practice of surgery and operative surgery; Adolph O. Pfingst, M. D., professor of physiology and histology; Harris Kelly, B. A., M. D., professor of chemistry and toxicology; August Schachner, M. D., associate professor of anatomy, demonstrator of anatomy.

There are besides 14 lecturers, directors, and instructors, who serve as assistants to the faculty proper in the various departments.

BIBLIOGRAPHY.

The material for this sketch has been obtained almost entirely through correspondence with Dr. George M. Warner, secretary of the faculty, and from catalogues and other sources of general information. A few facts have been secured from Collins's History; Williams's Ohio Falls Cities; and Louisville, past and present.

LOUISVILLE COLLEGE OF PHARMACY, LOUISVILLE.

The preliminary meeting looking toward the organization of the Louisville College of Pharmacy was held in the office of J. B. Wilder & Co., at Sixth and Main streets, in Louisville, on July 25, 1870, when the feasibility of establishing such an institution, "to supply a want that had long been felt in the Southwest,"[1] was fully discussed. This meeting was attended by leading pharmacists of Louisville, Ky., and of Jeffersonville and New Albany, Ind., among whom may be mentioned as especially active in furthering the proposed enterprise Dr. C. Lewis Diehl, George A. Newman, Thomas E. Jenkins, Dr. Emil Scheffer, L. D. Kastenbine, S. F. Dawes, F. C. Miller, R. J. Snyder, Edward Wilder, and R. A Robinson.

As a result of the previous discussion a corporation known as The Louisville College of Pharmacy was instituted on August 16, 1870, its first board of directors being composed of Thomas E. Jenkins, B. F. Scribner, George A. Newman, S. F. Dawes, John Colgan, Louis Eichrodt, Dr. C. Lewis Diehl, George A. Cary, J. A. McAfee, Dan B. Grable, Ferd. J. Pfingst, and Fred. C. Miller. Of this board Dr. C. Lewis Diehl was elected president and F. C. Miller and Louis Eichrodt secretaries. Dr. Emil Scheffer was made chairman of one of the important committees. Dr. Scheffer had already a national reputation as a pharmacist, as had also Dr. Diehl, the latter being one of the editors of the Pharmacopœia, the standard for compounding drugs in the United States.

A charter for the institution was later secured from the legislature of the State. It bears the date of February 10, 1873, and by its terms the college is empowered to confer the degree of graduate in pharmacy, while its management is placed in the hands of a board of 12 directors, one-third of whom are to be elected each year by the members of the corporation. All its funds in excess of its expenses are also to go to its further improvement and enlargement, and are not to be divided among its members, as it was not intended to be a source of profit to anyone but its students. According to this charter the school is also made, in a certain sense, a self-supporting State institution, as, if for any cause it should cease to exist, all of its property, both personal and real, is to go to the public school fund of Kentucky.

The funds for the opening of the proposed college in a modest way were secured by subscription from the members of the corporation, the apparatus needed to illustrate its lectures being at first either furnished by the professors or borrowed from the Louisville Female High School. Its first lecture rooms were in the Preston Pope Building, on Third street between Walnut and Guthrie streets, where its first session was opened on November 13, 1871 Its first faculty was

[1] First announcement, p. 4.

constituted as follows: Thomas E. Jenkins, M. D., professor of materia medica; L. D. Kastenbine, M. D., professor of chemistry; C. Lewis Diehl, professor of theory and practice of pharmacy.

The opening had been delayed about one month longer than the date that had been arranged for, and consequently the first session lasted about one month longer than usual, ending in the first week in April. Attendance upon two such sessions, together with four years' apprenticeship, was made a requirement for graduation.

In 1872 Dr. Jenkins resigned his chair, which was then denominated the chair of materia medica and botany, and it was filled by the appointment of Emil Scheffer, Ph. G. Dr. Scheffer held the chair until 1881, when he resigned, and Edward Goebel, Ph. G., was elected as his successor, Dr. Scheffer becoming an emeritus professor. Upon the death of Professor Goebel, in 1889, the chair of botany was separated from that of materia medica and Oscar C. Dilly, Ph. G., elected to the latter, while Otto E. Mueller, who had already been teacher of botany for at least a session previous, was selected to fill the former. Professor Diehl held the chair of pharmacy until 1882, when he retired on account of poor health, and B. Buckel, Ph. G., M. D., was chosen to fill the vacancy.

Meanwhile the institution had continued to prosper. Early in its history, through the liberality of the druggists of Louisville and the neighboring cities, it was furnished with apparatus and specimens sufficient to abundantly illustrate its lectures. In 1873 it sent out its first graduating class of 6 members, and in 1875–76 its means had so far enlarged that complete practical laboratories in chemistry and pharmacy were instituted. It soon outgrew its original quarters, and in 1878 moved to a larger and better adapted building on Green near Second street. In 1880–81 it had a class of 45 students, and at the end of that session had graduated 55 young men. In 1888–89 its 70 matriculates represented 8 States and 1 Territory, mainly in the South and West, and its graduating class of that year contained 17 members. Up to 1888, inclusive, it had had 129 graduates from 11 different States.

In 1889 the college removed to its present excellent building, on the corner of First and Chestnut streets, which had been purchased for the institution, and in which chemical and pharmaceutical laboratories, equal to any in the country, were established. Its faculty was then composed of veteran teachers of recognized ability. In 1890 women were admitted to all the privileges of the school upon the same terms as men, and the equivalent of a grammar-school certificate from a public school was made a necessary prerequisite to matriculation. In 1891 the faculty was enlarged by the appointment of the following assistant professors: Edward R. Constantine, of chemistry; H. Otto Haeusgen, of pharmacy; Burr Overton, of materia medica; and Louis Rominger, of botany.

Until August, 1894, both first and second year students had attended the same lectures, but at that time the course was rearranged and the students—except in botany, which was kept as before—divided into junior and senior classes. The junior instruction was placed in the charge of the junior professors, who, under the new management, were H. Otto Haeusgen, in chemistry; Gordon L. Curry, in pharmacy, and William G. Zubrod, in materia medica. A new microscopical laboratory was then completed and the chair of microscopy created and assigned to Professor Rominger. At the same time Prof. C. Lewis Diehl, who is one of the most gifted pharmacists and expert teachers in America, having recovered his health, returned to his old position as professor of pharmacy, in place of Dr. Buckel. The office of dean of the college was also created, and was filled by the election of Professor Curry, who has since efficiently discharged its duties. In 1895 a summer course in botany was established, which has since been maintained. In 1897 H. H. Koehler, M. D., succeeded Professor Rominger as professor of microscopy.

The average matriculation of the college in recent years has been about 60 annually, and its students have frequently represented as many as 9 States. The average number of graduates of late has been about 18 each year. The institution has altogether, up to 1898, inclusive, 335 alumni, who have come from as many as 18 States, principally in the South and West, but more largely from Kentucky and Indiana than any others. The college points with pride to its alumni as an evidence of the high character of its faculty and curriculum. Professors Dilly, Mueller, Haeusgen, Zubrod, and Curry of its present faculty are graduates of the institution. Whatever it has been able to accomplish has been due to the excellence of its own work, as it has risen from its humble beginnings without any endowment or other sources of revenue than the tuition fees of its own students. Its course still extends through two sessions of six months each, running from the 1st of October to 1st of March, as originally established, but the lengthening of the course has been favorably discussed, and while no definite action has yet been taken, it is probable that the period of graduation will soon be made three or four years instead of two. The system of instruction has recently been put more distinctively upon a university basis, in order to better adapt it to the needs of individual students, and the lengthening of the required course in chemistry for the coming session is at present under advisement. The course, as now constituted, requires attendance upon two years' lecture courses in the departments of chemistry, pharmacy, materia medica, and botany, together with two years' practical work in the pharmaceutical laboratory and one year each in the laboratories of chemistry and microscopy.

The present college corporation is composed of 72 members, of whom Oscar A. Beckmann is president, and Gordon L. Curry and Albert J. Shoettlin, secretaries.

The college faculty, as now constituted, is as follows: E. Scheffer, Ph. G., emeritus professor of materia medica and botany; L. D. Kastenbine, A. M., M. D., professor of chemistry; C. Lewis Diehl, Ph. M., professor of theory and practice of pharmacy; Oscar C. Dilly, Ph. G., professor of materia medica; Otto E. Mueller, Ph. G., professor of botany; H. H. Koehler, M. D., professor of microscopy. Junior professors: H. Otto Haeusgen, Ph. G., chemistry; Gordon L. Curry, Ph. G., pharmacy; William G. Zubrod, Ph. G., materia medica. Dean: Gordon L. Curry, Ph. G.

BIBLIOGRAPHY.

Catalogues and other sources of general information, with some reference to Williams's Ohio Falls Cities.

THE SOUTHERN NORMAL SCHOOL, BOWLING GREEN.

The usual title of this institution, as at present managed, is The Southern Normal School and Business College, as it is composed of what are really two separate schools under one management. Its normal department is worthy of being given a place among the professional institutions of the State. Its business department, being without the scope of this monograph, will only be noticed incidentally, the two schools being closely allied in management, and also, to some extent, in faculties.

The Southern Normal School is the only distinctively normal school in Kentucky that has had a continuous history for any length of time. It was organized as a training school for teachers at Glasgow, Ky., in the autumn of 1875 by Prof. A. W. Mell. Professor Mell was an enthusiastic teacher and was very much interested in normal work, having graduated at the National Normal at Lebanon, Ohio. His chief aim in establishing the Southern Normal was the education of teachers for higher professional service. As the school grew, the business department was later added as a further feature.

Soon after its opening the institution was chartered by legislative action. This charter provided for courses in music and art, as well as the usual literary course, and allowed the granting of the customary college degrees. Professor Mell conducted the school successfully for a number of years in Glasgow, having, after a time, associated with himself Prof. J. T. Williams, as joint proprietor and coprincipal. Professor Williams had more especial charge of the business department, which had grown to considerable proportions, although always subordinate to the normal idea.

In 1884 the school was moved by the proprietors to Bowling Green, which could furnish better accommodations than Glasgow, and was in some other respects a more desirable location. In its new situation the institution occupied the buildings formerly used by Bowling Green Female College, which had for many years been a flourishing female school, but had been lately suspended on account of financial difficulties. The buildings cost originally over $20,000 and were well arranged and well suited for educational purposes. In January, 1886, a more liberal charter for the school was received from the legislature, which granted to the holders of its higher degrees the right to teach in any county in the State without further license. This privilege was subsequently withdrawn by the legislature, as it was from all similar schools in the State.

The institution was fairly successful at its new location until 1890, when Professors Mell and Williams retired from its management. During the fifteen years which had elapsed since its foundation the school had had quite an able faculty which, besides Professor Mell, who had more than a local reputation as a teacher, included such men as T. F. McBeath in natural science, G. R. Klinkard in languages, and Florence Reese in elocution. During this period its average annual matriculation was about 250 students, and it turned out many well-equipped teachers and business men, among whom are numbered all of its later proprietors and managers.

In 1890 H. A. Evans and W. J. Davis, who were graduates of the school, succeeded Professors Mell and Williams in its management, but before the end of the school year they were succeeded by H. McI. Fletcher and J. R. Alexander. During the scholastic year 1891-92 Professor Alexander had sole charge of the institution. During this time, in shifting its proprietorship from one to another, it had naturally lost much of its former prestige. In September, 1892, H. H. Cherry and T. C. Cherry, together with Professors Alexander and Fletcher, alumni of the school, became its joint proprietors under the title of Cherry Brothers, and have since managed it very successfully. Professor Alexander is still a prominent member of its faculty.

The last six years in the history of the school have been a period of considerable expansion, so that, while its attendance had during the ten years prior to 1896 averaged about 400 annually, in 1896-97 it was about 600, and from September to May of 1897-98, 683 students were enrolled in the various departments.

Cherry Brothers, while maintaining the standing and reputation of the normal school, have emphasized the business department for which they have secured a charter which erects it into a separate institution under the same management. It has been given the title of the Bowling Green Business College. Besides the usual business courses in bookkeeping in all of its various practical forms, in shorthand, telegraphy, typewriting, and penmanship, it has also an English course for those who wish to take some literary work in addition to their commercial course; and all of its students are allowed to attend any of the classes of the normal school without extra expense. The business college has of late had about 80 graduates a year in all departments. Its sessions continue throughout the entire year and its work is so arranged that students can enter with profit at any time. The normal school has each year four terms of ten weeks each and a summer term of eight weeks. This last term is especially intended to furnish normal training to public school-teachers during their vacation.

In 1896–97 considerable improvements in the buildings of the institution were made, as well as additions to its educational apparatus. Its faculty was also materially enlarged, among the additions being Prof. J. C. Willis, who has considerable reputation as a teacher, especially in normal school work. He resigned the presidency of Southern Indiana Normal School, at Mitchell, Ind., to accept his present position. In January, 1898, superior accommodations were secured for the business college in the new Neale Building, centrally located in the business portion of the town, where it occupies the entire upper story of a large and handsome building, and has an excellent equipment.

The Southern Normal School has been coeducational from its foundation. It has also, throughout its history, been entirely unendowed, and has depended solely upon tuition fees for its support. Its objects and methods, in a general way, may, perhaps, best be seen from the following extracts, taken from a recent catalogue:

The objects set forth in the founding of the Southern Normal were twofold, viz: (1) To furnish the elements of a liberal education, under the following conditions: (a) The advantages of the school are shared by whites only—both male and female—without distinction; (b) the time required is the least possible consistent with thorough work in all departments; (c) classes and studies are so arranged that students who may not be able to complete a full course in any department may enter at any time, study what is most desirable, and get full credit for what they accomplish; (d) students in the Southern Normal can leave off at any stage, recruit their health or finances, and return to complete the course at any future time. (2) To bring the expense within the reach of all classes who may desire an education, and subject to the following conditions: (a) Tuition rates are kept sufficiently high to provide adequate facilities in all departments; (b) rates for board and other accommodations are kept at low figures of cost, as based upon the lowest wholesale cash rates for large quantities of goods.

By the use of such methods the institution has undoubtedly been able to do an important educational work in bringing better educational facilities within the reach of many not otherwise able to secure them. That there is a demand for instruction of this character is shown by the comparatively large matriculation of the school. This has grown so of late that the institution, probably with good foundation, claims to be the largest normal school in the South. Its students come from many of the States of the South and West outside of Kentucky and her neighboring States, 22 States being recently represented by its enrollment.

The institution offers a preparatory course, a regular teachers' course, a State teachers' course, and engineering, scientific, and classical courses, besides special courses in music, art, elocution, and physical culture. Special lecture courses are also provided. Its graduates in the B. S. course, its most popular higher course, have averaged about 15 annually of late. In 1897–98 there were 19 scientific graduates, and 150 graduates in the shorter teachers' course. Among the graduates of the school there are a number of teachers, editors, and public men of considerable note. The following is the list of the present faculty: H. H. Cherry, T. C. Cherry, J. C. Willis, J. R. Alexander, C. T. Bass, J. L. Harman, F. S. Broussard, A. B. Lyon, W. S. Ashby, Mrs. H. H. Cherry, Mrs. T. C. Cherry, Mrs. J. C. Willis, Miss Lissa Morris, Miss Mattie Lewis, Mrs. Josephine Fayne, Miss Ona Brock, Miss Mary Beisel, and Miss Mabel Fayne. A number of these give instruction both in the normal school and business college.

BIBLIOGRAPHY.

The Southern Educator for September, 1896, and March, 1898, a quarterly published by the school, supplemented by the usual sources of general information.

STATE NORMAL SCHOOL, FRANKFORT.

This institution is exclusively for colored persons, and may be called a branch of the State college at Lexington in the sense that the funds of the two institutions are drawn in general from the same sources, the State and Federal Governments, and their courses of instruction are required to be somewhat parallel.

The special demand that called the State Normal School into existence was the need of trained teachers for the colored public schools of the State, and those who may be mentioned as leaders in the effort to bring about its organization are Rev. William J. Simmons, Prof. J. M. Maxwell, Rev. C. H. Parrish, Hon. George W. Gentry, Prof. J. H. Jackson (who has been the principal of the school from its inception), and others, several of them being among the most prominent colored men in Kentucky.

The act establishing the school was approved May 18, 1886,[1] and declares its leading object "shall be the preparation of teachers for teaching in the colored public schools of Kentucky." An annual appropriation of $3,000 was given for the maintenance of the institution, the organization and management of which were committed to a board of trustees, consisting of one member from each of the three superior court districts of the State, to whom was added the State superintendent of public instruction as an ex-officio member and chairman of the board. This board, after receiving proposals for the

[1] Chapter 1297, laws of 1886.

location of the institution from Owensboro, Knottsville, Hopkinsville, Bowling Green, Danville, Lexington, and Frankfort, considered the offer of Frankfort the most advantageous, and accordingly located the school there. The State supplemented the donation of Frankfort by an appropriation of $8,700, and a substantial and commodious main building was soon erected on the land granted, which contained about 25 acres and was situated about a mile from the town limits.

John H. Jackson, A. M., a graduate of Berea College and a teacher of several years' experience, having been elected principal, the school was first opened on October 11, 1887. It was made coeducational from the beginning. Only a normal department was maintained for the first three years, during which time Principal Jackson had only one assistant. Tuition was free in the department to residents of the State who pledged themselves to teach twice as long in the public schools of the State as the period of their attendance. Fifty-five students, from 21 counties of the State, were present the first year, while in 1888–89 there were 87 from 32 counties, and in 1889–90, 74 from 26 counties.

The institution received its proportionate part[1] of the Congressional act of July 30, 1890, commonly known as the Morrill Act, and a considerable enlargement in its faculty and in the scope of its work was soon brought about. Its faculty was soon increased to five teachers, and by a legislative act, approved May 22, 1893, agricultural, mechanical, and domestic departments were regularly organized. At the same time the direction of the school was transferred to three trustees, selected from the county in which it is located, instead of the superior court districts, as before, thus securing more direct and therefore more intelligent supervision. Students in the new departments were also about this time relieved of the pledge to teach in the public schools of the State, to which only normal students were to be required to subscribe. The latter were also, upon graduation, to be granted State certificates, which entitled them to teach in any county of the State without further examination. The course of study was further systematized in such a way as to require a uniform period of three years for graduation in all the departments.

The equipment of the school was soon afterwards improved by the erection of a dormitory for girls, at a cost of $3,000, $2,000 of which came from a legislative appropriation and $1,000 from the trustees of the Slater fund. A mechanical shop, a laundry, and two neat cottages had either already been added or were soon afterwards. These increased facilities soon led to a considerably larger attendance, there being 122 students in 1895–1896 and 152 in 1896–97. Up to the end of 1896 the average attendance in the normal department had been about

[1] This is 14.5 per cent, and amounted to $2,175 in 1893, since which time, according to the provisions of the bill, it has increased $145 a year, which it will do until 1900.

100, in the mechanical department about 12, and in the agricultural department, including those to whom lectures were given, about 40. New demands have recently led to a further enlargement of the equipment and means of instruction. In 1896 a professor's cottage was erected, and in 1897, 5 acres of additional land were purchased for the agricultural department. Also, in the autumn of the latter year an addition was made to the main building, at a cost of $3,000, the appropriation for which had been provided for by a legislative act of March 5, 1896. In 1898 the school received its share of the land-grant fund of 1862 for agricultural colleges. This gives to it a permanent endowment fund of $23,925. Its property in 1897 was estimated to be worth about $19,000.

The institution offers a regular three years' normal course, also a course of the same length in agriculture, in the mechanic arts, and in domestic economy. It has also recently added a department of music, and maintains besides a preparatory course of two years. For the convenience of teachers who can only attend for two out of the three terms of the school year, it maintains a special teachers' course of four years, all of the last of which must be spent in the institution. Its means of instruction are ample, as it has very good workshops and a good complement of educational apparatus generally. It has also laid the foundations of a good working library.

The school has had, up to 1898, inclusive, altogether 66 graduates, mostly, if not entirely, confined to the normal department, which is doing an excellent work in furnishing the colored public schools of the State with well-equipped teachers. The industrial departments of the school are also an important feature, as they are now in a position to become a strong factor in developing the colored population of the State industrially by furnishing to them the opportunity for acquiring the rudiments of useful trades. The institution is doing much to raise the professional standard of the colored teachers of Kentucky as well as stimulating the colored youth of the State to greater industrial usefulness. Much of its success is due to the well-directed efforts of Principal Jackson, who enjoys a national reputation as a teacher among his people. The following is the present faculty, with the chair of each member: John H. Jackson, A. M., president, and professor of didactics, mathematics, and civics; W. D. Thomas, professor of natural sciences and of agriculture; Moses A. Davis, professor of mechanics and of manual training; Mary E. Jackson, professor in the normal department; T. Augustus Reid, professor in the preparatory department; Bettie M. Bailey, matron, and professor of domestic economy. The chair of vocal and instrumental music is at present unoccupied.

BIBLIOGRAPHY.

Reports of the State superintendent of public instruction, together with the usual sources of general information.

LOUISVILLE NATIONAL MEDICAL COLLEGE, LOUISVILLE.

As colored men were excluded from all of the other medical colleges of Kentucky, and, indeed, from those of most States of the Union, this institution was founded to furnish them the proper facilities for acquiring a medical education, but its advantages have not been offered to men only, as it has been coeducational from its establishment. One of the chief promoters of the enterprise was Dr. H. Fitzbutler, who was probably the first colored man in Kentucky to enter upon the regular practice of medicine. He has been dean of the institution since its organization. He had, as early as 1874, begun giving instruction to students in the rudiments of medicine. Dr. Rufus Conrad, also of Louisville, and Dr. W. A. Burney, of New Albany, Ind., had several years later become similarly engaged to some extent.

These preceptors, in 1886, applied to the State legislature for an act authorizing them to establish a regular medical college for their race in Louisville. The bill looking toward this end was introduced late in that legislative session and so was passed over in the rush of other business at the end, but it was taken up at the next session and approved on April 24, 1888.[1] This act incorporated the proposed institution under the name of the National Medical College of Louisville, made the 3 teachers above mentioned its first board of trustees, or regents, and conferred upon it the power of granting diplomas "in medicine or surgery, or in both medicine and surgery." This charter also required the students of the school to have studied medicine for three full years and to have taken two full courses of lectures prior to graduation. The practice of the institution from the beginning seems to have required three full courses of lectures for graduation.

Its incorporators constituted the principal part of the first faculty of the school, which was regularly opened in the fall of 1888 in a hall on the corner of Ninth and Magazine streets. Instruction had been carried on by the faculty for the past two years in anticipation of the granting of the charter, and so 6 students, all of whom had attended other medical colleges as well and had studied under preceptors for at least four years, were graduated at the first commencement in the spring of 1889, when, for the first time in Kentucky, the degree of M. D. was conferred on a colored man.

In the summer of 1889 the faculty was enlarged, chiefly by the addition of graduates of the school, for which a new and much more suitable building was purchased by the trustees. This building is situated on Green near First street, and had for the previous eleven years been used by the Louisville College of Pharmacy. It was occupied by the National Medical College in the autumn of this year and has since remained its home. Soon after the change of location the

[1] Chapter 1234, acts of 1888.

faculty completed arrangements for a free dispensary in connection with the institution, where all diseases might be treated and medicines furnished free of charge, thus furnishing clinical advantages to its students. New students entered the second session, but, as none of these had by its close come up to the required standard, only 2 honorary degrees were conferred in 1890 upon 2 aged practitioners. In 1891 there were 4 regular graduates, one of whom was the first woman in Kentucky to receive the degree of M. D. In 1891-92, 22 students from 7 States, mainly in the South, were in attendance, and at the end of the year 6 degrees were conferred.

In April, 1894, the institution was officially recognized by the Kentucky State board of health as one of the regular medical colleges of the State. In September of this year a preliminary course of about a month's duration, prior to the opening of the regular session, was established and has since been maintained. The regular session extends from October to April.

Beginning with 1896, the college required of all its students attendance upon four years of lectures as a prerequisite to graduation. It also, in this year, in order to furnish proper hospital privileges to its students, opened an auxiliary hospital at 1027-1029 West Green street. This hospital has 12 large rooms, with a capacity for 40 patients, and is open throughout the year.

The number of students in attendance upon the institution has gradually increased in recent years until in 1897-98 there were 42, who represented 10 States of the Union, and Jamaica. There have been from 4 to 8 graduates each year, the total number of degrees conferred up to 1898, inclusive, numbering 54. The school has received some contributions, but has no regular endowment. It was put into operation by funds obtained by subscription and has since been maintained practically entirely by tuition fees.

The course offered by the school embraces the departments of chemistry and toxicology, materia medica and therapeutics, theory and practice of medicine, physical diagnosis, obstetrics, gynecology, pathology, bacteriology, principles and practice of surgery, physiology, pharmacology, and anatomy and histology. The faculty as at present constituted is composed of: H. Fitzbutler, M. D., dean, professor of principles of surgery and materia medica, surgeon-in-chief to auxiliary hospital; W. A. Burney, M. D., professor of gynecology, gynecologist to auxiliary hospital; W. O. Vance, A. M., M. D., professor of chemistry and diseases of ear, throat, and nose; E. D. Whedbee, A. M., M. D., professor of obstetrics; William T. Peyton, A. M., M. D., professor of theory and practice of medicine; E. R. Gaddie, M. D., professor of physiology and diseases of the skin; James H. Fitzbutler, M. D., professor of anatomy, histology, and clinical surgery; Charles F. Maxwell, M. D., professor of pathology and bacteriology; B. F. Porter, M. D., professor of nervous diseases and insanity; B. B. Hall, M. D., professor of ophthalmology; R. F. White, Phar. D., demonstrator of chemistry in laboratory and professor of inorganic chemistry; H. W. Conrad, M. D., professor of electro-therapeutics; J. A. Agnew, D. D. S., professor of dental surgery; James R. W. Smith, LL. D., professor of forensic medicine. There are also 2 instructors and 1 demonstrator.

BIBLIOGRAPHY.

Historical notes in various catalogues have been the sole source upon which this sketch has been based.

SOUTHWESTERN HOMEOPATHIC MEDICAL COLLEGE, LOUISVILLE.

The Southwestern Homeopathic Medical College is the latest candidate for public favor among the medical colleges of Louisville, and is the only one of its kind in the section of the country in which it is located. It was organized for the promulgation of the principles of homeopathy, especially in the Southwest, whose students of medicine had hitherto been largely deprived of the opportunity of a regular study of this branch of the science, since, as a rule, they preferred for climatic reasons not to attend a Northern homeopathic college.

The proposed school had been talked of for perhaps two years prior to its actual organization in 1892. Its articles of incorporation were filed on August 30, 1892, under the general statutes of Kentucky, its incorporators being August Scheffel; A. L. Monroe, M. D.; C. P. Meredith, M. D.; S. M. Norman; Adam Given, M. D.; R. W. Pearce, M. D.; J. H. Dunn; J. A. Lucy, M. D.; Sarah J. Millsop, M. D; G. O. Erni, M. D.; M. Dills, M. D.; J. T. Bryan, M. D.; A. G. Smith, M.D.; S. B. Elliot, M. D.; and Allison Clokey, M. D., who may also be said to be those who were mainly instrumental in its establishment. The affairs of the corporation are by this charter placed in the hands of 9 stockholder trustees, elected, 3 each year for a term of three years, by the stockholders. The course was required to be a graded one of three years, and a first-class teacher's certificate, or ability to enter college, was made a preliminary requirement for matriculation. Women were also to be admitted upon the same terms as men. It was the first medical college for white students in the South to make such an arrangement.

With funds obtained by subscription from the members of the corporation a suitable building on Sixth street was leased and properly fitted up for the opening of the college, which took place on October 4, 1894.

The following were the members of the initial faculty, which, as will be seen, was largely composed of the incorporators of the institution: C. P. Meredith, M. D., and J. A. Lucy, M. D., professors of materia medica; A. Leight Monroe, M. D., professor of gynecology and orificial surgery; Adam Given, M. D., professor of theory and practice, pathology, and physical diagnosis; H. G. Bayless, M. D., and

Malcom Dills, M. D., professors of operative and clinical surgery; G. O. Erni, M. D., professor of anatomy; J. T. Bryan, M. D., professor of obstetrics; W. L. Hartman, M. D., professor of ophthalmology and otology; J. M. Higgins, M. D., professor of chemistry and toxicology; Allison Clokey, M. D., professor of physiology; Sarah J. Millsop, M. D., professor of hygiene and sanitary science. Edward Herzer, M. D., was demonstrator of anatomy; and Judge James H. Bowden, lecturer on medical jurisprudence. Dr. Meredith was dean of the faculty, and Dr. Clokey registrar or secretary. A dispensary was attached to the institution, in charge of A. G. Smith, M. D.

The appointments of the college building were ample for its purposes, its lecture and dissecting rooms being of good size and well lighted and ventilated, while its other apparatus was such as was needed. The method of instruction used from the beginning was that in which lectures and recitations went hand in hand, accompanied by demonstration, all students being required to perform all the operations for themselves during their course. Seventeen students, representing 4 States, were in attendance during the first session. Eight of these were women, and 2 of them, who had previously taken medical courses elsewhere, were granted diplomas in April, 1894.

In June, 1894, the college was recognized officially by the American Institute of Homeopathy as coming under that body's jurisdiction, with whose demands in regard to medical education its requirements have since been made to comply. The institution was also early given recognition by State boards of health, especially those of Kentucky and Illinois, as a reputable medical college. In 1895, after having experienced considerable opposition, it was granted equal privileges with the other medical colleges of Louisville in the city hospital, one of the largest and best equipped in the West, having 500 beds, for which it annually appoints 2 of its graduates as internes. In 1894 the clinical advantages of the institution had been considerably enlarged by the addition of a hospital, with accommodations for 12 patients, established under the management of the Ladies' Homeopathic League, and in 1895 its equipment was otherwise improved by the purchase of a complete outfit for demonstration in microscopy and bacteriology. In the latter year also, in compliance with the regulations of the American Institute of Homeopathy, a four years' graded course was required for graduation of students entering upon a new course of study.

In 1894–95 there were 47 students, who represented 8 States, 16 of the students being women. Two degrees were granted at the end of this session, but, as in the previous year, were conferred on graduates of other medical colleges. In 1895–96, 45 students were in attendance, and at the close of the session the first regular class, consisting of 2 men and 4 women, was graduated from the institution. The matriculation during the past two years has been somewhat reduced, owing probably, as in the case of the other medical colleges, to the greater requirements demanded for graduation, but larger classes have been graduated during the period—11 in 1897 and 13 in 1898. The college corporation is negotiating for the purchase of the building the institution now occupies, and should the change in proprietorship take place, it is probable that the equipment of the college will soon be considerably enlarged.

The departments of instruction in the institution are those of a modern medical education and will be sufficiently indicated by the chairs of the various professors as given below. The college has special laboratories for investigations in histology, microscopy, and bacteriology, as well as a regular chemical laboratory. The scholastic year is six months in length (extending from about the 1st of October to about the 1st of April). A number of changes have from time to time taken place in the faculty of the institution. In 1894, Drs. G. S. Coons and R. W. Pearce were also made professors, respectively, of surgery and gynecology, and obstetrics; and Dr. Herzer, professor of pedology and dermatology; Dr. Hartman resigned, and Drs. G. D. Troutman and G. W. Redmon were made joint professors of opthalmology, otology, and laryngology. In 1895, Drs. Lucy, Bayless, and Redmond severed their connection with the faculty, Dr. Higgins was transferred to the chair of mental and nervous diseases, and J. F. Elsom was made professor of medical chemistry, microscopy, histology, and bacteriology, while Dr. H. C. Kasselman became professor of pathology and physical diagnosis, and Dr. J. W. Clark of dental surgery. In 1896, Professor Elsom's chair was divided, chemistry being assigned to Dr. T. Cecil Hicks, while Dr. F. C. Askenstedt received microscopy and bacteriology; at the same time, Dr. Robert G. Reed became Dr. Troutman's successor. In 1897 the connection with the faculty of Drs. Given, Erni, Hicks, and Reed was dissolved, Dr. Meredith being transferred to the chair of theory and practice, Dr. William Pinkert becoming professor of descriptive and general anatomy, and Dr. M. H. Brown, who had previously been lecturer on embryology, being made also professor of chemistry. In the matter of administration Dr. Monroe, in 1894, was elected dean of the faculty, a position he has since capably and acceptably filled.

The following list of the present faculty will show the changes which occurred in 1898: A. Leight Monroe, M. D., professor of materia medica and clinical gynecology; H. S. Keller, M. D., adjunct professor of materia medica; C. P. Meredith, M. D., and C. A. Mayer, M. D., professors of theory and practice; H. C. Kasselman, M. D., professor of pathology and physical diagnosis; M. Dills, M. D., professor of operative surgery and genito-urinary diseases; George S. Coon, M. D., professor of clinical surgery and didactic gynecology; John H. Baldwin, M. D., adjunct professor of surgery and demonstrator of minor surgery; William Pinkert, M. D., professor of descriptive and general anatomy; J. T. Bryan, M. D., professor of obstetrics; H. L. Lott, M. D., adjunct professor of obstetrics and lecturer on embryology; Ellis H. Milton, M. D., professor of chemistry, toxicology, and urinalysis; Allison Clokey, M. D., professor of physiology and visceral anatomy; F. C. Askenstedt, M. D., professor of microscopy, histology, and bacteriology; Edward Herzer, M. D., professor of pedology; J. M. Higgins, M. D., professor of mental and nervous diseases; J. E. Mann, M. D., professor of ophthalmology, otology, laryngology, and rhinology; Sarah J. Millsop, M. D., professor of hygiene and sanitary science; R. W. Pearce, M. D., emeritus professor of obstetrics; J. W. Clark, D. D. S., professor of dental surgery. The faculty contains in addition 3 lecturers and demonstrators.

BIBLIOGRAPHY.

Information furnished by Dr. Allison Clokey, registrar of the faculty. The Louisville Times of September 30, 1892, and catalogues.

LOUISVILLE PRESBYTERIAN THEOLOGICAL SEMINARY, LOUISVILLE.

The Louisville Presbyterian Theological Seminary, although the most recently established institution of higher education of its own or any other rank in Kentucky, is not really new in idea, but dates back in spirit and conception to the earliest attempts of the Presbyterians of the State to establish a theological seminary in their midst which culminated, as we have seen, in the foundation of the Danville Theological Seminary in 1853. The new seminary really stands in the same relation to the seminary at Danville as Central University does to Centre College, Louisville Theological Seminary and Central University being representative institutions of the Southern Presbyterian Church, while Danville Seminary and Centre represent the original organization, ordinarily called, in contradistinction, the Northern Presbyterian Church. Both seminaries are, however, wider in their church relations than the colleges, as the former in a certain sense represent the whole of their respective churches, while the latter only represent the respective synods of Kentucky. As Louisville Seminary includes, as it were, in its jurisdiction any theological department which might be attached to Central University, it is not now probable that a department of that character provided for in the charter of that institution will ever be organized.

As a result of the establishment of the Southern Presbyterian Church in 1861 and of the division of the Synod of Kentucky between the two churches in 1866, the Southern Church, although representing by far the larger part of the former constituency of the institution, lost control of Danville Seminary, which had been founded for the whole church in the South and West, but in the disruption had remained under the original assembly. Thus deprived of any general institution in its midst for the higher professional education of its ministry, the Southern Synod of Kentucky, after an unsuccessful attempt to obtain an interest in the control of Danville Seminary upon what was deemed by them a desirable basis, determined, in the spirit of the fathers of the church in Kentucky, to establish a seminary of their own as early as practicable. The contemplated plan was held in abeyance for some time on account of the demands upon the church's resources of more pressing needs, but was never lost sight of, and finally reached its fruition in the establishment of the Louisville Presbyterian Theological Seminary in 1893.

About 1891, Rev. I. S. McElroy, D. D., as the financial agent of Central University and the Synod of Kentucky, began to take active steps to raise funds for the proposed institution. He succeeded in the next two years in obtaining in various parts of the State pledges for an endowment fund of $104,311 and for a building fund of $43,000.[1] In securing the latter fund especially, which was given by the denomination in Louisville on condition that the seminary be located there, he was very efficiently assisted by Rev. L. H. Blanton, D. D., chancellor of Central University. Among others who may be mentioned as especially instrumental in furthering the plan of the proposed school are Rev. E. M. Green, D. D.; Rev. T. D. Witherspoon, D. D.; Rev. C. R. Hemphill, D. D.; Rev. J. S. Lyons, D. D.; Col. Bennett H. Young; Col. T. W. Bullitt; A. J. Alexander, esq.; William T. Grant, esq.; and George W. Swearingen, esq.

The preliminary steps looking toward the immediate opening of the seminary were taken, in 1892, by the synods of Kentucky and Missouri, which agreed to join in the control of the institution. They invited the participation of the synods of the other Southern States, and appointed a provisional board of directors, with Rev. E. M. Green, of Kentucky, chairman, whose duty it was to draw up a charter as a legal basis for the school and frame a constitution for its organization and administration. The charter and constitution were adopted in the early part of 1893 by the associated synods of Kentucky and Missouri, by whom the first regular board of directors, composed of 10 members from each synod, was chosen. This board was soon afterwards organized in Louisville, Ky., where it was decided by them to locate the seminary on account of the large building fund offered by the city, the strength of its Presbyterian churches, its accessibility, and its admirable advantages in other respects. The organization of the institution may be said to have been complete when the supervision over it, provided for by its charter and constitution, was accepted by the General Assembly of the church, meeting at Macon, Ga., in the latter part of May, 1893.

[1] Minutes of the Synod of Kentucky for 1893, p. 502.

The charter bears the date of May 3, 1893, and constitutes the seminary a perpetual corporation under the general statutes of Kentucky, declaring its purpose to be—

> The education and training of young men as ministers of the gospel according to the Confession of Faith, catechisms, and other standards of the Presbyterian Church in the United States, commonly known as the Southern Presbyterian Church, and their support and maintenance while in attendance, as far as may be deemed advisable and practicable.[1]

It puts the proposed institution under the management, temporarily, of a board of directors consisting of 10 members from each of the synods of Kentucky and Missouri, as already constituted, but provision is made that this board in the future may consist of not less than 10 nor more than 50 members, chosen by the synods joining in its control, one-fifth of whom shall be elected each year. All direct control of the institution, both as to its property and other affairs, is vested in this board, but the General Assembly of the church is given the power to veto the election of any professor or his transfer from one chair to another.

According to its constitution, the funds belonging to the seminary are designated as (1) the building fund, (2) the endowment fund, (3) the library fund, (4) the current expenses fund, (5) the scholarship fund, and (6) the lecture-course fund. Its course of instruction is to be modeled upon the university plan in distinction from a fixed curriculum of study, and as originally outlined was divided into the 9 independent schools of Biblical introduction, Old Testament exegesis, New Testament exegesis, English Bible and Biblical theology, systematic theology, church history and polity, homiletics and pastoral theology, apologetics, and elocution. Students are required to be graduates of colleges or to pass a prescribed examination. Each professor upon entering office is required to publicly subscribe to the standard of the church. There are no distinctions in the faculty, except that the senior professor is its chairman. Dr. Marquess thus became the chairman of the first faculty of the institution, which was constituted as follows: Rev. William Hoge Marquess, D. D., professor of Old Testament exegesis and of the English Bible and Biblical theology; Rev. Charles R. Hemphill, D. D., professor of New Testament exegesis; Rev. G. D. Witherspoon, D. D., LL. D., professor of homiletics, pastoral theology, and of Biblical instruction; Rev. Francis R. Beattie, Ph. D., D. D., professor of systematic theology and apologetics; Rev. T. M. Hawes, professor of elocution; Rev. Edwin Muller, adjunct professor of church history and church polity

The seminary was first opened on October 2, 1893, a commodious house on Second street near Broadway being purchased for it, while another near by was rented and fitted up as a dormitory for students.

[1]Section III of charter, given in the minutes of the Synod of Kentucky for 1893, p. 478.

The Sunday-school and Bible-class rooms of the First and Second Presbyterian Churches were at first used for lecture rooms and for chapel exercises. Three valuable libraries especially suited to its needs, the gifts of Rev. Dr. J. B. Adger, of Rev. Dr. Symington, and of the heirs of Rev. Dr. Stuart Robinson, furnished it with 3,000 volumes as the foundation of a future collection. Twenty-five students were present at the opening, and before the end of the first session 31 were in attendance, who represented 9 States of the Union and 3 other countries. In 1895-96 the number had risen to 60, from 12 States and 1 foreign country. This has continued to be about the average attendance since. In 1895 the institution had 5 graduates; in 1896, 15, and in 1897, 13.

In 1895 Mrs. N. W. Muir, of Bardstown, Ky., donated to the institution an outfit of gymnastic apparatus of the latest and most improved designs, while other friends fitted up for it a reading room and provided it with current literature. Recently there have been numerous valuable contributions to the library. In the summer of 1896, through the liberality of one of its warm friends, it came into possession of a handsome property at the corner of First street and Broadway, which provides a chapel, lecture rooms, and additional rooms for students. Its endowment had also been added to until, by this time, it was about $200,000.

No material changes have since been made in the regular course of instruction of the seminary as originally outlined, but a number of advanced optional courses have recently been added. All the nine schools of the regular course must be completed for the student to obtain the degree of bachelor of divinity. This usually requires three years, the sessions extending from the 1st of October to the 1st of May following. The regular faculty also remains as at first, the instructor in music attached to it being the only member of the teaching force who has been changed. There have been only two changes in the personnel of the board of directors, which still consists of 10 members from each of the synods of Kentucky and Missouri.

BIBLIOGRAPHY.

Minutes of the sessions of the Synod of Kentucky, at Louisville, March, 1893, and at Winchester, October, 1893; Louisville, 1893. Other sources of general information, principally catalogues.

Chapter VIII.

EXTINCT COLLEGES OF SOME IMPORTANCE.

BETHEL ACADEMY, JESSAMINE COUNTY.

As already noticed in treating of the history of Kentucky Wesleyan College and Union College, those institutions, as well as Vanderbilt University, in a sense, are the present representatives of the early educational efforts of the Methodist Episcopal Church in Kentucky, which have finally found expression in them after the trial of several other educational experiments. The principal institutions, besides those previously described in other connections, established in Kentucky, either by the church as a whole or by its branches, have been Bethel Academy, Augusta College, and Warren College, a general view of each of which will be given here, both because of its own importance and that the movement just referred to may be given in all of its general outlines, Warren College being treated out of its chronological order that this may be done.

The beginning of this movement and the second[1] educational institution established by the Methodist Episcopal Church in America was Bethel Academy. It has been claimed[2] that the Methodists were the first Christian denomination in Kentucky to undertake a movement toward the establishment of an institution of learning. This claim is only true if it has reference to the undertaking of such an enterprise in a distinctively denominational capacity, as the date given for the inauguration of the movement to establish Bethel Academy, 1790, is prior to that of any other educational enterprise which may be called denominational in the State, although it is antedated ten years by the movement to establish Transylvania Seminary, which was, as we have seen, under Presbyterian auspices.

Collins[3] tells us that when Bishop Asbury first visited Kentucky, in May, 1790, and held the first annual conference, "a plan was fixed for a school called Bethel and £300 in land and money subscribed toward its establishment." The academy was located in Jessamine County,

[1]The first was Cokesbury College, at Abingdon, Md., planned as early as 1784, but not opened until December, 1787. It was chartered on December 26, 1794, about the time of Bethel's first incorporation. (See Steiner's Higher Education in Maryland, pp. 229-239.)

[2]Redford's Methodism, Vol. I, p. 84.

[3]History of Kentucky, Vol. I, p. 446.

on a high bluff of the Kentucky River,[1] on a tract of about 100 acres of land donated to it by Mr. I. Lewis. Here, in a fine native grove, a brick building, quite spacious for the time, being 80 feet by 40 feet and three stories high, was erected, and although never completely finished was used for school purposes for several years.

The institution was under the control of the Western Methodist Conference, whose ministers are said to have been kept poorer than usual for several years by having to beg for its support as well as their own. The conference often met in the academy building, many of its members from the distant settlements, such as those on the Holston River, in Tennessee,[2] having to travel to its sessions for several days on horseback along the Indian trails, subsisting on the way upon biscuit, broiled bacon, dried beef, and tree sugar.

We know comparatively little of Bethel Academy for the period of about twelve years, during which it seems to have been in active operation. Rev. Francis Poythress was mainly instrumental in having its building erected, and he, with Col. Thomas Hinde, Willis Green, I. Lewis, Richard Mastersen, and Isaac Hite, were its incorporators. It was first incorporated in the latter part of 1794,[3] and was reincorporated by an act of February 10, 1798.[4] By this act, although still remaining under denominational control, it became a part of the general academy system, and received from the State a donation of 6,000 acres of land. This put it upon exactly the same basis as Kentucky Academy, the Presbyterian school, was at the time. The records of the conference[5] show that the building had been erected in April, 1792, and that the school was probably in operation at that time. It was certainly in operation in 1794, when it had as its principal John Metcalf, who remained at the head of its English department for several years, probably until 1803.

The academy's course of study was intended especially to train ministers for the church, and was afterwards of a high classical order; but for the first few years of its history it only imparted the elements of a good English education, and its English department was always one of its prominent features.

In 1799 Rev. Valentine Cook, one of the famous pioneer Methodist ministers of the State, described by Collins[6] as "scholarly, profound,

---

[1] Near the present High Bridge on the Southern Railway.

[2] The conference of which Kentucky was then a part embraced practically all the country west of the Alleghenies.

[3] In giving this date as that of the first incorporation of the academy several authorities have been followed, but since the act can not be found in several collections which have been carefully examined and are otherwise quite complete, it appears quite probable that no regular legislative incorporation occurred at this time.

[4] For references to this act, see Chapter II.

[5] Given in Alexander's Earliest Western Schools of Methodism, pp. 363-364.

[6] History of Kentucky, Vol. I, p. 451. A sketch of Mr. Cook is also given in Sprague's Annals, Vol. VII, p. 153.

masterly in an argument, and overwhelming in the enforcement of the great truths of Christianity," became connected with the academy as the head of its higher or classical department, then first organized. Mr. Cook was the most distinguished graduate of Cokesbury College, Maryland, and was noted as a teacher as well as preacher. He, however, only remained at Bethel for one year. In 1803 a new charter was secured for the institution, conferring upon it the full powers and privileges of a literary institution, which its other acts of incorporation had, it appears, not bestowed upon it.

We are not informed of the exact number of students in attendance upon the academy, but are told that there were a considerable number, especially during the presidency of Rev. Valentine Cook. The conference regulations over the students, especially, we presume, over those preparing for the ministry, were very strict and would be considered quite an anomaly nowadays. They were compelled to rise at 5 o'clock in the morning and retire at 9 o'clock at night, while no games of any kind were allowed, and idleness was punished by confinement in a room constructed especially for that purpose.

The institution seems to have been fairly prosperous for a time, but the poverty of the church, combined with the unsettled state of the country, due to Indian hostilities and its own rather inaccessible position, caused its attendance to decline and resulted in its practical abandonment by the conference about 1804. Its building was afterwards used for a time for a neighborhood school, but was finally dismantled, a portion of it being used to construct an academy building in Nicholasville.

BIBLIOGRAPHY.

Collins's and Smith's History; acts of the legislature; Sprague's Annals; Redford's Methodism in Kentucky.

A few facts have been taken from Earliest Western Schools of Methodism, by Gross Alexander, S. T. D., Nashville, 1897.

AUGUSTA COLLEGE, AUGUSTA.

Although the Methodists of the West had been compelled by the force of circumstances to abandon Bethel Academy as a denominational institution, yet the idea of a Methodist college for that section had not been given up by the church and soon took definite shape in the foundation of Augusta College.

When the Kentucky conference held its first session at Lexington, in September, 1821, one of the most prominent questions before it was the establishment of an institution of learning for the church. The Ohio conference had a few days before appointed a commission to prepare the foundation of a college under the joint control of the two bodies. This plan was approved by Kentucky conference, and commissioners[1] were appointed by it to act in conjunction with those already appointed by Ohio conference in inaugurating the enterprise.

[1] For the names of the commissioners from the two conferences, see Alexander's Western Schools of Methodism, p. 367.

These commissioners, by agreement, met on the 15th of the following December, at Augusta, Ky., in a conference with the trustees of Bracken Academy, an institution established in that town and given an endowment of 6,000 acres of land by the State legislature in 1798. An arrangement was then made, whereby the proposed new college was to have the use of the funds arising from the sale of the academy lands, amounting to about $10,000, and was to be assisted by the latter's trustees in securing suitable ground and buildings. Considerable donations for this last purpose were also obtained from other local friends of the enterprise, especially Mr. James Armstrong. By reason of these inducements the commissioners located the college at Augusta, which was also otherwise desirable on account of its being somewhat centrally located with reference to the two conferences.

The aims of the church were now more ambitious than in the case of the inauguration of Bethel Academy, and so a regular college charter was obtained for the new enterprise from the Kentucky legislature on December 7, 1822,[1] which declared that "said seminary of learning shall be conducted on free, liberal, and enlightened principles," and placed it under the control of a self-perpetuating board of twenty-three trustees, twenty of whom were from Ohio and Kentucky conferences, while the other three were the trustees of Bracken Academy. The funds of Bracken Academy were also transferred by the instrument to the new institution, whose trustees were empowered to admit students free of tuition and whose property was exempted from taxation. Thus was chartered the third[2] Methodist college, at least under the name of college, in America, and one which was for a time the only real Methodist college in operation[3] in the world.

While Augusta bore the name of college from the beginning, it was really an academy[4] for the first three years of its existence. By the appointment of Conference in 1822 John P. Finley became the first president of the institution, and in the latter part of that year he opened its preparatory department, although its building was not entirely completed until October, 1823. This building was an excellent one for the time, and was a brick structure 80 feet by 42 feet and three stories in height. In 1825 Rev. J. S. Tomlinson, who had just graduated from Transylvania University and was later to become a doctor of divinity in his church and to remain connected with the institution for the most part during the remainder of its history, became a member of the college faculty, as professor of mathematics

[1] Acts of 1822-23, pp. 163-171.

[2] It was only antedated by Cokesbury (1787) and Asbury (1816) colleges, in Maryland.

[3] Cokesbury College went out of existence in 1796, and Asbury College, while it may have had a formal existence until about 1830, did not amount to anything after 1818, and Wesleyan University, Connecticut, did not originate until 1831. Madison College, Uniontown, Pa., had a desultory existence from 1827 to 1832.

[4] Barnard's American Journal of Education, vol. 27, p. 335.

and natural philosophy, and shortly afterwards John P. Durbin, A. M., became professor of Latin and Greek.

In 1827[1] Rev. Martin Ruter, D. D., became president of the college, a position which he retained until 1832. College classes seem to have been organized at the time of the accession of Professor Tomlinson to the faculty, as the first class was graduated in 1829. This class contained 4 members. In 1831 Professor Durbin, who had resigned, was succeeded by Rev. B. H. McCown, A. M., a graduate of St. Joseph's College, Kentucky, who was a noted professor at Augusta for eleven years and afterwards at Transylvania University for several years.

Upon the resignation of President Ruter, in 1832, Rev. Joseph S. Tomlinson,[2] D. D., already mentioned as an early professor in the college, became his successor in the presidency, an office which was held by him throughout the future history of the college,[3] except for short intervals when he was relieved of its duties on account of bad health. At the opening of his administration, Rev. H. B. Bascom, afterwards so prominently connected with Transylvania University, became a member of the Augusta faculty, as professor of moral science and belles-lettres, thus constituting a strong faculty, which, in 1833,[4] was composed as follows: Rev. J. S. Tomlinson, A. M., president and professor of mathematics and natural philosophy; Rev. H. B. Bascom, A. M., professor of moral science and belles-lettres; Rev. B. H. McCown, A. M., professor of languages; Fred. A. W. Davis, M. D., professor of chemistry and botany; Solomon Howard, assistant in academic department; John Vincent, teacher of primary school.

President Tomlinson was a versatile teacher and was often known to discharge the duties of many different departments, while Professor Bascom was noted for both energy and ability. The latter at once became prominent in the affairs of the institution, although he would never accept its presidency, which, we are informed,[5] was several times offered to him. As the agent of the two patronizing conferences, about 1837, he raised $10,000 in each of them toward the endowment of the college. These, together with other funds of the institution, seem, however, to have been soon afterwards lost by the mismanagement of its authorities. It was also soon hampered in its usefulness by differences which sprang up between the two conferences, especially in regard to slavery. These led, before long, to the practical withdrawal of the Ohio Conference from patronizing Augusta, because of its being in a slave State, and later to the establishment

---

[1] This date is given as 1828 in the sketch of Dr. Ruter in Sprague's Annals, Vol. VII, pp. 327, 329, but the date in the text seems best authenticated.

[2] Dr. Tomlinson's connection with Augusta has been taken mainly from Sprague's Annals, Vol. VII, pp. 706-707.

[3] According to the American Almanac, Nathan Bangs, D. D., was president of Augusta in 1835.

[4] From the American Almanac for 1834.

[5] By his biographer, Rev. M. M. Henkle, in his Life of Bascom.

by that body first of academies in its own midst and then of a college of its own in the Ohio Wesleyan University, which necessarily became a rival institution.

This state of affairs led Dr. Bascom and other friends of Augusta to lose hope in its success, and when the proposition came from the trustees of Transylvania University to turn over its academic department with all its funds and equipments to the church, they thought it wise and right to accept this offer, which they considered to have in it much greater prospects of advantage to the church than were likely to be realized from Augusta. Many friends of the latter, however, did not hold this view and resisted the proposed change. After this was carried out the college, although practically abandoned by the church as a whole, and still further weakened as was the university also by the divisions soon to begin in that body, was able to maintain itself in a decaying condition for several years, indeed as long as the new Transylvania University experiment, as its charter was repealed in 1849, the year in which Dr. Bascom gave up Transylvania as an unprofitable undertaking.

The repeal of the charter of the college was probably due to the conviction of the local community that its property would be of greater educational utility in the hands of the trustees of old Bracken Academy, to whom it reverted upon the withdrawal of its charter, than it was on its denominational basis. These trustees leased the property for a number of years to various teachers who conducted it as a high school or academy. Under this plan it was leased from 1879 to 1887 to Rev. Daniel Stevenson, D. D., who operated it as a collegiate institute for the Methodist Episcopal Church, thus in a sense returning it to its original denominational connection, but without the same conditions as to property rights. When Dr. Stevenson gave it up to establish Union College for his church it was made a part of the public school system of the town of Augusta. Quite recently[1] its building, which had been burned on January 29, 1852,[2] and been replaced by a plainer one, was demolished to make way for a modern public school building.

During the quarter of a century that the college was in operation in its best estate it maintained a high-grade classical curriculum and had in its faculty several able and prominent professors, particularly Dr. Bascom and Professor McCown; it had for the time an excellent building and a good equipment, having a library which at one period contained 2,500 volumes. The institution was never properly endowed and had to depend largely for its support on tuition fees, but, notwithstanding discouragements and embarrassments, was able for a time to make good progress and to fill an excellent educational sphere. In its most prosperous days it had from 100 to 150 students

[1] Alexander's Earliest Western Schools of Methodism, p. 371.

[2] Collins's History of Kentucky, Vol. I, p. 64.

annually, and sent forth a number of graduates who afterwards became distinguished. Among these may be mentioned Hon. William S. Groesbeck, Hon. W. H. Wadsworth, Hon. E. C. Phisten, Rev. George S. Savage, M. D., Bishop Randolph S. Foster, and Rev. John Miley, D. D., who with many others have occupied high positions in church and state. Dr. Redford[1] speaks of the services of the institution as follows:

Under all the embarrassments to which such enterprises are exposed, the vast amount of good that resulted to the church and the country from Augusta College can never be estimated. Over its fortunes some of the noblest intellects have presided: its faculty was always composed of men of piety, of genius, and of learning; and in all the learned professions in almost every Western and Southern State its alumni may yet [1870] be found. It gave to the medical profession, to the bar, and to the pulpit many of their brightest lights.

BIBLIOGRAPHY.

Collins's and Smith's History.

Acts of the legislature.

The Gospel Herald for November 30, 1830.

A communication from the Kentucky Conference Commissioners in reply to a memorial from the trustees of Augusta College.

Redford's Methodism in Kentucky.

Sprague's Annals.

Barnard's American Journal.

The American Almanac.

A small amount of additional information has also been obtained from Alexander's Earliest Western Schools of Methodism.

WARREN COLLEGE, BOWLING GREEN.

This institution represented, until comparatively recent years, the efforts of Louisville Conference of the Methodist Episcopal Church South in Kentucky to establish in its midst an institution of higher education after it and Kentucky Conference[2] had withdrawn, in 1850, from the joint control of Transylvania University.

Louisville Conference was little behind her sister conference in attempting to supply her educational needs, as, while the latter began in 1858 to lay the foundations of Kentucky Wesleyan College at Millersburg, the former, at its session at Bardstown in 1859, appointed 10 commissioners to take steps to establish a similar institution at Bowling Green.

These commissioners, acting under the authority given to them by the conference, soon secured the transfer of the charter of the Southern College of Kentucky, an institution chartered at Bowling Green in 1819 and having a desultory existence there for several years but

[1] Methodism in Kentucky, vol. 3, pp. 100–101.

[2] These two conferences are separated by a line running in general north and south just east of Louisville, Kentucky Conference being east of this line, and Louisville Conference west.

long since suspended. It still, however, possessed property and funds amounting to about $17,000, and the terms of its charter were full and liberal. The income from its funds was secured for the conference, and under the provisions of its charter the commissioners proceeded to organize a new institution, for which, by the autumn of 1860, they had laid the foundations of a fine new building to cost about $30,000. The advent of the civil war, however, soon after caused them to have to abandon for several years the erection of this building, and indeed the whole enterprise, which was never revived on the same basis.

A new charter was obtained from the legislature in 1866 under the name of Warren College, and in 1867 a board of education was incorporated to cooperate with the trustees of this college, seven in number, in securing funds for its endowment, the sale of the former site of the institution having been authorized in the latter year. Several agents of the board of education, chiefly Rev. J. F. Redford, secured, within the next three years, cash and subscriptions amounting to about $24,000, for the endowment of the proposed college, for which the property now occupied by Ogden College, then a large and handsome private residence, was purchased and improved in such a way as to become well adapted to educational purposes.

A preparatory school, which had been conducted in a rented building since 1866 by Prof. S. T. Scott, was, in February, 1872, transferred to the new building, Prof. G. B. Doggett becoming its principal at the latter date. In the autumn of 1872 the college proper was organized. It opened its doors on September 5, 1872,[1] and had as its first president, and indeed its only one, Rev. J. G. Wilson, D. D. Dr. Wilson was assisted the first year, at the beginning of which 80 students were enrolled, by Professor Doggett and Wilbur F. Barclay, A. B.

By this time the pledged endowment of the institution had reached about $30,000, of which only about $11,000, however, seems ever to have been paid in, with the aid of the income from which an additional professor, Rev. Gross Alexander, S. T. D., now of the theological department of Vanderbilt University, was employed in 1873. An excellent faculty of four members was maintained by the college and a good educational work done by it for the next three years, but the opening of Vanderbilt University on the one hand and the proposed early establishment in Bowling Green, according to the terms of the will of its donor, of Ogden College, an institution which was more largely endowed and would offer practically free tuition, caused the board of trustees of Warren College in 1876 to decide to close that institution whose work was already much crippled for lack of endowment and whose field in the future would necessarily be largely occupied by the institution just mentioned. The work of the college was therefore in that year finally discontinued. Its property was rented

[1] Collins's History of Kentucky, Vol. I, p. 231.

the next year to the trustees of Ogden College, by whom it was not long afterwards purchased.

In 1880, the income from the endowment fund of the board of education, which had gone to the aid of Warren College during its existence, was set apart by the conference to assist its theological students in Vanderbilt University. This arrangement led to a very wise step in 1884 whereby, instead of attempting to establish for itself a new college, the conference adopted the university as its educational institution, and was given in return a representation of two members in the latter's board of trust, the conference being admitted as one of the eight "patronizing conferences" whose representatives control the university. Thus the Louisville Conference has become joint owner of one of the greatest universities in the South, and has no real need for an additional institution for higher education. The conference has, since 1884, taken further steps to supply its educational needs. These have very properly taken the form, not of establishing another college, but of a training school, known as the Vanderbilt Training School, which was located at Elkton, Ky., in 1892, and is intended to furnish proper preparation for the lower classes of Vanderbilt University, and also to give the elements of a good English education to those who have not the desire or opportunity to pursue a college course. The school has an excellent equipment in the way of buildings and apparatus and has been doing a good work. Prof. R. E. Crockett has been its efficient principal since its establishment.

BIBLIOGRAPHY.

This sketch is based almost entirely on Alexander's History of Education in the Louisville Conference, with some information from Collins's History and Henderson's Centennial Exhibit.

ST. JOSEPH'S COLLEGE, BARDSTOWN.

St. Joseph's College is worthy of a place in this monograph, both because of its own importance, having been long one of the principal colleges of the State, and also because its history, in a sense, still continues in that of St. Mary's College, which has been made its successor. It was also the first college established in Kentucky by the Roman Catholics, and was one of the earliest denominational institutions in the State.

The Catholic church early established in Kentucky a seminary[1] for the education of its priests. This was, after a time, removed to Bardstown, then one of the most flourishing towns in the State and, as the

[1] This seminary was organized in 1811 on the Ohio River in the boat which brought Bishop Flaget to the State. It was conducted at St. Stephen's (Loretto) for a few months, but was moved in November, 1811, to St. Thomas, near Bardstown. It was moved to Bardstown on April 21, 1819. It was continued at Bardstown, St. Marys, St. Thomas, and Louisville until quite recently, when it was discontinued in favor of the larger seminaries of the church.

cathedral town, the center, as it remained for some time, of Catholic influence in Kentucky and the West. In the basement of the building of this seminary was opened, near the close of 1819, a day school, from which, as an humble beginning, soon sprang St. Joseph's College, the first Roman Catholic institution in the State for the higher education of young men. The school was maintained in the seminary building for about a year.

The one mainly instrumental in establishing this school and the president of the college for some time was Rev. G. A. M. Elder, who was born in Kentucky in 1793, and at the time of the establishment of the school had just finished his studies for the priesthood at Emmitsburg and Baltimore, Md. Just after his ordination[1] at Bardstown in the latter part of 1819, he received from Bishop Flaget, the pioneer Catholic bishop of the West, the commission to establish the school just referred to, the foundation of which had been long desired by the bishop, who had previously, however, not had the clergy to spare from other more pressing church enterprises for its proper supervision.

Father Elder's ability, combined with his amiability, made him popular with his students, and under his careful management the school soon grew in numbers. Largely from the proceeds of tuition, at first partly anticipated, a building was soon erected for it, and a boarding department added. The south wing of this building was completed at the close of 1820 and the school moved from the seminary at that time. The north wing was erected in 1823 and the front soon afterwards,[2] the whole costing about $20,000 and constituting one of the largest and best appointed educational buildings in the West at that time. Pupils then came in large numbers, about 50 being brought at one time, in 1825, from a Louisiana college by Rev. M. Martial. This was the beginning of a large patronage, which was long retained, from the South, especially from Louisiana and Mississippi.

The increasing attendance had caused Father Elder and other friends of the enterprise to become more ambitious in its behalf. So, on December 27, 1824,[3] a charter was obtained from the State legislature conferring upon it full collegiate powers and privileges, under the name of St. Joseph's College. It was by this instrument placed under the control of six trustees, of whom the bishop of the diocese was the moderator or chairman.

Father Elder became the first president of the new college, whose course, early in its history, became a high-grade, classical one, in comparison with similar institutions throughout the country. At his own request, Father Elder was relieved from its presidency from 1827 to

[1] This, as noted in connection with the history of St. Mary's, occurred at the same time as that of Father Byrne, the founder of that institution.

[2] Niles's Register, vol. 28, p. 416 (August 27, 1825), says the college has nearly finished a new brick building, four stories high and 120 feet long, and that it is in a very prosperous condition, having 200 students.

[3] Acts of 1824-25, pp. 65-68.

1830, during which time the duties of the office were ably discharged by Rev. I. N. Reynolds, subsequently bishop of Charleston, but in the latter year the first president resumed his former position and unselfishly devoted the remainder of his life to the further building up of the college. On January 25, 1838, the institution suffered the misfortune of losing its main building by fire, and eight months afterwards suffered the additional loss of its faithful president and founder, whose death was largely brought about from overexertion at the time of the fire. The building was soon reerected, but the result of the fire long remained in the shape of debt, which hung heavily over the diocese for a number of years.

By the end of Father Elder's administration, St. Joseph's was recognized as one of the first literary institutions of Kentucky and the South generally. It had annually, during this period, from 100 to 250 students, and soon began to send out good-sized graduating classes for the time, the class of 1833 numbering eight members.

Father Elder was succeeded in the presidency of the college by Rev M. J. Spalding,[1] then quite a young man, but destined later to become a very prominent figure in his church. He remained at the head of St. Joseph's for two years, becoming afterwards bishop of Kentucky, and later the seventh archbishop of Baltimore.

He was succeeded in 1840 in the presidency of St. Joseph's by Rev. J. M. Lancaster, who was in turn succeeded by Rev. Edward McMahon, the combined administrations of these two presidents extending to 1848. Under their excellent and careful management the college continued to prosper. Collins tells us in his Sketches[2] that it had 150 students in 1847, during the administration of Father McMahon. It had then a faculty of four professors, besides the president, and a library of 5,000 volumes. The faculty had been making self-denying efforts to pay off the debt weighing on the institution, of which $23,000 still remained in 1848. For a number of years they had each received from $75 to $150 a year for their services. We are informed[3] that up to about the end of Father McMahon's administration about 6,000 young men, coming from nearly all of the States in the South and West, had spent at least a year in study at St. Joseph's. Between 1823 and 1848 the college had sent forth many graduates who afterwards became distinguished in the different professions. During this

[1] Archbishop Spalding was born in Kentucky in 1810, and graduated at St. Mary's when 16 years old, having been a professor there at 14 years of age. He then studied theology at Bardstown and Rome until 1834, and was then pastor, editor, and president of St. Joseph's for several years. He became bishop of Kentucky in 1850 and archbishop of Baltimore in 1864. He died in 1872 greatly beloved and admired. More complete sketches of his life are to be found in Smith's History of Kentucky, p. 555, and Collins's History of Kentucky, Vol. I, p. 490.

[2] Sketches of Kentucky, p. 475.

[3] Spalding's Sketches of Bishop Flaget, p. 299.

portion of its history the institution was conducted by the secular clergy of the church, and was for most of the time operated in close connection with the diocesan seminary.

In June, 1848,[1] the Jesuits of the province of Missouri, at the solicitation of Bishop Flaget, who was always much inclined toward their order as a teaching organization, and had offered to them the control of the college in 1829, just prior to their assuming the administration of St. Mary's College, took charge of St. Joseph's, which was opened under their management in the following September, with Rev. Peter J. Verhaegen, formerly president of the University of St. Louis, as its new president. There was a fair showing of students at the opening of the new administration, and their numbers increased during the first session. The college afterwards had numerous students, particularly from the South, and was uninterruptedly prosperous until closed by the civil war in 1861.

The other presidents during the period of Jesuit control, besides Father Verhaegen, who remained at the head of the institution for three years, were Fathers Emig, D'Hoop, Coosemans, and de Bluck.

In 1852, during the administration of Father Emig, a large additional building, to be used as an infirmary and for class-room purposes, as well as to furnish splendid quarters for the college museum, was erected. A number of other additions and improvements to buildings and grounds were also made during this period, and the old college debt was finally fully expunged. The institution had continued to grow in public favor, but in 1861 its buildings were seized and occupied for some time by the Federal authorities for hospital purposes, and its exercises were not resumed for several years. The college was never reopened by the Jesuits, who, in 1868, owing to a misunderstanding with the bishop of the diocese in regard to a new college which they were proposing to establish in Louisville, gave up the management of St. Joseph's and withdrew from the State. The college property had only been held in trust by them, and upon their departure was transferred to the bishop free from the old debt which they had liquidated. It reverted to its former plan of management and was placed under the direction of the secular clergy.

From 1869 to 1872 the buildings were occupied by the preparatory Theological Seminary from St. Thomas, with Rev. P. de Fraine as superior. In 1872 a limited number of students, besides those studying for the priesthood, were again admitted, and Rev. M. M. Coghlan became president and remained at the head of the institution until his death in March, 1877. In September, 1877, Rev. W. J. Dunn became his successor and was in turn succeeded by Rev. C. J. O'Connell at the end of the next year. During this period of the college's history no regular degrees were conferred, but there were two regular

[1] This date is given in Maes's Life of Nerinckx, p. 476, as July, 1848.

courses maintained—the classical for the ministry and learned professions generally, and the commercial for mercantile pursuits.

At the beginning of Father O'Connell's administration the privileges of the institution were fully opened to all young men who were properly prepared, and when, in 1880, Rev. W. P. Mackin became president the A. B. degree was restored and a scientific course also instituted. The college had at that time a good library and extensive scientific apparatus, and was well prepared to supply the educational needs of the time. Its faculty between 1873 and 1885 contained from 5 to 7 members, and its students varied in number from 76 to 108.

During the later portion of the institution's history it had been under the charge of the secular clergy of the diocese, while St. Mary's College, the other male college of the church in Kentucky, was being conducted by the Fathers of the Resurrection, a strong and well-organized teaching order. As both of these institutions necessarily drew their students largely from the same territory, the competition of each was a considerable hindrance to the other, so, in August, 1890, the bishop of Louisville, thinking it wise to concentrate the educational efforts of the church in one institution, which might thus be better equipped and in every way more efficient, caused St. Joseph's to be closed and St. Mary's made the official college of the diocese as the successor of both institutions. So while St. Joseph's has ceased to exist as a separate institution, it yet, in a sense, lives in St. Mary's. The buildings of St. Joseph's since it was suspended have been used as one of the male orphanages of the diocese. The college has been closed in such a way as not necessarily to remain closed entirely in the future, and if future circumstances shall render its reopening advisable it may resume its historic career.

Its history, especially for about thirty-five years prior to 1861, is quite a distinguished one, and is the more remarkable from the fact that all of its work was accomplished without any endowment and solely upon the income derived from tuition fees. During its existence it graduated a number of students who afterwards reached positions of great prominence as governors, members of Congress, bishops, editors, preachers, jurists, physicians, lawyers, and politicians. United States Attorney-General Garland; Governor Powell, of Kentucky; Governor Wickliffe, of Louisiana; Hon. Thomas C. McCreery, and others are among its noted alumni.

BIBLIOGRAPHY.

Collins's Sketches, Allen's, Collins's, Smith's, and Perrin, Battle and Kniffen's History.

Spalding's Sketches of Early Catholic Missions.

Spalding's Sketches of the Life and Times of Bishop Flaget.

Biographical Sketch of Hon. L. W. Powell.

Maes's Life of Nerinckx.

Webb's Centenary of Catholicity in America.

The American Almanac.

Sadlier's Catholic Directory for 1878.

Cumberland College was established at Princeton, Ky., in 1826 by the Cumberland Presbyterian Church, from which it derived its name. It was one of the first, if not the first, of the institutions in the State to make anything like an adequate test of a system of manual labor as a part of its regular work. A large farm was attached to the college, upon which all students were required for some time to labor two hours each day. They also all took their meals at a general boarding house.

The preliminary steps looking toward the establishment of the institution were taken by Kentucky Synod of the Cumberland Presbyterian Church in 1825, when it was resolved by that body, with great unanimity, to found a college in which its ministry, especially, might be properly educated. The manual-labor system was ingrafted upon the institution in order to diminish the expense[1] of attendance and at the same time promote health and practical habits. The college was chartered by an act of the State legislature approved January 8, 1827,[2] by the terms of which it was placed under the management of a board of not more than eleven nor less than seven trustees, who were to be appointed by Kentucky Synod. The students also might be reqnired to labor as much as three hours a day "on the farm attached to the college." The institution was later taken under the care of the general assembly of the church, and became the representative institution of the whole denomination instead of Kentucky synod simply.

The college had been opened before its charter was secured, in March, 1826, and had as its first president, Rev. F. R. Cossitt,[3] D. D., who was assisted by Daniel L. Morrison, as professor of mathematics and natural philosophy, and by several young men as tutors. Dr. Cossitt was a native of New Hampshire and was educated at Middlebury College, Vermont. He was a man of culture and a writer of merit. He remained at the head of Cumberland College as long as it remained under the care of the whole church.

The original college building was a substantial two-story brick structure, 60 by 22 feet. To this was added in 1832 another similar building, 70 by 40 feet. There was at that time also a dormitory for students. Professor Morrison had resigned in 1830, but his place had been supplied, and another regular professor had been added to the faculty, which in 1833[4] was composed as follows: Rev. F. R. Cossitt, president, mental and moral philosophy and belles-lettres; Rev. R.

[1] The American Almanac for 1833 gives the total expenses of a student under the system as $80 a year.

[2] Acts of 1827–28, pp. 21–27.

[3] A sketch of Dr. Cossitt is to be found in Collins's History of Kentucky, Vol. I, p. 435, where the name is incorrectly spelled Cassitt.

[4] From American Almanac for 1834.

Beard, ancient languages; Livingston Lindsay, mathematics and natural philosophy; Rev. A. Shelby, steward and superintendent of farm.

In order to carry out one of the special objects of the institution, instruction in theology was also given by President Cossitt and Professor Beard.

The college had early in its history a library of several hundred volumes and a respectable chemical and philosophical apparatus, and did much excellent educational work, particularly in furnishing its church with well-trained ministers. It had up to 1842 an annual average attendance of about 60 students, and its graduates up to that time numbered 52. Its manual-labor feature, although we are informed it was considered a great benefit in 1832,[1] had before long proved not suited to the ideas and habits of those who could be chiefly depended on to patronize the institution, and so was not a success, while much financial embarrassment had also arisen and a number of changes in the faculty had taken place.

The state of its affairs had become such as to cause the church as a whole to lose hope in its success under the conditions then existing at Princeton, and so the general assembly of 1842 gave up the institution as a general church enterprise and transferred its patronage to Cumberland University, then founded at Lebanon, Tenn., which place had offered considerable financial inducements and was considered in other respects a more desirable location than Princeton for a general church institution. Dr. Cossitt, who became the president of the new university, with all of the professors at Princeton but one, removed to Lebanon in February, 1843, and so old Cumberland College may be said to exist yet in the newer Cumberland University, still the leading educational institution of the Cumberland Presbyterian Church.

The college at Princeton, after having been abandoned by the church at large, was taken charge of by Green River Synod, and, with its manual labor department discarded, remained until 1858 a church enterprise. It was, however, during this period never able to become much more than a local high school, depending on tuition fees for a rather precarious existence, and was finally abandoned altogether by the church.

BIBLIOGRAPHY.

Collins's Sketches.
Collins's History.
Davidson's Presbyterian Church in Kentucky.
Barnard's American Journal.
The American Almanac.
Acts of the Legislature.
Higher Education in Tennessee, by L. S. Merriam, Ph. D.; Washington, 1893.

[1] Barnard's American Journal of Education, vol. 27, p. 335.

The facts obtainable in regard to the history of Shelby College, at one time somewhat prominent among the educational institutions of the State, can be stated in a comparatively few words.

The college was founded at Shelbyville in 1836,[1] and in 1841 took on the denominational feature characteristic of most of the colleges of the State by coming under the management of the Episcopal Church. It was controlled by that church for thirty years, although it seems not to have been supported by the denomination with very great unanimity.[2]

The college building was a handsome brick structure, 142 feet long by 70 feet wide, and its grounds embraced 18 acres. There was also a president's house in addition to the main building.

The president of the institution during most of its history was Rev. W. I. Waller, M. D., a prominent Episcopal clergyman. The Episcopal Seminary, formerly associated with Transylvania University during the presidency of Rev. B. O. Peers, seems to have been operated for a time in connection with the college, which during its existence educated many young men for business life and for the various professions.

BIBLIOGRAPHY.

Collins's Sketches.
Collins's History.
Acts of the Legislature.
Historical Sketches of Christ Church, Louisville, by Rev. James Craik; Louisville, 1862.

EMINENCE COLLEGE, EMINENCE.

Eminence College furnishes in its history a good example of what can be done by individual ability and enterprise in the field of education. It is also an excellent illustration of the result of all educational undertakings which depend solely upon personal initiative. The history of Eminence College is an epitome of a large part of the educational services of its president, W. S. Giltner, and when he severed his connection with it the institution ceased to exist.

The college grew out of a high school established at Eminence by a number of public-spirited citizens of the community, who in 1855 had organized themselves into a stock company and founded a school, which was opened in September, 1857, with Prof. S. G. Mullins as principal. The school had been regularly chartered in 1857, but continued only one year under its original management, as the not

[1] The college was given the right on February 16, 1837 (acts of 1836–37, p. 219), to raise $100,000 by lottery. We have no account as to how much was thus realized.

[2] Craik, in his Sketches of Christ Church, Louisville, page 106, says that the vestry of that church on August 10, 1846, recommended that the college be abandoned by the church.

uncommon mistake had been made by those interested of going beyond their means in erecting and equipping the commodious building of the institution, so the property had to be sold and was acquired by a new company with Prof. W. S. Giltner, a graduate of Bethany College, West Virginia, at its head.

Under the new order of things, Professor Giltner, who had already had several years' successful experience as an educator, was made, in 1858, the principal of the institution, whose patronage, chiefly through his personal efforts and ability, soon became large and well sustained. So, in the natural order of things, the high school soon blossomed out into a college, through an amendment to its charter secured in 1861. It also soon became practically a private enterprise through the acquisition of at least a large part of its stock by its president.

The institution had sent forth its first graduating class of seven members in 1860, from which date it continued in successful operation for about thirty-five years, during which its annual matriculation was comparatively large, having been quite good even during the civil war. Up to 1877 it had an attendance annually of from 126 to 204 students, and its graduating class each year numbered from 1 to 18. Its attendance declined considerably after 1877, but continued fairly good even down practically to its close. During its existence its matriculates, who were about equally divided between the sexes, represented as many as eleven States of the Union and one foreign country.

The original high school had been coeducational, and this feature was ingrafted upon the college, which claims to have been the first college in Kentucky[1] to advocate and adopt the policy of coeducation. Separate boarding departments and study halls were maintained for the two sexes, but the general educational privileges of the institution were shared equally by them. The college maintained a special course for girls who did not wish to take the longer and stronger course intended primarily for boys. In this course diplomas and not degrees were conferred. The more advanced course, which was taken by many of the girls with eminent success, led to the degrees of bachelor of arts and bachelor of science, and embraced the departments of ancient languages, mathematics, physics and chemistry, mental philosophy, biblical literature, and modern languages. To suit the needs of individual students, departments of music and art were inaugurated from the beginning, while in 1880 a commercial department was instituted, and in 1885 a normal department, intended especially to train teachers for the public schools of the State, was added. The institution had early in its history a fair amount of chemical and physical apparatus, a good mineralogical cabinet, and a moderate-sized reference library. The faculty of the college contained as a rule

[1] Sketch of Eminence College, page 3.

from seven to nine members, and throughout its history it maintained four regular academic professorships.

Eminence College never had any endowment, and its prosperity, at least during most of its history, was due entirely to the personal exertions of its president. That it performed efficient educational services is shown by the success achieved by its graduates, who numbered altogether, up to 1893, inclusive, 235, and were pointed to by the institution rather than "magnificent buildings and munificent endowments in proof of the hale and vigorous life"[1] prevailing there. Many of its alumni have taken an honored rank in the various learned professions, there being among them prominent teachers, editors, ministers, lawyers, and physicians.

The college was closed in February, 1895, principally because it had ceased to be a financial success, President Giltner determining at that time to retire from active participation in its management. Its property has since been used for private purposes. When Professor Giltner's forceful personality was withdrawn and no similar impetus was at hand, nothing was left upon which the perpetuity of the institution might be based. On the other hand, if its equipment had been owned and controlled by some permanent organization, as, for instance, a religious denomination, it would have been much more likely, independent of any question of endowment, to have had a continuous existence and to have perpetuated its educational usefulness, although its efficiency at any given time would, of course, have largely depended upon the one actually in charge of its executive affairs. In the history of such institutions as Eminence College lies a useful public lesson.

BIBLIOGRAPHY.

Biographical Encyclopedia of Kentucky. Historical Sketch of Eminence College, **Eminence,** 1876–77.

[1] Historical Sketch, page 8.

Chapter IX.

THE PUBLIC-SCHOOL SYSTEM.

EARLY IDEAS.

We have seen, in treating of the early university system, that the leaders of educational thought in Kentucky, especially Judge Wallace, early contemplated a system of popular elementary education, as the academy plan, doubtless in the mind of Judge Wallace, at least, had in view an extension of the system to include more elementary schools, which, as we have seen, came last in such a system, according to the ideas then prevalent in Virginia and Kentucky. It was probably with the object of later adding the more elementary schools that such advanced steps were taken in appropriating public land for educational purposes to the academies. We have observed, however, that the academy plan, even as far as it was carried out, was in advance of the public opinion of the day, absorbed as the people generally were in the engrossing pursuits of a pioneer agricultural community and scattered as they were in a wilderness of forests in which lurked a savage foe, ever to be watched, and thus having little time or opportunity to think of such questions.

Most of the leaders themselves also seem to have been occupied with the practical questions of the day or devoted such time as they could spare from these to the promotion of higher education in the denominational form that it had early taken in the State. The higher educational feature was then considered much the most important part of the system, and in its development the educational energy of the State was for a considerable time mainly engaged. So we see little or no public notice of popular education in the early years of the State's history and no mention is made of it in the messages of its early governors or in the first two constitutions of the State, adopted in 1792 and 1799, respectively.

One of the first public utterances, if not the first, on the subject is to be found in the message of Governor Gabriel Slaughter, of December 3, 1816, in which he advocated the establishment of a State school fund by taxing banks and other corporations and by setting aside for that purpose the dividends on the bank stocks held by the State and the income from all escheated lands, provided this could be done "without materially increasing the public burdens." Again, in his message of December 2, 1817, about half of which he devotes to this subject, he says:

> I beg leave again to bring into view the subject of education, one of the first importance that can engage our attention, whether we regard its influence on human happiness or the permanency of our republican system.

He then recommended that the State be divided into districts of 5 or 6 miles square, in which schools should be supported, in part if not entirely, by the State and should be free to all poor children, saying in connection:

> We have many good schools, but nothing short of carrying education to the neighborhood of every man in the State can satisfy the just claims of the people or fulfill the duty of the Government.

In his message of December 8, 1818, he does not urge further his educational system, because the previous legislature seemed to "have thought it better to accommodate the country with a number of banks than with good schools," although he said:

> We neither have free schools for the education of the poor, nor colleges, nor universities sufficiently endowed to vie with the literary institutions of our sister States.

Again, however, on December 7, 1819, he advocated the setting apart for educational purposes of the public lands recently acquired by the State from the Indians and all other public lands then held by the State, to which were to be added all fines and forfeitures, together with all escheated lands and all other sources of revenue not actually needed for the expenses of the State.

These ideas were certainly quite liberal for the time and surroundings and were doubtless considerably in advance of public opinion, as they seem to have awakened no adequate response on the part of the legislature. They had, however, one deficiency not thoroughly remedied in Kentucky until comparatively recent years—the idea that the public schools were to be primarily not for the masses, but for the poor, thus giving to them an idea of charity and a tone of caste which necessarily resulted in their inefficiency, especially when coupled, as it was for a considerable time, with meager revenues.

THE FIRST SYSTEM, WITH THE STEPS PREPARATORY TO ITS INAUGURATION.

The recognized failure of the State academies by about 1820 began to call the attention of the State authorities and the people generally to the need of some other means of public education. So we find Governor John Adair, in his message of October 16, 1821, again urging upon the legislature the importance of a public-school system, as he had previously urged upon them the liberal support of Transylvania and the academies. He says of popular education:

> It is necessary to the purity and permanency of our civil and political institutions and to our relative dignity and influence in the council of the nation that it should succeed.

The legislature of this session thought somewhat in like manner, and after having, in conjunction with a similar action by Maryland and other States, instructed the representatives of Kentucky in Congress to apply for public land for educational purposes at the hands of the General Government, took the first step in establishing a public-school system for the State by setting aside by an act approved December 18, 1821, one-half the net profits of the stock held by the State in the Bank of the Commonwealth for a permanent public-school fund.

It also took an additional step at the same time in appointing an able commission, composed of William T. Barry, J. R. Witherspoon, D. R. Murray, and John Pope, to collect information and prepare and report a system of common schools suited to the peculiar circumstances and habits of the people, which report was to be presented to the legislature of 1822. This commission sought to ascertain the actual condition of the schools of Kentucky, and also inquired in regard to the success of the systems of other States, especially those of Massachusetts, Connecticut, and New York. In the course of its investigations it conducted a correspondence with John Adams, Thomas Jefferson, James Madison, Robert Y. Hayne, and other prominent public men in regard to pubic schools in their respective States.

Its report made in the latter part of 1822[1] was an able one and favored the State fostering Transylvania University and the academies as training schools for teachers, but advocated a public-school system, supported by State appropriations, augmented by local taxation, as in the New York system. The schools were to be for the public generally, and not for the poor only, and were to be made free as far as possible. The commission believed such a system practicable in Kentucky, although the State was then sparsely settled and the existence of slavery was likely to be somewhat of a hindrance. It was also recommended that there should be a State superintendent of schools, who might also at the same time hold some other State office, as that of secretary of state, and who should act in conjunction with the local judicial officers in inaugurating and carrying on the system.

Barnard[2] speaks of the report of this commission as "one of the

[1] The first report of the commission was issued November 30, 1822, and an additional one on December 2 following, to which the two additional names of David White and William P. Roper are attached.

[2] American Journal of Education, vol. 16, p. 353. The report of the commission was drawn up by Amos Kendall, subsequently Postmaster-General of the United States, then a teacher in Frankfort.

most valuable documents upon common-school education that had at that time appeared.") The only thing that seems to have been done in regard to it by the legislature of the time is that the committee on education highly approved of it, and it was ordered to be printed for general distribution. This was done soon afterwards, the letters of Adams, Madison, Jefferson, and Hayne being appended, and through its general circulation in the State it doubtless later had a favorable influence on public opinion.

The income from the bank stock set aside by the act of 1821 was at the time about $60,000 per annum, but this seems neither to have been applied to public education nor to have been properly husbanded. Rev. B. O. Peers tells[1] us that in 1829 it only amounted to a total of $150,000, and Barnard says[2] that in 1833 there was only about $141,000 of it remaining. Most of it had gone where the rest of it then threatened to go—to defray deficiencies in the general revenues of the State.

Meanwhile several other preparatory steps looking toward the establishment of a general system were taken. By an act approved December 21, 1825,[3] any five persons were given the right to associate themselves together and hold property for school purposes, trustees for its management being appointed by the county court. Governor Desha, in his message of December 4, 1826, recommended that in addition to the fund already created the remainder of the bank stock held by the State, the proceeds from vacant lands, and certain other funds should be invested in building turnpikes, the dividends from which were "to be forever sacredly devoted to the interest of education." This recommendation does not seem to have been adopted by the legislature; but had it been it is not probable that much income would ever have been realized from this source, as Kentucky seems never to have received much return financially from her investments in internal improvements. The preoccupation of the State in these improvements and the absorption of its revenues in carrying them out is one great reason why no more attention was paid to public education at this time.

On January 29, 1829, probably as an outcome, partially at least, of the report of the commission of 1822, the committee of the legislature on education called upon Rev. Alva Woods, D. D., then president of Transylvania University, and Rev. B. O. Peers, already a prominent advocate and exponent of advanced educational ideas and methods, for an expression of their opinion on the subject of common schools.

The report of this committee, published in January, 1830, had appended to it a letter from Rev. Mr. Peers, purporting, as far as possible, to give "the collective experience of the nation." It contained an able examination of the systems of the Middle and New England

[1] Letter of 1829.
[2] American Journal of Education, vol. 27, p. 335.
[3] Acts of 1825-26, p. 118.

States in comparison with those of Ohio and Virginia, and again, as in the case of the commission of 1822, indorsed the New York plan of having the State appropriation conditioned upon the levying of at least an equal amount by local taxation, especially in a State where public opinion was laggard. It also showed the necessity of legislative patronage and control as well as of an enlightened public sentiment for the success of any system.

Mr. Peers was also in advance of the country generally at the time in advocating the training of teachers by the State through the establishment of a State normal school. His letter and his subsequent agitation of the subject, by public discussion and through the press, awakened the public mind on the question. He was thus largely instrumental in arousing the people, and by his influence, in various ways, both before, during, and after his presidency of Transylvania University, may be considered, perhaps more than any other one man, the father of the public-school system of Kentucky.

He took a prominent part in various State educational meetings held at this period, and used other powerful means in influencing public opinion. The first of these was the State educational convention, which met in Lexington on November 7, 1833, and formed plans upon which a State common-school society was established at Frankfort in January of the following year. This society memorialized the legislature in behalf of common schools and a normal school, and took other steps to bring the matter of public education to the attention of the people of the State generally. Governor Breathitt, James T. Morehead, Rev. John C. Young, Rev. H. B. Bascom, Thomas Marshall, and Daniel Breck were, among others, prominently associated with Mr. Peers in these conventions.

At the same time that Mr. Peers had been called on by the legislature for his report on common schools the Representatives of the State in Congress had been again requested to ask for an appropriation of public land for the aid of schools, but before anything was received from the General Government an act was passed by the State legislature on January 29, 1830,[1] which bears the rather grandiloquent title of "An act to encourage the general diffusion of education in this Commonwealth by the establishment of a uniform system of public schools." This act provided that the county courts might lay off the various counties into school districts, which were to be under the management of three commissioners elected by the district and empowered to collect a poll tax of not over 50 cents per capita for school purposes, while a tax of not over 6¼ cents on the $100 might be voted by the district for the same object. No material result appears to have come from this act, as local sentiment was not in most cases sufficient even to inaugurate the system, much less to vote the tax needed for its support.

[1] Acts of 1829-30, pp. 272-281.

Not long after this the petitions of the States to Congress led to a tangible result, as that body, by an act approved June 23, 1836, determined to distribute the surplus then in the Treasury among the various States. This distribution was, partially at least, in lieu of the grants of public land requested, and was to begin on the 1st of the following January. Soon after the reception of the first installment, Kentucky, which had asked for the grant for educational purposes, established the foundation of its present public-school fund by an act (February 23, 1837) which declared that $1,000,000 of the amount received from the General Government should be "set apart and forever dedicated to the founding and sustaining a general system of public instruction."

As the amount received from the United States did not turn out to be as large as had been expected, an act of February 16, 1838,[1] reduced the amount previously set apart from $1,000,000 to $850,000, which was declared to be "dedicated and forever set apart to the purposes of education." By this same act what is really the first public-school system of the State was organized. The outlines of this system were as follows:

(1) The fund created by the act was to be distributed to the counties in proportion to the number of children of school age.

(2) A board of education was established, consisting of the secretary of state, the attorney-general, and a new officer—the superintendent of common schools, who was to be appointed by the governor and was chairman of the board, his duties being principally to prepare reports and apportion the school money.

(3) The State was to be divided into districts, each containing not more than 50 nor less than 30 children of from 5 to 16 years of age.

(4) Each district was allowed to tax itself to an amount equal to what it received from the State fund.

(5) Five commissioners were to be appointed in each county whose principal duties were to report the number of schools, the number of children of school age, and to distribute the money to these schools.

(6) Five trustees were to be elected by each district who were to build schoolhouses and organize schools, being, however, only empowered to levy a poll tax of 50 cents per capita for the former purpose.

To Judge William F. Bullock, of Louisville, is to be given a large part of the credit for the passage of this law, which was certainly not enacted before it was needed, as we are told that there were in Kentucky at the time 175,000 children of school age, about half of whom were without any previous opportunity for a common-school education, and one-third of the adult population of the State at the time were unable to write their own names.

The system was based largely upon Mr. Peers's ideas, although considerably below these, and had some excellent features. It was, how-

[1] Acts of 1837-38, pp. 274-283.

ever, defective in many ways, as in not giving the districts sufficient inducement and power to lay local taxes; not making adequate provision for supplying schoolhouses, inspecting schools, and securing the proper qualifications of teachers, but especially in making the superintendent a minor State officer and not giving to him the proper powers and privileges. The law was, moreover, cumbersome in many ways, and, most of all, was not yet backed by a proper state of public opinion, as was soon to be shown. It had great difficulties to contend with, due to the population of the State being scattered and its system of local government being somewhat defective, but its greatest obstacle was public indifference and lack of information in regard to the law and its operations. There was, on the part of the people at large, the lack of a proper standard of education and of a consequent demand that the law be properly enforced.

THE SOLIDIFICATION OF PUBLIC OPINION AND THE IMPROVEMENT OF THE ORGANIZATION OF THE SYSTEM.

As has been noted, the law of 1838 established in form a fairly good public-school system for the time, but we shall see that, owing to a lack of appreciation on the part of the people, and especially of the public men of the State, it was practically entirely inoperative for a dozen or more years. This time was not, however, wholly lost, as during the period, through the efficient labors of the superintendents and other friends of the system, public opinion, already somewhat educated, became more strongly solidified in its favor and made it possible for its organization to be so improved as to become really effective.

The first superintendent under the new system was Rev. Joseph J. Bullock, D. D., who went into office about February 28, 1838, and labored earnestly and faithfully to make it a success, but for some time the school system had only a nominal existence, for as early as 1840 the State refused to pay the interest on the school fund, owing to her system of public improvements having depleted her treasury and impaired her credit. Up to 1843 only $2,504 of this interest had been paid, while $116,375 remained unpaid, and by a legislative act of February 10, 1845, all the State school bonds were actually destroyed.

Superintendent Bullock had been succeeded in 1839 by Rev. H. H. Kavanaugh, D. D., who served until 1840. The office was held during the next seven years by B. B. Smith, D. D., who served from 1840 to 1842; George W. Brush, who served from 1842 to 1843, and R. T. Dillard, D. D., who served from 1843 to 1847.[1] These were able and conscientious superintendents, but, owing to the difficulties already noticed, combined with crude and unsympathetic legislation, the

[1] B. B. Sayre, A. M., was appointed to fill a vacancy on March 1, 1842, but soon declined. Rev. Robert Davidson, D. D., was appointed on April 26, 1842, but declined on May 15, 1842.

school system made little apparent progress, although public sentiment was somewhat cultivated in its behalf, as shown by the support given it in the next administration.

Rev. Robert J. Breckinridge, D. D., was appointed superintendent on September 14, 1847, and at once took up the cause of popular education with enthusiasm. It was largely through his indefatigable efforts that the next important steps in the progress of the system were made. He first secured, in 1847 and 1848, the issue of a new bond for the State school fund, which included all the arrears of interest due and made the bond a total of $1,225,768. Also, by an act of February 26, 1849, he secured the submission to popular vote of the proposition to levy a tax of 2 cents on each $100 of property in the State to furnish additional revenue for the school system. This proposition was ratified by the people at the polls in the following August by a large majority.

Dr. Breckinridge also, by the help of such members of the constitutional convention of 1849 as Larkin J. Proctor, John D. Taylor, William K. Bowling, Ira Root, Thomas J. Hood, Charles A. Wickliffe, and Thomas J. Lisle, succeeded in making another great gain for the system by having the school fund declared inviolable for the purposes of common-school education by the new constitution and also by having the superintendent of public instruction made a regular State officer, to be elected by the people. Article XI, section 1, of this constitution, proclaimed on June 11, 1850, declares that the former common-school fund, "together with any sum which may hereafter be raised in the State, by taxation or otherwise, for purposes of education, shall be held inviolable for the purpose of sustaining a system of common schools."

Another advance in progress was accomplished by Dr. Breckinridge when, in March, 1850, against the strenuous opposition of Governor Helm, he succeeded by legislative action in having the school fund considered a part of the regular State debt, the interest of which was payable out of the sinking fund and was one of the first charges against the State revenues. The year 1850, in which the last of these important gains was secured, may be said to be the one in which the public-school system of Kentucky was first regularly organized. Dr. Breckinridge's services in its behalf were certainly very great, and he may as truly be called the father of the actual system as Rev. B. O. Peers is of the public opinion which called it into existence.

Dr. Breckinridge's labors were indorsed in 1851 by his being elected superintendent by the vote of the people, and during the remainder of his administration he endeavored especially to bring the people as far as possible to a proper appreciation of their public schools. Like Mr. Peers, he made use of educational conventions for the purpose of bringing public opinion into line with his educational policy. A large convention of the friends of the public-school system met under his leadership at Frankfort in November, 1851, and another in 1852, which, by their discussion, did much for the cause throughout the State.

Dr. Breckinridge resigned his position as superintendent on October 22, 1853, to accept a chair in Danville Theological Seminary, of which he was one of the principal founders, and whose work he considered as of a higher character of usefulness. His services as superintendent may, in general, after the manner of his last report, be summarized as follows: He had had restored and augmented a large school fund, which had been made sacred to its object by the State constitution; had inaugurated a complete system of schools in their lowest stage; had had hundreds of schoolhouses erected, and had aroused a deep public interest in favor of education throughout the State. His predecessors had done much to create a healthy public sentiment, and upon the foundation they had laid he had built wisely and well.

In 1853 the common-school system was in operation in every county in this State, but its workings were crude and the quality of education it furnished poor, as the salaries it offered could only call into its service an inferior grade of teachers. The State educational fund at that time consisted (1) of the bond of the State, amounting to $1,326,-770; (2) of $73,500 in stock of the Bank of Kentucky, purchased by the superintendent in 1839; (3) of the 2 cents ad valorem tax of 1849, which had since been supplemented by some other small taxes. The income from the fund was about $80,000 a year, and that from taxes in 1852 $133,680. The combined revenue from all sources only furnished a per capita allowance of 60 cents to each child of school age in the State. How much the system lacked of being in anything like complete operation was shown by the fact that of the 207,210 school children reported as being in the State, only 76,429 were in school.

THE PROVISION OF AN ADEQUATE STATE REVENUE.

Dr. Breckinridge's able and persistent efforts had converted the public-school system from what had been largely a mere form into an organization which possessed the elements of vitality. The system, however, still lacked two things essential to its highest efficiency. One was the passage of laws needed to perfect the details of its organization and adapt it to the special educational wants of the people of the State; the other was to provide for it an adequate general revenue.

The State common-school laws had been revised in 1852, contrary to the desires of Dr. Breckinridge in a number of respects, but, although the important principle that all schools should be free was introduced, no material advance was made in organization and none was made for a number of years. The educational energy of the State for the next seventeen years was mainly absorbed in supplying the second of the above-mentioned needs, the lack of an adequate revenue, which, however, carried along with its most progressive step in 1869 a considerable improvement also in the legal status of the school system.

Dr. Breckinridge's successor as superintendent was John D. Mathews, D. D., who served from 1853 to 1859, having been appointed to fill out his predecessor's term and then elected by the people, in August, 1855. During his term of office, by an act approved March 10, 1854, and ratified by a very large popular majority in August, 1855, the ad valorem school tax was raised from 2 cents to 5 cents. We have already recounted in another connection how in 1856 Transylvania University was converted into a State normal school, as a much-needed head of the State public-school system, an experiment which was at that time a failure.

Robert Richardson, A. M., was superintendent from 1859 to 1863, and Daniel Stevenson, D. D., from 1863 to 1867. During this period, in which no material organic changes were made in the school system, it was ably and faithfully administered and made some progress, at least in public regard, if not otherwise. Its operations during part of the time were considerably disturbed by the civil war. The loss of property due to the overthrow of slavery had also caused its income to decrease, the per capita in 1867 being 72 cents, whereas in 1863 it had been $1.10. Dr. Stevenson said of the system, just before the close of his administration, that its condition was very much what it had been twenty-five years before.

In 1867, after peace and comparative order had been restored, a new era of progress began, under Supt. Z. F. Smith, who had been elected in August of that year, and served until 1871. Mr. Smith began his administration with a progressive programme of action, which he submitted to the people in a special report, accompanying Governor Stevenson's message of December 2, 1867. His ideas were based on having the means of the system increased and its organization improved.

The main features of his plan were as follows: To have the ad valorem State tax increased from 5 to 20 cents on the $100, to which a poll tax of from $1 to $2 per capita was to be added; to grant to districts the right to vote an additional tax of 30 cents on the $100, in order to provide schoolhouses, lengthen the school term, and pay better salaries to teachers. Also to have the school law so reconstructed as to secure improved schoolhouses, uniformity of text-books, better qualifications of teachers, greater power for local school officers, and other desirable results. His programme also included more advanced ideas, such as the establishment of a State normal school, the formation of teachers' institutes and associations, and other progressive features, many of which have since been adopted.

His proposition to submit the question of an additional tax of 15 cents to the people was passed by the legislature on January 22, 1869, and was approved by the people in the succeeding August. Soon after, a greatly improved school law was adopted, although it was not yet what Superintendent Smith would have had it, as it contained many objectionable features of the old law. When this new law went fully into effect, on July 1, 1870, the public-school system of Kentucky may be said to have entered upon a fourth era of progress.

Within a year a great and vital impetus was imparted to it, as may be clearly seen by a comparison of the statistics of the school years 1868–69 and 1870–71, the last full year under the old system and the first one under the new. The number of schools taught had increased from 4,477 to 5,177; the amount expended for schools from $275,113.61 to $779,672, the latter making a per capita allowance of $2 per scholar instead of 73 cents, as under the former, although there had been an increase from 376,868 children of school age to 389,836.

Besides these organic advances during Superintendent Smith's administration, the discussion of the cause in the legislature and the arguments advanced in its behalf by the superintendent and other zealous friends, through the State press and otherwise, did much to awaken in its behalf a deeper and more widespread public interest than formerly, and one which would later demand a more liberal and efficient system. The work accomplished during the administration may be summed up in general, according to Collins, as follows: The amount of State funds distributed had been greatly enlarged; the number of schools taught increased, as well as the average attendance on these; and the character of the teachers, and consequently the quality of education given, greatly improved.

LATER DEVELOPMENT.

The condition of the public-school system of Kentucky for the last twenty-eight years has been one of uniform and steady progress in almost all directions, particularly in the matter of the perfection of its organization and the continued growth of a healthy public sentiment, especially locally. Some notice will now be taken of the various progressive steps that have occurred under the different superintendents' administrations.

In 1871 H. A. M. Henderson, D. D., LL. D., succeeded Mr. Smith as superintendent and served efficiently for eight years, being indorsed by the people, by reelection, in 1875. Superintendent Henderson did much toward perfecting the statistical blanks of his department, in more completely organizing institutes, first inaugurated in the previous administration and very efficient in improving the qualifications of teachers, and also in remodeling the school law to suit the wants of the State. The general statutes of 1873 made important and valuable changes in this law, especially by reintroducing the plan of district taxation as supplementary to the income derived from the State.

In 1879 J. D. Pickett, LL. D., was elected superintendent. He served continuously until 1891, during which time several laws of importance were passed. By an act approved April 24, 1882,[1] the per capita for white and colored schools was equalized and a vote on an additional 2 cents ad valorem tax authorized, while at the same time the school fund secured its just proportion of the tax on railroads and other corporations. The additional 2 cents tax was ratified at the polls in the following August.

An act of May 12, 1884, secured quite an advance for the system by substituting county superintendents, elected by the people, instead of the previous county commissioners appointed by the county courts. It also improved the course of study, made better arrangements for building schoolhouses, reduced the size of districts, and provided for State as well as county institutes. It was amended on May 17, 1886, in such a way as to improve the qualifications of teachers. Several steps of advancement outside of these laws are noticeable during Superintendent Pickett's administration, such as the lengthening of the school term, the improvement in average attendance, the increase in the amount of local taxation levied, and the establishment of graded schools in a number of towns and cities.

E. P. Thompson became superintendent by popular election in 1891. The new State constitution adopted in this year, besides putting the former school fund, and its additions as well, on the old basis of being inviolably devoted to public schools, added, by section 188, to the previous school fund the direct-tax fund of $606,641.03, which had been returned to the State by a Congressional act of March 2, 1891. A new State bond, bearing 6 per cent interest, was issued for this amount on March 12, 1892. On July 6, 1893, the school laws were systematized and codified in conformity with the new constitution. Superintendent Thompson says[2] of this law: "Under its express and constructive provisions an organization is assured that will be not only symmetrical and consistent, but adapted to present needs and promotive of normal development." The principal new features of this law were, that it required all schools to be graded and to be at least five months in length each year; that it made county teachers' associations obligatory, and provided for county teachers' libraries.

The administration of Superintendent Thompson is marked especially by the establishment of well-organized graded schools in almost all the populous communities in the State. The average school attendance also considerably increased during his term of office, while

[1] Schools for the colored population of the State were first provided by the act of February 14, 1866, which appropriated for their schools all the taxes paid by the race in the State except enough to support their paupers. By an act of March 9, 1867, a poll tax for school purposes was laid on all males of the race over 18 years of age. By an act of February 23, 1874, all fines and forfeitures paid by the race were added to their school fund and all moneys from the sale of public lands set apart by the United States until the per capita of the race should equal that of the whites.

[2] Report of 1893-94, p. viii.

there was a considerable enlargement of local taxation supplementary to the State fund, already augmented by the direct-tax fund. These additional means made it possible for the average wages of teachers to be advanced somewhat, and consequently their qualifications were to some degree improved.

In January, 1896,[1] Superintendent Thompson was succeeded by W. J. Davidson, who is the present official head of the State public school system. The principal event of Superintendent Davidson's administration has been the passage by the legislature of a compulsory school law, approved March 28, 1896, which requires at least eight weeks' continuous attendance at school annually on the part of all children between 7 and 14 years of age. Statistics seem to indicate that this act has, during the past two years, considerably increased the average attendance of the public schools of the State.

The progress of the public school system of Kentucky in recent years may be readily seen by a comparison, in a general way, of the school statistics for the years 1870-71 and 1895-96. The number of schools taught had during this time increased from 5,177 to 8,143, and the amount expended for schools from $779,672 to $3,028,432.[2] This gave a considerably larger per capita allowance, although the number of children of school age had increased from 389,836 to 736,109.

The sources of State school revenue in 1897 were the following: (1) The interest at 6 per cent on the permanent school fund, composed of the fund of $1,327,000,[3] and the bank stock of $73,500 held by the State in 1870, and the direct-tax fund of $606,641.08 of 1891;[4] (2) of a State tax of 22 cents on each $100; (3) of forty-four eighty-fifths of all taxes on railroads, banks, and some other corporations.

The organization of the system, during the period referred to above, has also been greatly improved in almost all respects, especially in the raising in dignity and importance of the office of State superintendent and the conferring of greater powers upon its incumbent. The greatest weakness of the organization at present is the local trustee system, which is of such a character that, at least until public sentiment is greatly improved, it does not guarantee the appointment of efficient teachers for the schools, especially in the country districts. Local public opinion has much improved of late years, as is shown by the large increase during that time of local taxation for school purposes. The further enlargement of local taxation is, however, the one thing needful, in a financial way, for a larger general success of

[1] Under the State constitution of 1891 the superintendent goes into office in January, instead of in the summer, as before. This made Superintendent Thompson's term a little more than four years.

[2] Report of the Commissioner of Education for 1896-97, p. LXIX. Of this amount $1,079,254 came from local taxation and $1,804,360 from State taxation.

[3] Fixed at this amount by act of March 21, 1870.

[4] There is also a surplus fund going to the various counties of $381,986.08.

the public schools of the State. Kentucky already grants as a State one of the largest per capita allowances to her public schools of any State in the Union, and further increase of State taxation is, by those who are well informed on the subject, not thought to be desirable. An improvement in the local support of schools, which will cultivate the proper public interest, is, however, much needed in the State.

According to the recommendations of Mr. Davidson and other recent superintendents, other improvements are needed to bring the system up to what it should be and to make it compare to the best advantage with the more advanced systems of other States. Among these may be mentioned the lengthening of the required school year to at least seven months, the establishment of not less than two additional training schools for teachers, in addition to the one already connected with the State college, and also the introduction of better methods of employing teachers. This last object would be largely brought about by a proper change in the method of selecting local school trustees.[1] It can probably be fairly said that few, if any, of the States of the Union have, in recent years, made more rapid or better progress than Kentucky in the organization of an efficient system of public schools. Her school system is doubtless much less advanced than that of a number of the States more favorably situated in various ways, but its condition for the future is one of great hopefulness.

STATE ELEEMOSYNARY INSTITUTIONS.

The public-school system of Kentucky in its legal organization includes not only the public schools proper, but also the Agricultural and Mechanical College, the State Normal School, and the various institutions intended for the education of the children of the State who are defective in such a manner as not to be able to attend with advantage its public schools. Kentucky has provided well for these classes by the establishment of institutions for the education of the blind, of deaf-mutes, and of feeble-minded children. The other parts of the system having been described, a general idea will here be given of these institutions, in order to give a complete view of the State's educational policy.

The Kentucky Institution for the Education of Deaf-Mutes was established in 1823 and is located at Danville. It is open to all children who are deaf, between 8 and 18 years of age, to whom it gives a public-school education, in addition to which the boys are given manual-labor training and the girls are taught the domestic arts, all being required to labor two hours and a half each day. A department for colored children was added to the school in 1885. The institution

[1] An improvement in this regard was provided by the legislature of 1898 by having the trustees elected after the schools begin, thereby preventing to some extent the attempt of prospective teachers to influence their election.

uses the combined oral and manual methods of instruction. Augustus Rogers is the present superintendent.

The Kentucky Institution for the Education of the Blind was founded in 1842 and is located in Louisville. It has a fine main building, with accommodations for 100 pupils, used for white children, and a separate building for colored children, which will accommodate 25. Both buildings are splendidly located in a beautiful park of 25 acres. The school is under the charge of a board of nine citizens of Jefferson County, appointed by the governor. It receives all children between 6 and 18 years of age who can not see well enough to study in the public schools. To these it aims to furnish a good grammar-school education, with special instruction to all in manual training and domestic economy, and a good musical education to those who are capable of taking it. The present superintendent is B. B. Huntoon.

The Kentucky institution for the training and education of feeble-minded children is situated near Frankfort, and was organized in 1860. Its grounds contain 95 acres of good blue-grass land. The institution receives children between 6 and 18 years of age who are so defective as not to be able to pursue with success the educational methods ordinarily used in the public schools, and yet are capable of receiving some mental training. To these it imparts such elementary instruction as they are able to receive, while at the same time teaching them the rudiments of some useful trade. The school has been particularly unfortunate in the way of fires. The first building, a frame one, was burned about 1867. It was replaced by a handsome brick structure, which was burned in 1888. A new brick building which was then erected was also destroyed by fire on September 1, 1896. The present building, which is the best proportioned and most convenient of all, was occupied on January 1, 1898. This school, as well as all the other eleemosynary educational institutions of the State, requires the students attending it to pay a moderate charge for their education, as far as they are able. Dr. J. P. Huff is its superintendent.

BIBLIOGRAPHY.

Report of the commissioners of 1822; reports of various legislative committees on education, especially that of the committee on education of the house of representatives of 1829, second edition, Frankfort, 1830; the Common-school Assistant, 5 volumes, Albany, 1836-1840; messages of governors; acts of the legislature; reports of the State superintendent of education; inaugural address of president Green, of Transylvania University; Henderson's centennial exhibit; articles by Colonel Durrett in the Courier-Journal of January, 1881; articles by T. M. Goodknight in the Southern School of 1893-94; Collins's sketches; Butler's, Collins's, Shaler's, and Smith's histories; Biographical Encyclopedia of Kentucky; the Presbyterian Encyclopedia; the American Journal of Education; the American Annals of Education; Barnard's American Journal of Education; Niles's Register; the American Almanac.

PUBLIC-SCHOOL SYSTEM OF LOUISVILLE.

The development of a system of schools in the city of Louisville has been quite progressive, having been, as a rule, quite in advance of the educational policy of Kentucky and even, in some particulars, of the country at large. A sketch of it will therefore be historically valuable as well as interesting, and is accordingly given in this connection. Butler says,[1] in speaking of the little Kentucky had done for public elementary education in 1834, "To this remark the city of Louisville presents a proud exception and a model for the rest of the State."

We have already, in tracing the history of Jefferson Seminary, noticed that at the founding of that institution in 1816 there were in Louisville a number of schools of the "Old-field" type, for which the new seminary was to be a finishing school. None of these schools were, however, free, as tuition was charged in all of them, the usual rate being $2.50 a quarter.

The foundation of the present public-school system of Louisville is to be found in a provision of section 12, article 11, of its first city charter, granted on February 13, 1828, which says:

> The mayor and councilmen shall have power and authority to establish one or more free schools in each ward of said city, and may secure donations of real and personal estate to erect the necessary buildings and to provide the necessary means for their maintenance, and may supply the funds from time to time by a tax on the ward or wards where such school or schools shall be established.

This provision was somewhat deficient, especially in providing no funds for building purposes, but was in advance of any action yet taken by the State and even, as we shall see, somewhat of public opinion in the city at the time.

On April 24, 1829, the city council, upon the previous recommendation of John C. Bucklin, the first mayor of the city, "that steps be taken looking to the adoption of some well-digested system for establishing a permanent free school," passed an ordinance establishing a public school, on the Lancastrian or monitorial plan, to be free to all white children between 6 and 14 years of age. This school was to be managed by a board of six trustees, appointed each year by the mayor and city council.

Soon afterwards the trustees elected Mann Butler, then at the head of Jefferson Seminary, as the principal of the proposed school, and appropriated $150 for him to go east to examine the Lancastrian system, then in use in New York, Boston, and other cities. He returned in August heartily in favor of the system, which was first put in operation in the upper story of the old Baptist Church, on the southwest corner of Green and Fifth streets, where the first public school in Louisville and in Kentucky was opened on August 17, 1829, under

[1] History of Kentucky, p. 188.

Mr. Butler, with Edward Baker as assistant. The principal's salary was $750 annually; that of the assistant, $400.

This school was free the first year, the city appropriating $2,050 for its support. Public opinion, however, does not seem to have supported the granting of this appropriation, and in the second year tuition fees were charged. These were retained for a number of years, but were always moderate in amount. Pupils soon crowded into the new school, and before the end of its first year many had to be turned away for want of room. A report of a committee of the city council, made through its chairman, James Guthrie, on November 20, 1829, says there were then 257 pupils enrolled, of whom 150 were reading under monitors and 75 without, while 30 were learning their alphabet, the average daily attendance being 180.

Meanwhile, in August, 1829, a committee of the city council had purchased a lot on the southwest corner of Walnut and Fifth streets and begun the erection of a building for the school, which was occupied the following year, and had cost, including the lot, about $10,000, appropriated, it seems, from the city treasury. It was constructed of brick; had an imposing front of 40 feet, and a depth of 94 feet; was three stories in height, and was designed to accommodate 750 pupils. A city ordinance of August 20, 1830, divided the school into a primary, a female, and a grammar school department, each under a principal, the first two of whom were to receive $600 each annually and the last $700. At the same time the law instituted a system of tuition fees, which were made $1 per quarter in the primary department and $1.50 in each of the others, the trustees having the power to remit these fees, in part or in whole, whenever in their judgment the pupils were not able to pay them. Monitors were to be used as assistant teachers.

The school was opened in the new building on the first Monday in September, 1830, Mann Butler being principal of the grammar school, Rev. Daniel Banks of the female department, and Alexander Ewell of the primary, all ripe scholars. During this year there were 380 pupils in attendance. The teachers certainly earned their money, for they were required to teach from six to eight hours a day for eleven months of the year. The course was intended to give only an ordinary English education, although it included for a time considerable high-school work. The school had in 1832[1] $200 in apparatus, and its total annual cost to the city at that time was $5,070, $2,400 of which was paid by tuition fees. It had then 400 pupils in attendance.

The city received nothing from the State public-school fund until 1840, but by a legislative act of January 29, 1830, had been authorized to appropriate to her public schools all escheats of property in the city and all fines and forfeitures in the Jefferson circuit court and the courts held in the city by the mayor and by justices of the

[1] Louisville Directory for 1832, page 138, article by Mann Butler.

peace. We are not informed as to what income was received from these sources, but it was probably not large. We have seen that Jefferson Seminary was acquired by the city in 1830, and that it was soon made a high school, under the name of Louisville College. This gave the city quite a complete school system, composed of primary, grammar school, and high school departments.

Mann Butler remained in charge of the grammar-school department until 1834, when he resigned to accept a professorship in Transylvania University. In November of that year a remarkable step for the time was taken in establishing a night school for apprentices especially. The sessions of this school were to last four months, and its tuition fees were very small. It had, the first session, 2 teachers and 22 pupils, and the second session 1 teacher and 24 pupils. Barnard tells[1] us that, in connection with these schools, a school agent was appointed, whose duty it was to visit all the city schools quarterly and report on their condition. His yearly salary was $400. We see here one of the chief functions of a modern city superintendent. The records of the city school board of Louisville show that the duties of this school agent were soon enlarged, so as to be practically identical with those of the city superintendent of to-day.

Barnard calls[2] Rev. James Freeman Clark, appointed school agent by the mayor and city council on May 27, 1839, the first city superintendent of schools in America, but the records of the school board, then called the "board of visitors," show that as early, at least, as 1838 Samuel Dickinson had been appointed as their agent, with all the functions subsequently exercised by Rev. Mr. Clark. The title superintendent was not regularly applied to this agent until 1847, but the duties of the latter had undoubtedly been identical with those of the former for a number of years. Louisville is thus, according to Barnard, to be credited with having the first city superintendent of schools in the country, as well as establishing the first night schools.

Considerable was done between 1830 and 1840 in the way of enlarging the field of education in the city, as additional schools were established, some in buildings erected for them, others in rented buildings, so that by 1840 there were, besides the Louisville College, 7 primary schools, 6 grammar schools, and 1 night school, with an aggregate attendance of 1,287 and an average attendance of 948. The salary of the principal of the main grammar school had by this time been raised to $900, and that of the school agent to $800. The city received this year its first pro rata from the State fund, amounting to $831.20.

On May 27, 1840, an important ordinance was passed by the city council, which declared in its first section:

> That from and after the 1st of September next the monitorial system of instruction and all charges for tuition fees in the city schools be, and they are hereby, abolished.

[1] American Journal of Education, vol. 19, p. 537. [2] Ibid., vol. 24, pp. 253-255.

This made the whole city school system free, except Louisville College, which still charged tuition.

From 1840 to 1850 there was no advance in the free-school idea, except that an arrangement was made, about 1845, to supply poor children with books when necessary, but new schools were added to those already existing under the new method, until, in 1845, there were 5 grammar schools and 15 primary schools, with an aggregate attendance of 1,750, and an average attendance of 1,375; and in 1850 there were 5 grammar and 18 primary schools, which received for their support $3,850.80 from the State and $12,651.73 from the city and had on their rolls the names of 4,303 pupils. There were, in 1850, 43 teachers and assistants, who received salaries aggregating $16,050, and the value of the city school property at that time was $33,721.85. The city then had 45,000 inhabitants and was divided into eight wards.

The closing words of the fifth section of Article X of the second city charter, adopted March 24, 1851, were as follows:

> No fees for tuition shall ever be charged in said academical department of said university, in said high school for females, or in said public schools of Louisville.[1]

This charter placed the property of the public schools and their management in charge of a board of trustees, composed of two members from each ward of the city, elected by the people of the ward. It declared that the academic department of the university should be opened in its new location and a central female high school should be established in 1852. It also allowed the city to levy a tax of not less than 12½ cents or more than 25 cents on the $100, and to appropriate its portion of the State school fund and all fines and forfeitures in its courts, together with all escheats in its limits, to its own schools. In addition it was empowered to make a special appropriation of $75,000 to supply needed school buildings.

Early in 1852, in order to put the schools on a ward basis and have more desirable buildings, all the old school property was sold and new lots, suitably located, purchased, $68,405 being paid out for lots between May 3, 1852, and May 14, 1876, and between 1857 and 1873, 20 school buildings, all brick but one, were erected, the city having contributed, between January 1, 1853, and February 1, 1870, $610,000 in appropriations to its schools. When the third city charter was adopted, on March 3, 1870, there were 4 intermediate, 14 district, and 4 branch schools, most of them in much larger buildings than in 1850, with an enrollment of 13,593 pupils and an annual income of $151,539.23, of which $28,520.48 came from the State. There were 267 teachers and assistants, with annual salaries of $164,265.17.[2] In 1854 the study of German had been introduced into the schools, and, in 1870, 4,667

[1] This made the whole city school system free. The academic department of the university is old Louisville College, nominally made a part of the University of Louisville in 1846.

[2] The city then had 12 wards and a population of something over 100,000.

pupils were enrolled in the department, there being then 1 superintendent, 10 teachers, and 13 assistants connected with it, whose salaries were $15,700. In 1861 the Pestalozzian method of object teaching was introduced into the Louisville schools, mainly through the influence of Prof. W. N. Hailmann, professor of physical science in the male high school at the time, a normal school being temporarily established to facilitate its introduction.

The charter of 1870 made the tax for city schools 25 cents on the $100, a special levy of 8 cents for three years or longer, as the city council might decide, being allowed, in addition, to supply buildings as needed. In the matter of providing for the education of the negro only has Louisville ever been behind the State of Kentucky in educational policy. The State passed its first law looking to the establishment of schools for its colored population in 1866, but the first step looking in this direction was not taken by Louisville until 1867, when, by an amendment to the city charter, all taxes paid by the negroes of the city were set apart to provide separate schools for their children.

Nothing was accomplished under this act, but section 86 of the charter of 1870 made a similar provision, and, by a liberal interpretation of this charter, the city soon went far ahead of the State in providing schools for the race. In the latter part of 1870 two colored schools were opened with 3 teachers each and an enrollment of 457 pupils. The first colored high school building, a very handsome and well-equipped one, was dedicated on October 7, 1873, there being then three other buildings for the race accommodating 1,000 pupils. The running of these cost the city more than $3,000 a year above the taxes received from its colored population, which was something less than $2,000. The number of these schools was further increased in the next few years so that when, in 1882, the schools for the two races were put upon the same basis by State action, Louisville already had quite well provided for the education of her colored population.

The history of the school system of Louisville since 1870 has been one of continued and uniform progress in other directions besides that just indicated. In 1880 an additional tax of 5 cents on the $100 was imposed to meet growing needs. In that year the income of the schools from city taxation was $160,079, whereas in 1870 it had been $139,366. The amount received from the State fund in 1880 was $50,964. In 1881 the total income of the Louisville schools was about $300,000. At that time there were 31 schools with 328 teachers and an average attendance of 14,992 pupils, the city school property then being valued at $847,338.20.

The charter of 1893, passed in order to conform the city government to the new State constitution of 1891, retained practically intact the previous city school system, in the organization of which it made no material changes, the control of the system being vested in two trustees elected from each of the seven legislative districts of the city instead of two from each ward as formerly. According to it, the city tax, levied for school purposes, was made not less than 33 cents on the $100. The growth of the system in recent years may be seen from the following statistics for the school year ending June 30, 1897: There were then 44 schools, 39 ward schools, primary, secondary, and intermediate, besides 4 high schools (including the manual training school), and a normal school, with a total enrollment of 26,242 pupils, and an average attendance of 19,830; the total number of teachers being 556. The school property was valued at $1,047,280, and the school furniture and apparatus at $88,690. The money received from the State was $176,310.80; from city taxes $326,154.35, and the total expenses for the year were $526,360.10, of which $356,511.58 was paid for teachers' salaries.

Much of the success of the present school system of Louisville is due to the excellent superintendents of schools the city has had the good fortune usually to secure. Of these, George H. Tingley, jr., deserves especially to be mentioned on account of his long and able services. Mr. Tingley had become a pupil of the city schools almost from the inception of the system, was later a teacher and then a trustee. He was elected superintendent in September, 1863, and served continuously until his resignation on October 7, 1894, having labored faithfully in behalf of the system, either as teacher, trustee, or superintendent, for over fifty years. He was succeeded by the present efficient superintendent, E. H. Mark.

One of the most prominent features of the development of the school system of Louisville in recent years has been the more complete organization and enlargement of its higher departments. These consist at present of four high schools, including the manual training school, and a normal school, and are worthy of some notice in this connection.

We have seen that the school known at different periods in its history as Jefferson Seminary, Louisville College, and the academic department of the University of Louisville had long served as a high school for the boys of the city. By the charter of 1851 it was regularly converted into the city male high school, which it has since remained. This transformation and the change to the new location in the building of the law department of the university, which it has since occupied, do not seem to have been carried out until 1856, when William Harney became its first regular high school principal. It has since had 11 other principals, for longer or shorter periods of service. The school now has a faculty of 10 teachers and an excellent high school course, which prepares for the best colleges and universities and for business life. It usually has about 300 students and about 30 graduates annually.

A female high school was also provided for by the charter of 1851, to be established in the next year. It was not opened, however, until 1856, when it was located at the southwest corner of Fifth and Walnut streets, and had J. C. Spenser as its first principal. It has since had three other principals. After having had temporary quarters in three other buildings, the school was finally located in 1873 in the building it has since occupied on First near Chestnut street. This building when erected was one of the largest and finest of its kind in the country, costing with its furniture something over $115,000.

The course of the school is very similar to that of the male high school, but substitutes for Greek something in the way of what is usually denominated ornamental education. The present faculty is composed of 19 teachers. The usual attendance is about 600 annually, and the graduates generally number about 50. Its present building has been overcrowded for several years, and arrangements have consequently been made to erect for it a fine new building at Fifth and Hill streets. When the school has been transferred to this building, its present building will probably become a home for the male high school, which, besides having no permanent location, has also been cramped for space.

The importance of manual training had for some time been appreciated by the school authorities of Louisville, and efforts had previously been made to furnish facilities in this department before the first preliminary steps looking in this direction were actually taken in September, 1890, when a manual-training department was attached to the male high school. This had since been in operation with considerable success when, on May 2, 1892, Mr. A. V. Dupont, a wealthy citizen of Louisville and an enthusiast for such education, proposed to build and equip for the city, at his own expense, a first-class school building for manual training, with accommodation for 300 pupils, provided the city would establish a manual-training high school as a part of its regular school system. This proposition was accepted, and the building, which is a handsome one, with a complete modern equipment, was partly occupied in October, 1892.

The school was fully inaugurated in the autumn of 1893, with H. G. Brownell as its first regular principal. He is at present assisted by a faculty of 12 other teachers. The course of instruction, while putting great emphasis upon drawing and shop work of all kinds, also includes elementary science and mathematics, together with English, German, history, and civics. Something over 200 pupils have attended the school annually since its establishment, and the graduates during the last four years have averaged something over 20 each year.

A colored high school, known as the Central School, was, as we have seen, established in 1873. It has a faculty of seven teachers and a course including the departments of psychology and logic, English, history, mathematics, natural science, and Latin. Its annual matriculation averages about 200, of whom 20 are usually graduated.

A regular city normal school was established in 1871, as a necessary complement to the city school system, in order to supply it with trained teachers. The school was located in one of the city school buildings on Main street until its present building on Market street was erected. Hiram Roberts was its first principal, and remained so throughout its history until his death in 1897, when he was succeeded by the present principal, W. J. McConathy.

It was suspended in 1878 on account of the extra expense due to its operation, but was soon found to be almost indispensable and was reopened in October, 1881. The present faculty has four regular instructors and five critic teachers. The school receives each year 30 graduates from the female high school, and six others are admitted on examination. The regular course is two years in length, and there are usually about 30 normal graduates. A commercial department was attached to this school in 1891, and has commercial and business classes, each with a course of one year. These classes combined have usually about 150 pupils, with about 100 graduates. There are five additional teachers in this department.

BIBLIOGRAPHY.

The Louisville Directory for 1832, containing a sketch of the city by Mann Butler; Butler's History of Kentucky; Deering's Louisville; Louisville, Past and Present; Williams's Ohio Falls Cities; articles by Colonel Durrett in the Courier-Journal of January, 1881; Barnard's Journal of Education.

VITA.

Alvin Fayette Lewis was born near Bowling Green, Kentucky, October 9, 1861. He received his collegiate education at Ogden College, Bowling Green, Kentucky, and Princeton College, New Jersey, the former conferring on him the degree of A. B. in 1881 and of A. M. in 1885, and the latter the degree of A. B. in 1884 and A. M. in 1887. He was Principal of a preparatory school connected with Ogden College in 1881-1882, and an Instructor in Bardstown (Kentucky) Male and Female Institute in 1884-1885. He was then an Adjunct Professor in Arkansas Industrial University, Fayetteville, Arkansas, 1885-1887, and a Professor in the State Seminary at Tallahassee, Florida, 1887-1889, and the President of the last-mentioned institution, 1892-1898, being absent on leave during 1895-1896. He pursued graduate studies in Johns Hopkins University in 1889-1892 and 1895-1896, having given his attention mainly to Latin and Philosophy in 1889-1890 and to History and Economics during the remaining years, devoting about three and one-half scholastic years to the Departments of History and Economics and Philosophy, in which courses were pursued principally under Professors Adams and Griffin, Associate Professors Ely and Emmott, and under Dr. James Schouler, Lecturer in American History. The candidate spent the major part of the winter semester 1898-1899 at the University of Berlin, pursuing there special courses in the departments under different professors. His principal subject of study has been History, his first subordinate Economics, and his second subordinate Philosophy. At intervals between 1892 and 1898, he has collected, mainly on the ground, the facts for the accompanying dissertation on the History of Education in Kentucky.

www.ingramcontent.com/pod-product-compliance
Lightning Source LLC
Chambersburg PA
CBHW022257280326
41932CB00010B/896

* 9 7 8 3 7 4 4 7 6 4 6 7 4 *